British
Hotels &
Restaurants 2006

Les Routiers is an association of mainly owner-managed establishments. However, membership is not automatic. Many applications are refused because every establishment displaying Les Routiers' symbol must satisfy our rigourous quality criteria. All opinions included in the Guide entries are based upon the findings of external assessors.

Published in 2005 by:
Routiers Limited
190 Earl's Court Road
London SW5 9QG
Tel: 020 7370 5113
Fax: 020 7370 4528
Email: info@routiers.co.uk

Book-trade distribution:
Portfolio Books Ltd
Unit 5, Perivale Industrial Park
Horsenden Lane South
Greenford, Middlesex
UB6 7RL

ISBN 0-900057-23-8
Copyright © 2005 Routiers Limited

Maps © Routiers Limited 2005
Great Britain Digital Database and
Greater London Digital Data
© Cosmographics Limited.
Maps designed and produced by Cosmographics.
Reproduced by kind permission of Ordnance Survey.
Crown Copyright NC/01/365".
Including mapping content © Automobile Association
Developments Limited 2001 and
© Bartholomew Digital Database.
Greater London Map based on information derived
from satellite imagery and an original ground survey by
Cosmographics. Satellite data provided by USGS and
Infoterra Ltd.

British Library Cataloguing in Publication Data.
A catalogue record for this book is available from the
British Library.

Editor:
Melanie Leyshon

Production and Design Editor:
Holly Hall

Design:
Oliver Carter

Sub-editor:
Gill Wing

Editorial Contributors:
Julie Arkell
Anita Chaudhuri
Philip Moss

Location Photographers:
britainonview.com
Annie Hanson
Rebecca Harris
Simon Lunt
Nicholas Stanley

Cover Photography:
Claudia Riccio
Tel: 07990 604806

Maps:
Cosmographics Limited, Watford

Printed in Great Britain by:
London Print and Design plc, Warwick

For Les Routiers:
Chairman:
David Curry
Operations Director:
Imogen Clist
Marketing Manager:
Victoria Borrows
Membership:
Suzy Small

www.routiers.co.uk

Les Routiers Guide – De bons restaurants pas chers et pour tous was originally written for truck drivers who were looking for fairly priced hotels and restaurants. It soon became popular with travelling salesmen, and French and foreign tourists.

Today, the red and blue Les Routiers sign has become a cult symbol, standing alongside the Gitannes pack and the Ricard logo as the essence of French style, and the Routiers' original concept of a warm homely welcome and affordable good value is as strong today as when it was first conceived in the 1930s.

Les Routiers Guide – De bons restaurants pas chers et pour tous is a boon for travellers in France, listing simple, inexpensive roadside restaurants and hotels for both truck drivers and motorists.

To obtain a copy visit:

www.routiers.com

Contents

Features

🛏 Accommodation   🌶 Food shop

🛏 Residents only   📕 Set menu

☕ Pub or bar   ★ Award winner 2004

🫖 Teashop or café   ★ Award winner 2005

Food maps
Ever wondered where our members source their quality ingredients?
Our food maps pinpoint the top producers and suppliers of quality
foods in 12 culinary hot spots

Just off the motorway
Give the motorway services a miss and take a quick detour to one
of our conveniently placed members

ABOUT THIS GUIDE

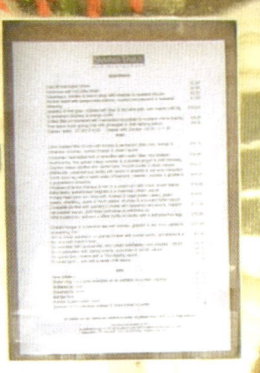

Individual, friendly, welcoming and value for money – you'll find all these attributes at Les Routiers' select collection of owner-managed hotels, restaurants, pubs and cafés around Britain. On their search of the regions, Les Routiers' inspectors look out for the most special places. Those that combine character, quality and have that special British quirkiness, be it a B&B in the far-flung Highlands of Scotland, an historic country-house hotel in the Cotswolds, or an Indian restaurant serving curry made with locally caught fish or haggis.

Les Routiers' approach and philosophy is very much in tune with the discerning traveller, who wants style but informality, without the anonymous atmosphere and impersonal service of some of the larger hotel chains. Our members champion regional foods and source most of their ingredients locally. This means you get to enjoy foods in season when they're at their most flavoursome, from regional cheeses and organic herbs and vegetables to game and speciality-breed meats. As well as offering good food, you will be assured warm and welcoming hospitality, comfortable, well-appointed bedrooms and excellent value for money.

How our members make the grade

Les Routiers employs eight regional inspectors/field managers who have previously worked in the hospitality industry, either as proprietor-chefs, food inspectors or hotel managers. Hotels and restaurants interested in applying for membership are fully inspected and have the marketing benefits of joining Les Routiers explained. Only after passing our rigorous criteria are new members accepted and invited to become part of our select group. There is a charge for inclusion in the guide, but this annual membership fee goes towards covering the inspections and producing the annual guide books.

LES ROUTIERS
Hotels & Restaurants 2006

Local foods

Over the last five years, there has been a huge surge of interest in local, seasonal and organic food. Hotels and restaurants are serving more game, beef, fruit and vegetables from local estates, farmers and fishermen. This year, we surveyed Les Routiers' members to find out what the next big food trend is going to be. The general consensus is that demand for locally-sourced, quality-food that leans towards the healthy is growing fast. The good news is that you will already find more local and seasonal foods on our members' menus than any other hotel or restaurant menu.

A taste of Britain traditional recipes

Often, when you eat out, you enjoy a dish so much you'd like to make it at home. That's why this year, several of our members share their most popular dishes from the regions. You'll find light and fluffy scones from Devon and Welshcakes (from Wales, of course), the popular Scottish soup starter, cullen skink, (a meal in itself), and hearty English mains such as shortcrust steak, kidney and mushroom pie. Puddings take in a luscious fruit crumble. All these recipes have been adapted for the home cook.

Food maps

Dotted throughout this guide you will find Food Maps, which identify Les Routiers' members who are champions of local foods. Each member shares his or her key local suppliers and some of the interesting food shops in the area, whether that's a farm growing asparagus or soft fruits, a small-holding that delivers organic vegetables or a local fishing boat that lands fresh fish and crab.

Quick-reference guide

Here you will find at a glance our selection of top hotels and restaurants, for alfresco eating, the best views and waterside locations. We also list the best places to eat seafood and game, and those offering private-dining facilities.

Now and then

Prawn cocktail, chicken and chips and gooey gateaux – you may think these dishes are a relic of the 1970s, but nostalgia food is still making a big impact on menus around Britain. National newspaper writer Anita Chaudhuri talks to Les Routiers' members who are serving more lavish and updated versions of these classics, which are proving to be just as popular as the first time round.

A festival of food

It's becoming the foodie event of the year – the annual Abergavenny Food Festival is a feast for the senses, and attracts more than 25,000 visitors over the two-day event. You can visit the many food stalls, or sit back and enjoy talks by celebrity chefs and cookery demonstrations by the experts. Restaurant reviewer and food writer Philip Moss is your guide to the best food suppliers and places to stay and eat in this culinary hot spot.

Just off the motorway

We've all been there: the motorway service station that short-changes you on food, but charges the earth. Check out the nine maps to find your detour off the motorway to a Les Routiers' member, not just the hotels and restaurants listed in this guide, but also Les Routiers' pubs and inns. The members suggested are just a short drive from the main motorway junction, but miles ahead on food and accommodation.

Matching food and wine: The grape and the good

Wine expert Julie Arkell deconstructs a typical restaurant wine list to help you find the best buys on the menu. She offers helpful advice, from choosing house wine and spotting other bargains to ordering speciality Champagnes. Her guide to grapes gives the lowdown on flavours and which foods go best with which grape variety. She also pinpoints the wines that are going up in popularity and those going down, as well as picking out the best bottles to look out for in the coming year.

How to use this Guide

Finding an establishment

Les Routiers British Hotels & Restaurants 2006 is sectioned into England, Scotland, Wales and the Channel Islands. The countries are listed alphabetically by county, listing town and establishment name. There are four ways to track down an establishment.

1. If you are seeking a place in a particular area, first turn to the maps at the back of the book. County boundaries are marked in lilac and each establishment has a relevant marker alongside their listing town, shown in bold. Once you know the locality, go to the relevant section in the book to find the entry for the hotel or restaurant.

2. Each page is colour-coded at the top so you can flick through the guide and find what you are looking for with ease. Turn to the contents pages for the colour key.

3. Turn to the index on page 274 where both establishment names and listing towns appear in alphabetical order.

4. Turn to the quick-reference guide on page 278 to help you find a place that will suit you whether it be somewhere with riverside seating or beautiful gardens.

How to read a guide entry

A sample entry is set out on the facing page. At the top of the entry you will find the establishment's name, address, telephone number and, if it has them, an email and website address. Also, any symbols that may apply to the establishment; an explanation of what these symbols stand for appears beside the sample entry. The middle part of the entry describes accommodation, atmosphere, food, wines and so on, while the final section gives additional statistical information and a map reference.

Listing town and county: Many of our establishments are in the countryside, so their listing town may be a location several miles away. If you are unsure of the county, look up the town in the index and it will refer you to the correct page.

Telephone: Numbers include the international code for dialling the UK from abroad. To dial from within the UK, start the number with the 0 in brackets; from outside the UK, dial all numbers except the 0 in brackets.

Last orders: Times to order lunch and dinner by are given for the bar and restaurant where applicable. Where there is only an evening time given, the establishment serves food throughout the day.

Closed: Where 'Never' is stated, the establishment is open throughout the year. Where 'Rarely' is stated, the establishment is open throughout the year except on important holidays (Christmas, New Year). Otherwise, dates and days closed are stated.

Directions: These have been supplied by the proprietor of the establishment. The map reference at the end refers to the map section at the back of the guide.

Listing town

Name

Address
Telephone: +44(0)870 000000
excellentpub@hotmail.com

This quintessentially English hotel dates back to the 18th century and has been revamped by its new owners…

Rooms: 15. Double room from £72, single from £57. Honeymoon suite available.
Prices: Set menu £18. House wine from £9.95.
Last orders: Bar: 23.30. Food: 21.00.
Closed: 25th December to 2nd January.
Food: Modern British.
Other points: No-smoking area. Children welcome. Garden. Car park. Licence for civil weddings.
Directions: Exit 22/M5. Turn right at the roundabout towards Weston-super-Mare on the A38. The hotel is one mile on the left. (Map 4, C6)

Symbols:

- Accommodation
- Residents only
- Pub or bar
- Teashop or café
- Food shop
- Set menu
- ★ Award winner 2004
- ★ Award winner 2005

All symbols are in their country's colour, apart from the award-winner stars. We do not have a good-food or good-wine symbol, as it is part of our requirements for membership that all Les Routiers establishments serve good food and wine at reasonable prices.

Rooms: For establishments offering overnight accommodation, the number of rooms is given, along with the lowest price for a double/twin and single room. Where this price is per person it is indicated. Prices usually include breakfast. Where the price includes bed, breakfast and dinner, it is indicated.

Prices: Set meals usually consist of three courses but can include more. If a set meal has fewer or more than three courses, this is stated. Where no set meal is offered, we give the price of the cheapest main course on the menu. House wine prices are by the bottle, unless otherwise stated.

Other Points:

Smoking – The majority of establishments are either totally no-smoking or have a no-smoking area. However, we also indicate where smoking is allowed throughout.

Credit cards – Very few places don't take credit cards; those that don't are stated here.

Children – Although we indicate whether children are welcome in the establishment, we do not list facilities for guests with babies; we advise telephoning beforehand to sort out any particular requirements.

Dogs – We indicate whether dogs are allowed in the public bar and/or overnight accommodation of the establishment. However, please mention this when booking.

Disabled – We indicate whether an establishment does have wheelchair access. If this does not apply to the WC, this is also stated. However, we recommend telephoning the hotel or restaurant of your choice to discuss your needs with the manager or proprietor directly.

NO. 7 ON THE LIST OF
TABLES FOR TWO

Number 9 is in the dining carriage of the Orient Express.
Number 8 is in Monte Carlo in front of a croupier.
Number 7 however, you practically levitate above.
A white mud treatment washes away any traces of tension and with Membership Rewards®
picking up the bill, there's no stress on your wallet either. In fact the points Members earn on everyday
purchases can be redeemed for almost any indulgence – from mud packs to Margaux.

For more ideas visit americanexpress.co.uk/dreams

FOR WHATEVER DREAMS ARE ON YOUR LIST

Hospitality and Service Award

This year, we have introduced a new award for hospitality and service, sponsored by American Express. American Express consistently delivers new business and high-spending Card members to its merchants, and works to support independent establishments across Britain. Good service deserves recognition. Offering customers a choice of payment methods contributes to good service, in both city centres and the countryside. Friendly, efficient staff and a slick front-of-house, all make for a pleasant, stress-free stay or dining-out experience. We believe the winners of this award ensure customers feel at ease and are well looked-after, from initial booking through to paying the bill.

Les Routiers
Hotel & Restaurant Awards 2005

Our annual awards recognise members that excel at meeting the standards required for Les Routiers' membership. There are six categories and, as always, it was a tough call to decide, as overall standards of accommodation, food and drink are excellent. Congratulations to our winners, who just had the edge, and will attend the Les Routiers' awards dinner.

Hotel of the Year

All our hotels are independently run, and this is evident from their friendly, personal service, individually designed interiors and comfortable accommodation. Our winners successfully combine warm hospitality with a high standard of décor, and often provide extras and that you would expect of deluxe hotels.

Restaurant of the Year
sponsored by Tabasco® Pepper Sauce

Les Routiers' restaurants are champions of fresh, local seasonal produce. This means we have a network of restaurants around the country that serve good food at its flavoursome best. Our winners source ingredients from specialist local suppliers, which they use imaginatively in their unpretentious, and often regional, dishes. Their appreciation of regional produce is what underpins Les Routiers' philosophy.

Bed & Breakfast of the Year

Gone are the days when bed and breakfast was considered second best. Our members offer first-class accommodation with a friendly, although not obtrusive, service. The bedrooms and public areas combine a comfortable home-from-home feel with stylish interiors. Our winners surpass in all these elements, and many offer good food options.

Wine List of the Year

This award recognises a passion and enthusiasm for choosing quality wines at value-for-money prices. We have chosen members who put as much effort into their house-selection as they do into choosing their fine wine collection. This year, we were particulary impressed by The Wynnstay Arms in Machynlleth, which has put together what must be one of the most comprehensive Italian wine selections in the UK.

Café of the Year

Les Routiers' cafés are a rare and varied bunch, ranging from traditional tearooms and cafés to contemporary conservatories serving all-day homemade snacks. The emphasis is on quality food and friendly service, and all our winners are shining examples of this combination.

Local Food Supporters of the Year

Hotels and restaurants in this category go out of their way to source the best local produce. These establishments are run by food-loving chefs or proprietors who would rather buy ingredients locally, whether that's fruit and vegetables; rare-breed or fully traceable local meats, often organic; line-caught fresh fish from day boats; or dairy and farm-shop deli lines. Our winners are excellent examples of supporters of the local economy.

Hotel of the Year

National Winner

London & the South-East – Langrish House, Petersfield, Hampshire

'Exactly how a country-house hotel should be: it's so relaxed, it's like visiting friends for the weekend. Beautiful grounds, a family home steeped in history, family run and with passion oozing from the kitchen.'

Langrish House

Regional Winners

Scotland – Highland Cottage, Tobermory, Isle of Mull
'This immaculate hotel is run by David and Jo Curry, who have furnished it beautifully. The standard of cooking, all by Jo Curry, is excellent.'

Wales & The Marches – Llansantffraed Court Hotel, Abergavenny, Monmouthshire
'A small, but comfortable, country-house hotel with a high level of service and a "can do" approach. The food is always well-thought out and well-presented. There is a good mix of formal spaces and places to relax.'

The North – Pheasant Hotel, Helsmley, North Yorkshire
'A charming hotel in a truly peaceful, rural village location, overlooking a picture-postcard pond. It has beautifully maintained grounds and a stylish, but relaxed, atmosphere.'

Central & East Anglia – The Lincoln Hotel, Lincoln, Lincolnshire
'This independently run hotel is beautifully situated overlooking the cathedral in the centre of Lincoln. Comfortable well-decorated rooms, quality fresh food and very friendly service. Relaxing.'

The South-West – St Vincent House, Hotel & Restaurant, Lynton, Devon
'You'll get a homely welcome in this quietly understated stylish hotel. The comfort of guests is paramount, and the Belgian owner is passionate about serving good food – and some excellent Belgian beers!'

Restaurant of the Year
Sponsored by Tabasco® Pepper Sauce

National Winner

Central and East Anglia – Thornham Hall & Restaurant, Thornham Magna, Suffolk

'The informal restaurant serves fresh local food cooked with plenty of creativity. A place worth travelling a long way to visit. Excellent value, too, at this very individual establishment.'

Coriander Restaurant & Deli

Regional Winners

Scotland – Let's Eat, Perth, Perth & Kinross
'One of the most highly regarded restaurants in Scotland. It majors in fresh Scottish food cooked creatively – expect quality, but no pomp and ceremony at this relaxed restaurant.'

The North – Ramsons, Ramsbottom, Greater Manchester
'Chris Johnson brings Italian flair and flavour to his well-thought out menu, which is a model of flexibility. Dishes are built around prime ingredients, impeccably sourced, and simply, but superbly cooked.'

Wales & The Marches – The Thai House Restaurant, Cardiff
'This is a cutting edge eating establishment, housed in a building designed by Welsh architect Huw Jones. They have a loyal following for fine cooking that brings together Thai flavourings with Welsh ingredients.'

The South-West – Elephant Bar & Restaurant, Torquay, Devon
'A classy and unusual setting with a hint of the colonial. The service and food is outstanding. It offers a complete social experience, whether you come for just a cocktail and drinks, or dinner.'

London & the South-East – Coriander Restaurant & Deli, Hove, East Sussex
'Interesting and different, with a friendly bohemian vibe in the restaurant (now open at lunchtimes as well), where they serve excellent adventurous and delicious dishes. Fun and knowledgeable owners and staff.'

Bed & Breakfast of the Year

National Winner

South-West – Anchorage House, St Austell, Cornwall

'This superbly run B&B comes with luxury touches, the rooms are wonderful and the food served is carefully sourced. The lap pool in the lovely grounds is an unexpected pleasure, as are the beautiful gardens.'

Oaklands

Regional Winners

Scotland – Balkissock Lodge, Ballantrae, South Ayrshire
'Delightful, peaceful and quiet surroundings. Very friendly welcome and warm hosts. The renovation of the farmhouse has been carried out to high standards. Excellent traditional Scottish food, too.'

The North – Marton Grange, Bridlington, East Yorkshire
'Genuine hospitality. The grounds and house are immaculately maintained. Bedrooms are well planned and decorated. Food is wholesome, using local ingredients where possible.'

Wales & The Marches – Aspen House, Hoarwithy, Herefordshire
'Excellent dinners are provided, using only the freshest of local organic produce. The gardens have undergone a radical reworking and now comprise several small, discrete terraces.'

London & the South-East – Oaklands, Rye, East Sussex
'Attractive building with lovely gardens and amazing views. Spotless and run with pride by the charming owners.'

Wine List of the Year

National Winner

Wales & The Marches – The Wynnstay Hotel & Restaurant
Machynlleth, Powys

*'There are more than 60 regional Italian wines on offer. It's refreshing
to see that the super-Tuscans and Chianti-shire favourites have been
replaced by whites from Liguria and bold reds from further north.'*

The Wynnstay Hotel & Restaurant

Regional Winners

Scotland – Inn at Lathones, St Andrews, Fife
'There are more than 150 wines on the list, with prices to suit every pocket. Champagnes up to £300, white wines
up to £600, reds up to £900. They can source a favourite tipple, if so required.'

The North – Tufton Arms Hotel, Appleby-in-Westmorland, Cumbria
'An extensive list with depth and quality. Much is sourced through Lay & Wheeler, but there is also some excellent
direct sourcing, as evidenced by their house wines. They offer a considerable choice of quality wines by the glass.'

South-West – The Priory House Restaurant, Stoke-sub-Hamden, Somerset
'The owners put a lot of thought and attention into the choice of the wines they offer. There is something for
everyone and always something to complement the menu. Many wines are offered by the glass.'

Central and East Anglia – Greens Restaurant, Witney, Oxfordshire
'Carefully constructed wine list offering great choice and value at this top-notch establishment. The list tempts you
to try more than you probably should.'

London & the South-East – Le Frère Restaurant, St Martin, Jersey
'Excellent wine list painstakingly put together by ex-Relais and Chateau owner. Wines mostly exclusive to Le Frère
complement the high standard of cuisine.'

Café of the Year

National Winner

The North – Quayside, Whitby, North Yorkshire

'Enthusiasm and professionalism. Stuart Fusco is nationally acknowledged as one of the best fish friers around. The café is kept in pristine condition and staff are always pleasant and attentive.'

The Curio Café

Regional Winners

Scotland – The Anstruther Fish Bar, Anstruther, Fife
'Light, bright and clean, with amazingly efficient service, especially when you consider there are nearly always queues. Its excellent fish and chips are served as fresh as can be – people travel from miles to sample a fish supper.'

Wales & The Marches – Juri's The Old Bakery Tea Shoppe, Winchcombe, Gloucestershire
'The setting is perfect. The Japanese eye for detail possessed by the eponymous Juri and her mother-and-father team really makes this establishment stand out. Local ingredients are used where possible.'

Central & East Anglia – The Curio Café, Newark-on-Trent, Nottinghamshire
'This attractive café serves wholesome and delicious all-day snacks and light lunches. It combines eating and shopping, as upstairs there are many display rooms selling antiques, especially Art Deco pieces.'

London & the South-East – Denmans Garden, Fontwell, West Sussex
'A total experience – divine gardens, plants and gifts to buy, and the attractive year-round Garden Café, offering uncomplicated but great value-for-money fare.'

Local Food Supporters of the Year

The Stonemill

Winners

Old Ferryman's House, Boat of Garten, Highland
'Liz Matthews nurtures her hens for fresh eggs, maintains a vegetable garden, sources honey from a nearby apiarist and gets her dairy produce and other vegetables locally. Game is from nearby estates.'

Watermill, Penrith, Penrith
'The Jones run the mill and café in a way that is totally committed to the organic/biodynamic ethos. While some of the grain purchased is not local, that's because it satisfies Anna's insistence on the quality and method of husbandry.'

The Stonemill, Monmouth, Monmouthshire
'This restaurant has hit a golden period. Its owners are passionate about using local food. With pasta and bread made in house, and duck and chicken eggs from the adjoining farm, dishes here can be seen as a bold representation of the locale.'

terroir, Cley next the Sea, Norfolk
'Very tempting array of the best local produce, all carefully sourced, in imaginative dishes. You will find all its suppliers listed on its menu. Friendly staff and a most attractive setting. The sort of place you have to return to.'

Browns Hotel & Brasserie, Plymouth, Devon
'A wonderful, affordable, chic establishment in the heart of Devon, whose two award-winning chefs pride themselves in serving creative dishes prepared with locally sourced ingredients.'

Food for Thought, London
'Long established and consistently good. Excellent sourcing from Borough and New Covent Garden markets means you can really taste the fresh flavours in their daily-changing vegetarian menu.'

Hospitality and Service Award

Sponsored by American Express

National Winner

San Carlo, Birmingham, Manchester, Bristol and Leicester

'This small chain of Italian restaurants serves authentically good food that is matched by top-notch service from its staff, who are predominately Italian too. They are friendly, knowledgable and carry off a slick service, however busy they are. San Carlo's friendly and consistent service made it a worthy winner.'

San Carlo, Birmingham

Readers' digest

Our countrywide survey of Les Routiers members reveals a feast of facts about eating out. **Melanie Leyshon** serves up the facts, from the most popular dishes to the top wines and ingredients, as well as revealing some of the more unsavoury customer behaviour when dining out

Our appetite for eating out continues to grow, but, at the same, we are eating less on these occasions. In Britain, we are becoming two-course rather than three-course diners and taking a less is more philosophy to food quality, according to our survey of 250 Les Routiers' members around Britain.

Twenty years ago, meals out began with a starter and finished with a full-on pudding, coffee and minted chocolate, but now we are more likely to opt for to a starter and main, or a main and pudding, and show a little more constraint when it comes to ordering calorie-laden dishes. Our list of ingredients falling out of favour, shows that high-fat foods are being sidelined, as healthier dishes appeal more to our palates and waistlines.

One Les Routiers' member noted, 'People are choosing smaller portions and fewer courses, and are more aware of what they are eating. They don't want cream in sauces. They will be tempted by a pudding, but as a special treat.'

Three-quarters of Les Routiers' members said they thought people were eating out more compared to 10 years ago and put this down to greater affluence, more disposable income, liking the social experience – and laziness. Frankly, who wants to cook supper when you can enjoy well-priced gastrofood at the revamped local?

And it's these Monday-night suppers and Thursday-lunchtime treats that are fuelling this growth in eating out. 'The demand for special-occasion meals appears to be at the same level, but everyday-menu options are clearly attracting much more business from busy people looking for a good, but moderately priced meal', said one member. Lunchtime dining is on the up thanks to time constraints, and the working lunch continues to be a favourite fixture.

The growing trend for eating good food means Les Routiers' members are leading the way by using local, seasonal produce. Microwavable, or 'ping' food, cooked at the beginning of the week and reheated on the day, is not what discerning customers are looking for. 'People are eating out more frequently, becoming more choosy and putting greater emphasis on quality,' said one member.

On the healthy-eating front, many restaurants noted that customers' main concern is more about weight loss than healthy-eating. Post-Atkins and the South Beach Diet, there has been a rise in the requests for low-carbohydrate meals. 'Customers are requesting Atkins and South Beach Diet meals, and are pleased they don't have to go into details because we are familiar with them and cook food to order with those eating plans in mind,' said one obliging member.

'The popularity of the coronary inducing full English breakfast shows little sign of diminishing'

If customers are to believed, food intolerance and allergies are also on the rise, according to more than 90 per cent of Les Routiers' members. Many restaurants were cynical, however, about the steep increase in gluten intolerance and nut allergies.

One member suspects that 'Many people declare a food intolerance when really they mean they dislike something, so it is misleading.' Another said: 'There are people with true food intolerances; and there are people (an increasing number) whose "intolerances" are a moveable feast; we've had people book as wheat-intolerant who've then devoured baskets of our homemade bread; a dairy-intolerant guest who asked for ice cream with her dessert and even a vegan who devoured a cheese course.'

One meal occasion where it's still no holds barred is breakfast. The popularity of the coronary inducing full English breakfast shows little sign of diminishing.

One member said: 'Weekenders on special deals eat huge breakfasts and can be greedy, although weekday guests and business people are more likely to choose a poached egg on toast, or fruits. The croissants and Danish pastries come back untouched.'

Another member trying to wean guests off the fry-up with delicious alternatives is making little ground: 'We offer a huge range of vegetarian and fish alternatives, but the take-up can be very disappointing.'

Ingredients in favour

Apart from the odd weird and wonderful ingredient, it's locally sourced meats, fish and dairy produce that are making an impact on Les Routiers' menus. Although chorizo, smoked paprika and balsamic vinegar are popular, diners are more interested in the local black pudding, special-recipe sausage, artisan cheese, fresh herbs and smoked fish and seafood. While members said delivery times, lack of supplies and poor quality of local foods can be a problem sometimes, it is these products that they prize the most.

Ingredients out of favour

Spicy foods, chilli, lemon grass, salt, butter, milk, cream, roux sauces, boiled potatoes, fried foods and after-dinner chocolates are less popular choices on menus.

Hard to source

Getting good fish inland can be a problem. In other areas, it's still hard to source ox tails post BSE, as well as fully traceable beef. Other members bemoaned the closure of local bakeries, as this makes finding good dried and fresh yeast, especially the organic variety, difficult. Ever resourceful, Les Routiers' members will turn their hand to growing or making their own if necessary, whether that's growing herbs or dry-curing bacon. Sourcing from abroad also brings its frustrations, as one member found when he failed to persuade an artisan producer of Italian limoncello liqueur in Amalfi to fill in documents permitting him to send supplies for the restaurant's lemon panna cotta.

The next big thing

While several members said the next country cuisine to take off would be tapas, it was the more general themes, such as fully traceable meats, cooking with local, home-grown produce and serving healthier, lighter and low-fat, low-salt meals that they believed would become more important to diners. A number also said it would be 'vegetarian meals taken seriously'.

Top choices on the menu

Under starter's orders

1st Soup is the favourite starter countrywide, with **smoked haddock chowder** or **smoked haddock and mussel chowder** coming top, but with an assortment of homemade flavours made using fresh seasonal produce proving big hits. One member said his customers are happy with bowls of 'Jerusalem artichoke, pea, broad bean, asparagus, or whatever is around…' The choices at the majority of members reads like a veritable market garden of daily-changing options taking in **curried parsnip, butternut squash and mango, leek and potato, Welsh cawl, borscht, langoustine and seafood**, to name just a few…

2nd Homemade pâté and chicken liver. Variations on this theme such as **chicken liver and raspberry pâté** were popular, as were duck-liver pâté and wild boar parfait, duck terrine and foie-gras terrine.

3rd Smoked salmon, another home-produced ingredient, continues to hold its own. When it's not served with brown bread and lemon, it comes with blinis and caviar, or is served as **hot smoked salmon with a lemon crème fraîche** and bruschetta, or with mussels or avocado.

4th Regional specialities such as **haggis and a whisky sauce** were popular in Scottish establishments, in north Norfolk it's **potted brown shrimps**, while in Wales **cockles and laverbread** got many votes.

5th Exotic salad combinations made a strong showing, with dishes such as **squid and chorizo salad, manti (spiced meatballs in pastry), and tiger prawns with sweet chilli mayo** holding their own.

'The soup choices at the majority of members reads like a veritable market garden of daily-changing options'

The main event

1st Fish has beaten beef to top spot and is the favoured main course on more than half of Les Routiers members' menus. This was true around the country, and not just at the well-stocked coast. But it's not only our national favourite, battered fish and chips, that is stealing the show – there are more sophisticated and healthier, lighter dishes among the top choices. One member says 'all varieties' of fish are popular, with **fresh from the bay** and **the local catch** appealing the most, especially simply grilled or baked fish, such as sea bass. **Sea bass baked with lemon and thyme** served with a tomato and basil sauce or **pan-fried with saffron sauce,** served with a herb risotto were among the popular recipes mentioned. **Plain white fish** with light sauces, especially Dover sole, plaice and halibut, were also winners, with recipes such as grilled **Dover sole with capers and fresh herbs** or **Dover sole with Swiss Chard, and vine tomatoes or monkfish stuffed with mussels and spinach,** and **white fish flash fried with butter then steamed in the oven with tarragon, cream and artichoke hearts** getting namechecks.

2nd Beef came a strong runner-up. **Fillets and rib-eyes**, followed by **roasts,** such as beef and Yorkshire pudding, were the most popular. Runaway favourites were fillet steaks traditionally cooked with a peppered sauce, steaks served with French fries or rib-eyes with mushrooms, red wine and pepper. Serving fillets simply with a good flavoured butter was another popular choice, and good old **steak with bèarnaise sauce** is still a crowd pleaser.

3rd Lamb trounced chicken and pork. **Lamb shanks** and slow-braised dishes are the top choices, but also featuring quite prominently were **Moroccan-inspired dishes**.

4th Chicken served as a casserole, with Cajun spices, roasted or cooked in rich sauces such as **Madeira** or **thyme and mushroom** is also popular. In Scotland, diners enjoyed **chicken stuffed with haggis wrapped in bacon with Madeira sauce.** Naturally, our members like to do things differently, and **chicken schnitzel on chorizo served with an oregano creamed tagliatelle** features on one Les Routiers' menu in Scotland.

5th Apart from at our vegetarian restaurants and cafés, vegetarian dishes trailed, but this was not from the lack of imagination shown in creating interesting dishes.

'It's not only our national favourite, battered fish and chips, that is stealing the show – there are more sophisticated and healthier, lighter dishes among the top choices'

Spuds u like

1st It's **mash** by a mile. This is the most requested accompaniment to main meals. Customers like it plain with butter and cream, but adding all kinds of flavourings proved popular. Thyme, celeriac, horseradish, herbs and saffron are some of the interesting variations that won votes.

2nd The old favourite, **chips**, which are served with everything from chicken and steak to lobster.

3rd **Roasts**, testament to the enduring popularity of Sunday lunches.

4th **Baked and sautéed**.

5th **Boiled new potatoes**.

The trend for crushed potatoes is definitely on the wane. As one member put it, 'English new potatoes, especially, don't need crushing as they're delicious as they are.' And if you want potatoes in a more unsual setting, opt for *latkes*, a cake of shaved onion and potato with spice and buckwheat, fried in olive oil at Les Routiers' The Russian Tavern, Scotland.

The drinking and smoking debates

■ Looks like you won't be drinking into the small hours at Les Routiers' establishments. Members gave late licences and 24-hour opening the big thumbs down, and only one per cent said they would be applying for a late licence.

■ Members favoured a complete ban on smoking in public places and in restaurants. One said, 'We enjoyed a holiday in Italy where all restaurants and bars were no smoking. It was great, as even the smokers enjoyed going outside and talking with strangers while smoking.'

Plum puddings

In this category, British puddings scooped the top places.

1st Nursery favourite **sticky toffee pudding**.

2nd **Crumble**, either apple or rhubarb.

3rd All things **chocolatey**, from mousses and tortes to gooey gâteaux.

4th Ice creams – homemade, of course.

5th **Crème brûlée** and **citrus tarts**. Meringue-based desserts, such as Pavlova, made a strong showing, too, as did bread-and-butter pudding, but falling out of favour are Italian favourite tiramisù, soufflés and cheesecakes.

Wine

French wine is still the top choice for house wines, followed by Australian, Chilean, South African and New Zealand. And you have plenty of choice by the glass, as more than 75 per cent of Les Routiers' restaurants and bars offer five-plus varieties this way. The most popular wine size was a 175ml glass, followed by 125ml. And when they're not drinking alcohol, customers opt for sparkling mineral water, followed by Coca-Cola-style drinks, although, in Scotland, Dandelion & Burdeck is a popular alternative.

Customers behaving badly

As you'd imagine, turning up late or not at all for a table you have booked can get restaurateurs hot under the collar. No-shows and late-arrivals were cited as the most annoying customer habits. In second place came lack of control over children, followed by chatting constantly on mobile phones. However, there were some customers whose antics were of quite another order, and here we list some of the more eccentric bad moments at Les Routiers' establishments in the last year.

- Walking in with muddy boots
- Taking more cutlery/serviettes from the waiter than needed
- Leaning over the counter to point/touch food
- An infuriating inability to choose from the menu
- Lifting precious ornaments to look underneath
- Placing an order then moving to another table
- Demanding service when a restaurant is on the point of closing
- Turning up late on a Sunday night and demanding a full dinner at nearly midnight
- Demanding salt without tasting the meal
- Meticulously filleting the smoked sprats
- Splitting the bill painstakingly, to the penny, at the end
- Taking away menus without asking, ditto branded mineral-water bottles
- Claiming to suffer an allergy, which may mean merely disliking a food
- Putting a napkin on top of a candle
- Smoking in the bedroom
- Dropping cigarette butts on the carpet
- Stubbing a cigarette out in a main course when told the restaurant was non-smoking
- Bringing their own karaoke machine
- Taking a gadget from a handbag to test the food was cooked
- Turning a plate of food upside down on a table
- Pulling flowers from vases and throwing them around the restaurant while uttering maledictions
- Stealing a picture
- Trashing a room
- Staff being physically attacked
- Allowing a child to urinate on the front doorstep
- Eating a live goldfish

now and then

Prawn cocktail, Black Forest gâteau and chicken and chips – they're perennial favourites, but have never tasted so good. Anita Chaudhuri takes a taste trip down memory lane and talks to Les Routiers' members giving old favourites a new lease of life.
Illustrations by Natalie Hall

Top designers are famous for reviving retro fashions, so it's no surprise that many of the country's most creative chefs are now following suit and resurrecting the culinary equivalents of flared jeans, ponchos and wedge heels. From prawn cocktail and steak Diane to Black Forest gâteau and profiteroles, there is a hunger for nostalgic flavours that recreate the feelgood factor of bygone decades.

'Back in the 1970s, people thought vegetarians were from another planet'

At the Shibden Mill Inn, West Yorkshire, they have gone as far as introducing a special 'retro menu' at lunchtimes, which features only dishes inspired by the glory days of the 1970s and 1980s. 'We wanted to find a way of boosting our lunchtime trade and going retro seemed like a fun idea to attract a younger crowd, many of whom were children when they ate the food first time around, if they remember eating it at all! It's been a huge success and we're planning to expand the theme into the dinner menu as well,' explains general manager Glen Pearson.

Chefs are given a free rein to invent a new retro menu each week in order to encourage their creative talents and make best use of local seasonal produce. 'We were sorely tempted to go OTT and have loud retro music and prawn cocktail in a glass dish, but decided we needed to stay true to what our kitchen does well: home-made, quality food. Also the fare that used to be so popular when people ate out was very unhealthy. Everything was deep fried or doused in double cream and brandy, or mayonnaise. Now there's a demand for healthier options. Back in the 1970s, people thought vegetarians were from another planet.'

So far the inn has featured a modern twist on the seafood classic using large shell-on prawns on a bed of peppery salad leaves with a light dressing on the side, mushroom stroganoff with a ramekin of wild rice, and poached haddock risotto, and they are currently working on ways to revamp the famous German chocolate cake without the lashings of double cream, kirsch and glacé cherries. There is definitely an element of customers yearning for the comfort food of their youth, and many restaurateurs and hoteliers are waking up to this demand. Jeake's House Hotel in the picturesque town of Rye in Sussex, has become famous for the only meal it serves – breakfast. The menu is unapologetically based on the cosy atmosphere of nursery favourites and includes haddock with poached egg on top, devilled kidneys, buttered kippers and, most popular of all, soft-boiled egg with Marmite soldiers.

'There is definitely an element of customers yearning for the comfort food of their youth, and many restaurateurs and hoteliers are waking up to this demand'

'People really do seem to respond well to all the old favourites – it's feelgood food. But we do have a job explaining to foreign tourists the concept of soldiers,' explains Jeakes's manager Richard Martin. 'And once we've got the message across that it's not some weird British cannibalist fetish, we then have to try to describe Marmite!' Jeake's sources all its ingredients from local farms and suppliers. 'Very often guests will wander off after breakfast in search of the butcher who makes our homemade pork and herb sausages and they'll pick up a pound to take home!'

These retro dishes may sound the same as they did 30 years ago, but the chances are that what you'll be served is a very different kettle of fish – more likely undyed organic haddock than the bright-yellow mush of yesteryear.

These days, the emphasis is on quality ingredients and subtle flavours. If you see chicken in a basket on a pub menu today, the chicken is likely to be organic, corn-fed and served with a lime-and-coriander tapenade rather than sweetcorn relish.

At Seatoller House in the Lake District, dinner is still announced at 7pm by the beating of a gong, and the visitors book goes back a century, but the food has gone retro with a very big twist – more of a jive, in fact.

Chicken terrine was a classic hotel dish, but this is now spiked with pancetta and served with cranberry-and-kumquat relish. They're still serving fish for tea, but now it's baked fillet of red sea bream with tomato-and-lime salsa. And yes, you can have steamed pudding, but nowadays, it's not syrup sponge but a sophisticated date-and-walnut blend.

'People really do seem to respond well to all the old favourites – it's feelgood food'

When it comes to retro menus, Italian menus are perhaps ahead of the game – some would argue that many of the old-style trattorias have never felt inclined to change their menus since Slade were in the charts. Even here, though, there are signs that, in order to revisit the past, you need to keep one step ahead. At La Parmigiana, a Glasgow institution since 1976, a quick glance at the menu will certainly take you down memory lane. Supreme of chicken is corn-fed, poached salmon is organic with a leek-and-saffron sauce, the scallops no longer come drowned in cream but are chargrilled with lemon and olive oil, and polenta, rocket and grape, and red-wine salsa have crept onto the menu. The traditional crêpes suzettes flamed at your table are still there, however, as unashamedly retro as the giant peppergrinders.

At the Cricketers Arms, Clavering, the pub and restaurant presided over by Jamie Oliver's parents, the menu is so influenced by yesteryear that it feels like taking a trip in Dr Who's tardis. Starters include baked avocado with crabmeat in thermidor sauce and sautéed chicken livers in port, while mains include rib-eye steak served with horseradish-and-whisky sauce, supreme of chicken sliced on a creamy wholegrain-mustard sauce and sautéed lamb's kidneys with pease pudding. And they still serve petits fours with their coffee. There are, however, some iconic foods of the seventies that are best consigned to history – namely Vesta Chow Meins, Angel Delight and Blue Nun wine, and that you won't find on Les Routiers restaurant retro menus.

What's the catch?

A new wave of enthusiasm for different fish varieties means there is a wider choice of exciting dishes on restaurant menus. We net a rich source of species from our coastline, and our chefs have devised fabulous ways of serving them

It is not only delicious and versatile, but seafood is low in calories, high in protein and rich in vitamins, minerals and natural oils – in fact, it is one of the most nutritious foods we can eat.

Fish features in many different guises on menus around the world, and in the UK it has become the star feature on many of Les Routiers members' menus. More restaurants are creating superb fish dishes from fish caught off the British coast.

Apart from the national favourite – battered and fried fish served with chips – fish offers plenty of cooking possibilities. You can oven roast it whole, stuffed with aromatic herbs, a simple and fuss-free option, or lightly pan-fry fillets and serve with a butter or caper sauce. White fish is a brilliant canvas for absorbing a range of spicy and citrussy marinades, and once flavoured, the fish takes no time to cook on the barbecue, on a griddle, or under the grill.

The cooking possibilities are endless, especially as we are widening our fish choices and buying alternatives to the ever-popular cod and haddock. Sea bass, sea bream, halibut and monkfish are among the top choices. But that's not all. There are more than 21,000 species of fish in the world, and more than 100 varieties widely available to try in the UK.

Many of the fish varieties caught off our coastline are served at Les Routiers' establishments. In winter, try sea bass, coley, red gurnard and brill; in summer, flounder, hake, sardines, megrim, lemon or Dover sole. All year round, we can tuck into marvellous monkfish, John Dory, redfish and mackerel – just a few to look out for on menus or at fishmongers around the country.

'There are more than 21,000 species of fish in the world, and more than 100 varieties widely available to try in the UK'

Seafish was set up in 1981 and works to help consumers find out more about the wide variety of seafood available and the many benefits that it offers, as well as to help all sectors of the seafood industry raise standards, improve efficiency and develop environmentally responsible practices.

A key date in the Seafish calendar is the annual **Seafood Week**, which is held every October. And the date is no coincidence, for it is at this time of year when the best stocks of many different types of seafood are available to buy.

During Seafood Week, Seafish will be advising on buying and cooking fish and shellfish. It will be running special promotions with many restaurants and retailers. For information about the week, and events at other times of the year, check out its website at **www.seafish.org.uk**. It offers a wealth of information, and a wide database of restaurants, pubs and fish-and-chip shops, and even recipes to try for yourself.

The grape and the good

Choosing wine is easy once you know how. **Julie Arkell** guides you through a wine list, helping you distinguish grape varieties and pick out the real corkers

In last year's guide, I confessed that there are times when I hate being handed the wine list. Following a recent Bad Restaurant Wine experience, may I change my mind?

With a group of 34 friends, I went for a celebratory meal at a popular London restaurant. We had a wonderful evening, the food was scrumptious and the service impeccable. But it was the most sober event of its kind, all because of the house wine. The red and white Turkish Shifting Sands (I think that was the translation!) was so gut-rottingly dreadful that I could not force myself to drink more than a sip of each – this was one occasion when water had never tasted so good.

The sad point of this tale is that this restaurant had some very decent grog that was only fractionally more expensive than the house wines, which proves the point that it is all too easy to be blinded by price alone. Mind you, this cuts both ways: on special occasions, many people are swayed into buying the most expensive bottle on the list on the premise that it is going to be the finest wine available, yet this is not always the case. Over the page, I have decon-structed a wine list to show how to spot a good wine, and find a bottle that won't break the bank.

Here is an example of a typical wine list you may be handed at a Les Routiers' restaurant, accompanied by Julie Arkell's helpful tips on what's a good buy and what's not.

Before you dismiss house wines out of hand, check to see if any of them are French Vin de Pays. These 'country wines' usually offer great flavour, great character and, very often, great value. Ask if you can try a sip before you commit yourself to buying a whole bottle – nothing ventured, nothing gained!

Top restaurateurs always provide the full name of each wine, where it has been made (down to regional level), by whom and in which year (the vintage). A list that merely states the likes of Cabernet Sauvignon/Merlot, Chile is meaningless and signals bad news – if the standard of the list is poor, then what hope is there for the quality of the wines it represents?

House wines

Cornellana Cabernet Sauvignon/Merlot, Rapel Valley, Chile, 2003 £14.95
Aromas of green pepper and mint are followed by soft, ripe blackberry and plum flavours, with just enough tannin to provide grip and texture.

Domaine Coussergues Viognier, Vin de Pays d'Oc, France, 2004 £13.95
The aromatic Viognier variety is both subtle and seductive, exhibiting fragrant peach and apricot aromas. The palate is well-balanced, with exotic fruit flavours and fresh acidity.

White wines

Jacob's Creek Dry Riesling, South East Australia, 2004 £14.95
A popular wine with dry, whistle-clean, fruity flavours of green apples and zippy citrus fruits.

Jordan Estate Barrel Fermented Chenin, Stellenbosch, South Africa, 2003 £20.50
A serious Chenin full of creamy, spicy complexity and citrus fruits.

Domaine M. Schaetzel Pinot Blanc d'Alsace, Cuvée Reserve, France, 2003 £20.50
A delightful white with a nutty and creamy flavour that lingers on the palate. A superb wine to complement food.

Gisborne Vineyards Barrel Fermented Chardonnay, New Zealand, 2003 £19.25
A lightly oaked style, with an aroma of toasted coconut and flavours of ripe peach.

Givry Blanc, Côte Chalonnaise, Burgundy, France, 2002 £33.75
A Chardonnay with plenty of ripe, exotic fruit and a lovely, toasty bouquet.

It is always worth comparing New World against Old. Here, the New Zealand Chardonnay shares many of the same delicious flavours as the classic Old World version, yet it costs much less.

Alsace Pinot Blanc is indeed a food-friendly wine that can be drunk with all kinds of different dishes. Other highly versatile wines include most Italian whites, alongside New World Cabernet Sauvignon, Merlot, Semillon, Riesling and Chardonnay.

Jacob's Creek is the best-selling wine in the country, so 'popular' is something of an understatement here! Don't be shy of buying brands when eating out – they are usually extremely reliable and can be the ideal choice in restaurants that do not give much information on their wine list, or when you do not recognise any other familiar names.

Wine that has been fermented and/or aged in oak is always well-rounded, creamy and full-bodied, with unmistakable aromas and flavours of vanilla, hot buttered toast and spice. Key words to look for are oaked, oak aged, *fûts de chêne*, barrel fermented, barrel aged, *riserva*, *reserva* and *crianza*.

High-quality wine lists feature a description of each wine and the best also include hints on suitable food matches. Treat them with some caution, however, because they may have been written by the merchant who sold the wine to the restaurant – they are less likely to be entirely honest about a wine that in reality sports flavours of swamp and boiled cabbage!

Red wines

Alamos Ridge Malbec, Bodegas Esmerelda, Mendoza, Argentina, 2003
Rich and powerful, with plummy, chocolatey fruit and creamy, vanilla notes, matured in French oak to add depth. — £16.95

This sounds – and is! – every bit as tasty as the more expensive reds on this list. It therefore pays to look for wines from less popular countries and/or grapes – there are great bargains to be unearthed.

Bogle Old Vine Zinfandel, Clarksburg, California, 2001
A robust yet refined red made from old vines. This gives a wonderful concentration of red and black fruit aromas and flavours. — £26.95

Tommasi Amarone della Valpolicella, Veneto, Italy, 1998
Rich, complex and full-bodied, with a warmth and intensity of raisin fruit and hints of smoke and charcoal. Ideal on special occasions, with red meat, roasts, game and ripe cheeses. — £39.95

Given the similarity of these wines in quality, taste and price, how do you choose between the two? Well, in this particular example, the less expensive bottle is the better wine because 1996 was a far superior vintage to 1997. So, either bone up on vintages before you leave home, or take a vintage guide to the restaurant.

Château Chasse Spleen, Cru Bourgeois Moulis, Bordeaux, France, 1996
Full-bodied, with great finesse, vivid colour and a luxuriant, creamy, rich flavour of cassis and chocolate, and warm, spicy, vanilla undertones. — £52.50

Château Meyney, Cru Bourgeois St. Estèphe, Bordeaux, France, 1997
Rich and full, with flavours of chocolate, spice and blackcurrants. Ample, generous and very classy. — £58.75

Rosé wines

Kumala Rosé, Western Cape, South Africa, 2004
An easy-drinking, crisp and refreshing rosé made in a fruit-driven style – strawberries and raspberries are the key flavours. — £12.00

As soon as you read words such as easy-drinking, crisp and refreshing, you should be checking the vintage of the wine on sale. Rosés are designed to be drunk while they are young and fresh, ideally within 12 months of the vintage date. Any-thing older suggests that the wine may be tiring, or that it is already past its best.

Champagne and sparkling wines

Mumm Cuvée Napa Brut, California, USA, NV
An excellent champagne lookalike, based on the same grape varieties and produced by the same method, this sparkling wine has the characteristic biscuity aroma and delicate mousse. — £22.00

JM Gremillet Brut, Balnot-sur-Laignes, Aube, NV
Excellent 'growers' champagne, with tiny bubbles and masses of soft brioche flavours. — £29.50

Moët et Chandon Brut Imperial, Epernay, NV
Soft and biscuity, with a fine mousse. — £43.00

Look at these three descriptions. Can you spot the difference? In reality, there is very little to separate the style of these wines and yet you are asked to pay a whopping £21 more for the brand name! Growers' champagnes and many New World sparklers offer identikit flavours to their big-name cousins and are always less expensive.

The grape variety is the biggest clue to the aromas and flavours in the bottle, and each has its own signature. To learn more, see our accompanying guide to top grape varieties over the page.

Top grape varieties
matching food and wine

Reds

Cabernet Franc
Flavours of raspberries, blackcurrants and tobacco, with good texture and body, in a grassy, leafy style.
Good with: lamb and goose.

Cabernet Sauvignon
Rich and complex, boasting flavours of blackcurrants, cherries, blackberries, chocolate and, sometimes, mint, eucalyptus or cedar.
Good with: red meat.

Grenache
Brimming with untamed flavours of black and red fruits, smoke, nuts, white pepper, toffee, chocolate and coffee.
Good with: beef.

Merlot
Oozes plump, mellow flavours of brambles, damsons, blackcurrants, chocolate, black cherries and coffee beans.
Good with: chicken and shepherd's pie.

Nebbiolo
Inky and tarry, with flavours of prunes, plums, cherries, blackberries, red fruit, raisins and liquorice.
Good with: pheasant and duck.

Pinot Noir
Elegant, silky, strawberry, raspberry and cherry flavours, mellowing to a gamey style with maturity.
Good with: calves' liver and duck.

Sangiovese
All soft red fruits, plums, earth, tobacco, leather and herbs, rounded off by a bitter twist.
Good with: pasta dishes.

Syrah/Shiraz
A fusion of majestic structure, heady aromas and flavours of spice, liquorice, chocolate and sun-baked black fruits.
Good with: steak.

Tempranillo
From soft to intense, every style shares flavours of strawberries, cocoa, spice, tobacco and herbs.
Good with: pork and goulash.

Zinfandel/Primitivo
Lush flavours of blackberries, raspberries, cherries, dried fruit, mixed spice, dates, mint and black pepper.
Good with: Mexican food and cheese.

Whites

Chardonnay
Unoaked styles are lemony. Richer, oaked versions boast cream, spice, tropical fruit and butterscotch flavours.
Good with: chicken and fish.

Chenin Blanc
Makes crisp, dry wines and rich, honeyed sweeties sharing flavours of apples, melon, pear and guava.
Good with: cold meats.

Gewürztraminer
Pungent and almost oily-textured, bursting with exotic flavours of ginger, melon, lychees and Turkish Delight.
Good with: Thai and Chinese.

Muscat
Muscat smells and tastes of grapes and three styles are made: delicate, dry versions; luscious, fortified styles; and sweet fizz.

Pinot Blanc
An easy-drinking, appley style sporting a lick of citrus acidity, although some can be herbaceous.
Good with: fish and seafood.

Pinot Gris/Pinot Grigio
Light, crisp and spicy, or intense and pungent, with ripe peach flavours and a whiff of smoke.
Good with: pasta.

Riesling
Floral and peachy, streaked with lime juice, developing flavours of honey, pineapple and hints of kerosene.
Good with: spicy seafood.

Sauvignon Blanc
Flaunts pronounced aromas and flavours, including gooseberries, nettles, elderflower, tomato leaf, asparagus and grapefruit.
Good with: fish and goat's cheese.

Sémillon/Semillon
Young wines are lean, grassy and citrussy. Older styles become lanolin-soft, honeyed, custardy and nutty.
Good with: gammon and satay.

Viognier
Graceful and sophisticated, with a spring-flowers scent and apricot, white peach and nutmeg flavours.
Good with: chicken and duck.

20 Reasons to drink...

1 **1980 Vintage Port (£80)**
These delicious, fruit-driven wines are now ready for drinking and are the perfect after-dinner treat.

2 **1995 Vintage Champagne (£65+)**
This vintage is starting to drink beautifully now and although it may be expensive, each sip makes every penny worth it!

3 **Anything made from the Verdelho grape (£15)**
These lovely, soft, peach-and-lime-flavoured wines are so versatile that they can be drunk with a whole spectrum of foods, from seafood salad to spicy noodle dishes.

4 **Australian Semillon (£30)**
These wines are one of the wonders of the New World – waxy, custardy, creamy, lush, fleshy, lanolin-soft and well-rounded, with flavours of honey, ripe tropical fruits, nuts and slices of lemon and lime.

5 **Australian Sparkling Shiraz (£15)**
If you haven't tried this fun fizz before, expect aromas of rich, chewy, liquorice toffees and flavours of melted treacle, brown sugar and pure blackcurrant cordial.

6 **Boschendal Grande Cuvée Sauvignon Blanc, South Africa (£15)**
A classy white boasting all the zippy, grassy, tropical fruit flavours of Sauvignon, but without the rasping acidity, so it is much softer.

7 **Brown Brothers Tarrango, Australia (£12)**
A unique, 'must-try,' juicy, fruity Beaujolais lookalike that everyone falls in love with on first taste, created by one of Australia's finest and most innovative producers.

8 **Central Otago Pinot Noir, New Zealand (£45)**
This fine, sophisticated and elegant red is the nearest thing in taste to top-notch red Burgundy without carrying the same price tag.

9 **German Spätburgunder (£25)**
Some stunning reds are now being made from this grape (the German name for Pinot Noir). The best ripple with delightful raspberry and cherry flavours.

10 **Manzanilla (£12)**
Ditch the pre-dinner G&T in favour of this cracking, breathtakingly dry and refreshingly tangy sherry, which boasts a delicate style and a faintly salty, sea air twang.

11 **Marchese de' Frescobaldi, Nippozano, Chianti Rufina Riserva 2001, Italy (£25)**
Classic Chianti and a Decanter Magazine World Wine Awards trophy winner.

12 **Nyetimber Classic Cuvée Brut, West Sussex (£40)**
No, don't laugh! This English sparkling wine is every bit as good as Champagne – indeed, it has often been mistaken for it.

13 **Quinta do Crasto Vinha Maria Teresa, Douro, Portugal (£40)**
Portuguese reds are often sorely underestimated, so sample this big, powerful style to see what you have been missing!

14 **Tokaji Aszú 5 Puttonyos, Hungary (£20)**
A fascinating and delectable sweet wine, with enticing apricot, lime-skin and quince marmalade flavours – try it with rich, smooth pâtés.

15 **Top 1982 Bordeaux reds (£40+)**
If you are lucky enough to find a wine from this fabulous, rich and concentrated vintage, then buy it while you can!

16 **Top 1990 Bordeaux reds (£35+)**
Wines from this magnificent vintage are beginning to soften and become drinkable now.

17 **Top 1990, 1995, 1996, 1997 and 2000 white Burgundies (£35+)**
All these vintages are superb and are now ready for drinking.

18 **Top 1990, 1993 and 1995 red Burgundies (£40+)**
Once again, these wines from excellent vintages are approachable now.

19 **Villa Maria Seddon Vineyard Pinot Gris, New Zealand (£20)**
Although this wine is slightly off-dry, it is an ideal partner to smoked salmon – and, yes, this does go against all the textbook smoked salmon-and-wine-matching rules, but it is a magical combination!

20 **And finally ...**
Explore the world of wine by being more adventurous – drink something that you have never tasted before.

On the up

A Sideways move?
Impress your date by ordering Californian Pinot Noir to show that you're into the latest hot movies. Since last year's release of the Oscar-winning *Sideways*, CPN sales have shot up by an astonishing 30 per cent!

PG tip
No, not the tea that chimps like to drink! This is Pinot Grigio, aka Pinot Gris, the grape that gives us fresh, spicy white wines that are terrific with or without food. And if you want full-frontal, go for one from France's Alsace region.

It's all Greek to me
Did the 2004 Athens Olympics turn the tide? Who knows, but modern Greek wines are fresh, well-made, stylish and trendy. Based on original grapes such as Agiorghitiko – difficult to spell, never mind pronounce – they're proof that there is life beyond Retsina.

Going down

ABC
The Anything But Chardonnay brigade is finally winning the war, yee-ha! This is not to denigrate Chardonnay, because this grape can create sublime wines, but it was beginning to dominate wine lists at the expense of equally interesting whites. If this argument is not enough to convince you, then consider that no less than 51 baby girls have been christened Chardonnay in the wake of the television drama *Fooballers' Wives*!

Snapping at les talons
France has already lost out to Australia as the UK's largest wine supplier and now California is threatening to push it into third place. Definitely not a sideways move...

All screwed up?
How many corked wines have you come across over the past 12 months – the ones with the off-putting, musty smells and flavours? Even one is too many, so it's great to see more and more bottles losing that potentially dodgy piece of tree bark in favour of a taint-free piece of metal.

ENGLAND

'On the Continent people have good food; in England people have good table manners', wrote George Milkes in *How to be an Alien* in 1946.

Happily, this is not the case today. England is world-renowned for being a culinary champion rather than for its dining etiquette, and that's not just in London, but in the regions, too. Our restaurants have undergone something of a renaissance in the last 10 years: a refocusing on quality ingredients and a growing interest in local ingredients and organic foods has put flavour firmly back on the menu.

Les Routiers' members are at the forefront of this change, excelling at all things gastronomic. Recognising that good food begins at home, they are drawing on fabulous local ingredients, highlighting the different strengths and flavours of each of our regions. You can feast on hearty Lancashire hotpot in the north or the freshest Cornish seafood and Devon scones in the south.

Our members have created their own individual style and settings, too, from the quaint and quirky to the smart and contemporary, so you could choose to eat in a dining room steeped in history and filled with antiques or luxuriate in the minimalism of one of our modern boutique-style hotels. We can't offer you Michelin stars and TV chefs, but what we can guarantee is good, honest food that is based on quality, friendly service and good, old-fashioned hospitality.

Bath

Eastern Eye

8a Quite Street, Bath BA1 2JS
Telephone: +44(0)1225 422323
manager@easterneye.co.uk
www.easterneye.com

Fancy eating Indian food in a setting that's as majestic as the Taj Mahal? Then head to the Eastern Eye, where you can enjoy spicy specialities in Georgian splendour. The large, open-plan room has three glass ceiling domes, large windows, stunning ceilings, columns and fanlights, which turn dining into quite an occasion. The menu specialises in northern India and Bengal cooking. Start with the usual platter of poppadoms and chutneys and a cold Indian lager (Bangla comes highly recommended), while you check out its extensive enticements. There's much to tempt you away from the usual selection of jalfrezis or dansaks. If you're not sure where to head, check out the chef's recommendations first, which includes splendid seafood and vegetarian dishes. The butty kebabs from Bengal, small slices of delicately spiced and tender lamb cooked in a tandoori oven, are a perfect partner to another Bengali dish of channa bhaji – fried chickpeas in a spicy sauce. Main courses such as Karali lamb and garlic chilli masala chicken are produced with panache and the pilau rice is fresh and fluffy. The combination of freshly cooked food, reasonable prices and swift, friendly service means the Eastern Eye is always busy and we recommend you book.

Prices: Main course from £7.50. House wine £11.95.
Last orders: Food: lunch 14.30; dinner 23.30.
Closed: Rarely.
Food: Indian.
Other points: No-smoking area. Children welcome.
Directions: J18/M4. (Map 4, B7)

Bath

Rajpoot

Rajpoot House, 4 Argyle Street, Bath BA2 4BA
Telephone: +44(0)1225 466833/464758
www.rajpoot.com

This popular restaurant close to Pulteney Bridge has won many accolades for its exquisite food. And it's easy to see why, as everything is done with style, from the smartly turboned waiters to the vibrant décor and menu. The basement is divided into three snug, but cool, air-conditioned rooms, each individually themed along the lines of Old India, Indian Cottage and Kamra. The authentic feel is further enhanced by the traditionally decorated bar and richly coloured ceilings, while exposed brick walls and crisp white tableclothes provide contemporary touches. The menu brings together a comprehensive selection of tandoori, vegetarian, biryani and curry specialities such as massala, punjabi and charga dishes. Fish is also a star feature, from the unusual Rajpoot salmon to the fish Himshore – cod chunks cooked in coconut milk garnished with prawns, and green pepper. The choice of extras and sides is just as impressive. For those who would rather not agonise over the extensive list, there are two very appealing set menus. The wine cellar also covers a wide spectrum, from light-bodied dry whites to full-bodied reds, and includes a trio of half bottles and, interestingly, two Indian varieties worth trying.

Prices: Set lunch £7.95 and dinner £25. House wine £12.50.
Last orders: Food: lunch 14.30; dinner 23.00.
(Friday and Saturday 23.30).
Closed: Rarely.
Food: Indian.
Other points: No smoking in the restaurant. Children welcome.
Directions: J18/M4. City centre, off Pulteney Bridge.
(Map 4, B7)

Bath

Tilley's Bistro

3 North Parade Passage, Bath BA1 1NX
Telephone: +44(0)1225 484200
dmott@tilleysbistro.co.uk
www.tilleysbistro.co.uk

Set over three floors in one of Bath's oldest houses, Tilley's has bags of character, thanks to its many cosy nooks and crannies. The main beamed dining room, with an original stone fireplace at either end, has a wine-bar atmosphere. Up windy stairs is a comfortable lounge, small bar and private dining room. Good food at good prices means that David and Dawn Mott's bistro remains popular, even after 13 years in business, so it's always best to book. The set lunches are freshly flavoursome with carrot and potato soup sprinkled with crispy croûtons and a hint of cumin, or avocado calypso with pineapple, grapes, melon and Marie-Rose sauce to start. Second courses of spaghetti in a cream sauce with baby spinach and Bleu d'Auvergne cheese or fish of the day come with a choice of accompaniments. In the evening, the carte and separate vegetarian menu offers a wide choice. The carte ranges from Cornish brown crab with cherry tomato tart to escargots à la bourguignonne through to fillet steak au poivre. Fabulous Salcombe Dairy ice cream set standards of the pudding bar high. There's a global selection of wines, nearly all under £20, with about nine available by the glass.

Prices: Set lunch £12.50 and dinner £20 and £25. Main course from £10. House wine £13.
Last orders: Food: lunch 14.30; dinner 23.00.
Closed: Sunday.
Food: French and English.
Other points: Totally no smoking. Children welcome. Wheelchair access.
Directions: J18/M4. In the centre of Bath, near to the Abbey.
(Map 4, B7)

Chillcompton

Court Hotel

Linch Hill, Emborough, Chillcompton,
Bath and NE Somerset BA3 4SA
Telephone: +44(0)1761 232237
reception@courthotel.co.uk
www.courthotel.co.uk

Close to Bath and Bristol, and with Cheddar Gorge, Longleat and Glastonbury nearby, this traditional hotel makes an excellent touring base. Restored by the current owners in 1992, its Edwardian-style interiors marry very well with the architecture. If you don't want to follow the tourist trail, it's easy to lose yourself in the three and a half acres of attractive grounds. The hotel's friendly and efficient staff will also ensure your stay is relaxing and comfortable. Bedrooms in the main house are traditionally decorated, and there are further ground-floor rooms in an adjacent wing and bedrooms in the separate lodge. However, it's the coach-house bedrooms that are the most contemporary. Dining options include informal meals in the bar and conservatory and a more formal full menu in Browne's Restaurant. Modern European in style, start with an insalata Caprese or breaded and deep-fried frogs' legs, before choosing from the many meat, fish and steak and grill dishes, which include chicken Grand Marnier, a huge mixed grill or a fruits de mer platter. On Sundays, there's a well-priced traditional lunch menu. The wide-ranging wine list is reasonably priced.

Rooms: 18. Double room from £65, single from £45.
Prices: Sunday lunch £11.50. Main course from £12.
House wine £9.50.
Last orders: Food: lunch 14.30; dinner 22.00. No food on Bank Holidays.
Closed: Rarely.
Food: Traditional British.
Other points: No-smoking area. Children welcome. Garden. Car park.
Directions: Take the A367 from Bath to Radstock, then Wells Road to Chillcompton. Take the A37 from Bristol. (Map 4, C7)

East Harptree

Harptree Court

East Harptree, near Bristol,
Bath and NE Somerset BS40 6AA
Telephone: +44(0)1761 221729
linda.hill@harptreecourt.co.uk
www.harptreecourt.co.uk

This handsome Georgian house, built in 1796, is set in 17 acres of landscaped gardens. You will feel deep in the countryside, but Harptree is conveniently near Bristol, Bristol Airport and Bath. Despite the grandness of its long drive that takes you past water features and ornate bridges, the hotel retains the warmth and friendliness of a family home. Tea on arrival makes you feel immediately welcome. Guests have a choice of sitting rooms: a smaller upstairs room with log fire and owner Charles Hill's 1970s record collection, or downstairs a larger room attired in period style. All the downstairs rooms, including the dining room, have wonderful views over the grounds. Breakfast is light and healthy, continental or the full-on English, and can be taken in the dining room or in the hall in front of a roaring fire. Dinner prepared by Linda Hill needs to be pre-booked, or you can walk to the village pub. The three bedrooms are large and furnished with antiques and Persian rugs, with stunning garden views. In-room entertainment runs to DVD players, tea/coffee-making facilities, books, magazines, chocolates, fresh fruit and flowers.

Rooms: 3, 1 en suite. Double/twin from £80, single from £60.
Prices: Set dinner £20.
Closed: Christmas.
Food: Traditional British.
Other points: Totally no smoking. Garden. Children over 12 welcome. Car park. Tennis court. Croquet.
Directions: Exit 18/M4 and Exit 18/M5. Turn off the A368 on to the B3114 for Chewton Mendip. After approximately half a mile, turn right into the drive just after the crossroads. (Map 5, C1)

Ivinghoe

The Kings Head

Station Road, Ivinghoe, Leighton Buzzard,
Bedfordshire LU7 9EB
Telephone: +44(0)1296 668388/668264
info@kingsheadivinghoe.co.uk
www.kingsheadivinghoe.co.uk

This 17th-century coaching inn more than holds its own in the charm and character stakes in the pretty village of Ivinghoe. It fills a prime site alongside one side of the village green. Low beams, oak panelling, antique furniture and period portraits create even more ambience. Enjoy a drink in one of the bars, or head to the restaurant or up to the banqueting suite. Chef Jonathan O'Keefe cooks to suit all diners, from his Bon Appetit lunch menu to the carte. Three-course set lunch menus feature starters of warm goat's cheese salad, followed by pan-fried fillet of sea bass and a selection of homemade puds. Vegetarians have a separate menu and the carte is another veritable feast of well-sourced dishes, from starters of fillet of red mullet to fillet of beef from Buccleuch and Aylesbury duckling. The banqueting suite, featuring paintings from Woburn Fine Arts, is available for business or pleasure and is an excellent setting for private functions.

Prices: Set lunch £16.95 and dinner from £33 including coffee. House wine £19.50.
Last orders: Food: lunch 14.15; dinner 21.30.
Closed: Sunday evening and 27-29 December.
Food: Modern British.
Other points: No smoking in the restaurant. Children welcome. Car park. Private banqueting. Wheelchair access to the restaurant/pub.
Directions: M25. Take the A41 to Tring. Turn right onto the B488 to Ivinghoe. The restaurant is on the right at the junction with the B489. (Map 5, B4)

Barkham

The Bull Inn

Barkham Road, Barkham, Wokingham,
Berkshire RG41 4TL
Telephone: +44(0)1189 760324
barkhambull@barbox.net
www.thebullatbarkham.com

At one time, this village pub doubled as the village blacksmiths. Today, the original forge still stands in the centre of The Bull's restaurant and scorch marks are visible on the adjacent beams. You can't fail but be won over by this pub's traditional pedigree; it's full of character and history. The main building was originally a brewhouse and the restaurant extension was the working blacksmith's forge from 1728 until it closed in 1982. You can eat informally in the bar or in the large attractive garden. In the restaurant, linen-clothed tables set beneath huge exposed beams create a more formal setting for chef-proprietor Adrian Brunswick's traditional country cooking. Expect a modern twist to familiar dishes – perhaps calves' liver on a rocket potato cake, venison steak on a bed of braised red cabbage with a spiced port and orange sauce or smoked haddock in a leek and prawn sauce. Chocoholics will appreciate the moist chocolate fudge cake with lashings of cream. As well as the hearty pies, chillies and battered fish, lighter dishes are available at lunchtime. Wife Susie oversees the large and attractively refurbished bar, dispensing Adnams ales and well-chosen wines.

Prices: Main course from £7. House wine £11.95.
Last orders: Bar: lunch 14.50; dinner 22.50 (Sunday 22.20). Food: lunch 14.15; dinner 21.15.
Closed: Rarely.
Food: Modern and Traditional British, and continental.
Other points: No smoking in the restaurant. Garden. Car park. Dogs welcome in the bar.
Directions: Exit10/M4. Head towards Wokingham and follow signposts to Barkham. The Bull Inn is in the centre of Barkham. (Map 5, C4)

...for the latest news

Newbury

The Bunk Inn

Curridge Village, Newbury, Berkshire RG18 9DS
Telephone: +44 (0)1635 200400
thebunkinn@btconnect.com
www.thebunkinn.co.uk

Travel-weary M4 drivers in need of a bed can now bypass the rather anonymous Chieveley Travel Inn, for a comfortable room at Mickey Liquorish's ever-popular Bunk Inn. All the bedrooms are kitted out with quality fabrics and fittings and smart en suite facilities. The accommodation should also appeal to those looking for a bustling and informal pub, and the present food set-up should not disappoint either. On the menu, you'll find sound traditional favourites alongside more modern pub dishes starring on the daily chalkboard and weekly changing carte. Bangers and mash or a 'Bunk' long loaf snack are hearty, comforting fare. Alternatively, head for the attractive conservatory dining room for the posher dishes of ham hock and caper terrine with apple chutney, followed by half-shoulder of lamb with port and redcurrant gravy, with stem ginger brûlée or a plate of cheese with chutney to finish. Altogether, the newly extended beamed bar and front terrace with upmarket tables and chairs create a civilised atmosphere.

Rooms: 8. Double room from £85, single from £70.
Prices: Restaurant main course from £9.95. Bar main course from £5.95. House wine £13.50.
Last orders: Bar: 24.00. Food: lunch 14.30 (weekend 15.00); dinner 22.00 (Sunday 21.30).
Closed: Rarely.
Food: Traditional and modern British.
Other points: No smoking in the restaurant. Children welcome. Dogs welcome in the bar. Garden. Car park. Wheelchair access.
Directions: Curridge is signposted off the B4009 (Goring road) three miles north of Newbury. J13/M4. (Map 5, C3)

Reading

London Street Brasserie

2-4 London Street, Riverside, Reading,
Berkshire RG1 4SE
Telephone: +44(0)1189 505036
www.londonstbrasserie.co.uk

Ironically, one of the oldest buildings in Reading now houses one of its most contemporary restaurants. Once the toll gate on Duke Street bridge, the Brasserie's interiors have been given a makeover and an appealing modern menu to match. It's an uplifting and pleasant experience eating in the bright restaurant with its white walls, polished wooden floors and tables, scanning the art for sale. In fine weather, the dining room opens out onto an attractive small decked area. The modern British carte also takes in the flavours of the Mediterranean, the Orient and Asia. If you deserve a treat, start with Sevruga caviar, smoked salmon blinis and a miniature frozen vodka or the rich game terrine. Mains include an exotically assembled oriental crispy duck dish, classic brasserie dishes made from local meat and game such as an entrecôte with béarnaise, or more modern teamings of venison fillet and McSween's haggis, figs, baby spinach, port, redcurrant and juniper sauce. The superb bread is care of the Degustibus bakery, and there are excellent cheeses. Puddings are indulgent, none more so than hot-chocolate fondant with Baileys ice cream. The 40-bin globetrotting wine list offers much by the glass. Under the same ownership as the Crooked Billet, Stoke Row.

Prices: Set lunch £13.50 (2 course, 12.00-19.00 daily). Main course from £11. House wine £13.50.
Last orders: Food: 22.30 (Friday and Saturday 23.00).
Closed: Rarely.
Food: Modern British and European.
Other points: Riverside terrace (heated).
Directions: Exit 10 or 11/M4. Follow signs to Oracle park in Oracle multi-storey car park. (Map 5, C4)

Bristol

The Ganges

368 Gloucester Road, Bristol BS7 8TP
Telephone: +44(0)117 924 5234

The long-established Ganges consistently serves authentic Indian food in glitzy surroundings. The restaurant is vividly decorated with large glittering chandeliers, giving it the edge in the glamour stakes. The menu is just as vibrant, focusing on the three main regions through which the River Ganges flows: it rises in Tibet, flows through India and reaches the sea at Bangladesh. The major influence, though, comes from north India and so you'll find the most popular curries, from mild lamb pasanda to a fiery vindaloo king prawn, alongside biryanis on the menu. If you tend to stick to your favourite dish, this is the place to branch out, as the chef has half a dozen well-thought-out and well-priced set menus, plus there's an all-encompassing thali of tandoori murg, lamb tikka, shish kebab, naan, pilau rice, and chicken tikka. Vegetarian dishes, including a vegetarian thali, are a high point, as the vegetables are always fresh, never frozen. The wine list is a cut above, too, and includes classics such as Sancerre and Barolo. There's a refreshing selection of bottled and draught beers, including Cobra, Kingfisher and Lal Toofan.

Prices: Set lunch and dinner from £14.50. House wine £8.95.
Last orders: Food: lunch 14.30; dinner 23.30.
Closed: Rarely.
Food: Indian and Bangladeshi.
Other points: No-smoking area. Children welcome.
Directions: On the A38 Gloucester Road. (Map 4, B6)

Bristol

San Carlo Restaurant

44 Corn Street, Bristol BS1 1HQ
Telephone: +44(0)117 922 6586
www.sancarlo.co.uk

Authentic Italian cooking and a city-centre location mean this restaurant is always busy, but plenty of seating means you should get a table without having to book. The tall Victorian building stands in an attractive pedestrianised area. Inside, clever décor means the long, narrow room is light, bright and airy. The atmosphere is unmistakeably Mediterranean, an ambience that is common to all four restaurants in this small, stylish group. It has adopted a contemporary theme: mirrored walls, white-tiled floor and colour in the form of potted plants and trees of different shapes and sizes. It serves all the popular favourites at reasonable prices, and the cooking is a cut above the norm for a city-centre eaterie majoring in pizzas and pastas. The lengthy menu lists familiar trattoria dishes: fritto misto; buffalo mozzarella with tomato, basil and avocado; saltimboca alla Romana; piccata al limone; and suprema di pollo Genovese. Blackboard specials extend the choice with a range of seafood that could include dressed crab, grilled Dover sole and mixed grilled fish with a good selection by the glass, and France and the New World bringing up the rear. San Carlo's buzzy atmosphere and friendly service are bound to raise your spirits.

Prices: Main course from £11. House wine £11.20.
Last orders: Food: 23.00.
Closed: Rarely.
Food: Italian.
Other points: Children welcome.
Directions: In Bristol city centre. (Map 4, B6)

Bristol

Westfield House

37 Stoke Hill, Stoke Bishop, Bristol BS9 1LQ
Telephone: +44(0)117 962 6119
guest@westfieldhouse.net
www.westfieldhouse.net

Set in the prosperous area of Stoke Hill in Sneyd Park, this friendly, family-run guest house is ideal for those who want to be within easy reach of Bristol city centre, but prefer calmer surroundings. Neo-Georgian in style, Westfield House has two and a half acres of gardens, with plenty to see as the owners are wildlife enthusiasts. The ground-floor rooms are well proportioned and decorated in pleasant pastel shades. There's a comfortable living room with seating around the fireplace and large french windows that lead onto the garden terrace. Upstairs, the bedrooms are beautifully appointed, en suite, and have TV and coffee-making facilities. Food is pretty much bespoke, as Ann Jell cooks more or less to order, be that a simple breakfast or a full-cooked meal. Whichever you choose, you'll find all ingredients are from good local suppliers or Bristol's farmers' market. Typical evening meals might include salmon en croute with puréed spinach and hollandaise sauce with potatoes dauphinoise, followed by apple pie or chocolate mousse. Attention to detail is evident, from the home-made jams and butter pats to the excellent coffee.

Rooms: 3. Double/twin from £79.50. Single from £55.
Prices: Set lunch £15. Set dinner £20. Restaurant main course from £10. Room-service sandwiches/snacks from £7.
Food: Traditional British.
Other points: Totally no smoking. Garden. Children over 12 welcome. Car park.
Directions: J17/M5. Follow the A4018 to Durdham Downs. At Blackboy Hill roundabout turn right, crossing the Downs on Stoke Road through traffic lights into Stoke Hill. Westfield House is the fourth entrance on the left after Church Avenue. (Map 4, B7)

Chalfont St Giles

The Ivy House

London Road, Chalfont St Giles,
Buckinghamshire HP8 4RS
Telephone: +44(0)1494 872184
enquiries@theivyhouse-bucks.co.uk
www.theivyhouse-bucks.co.uk

This much-loved 17th-century brick-and-flint freehouse set in the heart of the Chiltern Hills has views across the Misbourne Valley. Spick-and-span throughout, it sports an extended dining room, a smart patio for alfresco eating and five en suite rooms. The wood and slate-floored bar, with its old beams, cosy armchairs and wood-burning fires is full of traditional charm. A menu of modern British dishes reveals a happiness to experiment with ingredients to produce unusual dishes – look to the blackboard for the day's creations. Starter choices include homemade soups and giant prawns with basil oil and sweet chilli sauce. Main courses extend to pan-fried ostrich with mango and orange sauce, and chargrilled steaks with a choice of sauces, plus winter casseroles, summer salads, pasta meals, vegetarian meals and homemade puddings, perhaps Baileys dark chocolate truffle torte. Retire to one of the individually furnished bedrooms and wake up to a hearty breakfast.

Rooms: 5. Double room £95, single occupancy £75.
Prices: Main course from £9.95. House wine £11.95.
Last orders: Bar: lunch 15.00; dinner 23.00 (open all day at the weekend). Food: lunch 14.30; dinner 21.30 (all day at the weekend).
Closed: Never.
Food: Modern British and global.
Other points: No-smoking area. Children welcome. Dogs welcome in the bar. Garden and courtyard. Car park. Wheelchair access to the restaurant.
Directions: J2/M40. Situated between Amersham and Gerrards Cross on the A413. (Map 5, B4)

Mentmore

The Stag

The Green, Mentmore, Buckinghamshire LU7 0QF
Telephone: +44(0)1296 668423
reservations@thestagmentmore.com
www.thestagmentmore.com

The Stag stands in a picture-postcard village and has a lovely garden overlooking Mentmore House. It is run by Mike and Jenny Tuckwood, whose fresh modern approach to overseeing a traditional country pub has proved a great success. The classic bar is the place to sample Charles Wells ales and some good bar food: hot beef and onion sandwiches for example, one-dish meals of local spicy sausages with mash and onion gravy, or an evening dish such as Moroccan braised lamb with vegetable couscous. Imaginative, seasonally changing evening menus are served in the stylish two-tiered restaurant, which has direct access to the garden. A plate of buffalo mozzarella (from a local herd) with balsamic and black-pepper strawberries makes an unusual starter. Thoughtful attention to inherent flavours produces main courses such as roast cod with coconut and lemon sauce. An alternative to a dessert of baked American cheesecake is a plate of British cheeses.

Prices: Restaurant set lunch £15 and dinner £28, main course from £16. Bar lunch £45.50 and dinner from £8.50.
Last orders: Food: lunch 14.00; dinner 21.00; Sunday 20.30.
Closed: Rarely.
Food: Modern British.
Other points: No smoking in the restaurant. Children welcome at lunch and, over 12 years old, in the evening. Dogs welcome in the bar. Sloping garden with seating. Limited car parking. Wheelchair access (no WC).
Directions: Five miles north east of Aylesbury off A418 towards Leighton Buzzard. (Map 9, B4)

The Ivy House, Chalfont St Giles

Chef/proprietor Jane Mears and her team are always keen to try new recipes. They have sourced a wealth of local ingredients to achieve their exciting menus, which are modern British with a Mediterranean flavour. Here, Jane shares her top suppliers in the Chiltern Hills area.

Visit the local Farmers' Market

There is an excellent French farmers' market, which periodically comes to both Amersham and Chesham. It sells a wide range of quality fresh produce, including olives, garlic and cheeses from France.

Lovely Lee Seafood, Buckland Common

Sycamore Services Ltd Wendover

A413

A4128

Beechdean Ice Cream, North Dean

A404

High Wycombe

Beaconsfield

Lovely Lee Seafood
Dorriens Farm, Buckland Common
Tel: 01494 758978

One of three fishmongers that supplies The Ivy House. It offers a great selection of fresh fish and shellfish, including outstanding fresh Cromer crabs and excellent kiln-roasted salmon. The chef is looking forward to trying many more of its seasonal specialities.

Beechdean Ice Cream
Old House Farm, North Dean, High Wycombe
Tel: 01494 562829
www.beechdean.co.uk

This rich, creamy ice cream is made on the family farm using fresh Jersey whole milk from the pedigree herd. Flavours run from classic vanilla to sticky toffee fudge, and you will find it served at events as grand as Buckingham Palace tea parties to prestigious venues such as the Royal Albert Hall, as well as being sold in farm shops.

Sycamore Services Ltd
Station Approach, Wendover
Tel: 01296 624400

Former owners of Aldridges of Gerrards Cross, David and Margaret sold their greengrocers. They still supply trade customers, and you can sample their vegetables at The Ivy House.

Goddens Butchers
Chesham
Tel: 01494 772997
www.goddens.co.uk

A local Chesham family butchers, which closed its high street shop after the death of the founder Clive Godden. It continues to supply its favoured customers under the guidance of the sons. Excellent steaks, ostrich, boar and award-winning sausages.

Tom Robertson Butchers
10 Chenies Parade,
Station Road, Little Chalfont
Tel: 01494 763084

A long-established family butchers, with an outstanding reputation locally, from which The Ivy House buys top-quality game (including Balmoral wild venison), superb cooked meats and Gressingham duck.

G D Swerling & Sons
Upper Bottom House farm,
Bottom House Farm Lane,
Chalfont St Giles
Tel: 01494 872492

The Swerlings, who own fields opposite, have farmed the local area as long as any-one can remember. Graham should have retired years ago, but won't give up his round, and supplies all of The Ivy House's milk and cream and many of its cheeses.

Goddens Butchers, Chesham

A416

A404

Amersham

Tom Robertson Butchers, Little Chalfont

G D Swerling & Sons, Chalfont St Giles

The Ivy House, Chalfont St Giles

LES ROUTIERS

A413

A40

Waddesdon

Five Arrows Hotel

High Street, Waddesdon, Aylesbury,
Buckinghamshire HP18 0JE
Telephone: +44(0)1296 651727
bookings@thefivearrowshotel.fsnet.co.uk
www.waddesdon.org.uk

Built by the Rothschilds in 1887 to house the architects and craftsmen building Waddesdon Manor Baron Ferdinand's Renaissance-style château is set on a hill in the vast estate behind the inn. It's a delightful Victorian confection of turrets, gables and balconies, now a stylish small hotel-cum-inn. You enter straight into the bar, which leads off to several civilised dining rooms with rug-strewn wood or stone floors, antique tables, and pictures from Lord Rothschild's collection. Locally sourced ingredients plus garden herbs influence the menu; salmon fishcakes with a coriander jam, for example, or crayfish tails on a bed of leaves with dill mayonnaise. Main courses of pan-fried fillet steak with red shallot butter and confit of duck, served with pak choi and a sweet-and-sour sauce give a modern slant to the classics. To finish, choose between the cheese table or hazelnut meringue and homemade honeycomb ice cream. There are also blackboard specials and lighter lunchtime meals. The good wine list majors on the various Rothschild wine interests. The good-sized bedrooms are individually decorated and have all the modern comforts. There are grander suites in the converted courtyard stables.

Rooms: 11. Double room from £85, single from £70.
Prices: Main course from £13.50. House wine £12.50.
Last orders: Bar: lunch 15.00; dinner 23.00. Food: lunch 14.30 (Sunday 14.00); dinner 21.00 (Sunday 20.30).
Closed: Rarely.
Food: Modern British and continental.
Other points: No smoking in the restaurant. Children welcome. Garden. Car park. Wheelchair access.
Directions: Six miles north west of Aylesbury beside the A41 in Waddesdon. (Map 5, B4)

Waddesdon

Waddesdon Manor Restaurant

Waddesdon Manor, Waddesdon, Aylesbury,
Buckinghamshire HP18 0JH
Telephone: +44(0)1296 653242
www.waddesdon.org.uk

One of the last remaining complete examples of 'le style Rothschild' in Europe, Waddesdon Manor, built for Baron Ferdinand de Rothschild and completed in 1889, ranks as one of the finest places to visit in Britain. Built in the style of a 16th-century French château, the Manor is set in acres of parkland. It's now run by the National Trust, which charges for tours of the grounds and Manor. For a taste of the grandeur, book a table in the relaxed surroundings of the ground-floor servants' hall, where you will find one of the most original restaurants. The kitchen mixes National Trust tearoom classics with a lunch menu that is an inspired juxtaposition of traditional dishes from the Rothschild menu books and modern alternatives. Local meat, bread, organic vegetables and eggs are used in dishes such as smoked haddock chowder with curry oil, or braised ham hock with mustard mash. The kindly priced wine list, with its full range of Rothschild family wines, will appeal to serious oenophiles. The Stables Restaurant in the grounds is more casual and offer snacks and cakes. The food and wine here make it well worth the £4 entry fee. Check the website for foodie details.

Prices: Restaurant main course from £9.50. House wine £12.
Last orders: Food: Morning 12.00; Lunch 15.00; Afternoon tea 17.00. Telephone for monthly evening openings.
Closed: Monday and Tuesday except for Bank Holidays, and weekdays in January and February.
Food: Modern European.
Other points: Totally no smoking. Garden. Children welcome. Car park. Wheelchair access.
Directions: Off the A41 between Bicester and Aylesbury. (Map 5, B4)

Huntingdon

Old Bridge Hotel

1 High Street, Huntingdon, Cambridgeshire PE29 3TQ
Telephone: +44(0)1480 424300
oldbridge@huntsbridge.co.uk
www.huntsbridge.com

This 18th-century townhouse has been transformed into a slick hotel and is a top destination for wining and dining. Modern touches such as sea grass and wicker work well alongside the antiques. The 24 bedrooms make up an eclectic range of individually styled rooms; some are traditional, others have striking design statements. The main dining room is elegant and the menu is one to linger over. The bargain lunch menu is either a set-price two- or three-course affair, with starters of butternut squash soup with marjoram and Tuscan oil or warm salad of beetroot, goat's cheese, spring onion and pecan nuts, followed by bread and butter pudding Lighter snacks include hot sandwiches or a platter of prosciutto di San Daniele. The terrace restaurant is just as striking a room, decorated with Julia Rushbury murals. Chef/patron Martin Lee interprets the Huntsbridge Group philosophy of sourcing quality ingredients and turning them into imaginative dishes such as warm salad of confit pheasant with pomegranate, shallots, walnuts and a walnut dressing, and braised Cornish lamb with cumin potatoes, red cabbage and parsnip crisps. The wine list offers a top-class selection.

Rooms: 24. Double room from £120, single from £80.
Prices: Set lunch £16.75. Main course from £12.75. House wine £12.50.
Last orders: Food: lunch 14.30; dinner 22.00.
Closed: Rarely.
Food: Modern British and European.
Other points: No-smoking area. Children welcome. Garden. Car park.
Directions: At the intersection of the A1 (north-south) and the A14 (east-west). (Map 10, D5)

Werrington

Cherry House Restaurant

125 Church Street, Werrington, Peterborough,
Cambridgeshire PE4 6QF
Telephone: +44(0)1733 571721

The quaint thatched cottage that's home to the Cherry House Restaurant comes with a manicured lawn and pond, and just as picturesque interiors. It's comfortably olde worlde inside: the dining room has beams, exposed stone and an open fireplace. The time-honoured style follows through to the kitchen, where regional ingredients figure and cream and butter sauces are popular. French-trained Andrew Corrick is passionate about food and has created a loyal following for his cooking for both the set-price lunch and dinner menus. He's conceived an exciting menu that includes many French and British classics, including timbale of fresh salmon mousse wrapped in Scottish smoked salmon with locally grown asparagus tips and French onion soup to start. Mains offer roast breast of Gressingham duck with a raspberry vinegar and pink peppercorn sauce or tournedos of Scottish beef fillet, served with a creamy Stilton and port sauce and a julienne of celeriac. Alternatively, tuck into medallions of Grasmere Farm pork with a creamy tarragon mustard sauce. For simpler tastes, and at a supplement, there is a selection of grilled steaks. The wine list, helpfully organised by style, offers a comprehensive selection at fair prices.

Prices: Set menu £21.95. House wine £10.95.
Last orders: Food: lunch 14.00 (Sunday 14.30); dinner 21.30 (Saturday 22.30).
Closed: Monday.
Food: Modern British with French influence.
Other points: No-smoking area. Garden. Children welcome. Car park.
Directions: North of Peterborough, the Cherry House is signposted off the A15. (Map 10, D5)

Tattenhall

Mitchell's Wine Bar & Brasserie

Lyndale House, High Street, Tattenhall,
Cheshire CH3 9PX
Telephone: +44(0)1829 771477
info@mitchellswinebar.co.uk
www.mitchellswinebar.co.uk

Proprietors Martin and Peterene Cocking and their staff have moved en masse from the Fox and Barrel at nearby Tarpoley, and are continuing their excellent team spirit and good work at this friendly wine bar and brasserie. Set in the delightful village of Tattenhall in an early 19th-century building, the brasserie has attractive gardens to the front and hardwood floors, comfortable furniture and large windows inside, making it a pleasurable experience before you even get to chef Kevin Morris's consistently good food. His brasserie-style menu starts with his freshly baked breads, which come with butter and olives. Starters include soup or duck liver and orange pâté, and are followed by sautéed medallions of prime fillet of beef in a sage and garlic sauce with lyonnaise potatoes or pan-seared loin of tuna with a warm smoked salmon and potato salad with lime dressing. Steaks come plain or with a classic sauce, and the fresh fish choice, say freshwater bream with olive mash and basil cream, changes daily and is cooked with imagination. Mitchells' wine includes interesting choices among its mainstream collection, all favourably priced.

Prices: Set lunch £13.95. Set dinner £13.50. Restaurant main course from £8.95. Bar main course from £4.50.
Last orders: Bar: lunch 15.00; dinner: 23.00. Food: lunch 14.15 (Sunday 15.00); dinner: 21.00 (Friday and Saturday 21.30). Open all day Saturday.
Closed: Monday.
Food: International.
Other points: No smoking in the restaurant. Garden. Car park. Wheelchair access.
Directions: M53, Chester exit. Just off the A41, seven miles outside Chester on Tattenhall High Street. (Map 8, B5)

Warmingham

The Bear's Paw Hotel

School Lane, Warmingham, Sandbach,
Cheshire CW11 3QN
Telephone: +44(0)1270 526317
enquiries@thebearspaw.co.uk
www.thebearspaw.co.uk

This late-Victorian brick-built hotel beside the River Weaver overlooks willow-dappled water meadows and Warmingham's pretty parish church. If you put a premium on spacious bedrooms and bathrooms, then you've come to the right place. Seven new large en suite bedrooms have recently been added to the existing line-up of six. Overall, the public room décor leans towards the traditional, but this is part of its down-to-earth charm. The open-plan lounge surrounds a spacious central bar and there are log fires and plenty of traditional-style wood panelling and seating to make it feel cosy. The bar menu offers light bites such as club sandwiches or a good-value, weekly changing set-lunch menu. Real-ale fans will be delighted to learn that there are micro-brewery ales on hand pump, perhaps Slater's Premium or Khean's Fine Leg Bitter. In the restaurant, the carte menu offers a range of traditional fare and steaks as well as the more unusual. Start with smoked haddock fishcakes before moving on to rack of lamb, loin of wild boar, red mullet or barramundi. The short wine list travels far in terms of grapes and varieties.

Rooms: 12. Double room from £70, single from £60, family from £80.
Prices: Set lunch £14.95. Restaurant main course from £11.95. Bar main course from £7.95. House wine £9.95.
Last orders: Bar: 23.00 (weekends). Food: dinner 21.00 (21.30 weekends).
Closed: Monday to Friday daytime.
Food: Modern British.
Other points: No-smoking area. Children welcome. Garden. Car park. Wheelchair access to the restaurant/pub.
Directions: Junctions 16,17,18/M6. (Map 8, B6)

Romaldkirk

The Rose and Crown at Romaldkirk

Romaldkirk, Barnard Castle, Co Durham DL12 9EB
Telephone: +44(0)1833 650213
hotel@rose-and-crown.co.uk
www.rose-and-crown.co.uk

Built in 1733 as a coaching inn, the imposing, stone-built Rose and Crown stands beside a Saxon church and one of the beautifully maintained greens in this most picturesque of Teesdale villages. High standards of hospitality, service and cooking have created one of the finest all-round inns in the country. Much of this success can be attributed to consistent cooking that is inspired by the seasons and backed by first-class local produce. Lunchtime filled baps are well presented and traditional favourites such as salmon fishcakes with chive cream sauce are always cooked with flair. Weekly changing menus may also list sea bass with red wine jus, and belly pork with baked bean cassoulet. Exemplary desserts are typified by sticky toffee pudding, but there are also perfectly selected local cheeses. Four-course dinners are served in the civilised, part-panelled restaurant. The spotlessly maintained en suite bedrooms have wooden floorboards, beams, well-chosen antique furniture, stylish contemporary fabrics, and a host of extras. A class act!

Rooms: 12. Double/twin room from £120.
Prices: Set lunch £15.95 and dinner £26. Bar main course from £7.95. House wine £12.95.
Last orders: Bar: lunch 15.00; dinner 23.00. Food: lunch 13.30; dinner 21.30 (Sunday 21.00).
Closed: Rarely.
Food: Modern British.
Other points: No-smoking area. Children welcome. Car park.
Directions: Six miles north west of Barnard Castle on the B6277 towards Middleton-in-Teesdale. (Map 12, C5)

Lostwithiel

Trewithen Restaurant

3 Fore Street, Lostwithiel, Cornwall PL22 0BP
Telephone: +44(0)1208 872373
brianrolls1@supanet.com
www.trewithenrestaurant.supanet.com

During his 24 years in charge, Brian Rolls, and his co-chef Kathryn Rowe, have been cooking up a storm and building a loyal clientele. It may be small but this restaurant is perfectly formed and really cosy. The emphasis is on homemade, from breads to the after-dinner chocolates, and West Country specialities. Locally reared meats, such as venison served with a juniper berry sauce and pork from Tywardreath with a mushroom and basil sauce, are perennial favourites. The daily fish catch is used creatively in the Trewithen platter starter of prawns in sweet-and-sour sauce, melon, homemade paté and Cornish smoked fish or fresh South Coast scallops in a Pernod and cream sauce. Other notables include cheese soup with Cornish Yarg and local venison served in a juniper sauce with smoked bacon and mushrooms. The restaurant's original walls date from the 16th century when it was part of the Duchy Palace Complex. The Duchy Palace next door was the seat of the Cornish Parliament in the 13th century.

Prices: Set dinner £26. Main course from £15. House wine £11.50.
Last orders: Food: dinner 21.30.
Closed: Sunday and Monday except for Bank Holiday weekends and Mondays during the summer.
Food: Modern British with global influences.
Other points: No-smoking area. Children welcome. Patio. Wheelchair access.
Directions: M5, A390, halfway between Liskeard and St Austell, five miles south Bodmin (A30) and five miles east of the Eden Project. (Map 3, E3)

St Austell

Anchorage House

Nettles Corner, Boscundle, Tregrehan Mills, St Austell, Cornwall PL25 3RH
Telephone: +44(0)1726 814071
stay@anchoragehouse.co.uk
www.anchoragehouse.co.uk

This extended Georgian-style lodge offers home-from-home comforts, with the bonus of a having a 15-metre-long pool in its landscaped gardens. The décor is smartly executed, but with comfort in mind. The spacious lounge is perfect for relaxing: dip into the abundant reading matter or settle in for a pre-dinner complimentary sherry. This room leads off to the informal plant-filled conservatory, where breakfast and dinner are served around one large table. Breakfast is a feast of yogurts, berries, fruits, cereals and the full traditional British, newspapers included. They don't have a licence, but you can bring your own wine for the four-course dinner, which is prepared prior to arrangement. Jane and Steve Epperson are welcoming, and refreshingly, laid-back hosts. They've spent over 10 years improving the property to deluxe standards. Each of the bedrooms is individually styled. The two-storey loft suite come with luxury touches: chocs, biscuits, flowers, a turn-down service, king and super king-size beds. Magnificent bathrooms have large baths, separate power showers, and toiletries. There's also a Jacuzzi.

Rooms: 3. Double room from £50 per person, single from £75.
Prices: Four-course dinner by prior arrangement from £30. Suppers from £18. Unlicenced.
Last orders: 19.30.
Closed: December-February.
Food: Traditional British.
Other points: Totally no smoking. Garden. Jacuzzi Spa (BlisSpa) and outdoor swimming pool.
Directions: A30/A391. Two miles east of St Austell on the A390; take the turning for Tregrehan across from the St Austell Garden Centre. Then immediately turn left into the driveway leading into the courtyard of the lodge. (Map 3, E3)

Anchorage House, St Austell

Jane and Steve Epperson like to do things well, and this applies to the menu at Anchorage House as much as their immaculately turned-out guest rooms. Their breakfasts of fresh berries, yogurts and full English showcase many of their key suppliers, and this high standard of ingredients is carried through to their dinner menu. The couple delved into their contacts book so you can enjoy a taste of Cornwall at home.

Richard's
Harbour Road, Par
Tel: 01726 812550

Fish, fruit and vegetables are at Richard's are straight from the local coastline and local farms. Its shelves are stacked with the best fresh produce in the area, and they deliver, too!

A30

Charlie Harris at Tywardreath Butchers
41 Church Street, Tywardreath, Par
Tel: 01726 812051

You can't visit this black-and-white painted, attractive-looking butchers shop without leaving with some of the famous sausages. Charlie Harris makes around 34 different varieties and all are closely guarded recipes. He was the winner of the 1993 National People's Sausage Quest, which was sponsored by *The Guardian* newspaper. Only the best-quality pork goes into his meaty creations, which include pork--and-leek and pork-and-apple, as well as the more unusual pork-and-banana and pork-and-Thai. Anchorage House features its Greenback bacon, sausages, special black puddings, fillet steaks and tender duck breasts on its menu. If you can't find time to visit the shop, order online at www.thelocalbutcher.co.uk.

A390

Visit the local Farmers' Market

The area's farmers' market is held fortnightly on Fridays at Cornerstones Community Centre, Trinity Street. Call 01726 74507 for details, or visit www.foodfromcornwall.com, which also lists food-and-drink events throughout the year, from the Falmouth Oyster Festival to the Cornish Food and Drink Fair.

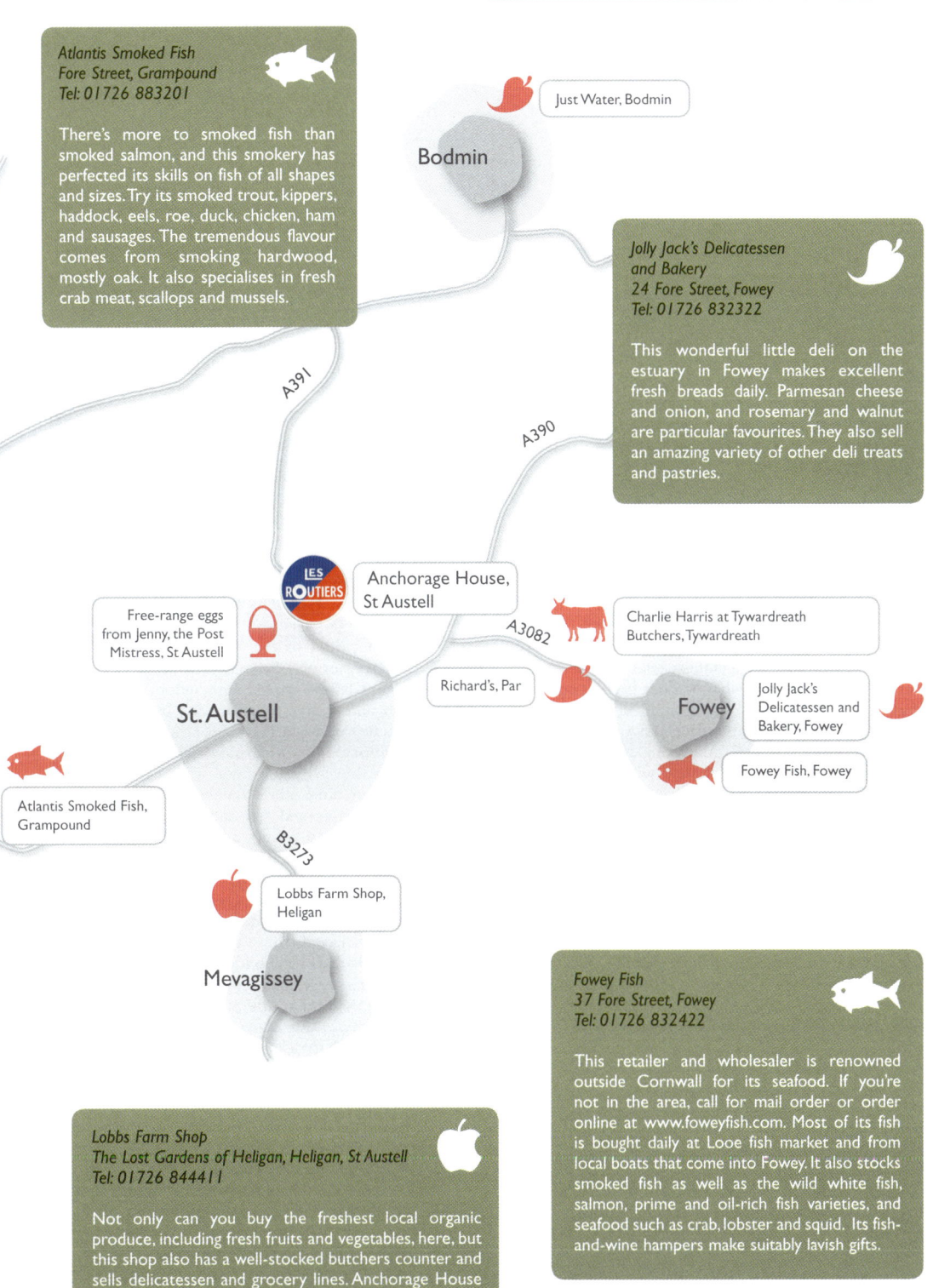

Atlantis Smoked Fish
Fore Street, Grampound
Tel: 01726 883201

There's more to smoked fish than smoked salmon, and this smokery has perfected its skills on fish of all shapes and sizes. Try its smoked trout, kippers, haddock, eels, roe, duck, chicken, ham and sausages. The tremendous flavour comes from smoking hardwood, mostly oak. It also specialises in fresh crab meat, scallops and mussels.

Just Water, Bodmin

Bodmin

Jolly Jack's Delicatessen and Bakery
24 Fore Street, Fowey
Tel: 01726 832322

This wonderful little deli on the estuary in Fowey makes excellent fresh breads daily. Parmesan cheese and onion, and rosemary and walnut are particular favourites. They also sell an amazing variety of other deli treats and pastries.

A391

A390

Anchorage House, St Austell

Free-range eggs from Jenny, the Post Mistress, St Austell

A3082

Charlie Harris at Tywardreath Butchers, Tywardreath

Richard's, Par

St. Austell

Fowey

Jolly Jack's Delicatessen and Bakery, Fowey

Atlantis Smoked Fish, Grampound

Fowey Fish, Fowey

B3273

Lobbs Farm Shop, Heligan

Mevagissey

Fowey Fish
37 Fore Street, Fowey
Tel: 01726 832422

This retailer and wholesaler is renowned outside Cornwall for its seafood. If you're not in the area, call for mail order or order online at www.foweyfish.com. Most of its fish is bought daily at Looe fish market and from local boats that come into Fowey. It also stocks smoked fish as well as the wild white fish, salmon, prime and oil-rich fish varieties, and seafood such as crab, lobster and squid. Its fish-and-wine hampers make suitably lavish gifts.

Lobbs Farm Shop
The Lost Gardens of Heligan, Heligan, St Austell
Tel: 01726 844411

Not only can you buy the freshest local organic produce, including fresh fruits and vegetables, here, but this shop also has a well-stocked butchers counter and sells delicatessen and grocery lines. Anchorage House is a big fan of its locally pressed apple juice. Children and city-weary visitors should find the 'farming in action' displays of interest.

St Austell

Auberge Asterisk

Mount Pleasant, Roche, St Austell, Cornwall PL26 8LH
Telephone: +44(0)1726 890863
ferzan@l-auberge.freeserve.co.uk
www.auberge-asterisk.co.uk

A warm and friendly welcome awaits at Ferzan Zola's French-style auberge in the Cornish countryside. This cream-coloured, squarely solid old house with its plaque prominently displayed wouldn't look out of place in rural France. It's a simple restaurant-with-rooms run with dedicated enthusiasm by Ferzan, who puts all his efforts into what he does best – cooking. Fresh produce delivered daily is used superbly in his eclectic menu that delights with classics and interpretations of modern dishes. A starting point could be the house speciality, coconut soup with water chestnuts and straw mushrooms, or Thai beef marinated in chillies and vinegar. Follow with a venison steak with a creamy Calvados sauce or monkfish with saffron. Puddings are also a speciality, and Ferzan has a flair for meringues, soufflés and profiteroles. The wine list is short, but wide ranging, and prices are a steal. The cosy atmosphere and the simple, rustic pine furniture makes this a particularly laid-back place to dine. Upstairs are three neat en suite bedrooms. They have pretty views and offer very good value in an area that is becoming increasingly short of bed space thanks to the runaway success of the Eden Project.

Rooms: 3. Double room from £49.50, single from £34.75.
Prices: Main course from £12. House wine £8.
Last orders: Food: dinner 21.00 (Wednesday-Saturday for non-residents).
Closed: Rarely.
Food: Modern European.
Other points: Children welcome. Garden. Car park.
Directions: On the A30, two miles west after Innisdown roundabout (Bodmin bypass). About five miles from the Eden Project. (Map 3, E3)

St Ives

The Garrack Hotel and Restaurant

Burthallan Lane, St Ives, Cornwall TR26 3AA
Telephone: +44(0)1736 796199
les@garrack.com
www.garrack.com

Set above Porthmeor Beach with views of 30 miles of coastline, the Garrack Hotel occupies one of the top spots in St Ives. The Kilby family has been at the helm for 36 years and has perfected its offering, from the facilities to the food. It's homely but has all the amenities of a more expensive hotel. The sun terrace and leisure centre with indoor pool, sauna, solarium and gym are surrounded by two acres of gardens. Bedrooms in the main house are decorated in an unfussy country fashion, while rooms in the sea-facing, lower-ground-floor wing cater for those wanting something more contemporary. Some rooms have four-posters and spa baths. In the restaurant, chef Phil Thomas adopts a classic modern British approach, using excellent local seafood and meat. There is a separate section for the many lobster options. The homemade ice creams and speciality coffees are fine ways to end a superb meal. The wine list is carefully selected from various suppliers to offer a global choice and the good local Camel Valley wines. Fair wine prices are achieved by applying fixed mark-ups, rather than the traditional percentage.

Rooms: 18. Double room from £114, single from £68.
Prices: Set dinner £25.50 (four courses). House wine £10.
Last orders: Food: dinner 21.00.
Closed: Rarely.
Food: Modern British.
Other points: Smoking area. Garden. Children welcome. Car park. Wheelchair access to the hotel.
Directions: Leave the A30 and follow the signposts to St Ives, A3074. At the second mini roundabout take the first left, B3311, signposted St Ives. In St Ives, at the first mini roundabout, take the first left and follow the signs for The Garrack Hotel. (Map 3, E2)

Tolverne

Smugglers Cottage of Tolverne

Tolverne, Philleigh, Truro, Cornwall TR2 5NG
Telephone: +44(0)1872 580309
tolverne@btconnect.com
www.tolverneriverfal.co.uk

Good home cooking and hospitality are the bywords at this thatched 15th-century cottage on the banks of the River Fal. It's a truly unique place, full of history and nautical memorabilia. The Americans used the cottage and slipway as an embarkation point for the D-Day landings, and General Eisenhower visited the troops here. One of the dining rooms is devoted entirely to the SS Uganda. The Newman family has run the restaurant and tea gardens since 1934, and has gained a well-deserved reputation for its Cornish specialities. The menu changes daily and uses fresh ingredients, which are cooked in the Newmans' Aga. At lunch, tuck into a proper Cornish pasty, the Smugglers' Special of soup with a filled baguette, fish pie or filled jacket potatoes and salad. The fruit crumble with Rodda's clotted cream is unmissable and, if you come in the afternoon, there is a fine selection of scones and muffins that are also freshly baked in the Aga. There are non-smoking dining rooms and the bar has a collection of more than 100 malt whiskies. When planning your route here, take the boat – much more fun and picturesque than coming by car.

Prices: Main course from £6. House wine £11.
Last orders: Food: 17.30 (Summer 20.30).
Closed: November-May.
Food: Modern British.
Other points: No smoking in the restaurant. Children welcome. Garden. Car park. Tea gardens.
Directions: Near the King Harry Car Ferry, on the Roseland Peninsula, on the banks of the river Fal. (Map 3, E3)

Appleby-in-Westmorland

Tufton Arms Hotel

Market Square, Appleby-in-Westmorland,
Cumbria CA16 6XA
Telephone: +44(0)1768 351593
info@tuftonarmshotel.co.uk
www.tuftonarmshotel.co.uk

This 16th-century building, which became a coaching inn in Victorian times, has been beautifully restored by the Milsom family. The ambience of the Victorian period is reflected in the attractive wallpapers, lots of prints in heavy frames, drapes, old fireplaces and large porcelain table lamps. Light lunch and supper menus are served in the clubby bar, with a more formal choice available in the stylish restaurant with its conservatory extension. Cooking is of a high standard, be it rack of Cumbrian fell-bred lamb, or game from the local Dalemain Estate. Fish is delivered from Fleetwood, to create, perhaps, paupiette of lemon sole stuffed with smoked salmon with a white dill wine sauce. There is a French accent to the carefully selected, well-annotated wine list of 160 bins. Bedrooms vary from suites with period fireplaces, antique furnishings and large old-style bathrooms to more conventional well-equipped en suite rooms.

Rooms: 21. Double/twin from £95.
Prices: Set dinner £24.50. Restaurant main course from £9.75. Bar main course from £6.95. House wine £9.50.
Last orders: Bar: 23.00. Food: lunch 14.00; dinner 21.00.
Closed: Rarely.
Food: Traditional English and French.
Other points: Children welcome. Dogs welcome overnight. Car park. Licence for civil weddings. Wheelchair access, not WC.
Directions: Exit 38/M6. Take the B6260 to Appleby via Orton. (Map 11, D4)

Bassenthwaite Lake

Ouse Bridge Hotel

Bassenthwaite Lake, Dubwath, Cockermouth,
Cumbria CA13 9YD
Telephone: +44(0)17687 76322
enquiries@ousebridge.com
www.ousebridge.com

Once a prestigious Lakeland home, this hotel enjoys wonderful views over Bassenthwaite Lake and Skiddaw. Owners Stephen and Kate Barrie are attentive and make every effort to ensure your stay is relaxing and comfortable. The interiors have been updated, giving the hotel a fresh look and feel. The lounge and small bar with their pale leather sofas are ideal spots to relax and admire the lovely views. Bedrooms and en suite bathrooms are pristine, uncluttered and comfortable, and many have lake views. Andrew is passionate about good food and takes time to source good local produce. The daily changing menu might be concise but reflects the best of what's available, and it doesn't stint on flavour. Start with fresh asparagus with parmesan and prosciutto on dressed leaves. Mains include breast of chicken with lemon and herbs or pork loin steaks stuffed with mozzarella and mushrooms with fresh vegetables, and there is always a good vegetarian option. A simple, good-value wine list should satisfy all tastes. Breakfast is also something quite special and includes local meats and free-range eggs.

Rooms: 10, 2 with private bathroom. Double room from £31, single from £23 per person per night.
Prices: Set dinner £16. House wine £9.50.
Last orders: Dinner served between 19.00 and 20.00.
Closed: From Christmas to the end of January.
Food: Modern British.
Other points: No-smoking area. Children over 10 welcome. Car park.
Directions: Exit 40/M6. Take the A66 towards Keswick for 25 miles. Turn right onto the B5291 and Ouse Bridge is 50 yards along on the left. (Map 11, C3)

Borrowdale

Scafell Hotel

Rosthwaite, Borrowdale, Cumbria CA12 5XB
Telephone: +44(0)1768 777208
info@scafell.co.uk
www.scafell.co.uk

In the 19th century, this elegant house received several famous visitors: Wordsworth, Coleridge and Southey stayed to walk nearby. During World War ll, after it had become a hotel, Sir Barnes Wallis visited for three months when he was working on the Bouncing Bomb project. It's easy to see its many appealing attractions; the scenery is breathtaking, and the hotel's elegant style reflects its 19th-century heritage, while the food and wine is along contemporary-classic lines. Proprietor Miles Jessop, who has been here for 40 years, is a friendly host. Most of the bedrooms have good views, are comfortable and furnished in country style. The public areas are spacious and relaxing. In the refurbished dining room, they serve a fine table d'hôte, which showcases local ingredients, such as fresh farm chicken, while Cumbrian pork and lamb are used in other dishes. A simple cocktail bar is set in one room around an open fire, while at the rear of the hotel is the public bar which has slate floors and outdoor seating, serving good bar food, local cask ales and a fine selection of wines.

Rooms: 24. Double from £145, single from £72.50. Rates are for dinner, bed and breakfast. Seasonal price variations apply.
Prices: Set lunch £11.95. Set dinner £20.50-£24.50 (five courses). Restaurant main course from £9.50. Bar/snack from £6.50. House wine £11.95.
Last orders: Bar: 23.00. Food: lunch 14.00; dinner 21.00.
Closed: Restricted bar hours January and early February.
Food: British and International.
Other points: No-smoking area. Children welcome. Dogs welcome. Garden. Car park. Licence for civil weddings.
Directions: Exit 40/M6. Take the A66 towards Keswick and then the B5289. (Map 11, D3)

Burton

Watergarden Restaurant

A6 Road, Burton, Cumbria LA5 9RW
Telephone: +44(0)1524 782888
jasonyorke@btconnect.com
www.watergardenrestaurant.co.uk

True to its name, there are water features galore outside this attractive restaurant. Its two proprietors, Jason and Karen Yoke have ensured it looks good inside too and have combined comfortable furnishings with attractive plants. Before extending and refurbishing the premises, the restaurant offered a simple café-style menu, and Jason has built on this. Dinners can still enjoy good traditional dishes, such as Cumberland sausages or gammon from an excellent local source, or start with fresh-baked black pudding roulade with Dijon cream or pork, spring onion and watercress rillette and continue with char-grilled Cajun-spiced salmon fillet. Other dishes show the same understanding of quality ingredients and an ability to cook to perfection. Finish with black-and-white chocolate soup or sticky toffee pudding with butterscotch sauce. The wine list is very well priced and offers a good range of grape varieties.

Prices: Set lunch from £15.95. Set dinner £25.95. Restaurant main course from £7.95. House wine £11.95.
Last orders: Food: 20.30 (Saturday 21.30 and Sunday 20.00).
Closed: Rarely.
Food: Modern European.
Other points: Totally no smoking. Garden. Children welcome. Car park. Wheelchair access.
Directions: Exit 35/M6. Follow signs for Lakeland Wildlife Oasis. Watergarden Restaurant is on the left. (Map 11, D4)

Cockermouth

Winder Hall Country House

Low Lorton, Cockermouth, Cumbria CA13 9UP
Telephone: +44(0)1900 85107
nick@winderhall.co.uk
www.winderhall.co.uk

This historic manor house, dating back to the 15th century, has all the comforts of a small country-house hotel. Nick and Ann Lawler have updated the décor and created a warm and friendly atmosphere. The small lounge with sink-into sofas and open fire is inviting, while each of the lovely en suite bedrooms is spacious and individually decorated in tasteful colours and fabrics. The couple have made their quality mark on the food, too. Dinner is served in the striking oak-panelled Arts and Crafts dining room, complete with a log fire and grand piano. Enjoy a complimentary apéritif before dinner. The menu incorporates local ingredients, organic meats and home-grown free-range eggs and pork and is flavoured with spices and fresh herbs. The choice may be limited, but what they cook, they do exceptionally well. Start with sweet pepper and garlic soup and follow with organic pork medallions or poached salmon with hot cucumber butter. The delightful desserts include warm lemon tart with raspberry coulis and bread and butter pudding with Baileys or a selection of local cheeses. The wine list offers value and character and is divided into helpful style categories.

Rooms: 7. Double room from £50, single room from £75.
Prices: Set dinner £29.50 (four courses). House wine £11.25.
Last orders: Food: dinner 19.00-20.00.
Closed: Occasional family holiday.
Food: Modern British.
Other points: Totally no smoking. Children welcome. Garden. Car park. Licence for civil weddings. Fishing rights. Wheelchair access to the restaurant.
Directions: Exit 40/M6. From Keswick take the A66 west to Braithwaite, then the B5292 Whinlatter Pass to Lorton. Take a sharp left at the B5289 signed to Low Lorton. (Map 11, C3)

Grange-over-Sands

The Hazelmere Café and Bakery

1 Yewbarrow Terrace, Grange-over-Sands,
Cumbria LA11 6ED
Telephone: +44(0)15395 32972
hazelmeregrange@yahoo.co.uk

They've been serving refreshments in this Victorian café since 1897, but never better we should think than under current owners Ian and Dorothy Stubley. Their bakery alone bakes 30-40 different breads and morning goods, from Lakeland plum bread and vanilla slices and strawberry tarts to authentic French sticks and ciabatta. Next door in the café, an array of these homemade goodies and other local produce is on offer, plus an impressive selection of speciality teas. Tea is Dorothy's passion and she is a globetrotter when it comes to sourcing the 30 or so single-estate teas on her list. Cake fans are also spoilt, and everyone should try a piece of the Cumbrian rum nicky, a sweet pastry case filled with a mix of cherries, dates, rum butter, spices and stem ginger. The Stubleys serve a tempting range of savoury dishes, from the light meals of grilled Cumbrian goat's cheese and potted Morecambe Bay shrimps to the filled toasted sandwiches. They also have amazing homemade preserves and Lakes ice creams. Children are very welcome and have their mini menu of adult dishes.

Prices: Set lunch £6.95. Main course from £6.45. House wine £2.10 a glass.
Last orders: Food: 14.30 (winter 16.00).
Closed: Rarely.
Food: Traditional English.
Other points: Totally no smoking. Children welcome. Dogs welcome. Wheelchair access.
Directions: Exit 36/M6 take the A590 then the B5277, signposted Grange-over-Sands. Pass Grange Station and at the mini roundabout take the first exit, 25 yards on the right. (Map 11, D4)

Grange-over-Sands

Netherwood Hotel

Lindale Road, Grange-over-Sands, Cumbria LA11 6ET
Telephone: +44(0)15395 32552
blawith@aol.com
www.netherwood-hotel.co.uk

This family-run mansion, built in 1893, with its attractive woodland backdrop and terraced formal gardens makes an excellent first impression. The interiors are just as pleasing. Its relaxed country-house feel is complemented by the modern amenities of a gym, pool and business and function facilities. The Fallowfield brothers are constantly working to improve the décor. Updated lounges are designed for comfort and the spacious bedrooms are refurbished on a rolling basis with elegant furnishings and immaculate bathrooms. Dining is a pleasure, from the imaginative set menus to the stunning views over the gardens to Morecambe Bay. Local produce includes Kendal Roughfell and North Lakes lamb, but you will also find the exotic as well as the traditional on this menu. Start with black tiger prawns and snapper or cream of cauliflower and caraway soup, then opt for medallions of wild boar with a Brazilian sauce or roast rump of beef with Yorkshire puddings. Luscious desserts, such as chocolate and Grand Marnier torte, add a fitting flourish of extravagance.

Rooms: 32. Rooms from £70 per person, family room from £150.
Prices: Set lunch £16 and dinner £32. Bar lunches available. House wine £14.
Last orders: Food: lunch 14.00; dinner 20.30.
Closed: Never.
Food: Global.
Other points: No smoking in the restaurant. Children welcome. Dogs welcome overnight. Garden. Car park. Licence for civil weddings. Wheelchair access.
Directions: Exit 36/M6, then A590 for Barrow-in-Furness. Left at the roundabout onto the B5277, then left again at Lindale roundabout. The hotel is on the right before the train station. (Map 11, D4)

Grasmere

The Jumble Room

Langdale Road, Grasmere, Cumbria LA22 9SU
Telephone: +44(0)15394 35188
thejumbleroom@which.net
www.thejumbleroom.co.uk

This contemporary café-restaurant in traditional Lakeland offers a colourful range of exciting dishes. The Jumble Room has been in Andy and Chrissy Hills' family for more than 50 years. It started life at the beginning of the 18th century as Grasmere's first shop where, among other things, Grasmere Rushbearing Gingerbread was made. During the day, the café serves snacks, sandwiches and light meals with the emphasis on local and organic produce. Aubergine and goat's cheese stack, Thai chicken, Szechuan chilli beef with stir-fried noodles, or homemade lamb sausages are a far cry from the usual run-of-the-mill fare. In the evening, The Jumble Room dresses for dinner: vinyl tablecloths are replaced with crisp linen, and dining is by candlelight. The menu has influences from Troutbeck to Thailand, with starters such as Soul soup made from local organic ingredients, and mains of Moroccan lamb tagine or Goosnargh corn-fed chicken. The puds change frequently and all are truly indulgent. There's an eclectic mix of wines from around the world with six European organics at good-value prices.

Prices: Restaurant main course from £10. Bar main course from £5. House wine £10.95.
Last orders: Food: lunch 16.30; dinner 22.30.
Closed: Monday, Tuesday, 23 -27 December, lunchtimes during the winter.
Food: Global.
Other points: Totally no smoking. Children welcome. Wheelchair access.
Directions: From Ambleside take the A590 and turn left into Grasmere. Turn left again at the church and take the first right opposite the Tourist Information Centre. The Jumble Room is 200 yards along on the right. (Map 11, D4)

Hawkshead

Queen's Head Hotel

Main Street, Hawkshead, Ambleside, Cumbria LA22 0NS
Telephone: +44(0)15394 36271 / +44(0)800 137263
enquiries@queensheadhotel.co.uk
www.queensheadhotel.co.uk

Set in the pedestrianised centre of this pretty little Lakeland village, this 16th-century inn-cum-hotel appeals to visitors and locals alike. It has period character from its black and white painted frontage to the traditional beamed bars with open fires. Ales are dispensed by bow-tied barmen, perhaps Robinsons Bitter or the aptly named Cumbria Way. The interesting menu travels far and wide, but they haven't forgotten how to do the basics well. A harvesters' platter of four generous wedges of organic cheese comes with delicious walnut bread and salad. Other choices include the salad bar, which offers Cumbrian roast beef with watercress, chilli, radish and soy sauce, or the separate Herdwick lamb menu, which could include lamb Henry. Otherwise, a meal might include Westmorland pie, or Woodhall's Cumberland sausage with ale and white onion sauce. There's a good vegetarian menu, too. Fifteen small, prettily decorated bedrooms are charming in a rural-chic style. Rooms at the front have the best views over the village.

Rooms: 14, 2 not en suite, 2 with private bathroom. 2 four-poster beds and 2 family rooms. Double room from £34 per person, single from £47.50.
Prices: Main course lunch from £7.25. House wine £10.95.
Last orders: Bar: 23.00. Food: lunch 14.30; dinner 21.30.
Closed: Rarely.
Food: Modern British.
Other points: No-smoking area. Children welcome.
Directions: Exit 36/M6 and follow the A590 to Newby Bridge. Take the second right and follow the road for eight miles into the centre of Hawkshead. (Map 11, D4)

Orton

New Village Tea Rooms

Orton, Penrith, Cumbria CA10 3RH
Telephone: +44(0)1539 624886

Appetising alternatives to motorway services can be hard to find, but this tearoom in the pretty village of Orton fits the bill perfectly. Christine Evans has honed her menu to suit locals and passing trade over the decade she has been in business. Her home cooking attracts regulars for lunch, tea, or to buy her homemade ready meals. The tearooms were originally four separate rooms for farm labourers, but have been cleverly converted in this homely Lakeland-style café. The cream walls, open fire, wooden tables with dark green and lace cloths and a dresser laden with homemade bakes add to its country charm. There are six tables downstairs and five up, plus seating in the small garden. The printed menu is packed with homemade goodies such as scones, sandwiches, toasties, jacket potatoes and Lakeland ice cream. There's also a blackboard detailing the day's specials, which include soups such as lentil and bacon or curried parsnip, hearty bakes in the shape of chicken and broccoli, or broad bean, onion and tomato, and homemade desserts of sticky toffee pudding or chocolate and orange crumble. Cakes and a large choice of takeaway frozen ready-made meals are available.

Prices: Lunchtime special from £5.50.
Last orders: Food: 17.00 (winter 16.30).
Closed: Sunday before 25 December to 2 January.
Food: Teashop.
Other points: Totally no smoking. Garden. Car park. No credit cards accepted. Unlicensed.
Directions: Exit 38/M6 Take the road signposted to Appleby. In Orton take the Shap Road in front of the George Hotel. The New Village Tea Room is located straight ahead opposite the post office. (Map 11, D4)

Penrith

Alan's Cafe Restaurant

Poet's Walk, Penrith, Cumbria CA11 7HJ
Telephone: +44(0)1768 867474
alanschef@btinternet.com

A café on weekdays, serving cakes and light lunches, Alan's becomes a stylish restaurant on Friday and Saturday evenings. Chef-owner Alan Potter pulls off both of these guises with aplomb. The modern décor – light colours and whitewashed wood furniture – is an inviting setting in which to enjoy the fine selection of teas, coffees, freshly baked breads, cakes and scones, or you can opt for one of the lunchtime specials, such as hot chicken and bacon salad or grilled avocado and brie with a cranberry dressing and salad. At weekends, the atmosphere becomes more sophisticated with soft lighting and subtle background music, creating the right ambience for a special night out. The fixed-price evening menu offers four or five choices per course and includes a fair selection of meat, fish and vegetarian options. Cream of parsnip soup or pan-fried scallops served on egg noodles kick things off, and can be followed by fillet of beef Wellington, venison steak or paupiette of lemon sole. Round off with a wicked traditional dessert such as bread and butter pudding with apricot coulis or crème brulée with fresh strawberries.

Prices: Set dinner £25. Restaurant main course from £11.50. Bar main course from £7. House wine £11.50.
Last orders: Lunch 14.30; dinner served from 19.00 (Friday and Saturday only).
Closed: Monday to Thursday evenings and all day Sunday.
Food: Modern British.
Other points: Totally no smoking. Children welcome. Wheelchair access.
Directions: Exit 40/M6. Just off the Market Square in the town centre. (Map 11, C4)

Penrith

Edenhall Country Hotel

Edenhall, Penrith, Cumbria CA11 8SX
Telephone: +44(0)1768 881454
info@edenhallhotel.co.uk
www.edenhallhotel.co.uk

This charming country house in the picturesque Eden Valley is steeped in history. Many of the cottages in the sandstone conservation village of Edenhall date back to 1240, and the house itself is best-known for the legend and poems that surround the 'Luck of Edenhall', a 10th-century goblet, which can now be seen at the Victoria & Albert Museum. The house is spacious, but remains cosy and has an appealing air of informality. The lovely large lounge with open fire and bar area overlooks the gardens. Dinner served in the dining room is a relaxed affair. The kitchen turns out classics, showing a flair for the contemporary and using mainly Cumbrian produce. The local meats and breads are well worth singling out for praise. Starters such as Barbary duck and Cajun chicken terrine with salad and homemade plum chutney, followed by fillet of salmon on a Mediterranean vegetable salad with a pesto cream sauce are examples of the imagination at play. A decadent line-up of puds rounds things off nicely, while a delectable wine list doesn't have a bad choice among its selection. The bedrooms are roomy, freshly painted and have comfortable beds.

Rooms: 25. Double/twin room from £80, single from £35, family room from £90.
Prices: Restaurant main course from £12.95. Bar main course from £7.95. House wine £11.95.
Last orders: Bar: 23.00. Food: lunch 14.00; dinner 21.00.
Closed: Never.
Food: Modern British.
Other points: No-smoking area. Garden. Children welcome. Car park. Licence for civil weddings.
Directions: J40/M6. Follow the A66 east to the roundabout. Exit the A686 for Alston. After approximately three miles turn right for Edenhall. (Map 11, C4)

Penrith

Watermill

Little Salkeld, Penrith, Cumbria CA10 1NN
Telephone: +44(0)1768 881523
organicflour@aol.com
www.organicmill.co.uk

Combine sightseeing with a sustenance break at this mill, which has quite breathtaking scenery as a backdrop. The pink-painted buildings are tucked away at the bottom of the village beside Sunnygill Beck, the waters that are channelled down the mill race to turn the wheels. Nick and Ana Jones restored the mill in 1975, and are committed to producing flour from grain grown to bio-dynamic organic standards by English farmers. Take a tour of the water-powered corn mill, one of the few in the country, before treating yourself to delicious homemade goodies in the tearoom. The food they serve is organic vegetarian, and the couple were granted a Soil Association licence in 2002. Come in the morning to enjoy a late breakfast of, say, porridge with maple syrup and toast with Watermill marmalade; at teatime, you can feast on delicious tea and scones with homemade jam, or organic Arabica coffee with a flapjack or rich chocolate brownie. In between, you can have a miller's lunch of Loch Arthur cheese and homemade chutney, quiche with salads or homemade soup with a selection of different breads. Budding bakers will be pleased to learn that the Joneses also run breadmaking courses.

Prices: Main course lunch from £6.
Last orders: Food: 16.30.
Closed: 24 December-30 January.
Food: Totally organic and vegetarian.
Other points: Totally no smoking. Children welcome. Car park. Wheelchair access.
Directions: Six miles from exit 40/M6. Take the A686 for five miles to Langwathby, left at the village green, then two miles to the mill. (Map 11, C4)

Seascale

Cumbrian Lodge Hotel

Gosforth Road, Seascale, Cumbria CA20 1JG
Telephone: +44(0)19467 27309
cumbrianlodge@btconnect.com
www.cumbrianlodge.com

Former corporate banker David Morgan has brought good taste in food and furnishings to this grand old house that sits on the attractive West Cumbrian coast. It became a hotel in 1999, and David's additional refurbishments combine 21st-century comforts and contemporary touches. In the bedrooms, you will sink into super-comfortable light goose-down duvets with Egyptian linen to watch the flat-screen TV. Downstairs you can enjoy the finer things, too: wine is served in Riedal wine glasses favoured by professional tasters and much thought has gone into sourcing quality local food – Royal Warrant holder Richard Woodall's meats and dairy produce from Crofton Dairies. The bar (with its maple woodwork and faux suede seating) is relaxing and plush. Dine in the restaurant on lunches of light snacks, hearty traditional Cumbrian hot pots or Swiss specialities, such as rösti and rahm schnitzel, or from an expansive dinner menu that brings together local produce. The wine list offers a good selection of interesting New World wines as well as the French stalwarts.

Rooms: 6. Double room from £50, single from £45, family from £55.
Prices: Restaurant main course from £7.95. Bar main course from £4.25. House wine £10.95.
Last orders: Bar: lunch 15.00; dinner 23.00. Food: lunch 14.00; dinner 21.30. No food all day Sunday and Monday.
Closed: Rarely
Food: Modern British and Swiss.
Other points: No-smoking area. Children over 12 welcome. Garden. Car park.
Directions: Exit 36/M6. Take the A590 west to Greenodd then take the A595 towards Whitehaven. Near Gosforth turn left on the B5344. The hotel is two miles along. (Map 11, D3)

Silloth on Solway

Cafe 14/16

14-16 Eden Street, Silloth-on-Solway, Wigton,
Cumbria CA7 4AD
Telephone: +44(0)1697 332541
fourteensixteen@waitrose.com

Jay and Morven Anson have bags of experience as previous owners of Seatoller House in the Borrowdale Valley. They have brought their flair and passion for authentically good food to their café, which offers an extensive all-day lunch menu and evening specials on Fridays and Saturdays. The café is simply decorated and has a welcoming atmosphere. In chillier weather, a fire roars in the original Victorian marble fireplace. It's popular not only because it offers great value, but customers recognise the quality and emphasis on flavours. You can start the day with breakfast, then there's tea or coffee (Fairtrade) with homemade scones and jam, or homemade soups such as organic tomato, basil and courgette with homebaked organic bread, made using Little Salkeld's organic flour, and plenty of sandwich and wrap options. Main dishes include gratin of Solway shrimp, salmon and cod in a parsley sauce topped with a king scallop, or free-range corn-fed chicken with a Cumberland honey mustard, brandy and five-spice sauce. The evening menu includes casseroles and fish specials, mainly made with organic ingredients. A bring your own wine policy keeps the bill well within budget.

Prices: Restaurant main course from £8.
Main course snack from £4.50.
Last orders: Café: Lunch 14.30 (Sunday 14.00); Bistro 20.30 (Friday and Saturday).
Closed: Monday.
Food: Traditional and Modern British.
Other points: Totally no-smoking. Children welcome. Credit cards not accepted. No car park. Wheelchair access.
Directions: J41/M6. Take the B5305 to Wigton, then the B5302 to Silloth. Turn left at the Tourist Information Centre, then right onto Eden Street. (Map 11, C3)

Ulverston

Dusty Miller's Tea Shop

Gleaston Water Mill, Gleaston, near Ulverston,
Cumbria LA12 OQH
Telephone: +44(0)1229 869244
dustymillers@watermill.co.uk
www.watermill.co.uk

This enterprising business is another superb example of Cumbrian initiative by two dedicated foodies. Vicky and Mike Brereton have turned the 18th-century Grade II-listed Gleaston water mill into a culinary cornocopia, which not only serves good food, but has an excellent shop selling homemade goodies and crafts, including collectable pigs. Visitors can also see the restored 18-foot wooden water wheel in action and honey being made at its observation hive. And if that's not enough, you can pop next door to explore the ruins of Gleaston Castle. A highlight of a visit, though, is the teashop. Brunch is served from 10.30am, which can be a light bite or the full Country Bunch, including Richard Woodall's famous dry-cured bacon and Cumberland sausages. Through the week, they serve hearty lunch dishes of, say, pork in a rich apple and cider sauce or a rustic vegetarian pie, soups, specials and cakes as well as a good choice of country wines, local beers and soft drinks. Their traditional Sunday lunches are popular. The Miller's Apprentice menu offers children's portions. Free bee-keeping courses run on Saturdays throughout late spring and summer.

Prices: Main course from £5.99. House wine £7.95.
Last orders: Food: 16.45.
Closed: Monday.
Food: Traditional British.
Other points: Totally no smoking. Patio. Children welcome. Car park. Wheelchair access.
Directions: Exit 36/M6. Travel west on the A590. At Ulverston turn left onto the A5087 and take the coastal route towards Barrow. Follow brown Gleaston Water Mill signs from Aldingham. (Map 11, D4)

Wasdale

Wasdale Head Inn

Wasdale, Gosforth, Cumbria CA20 1EX
Telephone: +44(0)19467 26229
wasdaleheadinn@msn.com
www.wasdale.com

At the head of unspoilt Wasdale, at the foot of Great Gable, in a setting of romantic grandeur, with steep fells by way of backdrop, is this famous, traditional mountain inn, popular with serious walkers and climbers. Ritson's Bar, named after its first landlord (said to be the world's biggest liar), has high ceilings, a polished slate floor, wood panelling, climbing memorabilia and stunning photographs of the surrounding fells. Here you can enjoy a top pint of home-brewed Great Gable beer and informal, hearty bar meals. Steak and ale pie, hotpots, thick soups and Cumbrian sausages from Woodalls of Waberthwaite served with onion gravy are perfect for reviving tired walkers. Alternatively, spoil yourself in the restaurant, which puts together some of the best local produce in its short, but excellent, four-course set-menu. Dinner may take in air-dried Cumbrian ham, local farm-reared Herdwick lamb or fillet steak, and classic puddings. The pick of the 14 bedrooms is the garden room, with its muslin-draped four-poster.

Rooms: 14. Room from £49 per person.
Prices: Bar meal from £7.50. Set dinner (4 course) £25. House wine £12.90.
Last orders: Bar: 23.00. Food: 21.00.
Closed: Rarely.
Food: Traditional British.
Other points: Totally no smoking. Children welcome. Dogs welcome overnight. Garden. Car park.
Directions: Wasdale Head is signed off the A595 between Egremont and Ravenglass. (Map 11, D3)

Windermere

1 Park Road

1 Park Road, Windermere, Cumbria LA23 2AW
Telephone: +44 (0)15394 42107
enquiries@1parkroad.com
www.1parkroad.com

Conveniently located five minutes from Windermere town centre, this stylish Victorian villa certainly stands out from the more traditional guesthouses. You will quickly feel at home thanks to the friendly welcome from owners Mark and Alexandra Soden. They have a good eye for interiors and have made the most of the building's attractive features. Its elegant rooms are decorated with Art Deco and Art Nouveau prints and ornaments. The wonderful tiled hall floor and the pine wood features are beautifully polished, but the period pieces don't overwhelm and the overall feel is contemporary and uncluttered. The bedrooms are havens of calm – spacious, with extras including CD players. Bathrooms are pristine and the beds especially comfortable. Mark is also a talented cook and devises an Italian-themed candlelit dinner menu daily. All the ingredients are sourced locally and everything is freshly prepared. Starters offer a soup of the day or garlic mushrooms in a creamy sauce, followed by a choice of five mains that take in spaghetti bolognese and Italian beef casserole. The sticky toffee pudding with fudge sauce and ice cream is a must.

Rooms: 6. Double/twin room from £35 per person, single from £50, family from £90. House hire also available for special occasions.
Prices: Set dinner £16.95. Restaurant main course from £9.95. House wine from £8.95.
Last orders: Pre-order dinner for night of arrival.
Closed: 20-26 December.
Food: Modern European and seasonal specials.
Other points: Totally no smoking. Well-behaved children welcome. Car park.
Directions: Exit 36/M6. In the centre of Windermere village. (Map 11, D4)

Windermere

Jambo Restaurant

7 Victoria Street, Windermere, Cumbria LA23 1AE
Telephone: +44(0)15394 43429
kevatjambo@aol.com
www.jamborestaurant.co.uk

Once a corner shop, this unprepossessing building is now home to some remarkably fine cooking, care of the talented Master Chef of Great Britain, Kevin Wyper. He runs this restaurant with his partner Andrea and together they have put together an exquisite menu based on homegrown fruits and vegetables and meat, mainly from local producers. The décor is simple, with tables laid with shining cutlery and glasses. The bar is on one level and the eating area on another. The menu displays a real understanding of how to prepare seasonal produce to the best effect and dishes are presented in a way that looks mouthwateringly appetising as well as attractive. Starters offer confit of rabbit glazed with honey, caramelised apples, radicchio and a roasted pepper salsa, or a trio of seared king scallops on a lemon and herb mash drizzled with avocado oil and tomato. Mains take in game such as pan-roasted Grizdale wild venison, roast rack of Cumbrian lamb, and fish specials, to name but a few delights. However, it's the combination of quality ingredients, complementary flavours and fine cooking that raises this restaurant to a special level.

Prices: Main course from £14.50. House wine £11.95.
Last orders: 22.00.
Closed: Closed for lunch (open for dinner from 18.30), all day Thursday, 25-26 December and two weeks in January.
Food: Modern British.
Other points: No smoking in the restaurant. Chilldren over 12 welcome.
Directions: From the M6, take junction 36 heading for Windermere/Bowness. On reaching Windermere, turn left into the village. Pass the Tourist Information Centre and the restaurant is 100 yards down on the left. (Map 11, D4)

Windermere

Kwela's Restaurant

4 High Street, Windermere, Cumbria LA23 1AF
Telephone: +44(0)15394 44954
booking@kwelas.co.uk
www.kwelas.co.uk

This unusual restaurant offers the best of both worlds, reflecting the partnership of South African chef-owner Jess Rossouw and his Cumbrian partner, also called Jess. The colonial décor is more *Out of Africa* than Lakeland and creates a relaxed, contemporary look, and the upstairs/downstairs dining rooms are both cosy and inviting. The couple's partnership works well on the menu, where they use quality local ingredients to interpret traditional African recipes. North African seasonings and authentic ingredients produce vibrant dishes that start with a homemade soup of pumpkin and coconut, which is rich, satisfying and nicely spicy, Tunisian crab brik (flaked crab meat with North African seasonings, wrapped in warka pastry and shallow fried and served with a harissa sauce), or pan-fried breast of quail wrapped in flatbread with pistachio sauce, mizuna salad and bramble vinaigrette. The main courses of lamb shank tagine, ostrich steak and traditional South African bobotie are just as adventurous and exciting. Desserts are just as enticing, or there's a good choice of cheeses. Moroccan red wines make a good robust match for this hearty food.

Prices: Restaurant main course from £10.95. House wine £10.
Last orders: Dinner: 22.00 (Sunday 21.30).
Closed: Lunchtimes, Monday all day, one week in November, 24-26 December and two weeks in January.
Food: Modern African.
Other points: No-smoking area. Children welcome.
Directions: Exit 36/M6. Take the A591 to Windermere village, first left and Kwela's is 100m along on the right.
(Map 11, D4)

Hardwick

Hardwick Inn

Hardwick Park, Chesterfield, Derbyshire S44 5QJ
Telephone: +44(0)1246 850245
batty@hardwickinn.co.uk
www.hardwickinn.co.uk

Dating from around 1600 and built of locally quarried sandstone, this striking building was once the lodge for Hardwick Hall, which is owned by the National Trust, so the inn draws much of its trade from visitors exploring the magnificent park and lovely Elizabethan hall; it can be very busy at weekends. The inn, owned by the Batty family for three generations, has a rambling interior that features good period details such as stone-mullioned windows, oak ceiling beams, large stone fireplaces with open fires, and a fine 18th-century carved settle. Traditional bar food (served all day) takes in ploughman's lunches, and a whole range of steaks and sandwiches, with blackboard daily specials offering hearty homemade pies, and fresh fish delivered daily from Scarborough. Look out for sea bass with orange and dill, beer-battered haddock and game and ale casserole, or opt for one of the daily carvery roasts, served with Yorkshire pudding and three vegetables.

Prices: Set lunch £12.60 and dinner £13.60 in the carvery restaurant. Bar main course from £6.50. House wine £7.95. Plus an extensive bar menu.
Last orders: Bar: 23.00. Food: lunch 21.30 (Sunday 21.00).
Closed: Rarely.
Food: Traditional British.
Other points: Totally no smoking. Children welcome. Garden. Car park. Wheelchair access to the restaurant and pub.
Directions: Two and a quarter miles from Exit 29/M1. Take the A6175, then after a quarter of a mile turn left and follow the tourist-board signs to the pub. (Map 9, B3)

Bideford

Riversford Hotel

Limers Lane, Northam, Bideford, Devon EX39 2RG
Telephone: +44(0)1237 474239
riversford@aol.com
www.riversford.co.uk

The Jarrard family run their homely hotel with style and simplicity, and have built up loyal support over the last 30 years. As well as offering quality accommodation and food, the hotel is well placed and there are good family beaches nearby. All 15 en suite bedrooms are well appointed and individually decorated in light, relaxing colours; the large suites have four-poster beds. Pleasant public rooms include the light, airy restaurant with lovely garden views to the River Torridge and beyond. Nigel Jarrard presides over the kitchen and is to be praised for sourcing quality local ingredients. Game comes from local shoots, Somerset and Dorset cheeses are from Hawkridge Farm, vegetables are grown locally, meat comes from a local supplier and cream is from Definitely Devon Dairies. The menu is strong on the traditional with dishes such as tournedos Rossini, and Devon lamb chops with mustard and brown sugar. Fish is a speciality, and local sea bass could be teamed with dill and orange sauce or king scallops sautéed in garlic, ginger and Thai spices. The short selection of wines continues the good-value theme.

Rooms: 15. Double room from £80, single from £50.
Prices: Set lunch £14, set dinner £18. Main course from £8. House wine £12.
Last orders: Food: lunch 15.00; dinner 21.30.
Closed: Never.
Food: Specialises in fresh produce and local seafood.
Other points: No smoking in the restaurant. Children welcome. Dogs welcome overnight. Garden. Car park. Full wheelchair access.
Directions: J27/M5. One mile north of Bideford on the A386, Limers Lane is on the right. (Map 3, C4)

Dartmouth

Stoke Lodge Hotel

Cinders Lane, Stoke Fleming, Dartmouth,
Devon TQ6 0RA
Telephone: +44(0)1803 770523
mail@stokelodge.co.uk
www.stokelodge.co.uk

Set high above Start Bay, this charming country house hotel has magnificent views. You can't fail to be impressed by the comfortable décor in the lounge-cum-bar and restaurant, and by the relaxed ambience and friendly welcome. The south-facing building, which is mainly 17th-century with an 18th-century façade, has been sympathetically extended. Lawns, terraces, a tennis court and outdoor and indoor swimming pools, sauna, spa and a snooker table mean guests can unwind or pursue a number of leisure activities. Several of the individually designed bedrooms have four-poster beds, and all are bang up to date. Meals are based around quality local ingredients, and the daily changing set menu offers a choice of traditional but superbly executed dishes, such as smoked eel with horseradish sauce, cream of leek soup, and grilled lamb cutlets with Cumberland sauce. Old favourites appear on the dessert menu, notably bread and butter pudding with custard, and sherry trifle. This makes a tremendous holiday base, and there's plenty to keep the children amused.

Rooms: 25. Double room from £87, single from £58.
Prices: Set lunch £14.95 and dinner £21. Main course from £12.95. House wine £10.75.
Last orders: Food: lunch 13.45; dinner 21.00.
Closed: Never.
Food: Modern British.
Other points: No smoking in the restaurant. Children welcome. Dogs welcome overnight. Garden. Car park. Indoor and outdoor swimming pools.
Directions: From the M5 at Exeter take the A38 towards Plymouth. Turn off at Buckfastleigh and follow the signs to Totnes and then Dartmouth (A381 or A3122). Turn right to Stoke Fleming. (Map 4, E5)

Lynton

Highcliffe House

Sinai Hill, Lynton, Devon EX35 6AR
Telephone: +44(0)1598 752235
info@highcliffehouse.co.uk
www.highcliffehouse.co.uk

Highcliffe is an ideal base for exploring Exmoor National Park and North Devon. From its elevated position in the National Park itself, there are stunning views. If you're not a keen walker, simply sit back and take it all in from the comfort of this former Victorian gentleman's summer residence. The house has retained its suaveness, and its bold furnishings in the sitting room and en suite bedrooms create a distinctive period style. Bedrooms have a Rococo, Tudor, Colonial or French theme and each features a huge hand-carved bed. There are useful extras, too, such as DVD/CD players and perfumes, and a sherry to enjoy before dinner. The warm welcome starts on arrival as you unwind with coffee and biscuits in the quiet room. Breakfast is served in the dining room, and at weekends, you can return later to enjoy a candlelit menu that changes daily and is modern European in theme. Start with a refreshing courgette, ginger and lemon soup then move on to chicken Calvados or Gressingham duck. And don't worry about tucking into the homemade puds and West Country cheeses, there are plenty of walks and National Trust gardens to explore nearby.

Rooms: 6. Double/twin from £38 per person per night. Single from £50.
Prices: Set dinner £23.50 by prior arrangement on Friday, Saturday and Sunday only.
Closed: December and January.
Food: Modern European.
Other points: Totally no smoking. Garden. Children over 14 welcome. Car park.
Directions: Exit 27/M5. From north Devon take the A361 to South Molton and then the A399 to Blackmoor Gate, A39 to Lynton and follow the signs to the Old Village. (Map 3, C5)

Lynton

St Vincent House Hotel & Restaurant

Castle Hill, Lynton, Devon EX35 6JA
Telephone: +44(0)1598 752244
welcome@st-vincent-hotel.co.uk
www.st-vincent-hotel.co.uk

Tastefully and elegantly furnished, you'll find it easy to feel at home at this smart hotel. The Grade II-listed house, built by Captain Green who served with Admiral Nelson, is named after the battle of St Vincent off the coast of Portugal. The bedrooms, named after ships, give a nod to its nautical heritage, as does the artwork and the design of the upper-floor bedrooms which resemble roomy cabins. Some fine food is served in the breakfast/dining room. The menu draws on local, seasonal produce: fish is landed at Appledore and venison, beef and lamb is from Exmoor. Jean-Paul, who is Belgian, includes some of his country's specialities in his menu as well as his home-grown herbs and imaginative combinations, such as lavender in his fillet mignon of free-range pork with caramelised lemon and garlic confit and honey. His signature dish is a fabulous Provençal bouillabaisse. There's a well-chosen wine list, Belgian beers, an apple apéritif and a Somerset pomana.

Rooms: 6. Double/twin room from £50, single from £38. Family room from £75.
Prices: Set dinner £23.95. House wine £11.
Last orders: Food: Dinner 21.00.
Closed: Mid-January to Mid-February and lunchtimes.
Food: Belgian and French, fresh fish and shellfish.
Other points: Totally no smoking. Children over 10 welcome. No wheelchair access but one ground floor bedroom for those with impaired mobility. No pets.
Directions: J27/M5. A361 to South Molton. Turn right at the roundabout, and take the A399 to Lynton at Blackmore Gate. Turn right on to the A39 to Barbrook and then left at the petrol station, continuing towards Lynmouth. Up the hill, take the second left and the hotel is adjacent to the Exmoor Museum. (Map 3, C5)

Plymouth

Browns Hotel & Brasserie

80 West Street, Tavistock, Plymouth, Devon PL19 8AQ
Telephone: +44(0)1822 618686
enquiries@brownsdevon.co.uk
www.brownsdevon.co.uk

This elegant townhouse hotel, once a former coaching inn, has been modernised for style and comfort. It's ideally placed in the bustling town of Tavistock in west Devon, which offers smart shops and the countryside on the doorstep. It is the oldest hostelry in the town, and water from the Tavistock spring has been served here as far back as Roman times and is now bottled from the well in the hotel's atrium as Dartmoor Spring. The en suite rooms are all beautifully appointed and come with added extras, including satellite TV, data port and coffee-making facilities. The hotel provides all-day eating, from morning coffee through to a fine dinner. For lunch, head to the Wine Bar with its comfortable sofas and open log fire or to the light and airy conservatory. Dinner is served in the brasserie and head chef John McGeever puts local ingredients such as fresh fish from Brixham and organic meats to superb use in his menu. Begin with baked goat's cheese Charlotte or paupiette of organic smoked salmon and trout. Mains include roasted local venison and Devon duckling. The wine list is impressive. Browns offers a warm and friendly atmosphere to slick, professional standards.

Rooms: 20. Double/twin from £90, single from £65, family from £140.
Prices: Restaurant main course from £10.50. Bar snacks from £7.50. House wine £14.50.
Last orders: Food: lunch 14.30; dinner 21.15.
Closed: Never.
Food: Modern British.
Other points: No-smoking area. Garden. Children welcome. Car park. Gym.
Directions: M5 joining the A30. (Map 3, D4)

Slapton

The Tower Inn

Church Road, Slapton, Kingsbridge, Devon TQ7 2PN
Telephone: +44(0)1548 580216
towerinn@slapton.org
www.thetowerinn.com

The 14th-century Tower Inn takes its name from the ancient ruins of a tower it stands beside, all that remains of a monastic college. That has long gone, but the pub remains, as charming as ever, tucked away in a sleepy village just inland from Slapton Sands. Visitors will be warmly welcomed by Annette and Andrew Hammett who bought the pub in December 2003. The welcome is followed by pints of local ale and plates of good modern pub food. Expect hearty sandwiches (try the local crab) and more traditional dishes such as sausage and mash at lunchtime. From the evening menu, there are treats along the lines of ham, leek and asparagus terrine, followed by lamb shank, pheasant supreme, salmon and sea bass. Stone walls, open fires, scrubbed oak tables and flagstone floors characterise the interior, and the atmosphere is enhanced at night with candlelit tables. There are three cottage-style en suite bedrooms and a super rear garden.

Rooms: 3. Single from £40, double from £60.
Prices: Restaurant main course from £9. House wine from £10.
Last orders: Bar: lunch 14.30 (Sunday 15.00); dinner 23.00. Food: lunch 14.15 (Sunday 14.30); dinner 21.30.
Closed: Rarely.
Food: Modern British.
Other points: No-smoking area. Garden and courtyard. Children welcome. Dogs welcome overnight. Car park.
Directions: Off the A379 between Dartmouth and Kingsbridge, or off the A381 between Totnes and Kingsbridge. (Map 4, E5)

Tavistock

Tor Cottage

Chillaton, Lifton, near Tavistock, Devon PL16 0JE
Telephone: +44(0)1822 860248
info@torcottage.co.uk
www.torcottage.co.uk

It's not so much the attractive Devon longhouse that sets Tor Cottage apart from the norm, but the fact that its five rooms are spread out in its extensive acres of beautiful gardens. The privacy and seclusion these rooms afford would appeal to a publicity-shy celebrity, although all the rooms are within walking distance of the main house. The most private rooms are Laughing Waters, next to the stream. All are en suite and come with private terrace, fridge, tea and coffee-making facilities, plus other useful items such as torch, umbrella, magazines and a welcoming trug of champagne truffles, sparkling wine and fruits. You could base your whole break around your room, as a breakfast hamper can be delivered if you don't feel like eating in the bright and airy conservatory in the main house. No meals are served in the evening as such, but hampers full of local goodies such as home-made sandwiches made with organic bread, chutneys, West Country cheese, salads and homemade scones with Devonshire cream and strawberries are available to order. Tor Cottage is an excellent base for exploring Dartmoor and the Tamar Valley, but just as nice is losing yourself in these beautiful grounds and lounging around the very private outdoor heated pool.

Rooms: 5. Double from £130, single from £89.
Prices: Picnic platters for two £28.
Tray suppers available by prior arrangement £22. BYO.
Closed: Mid December to mid January.
Food: Modern British and vegetarian/special diets.
Other points: Totally no smoking. Garden. Car park.
Directions: M5/A30. Keeping Chillaton post office on your left, go up the hill for 300m and turn off to the right down a bridleway track. (Map 3, D4)

Torquay

The Elephant Bar & Restaurant

3-4 Beacon Terrace, Torquay, Devon TQ1 2BH
Telephone: +44(0)1803 200044
orestone@btconnect.com
www.elephantrestaurant.co.uk

Two Georgian houses have been combined to form an elegant downstairs dining room with a luxurious feel. Like its sister hotel, Orestone Manor, the smart décor, supplemented with tall palms, ornate mirrors and stunning artwork, recreates visions of the Raj. The lavish modern European menu is ideally suited to the surroundings. Chef Simon Hulstone uses the best ingredients – meats from butcher Steve Turton, fresh produce from local farms, fish from day boats in Brixham and shellfish from Start Bay – to great effect. The menu rapide lunch is excellent value, offering starters of risotto of wild garlic and mozzarella and Iberico ham or smoked venison salad, followed by mains of boudin blanc with wild mushrooms, butter beans and Madeira cream and a fragrant pudding of rose panna cotta or West Country cheeses. The full carte offers even more delightful combinations, with lavish touches of, say, fillet of line-caught sea bass with truffled savoy cabbage and scampi tortellini. For a more informal experience, head upstairs to the smart bar that serves cocktails and bar food, where you can recline on bean bags.

Prices: Set lunch £13.75-£16.75. Restaurant main course from £14.50. Main course bar/snack from £5.50. House wine £12.50.
Last orders: Bar: lunch 15.00; dinner 23.00. Food: lunch 15.00; dinner 21.30.
Closed: Sunday, Tuesday and two weeks in January.
Food: Modern European brasserie.
Other points: No-smoking area. Children welcome. Wheelchair access.
Directions: A380 towards the seafront in Torquay. Turn left to the harbour and at the clocktower turn right. The Elephant is 200 yards along on the left. (Map 4, D5)

Torquay

Orestone Manor

Rockhouse Lane, Maidencombe, Torquay,
Devon TQ1 4SX
Telephone: +44(0)1803 328098
enquiries@orestone.co.uk
www.orestone.co.uk

Set on the Torbay coastline, Orestone Manor has a magical continental feel with a touch of the Raj. This stylish hotel is superior in so many ways: views from the hotel across to Lyme Bay are superb, the bedrooms magnificent and the food and service first class. Its inspired décor successfully combines several styles. The dining room, for example, has a colonial feel. The smart interiors continue through to the individually furnished suites and bedrooms. All are en suite and have sea views. Dining is a real treat, as the menu offers contemporary dishes using the best local ingredients and produce from the hotel's gardens. Set course lunches include moules to start, with mains of wild mushroom risotto or baked free-range chicken with sautéed thyme and garlic gnocchi. For dinner, start with pan-seared scallops or Gressingham duck roulade and follow with roasted pheasant or sautéed black bream. The 100-strong wine list includes fab options at good prices. Snacks, lunches and teas can be enjoyed in the conservatory all day.

Rooms: 12. Double/twin from £125, single from £89.
Prices: Set lunch £14.95. Restaurant main course from £16.50 at dinner. Bar snack from £7.50. House wine £12.95.
Last orders: Food: lunch 14.00; dinner 21.00. Open for afternoon tea.
Closed: Never.
Food: Modern British.
Other points: No smoking in the restaurant. Garden. Children welcome. Dogs welcome. Car park.
Directions: From Torquay, follow the A379 (signposted Teignmouth) up Watcombe Hill. Then look out for Brunel Manor and turn right down Rockhouse Lane about 50 yards further on. There is a signpost to the hotel on the main A379 road at the top of Rockhouse Lane. (Map 4, D5)

Studland Bay

Manor House

Beach Road, Studland Bay, Dorset BH19 3AU
Telephone: +44(0)1929 450288
themanorhousehotel@lineone.net
www.themanorhousehotel.com

Nestled in 20 acres of secluded grounds with views over Studland Bay, this early 18th-century Gothic manor house makes for an elegant and comfortable stay. Despite its olde worlde charm, it offers the latest conveniences and top-notch service. The baronial-feel, oak-panelled dining room with fireplace and dark-wood furniture and its adjoining bright conservatory, and comfortable, country-style lounge all have sea views. Bedrooms are light and spacious with period furnishings. All are en suite with every convenience and many have sea or garden views. There's a four-poster suite in the Coach House annex and a further four in the main house. Facilities include a bar and tennis courts. Dinner is a meal to look forward to, with chef Giuseppe Singaguglia sourcing many ingredients locally. Venison comes from local estates, while shellfish is delivered from Weymouth, and regional cheeses include Dorset Blue Vinney, Stinking Bishop and Somerset brie. The evening menu may include tian of crab and avocado with a dill dressing, followed by pan-fried skate wing with chargrilled vegetables and red-pepper butter. Around 40 affordable wines are bolstered by a few specials.

Rooms: 21. Double room from £75 per person, single £100, including dinner.
Prices: Set dinner £30 (4 courses). House wine £12.
Last orders: Food: lunch 14.00; dinner 21.00.
Closed: Never.
Food: Modern British and European.
Other points: No smoking in the restaurant. Children over five welcome. Dogs welcome overnight. Garden. Car park. Wheelchair access to the restaurant.
Directions: Three miles from Swanage, three miles from Sandbanks Ferry. (Map 4, D8)

Weymouth

The Roundhouse Restaurant

1 The Esplanade, Weymouth, Dorset DT4 8EA
Telephone: +44(0)1305 761010
michael.clough@btopenworld.com
www.roundhouserestaurantltd.co.uk

It's hard to believe that this elegant restaurant was once a tram-ticket issuing office. American soldiers stayed here before the D-Day landings. It's in a fabulous location overlooking the harbour, and the interiors have benefited from a recent revamp. Both the restaurant rooms are non smoking. There is much to tempt on the menu on which everything is homemade, including the breads, sweets and sauces. Local ingredients feature prominently and fish is a speciality. You could start with Weymouth Bay crab and mushroom parcel, then move on to one of the many fish specials or delicious alternatives such as lamb's liver braised and served on colcannon mash with a bacon and shallot gravy, or carbonnade of venison served on a wild mushroom savoury bread and butter pudding or a Roundhouse favourite, shank of lamb with a mint and spiced chutney glazed with a minted mash. The wide wine list means you'll easily find the ideal match for whatever you decide to order. Stunning views, good food and smart guest bedrooms are a winning combination that's hard to beat.

Rooms: 1. Double from £50.
Prices: Set lunch £15, set dinner £25. Restaurant main course from £14. Bar main course from £4. House wine £12.50.
Last orders: Lunch: 15.00; dinner: 22.30.
Closed: For lunch out of season.
Food: Modern British.
Other points: No smoking in the restaurant. Children welcome. Dogs welcome. Car park.
Directions: M3. In Weymouth head towards the seafront and turn right. The Roundhouse is the last building before the pavilion. (Map 5, E1)

Great Dunmow

The Swan at Felsted

Station Road, Felsted, Great Dunmow, Essex CM6 3DG
Telephone: +44(0)1371 820245
info@theswanatfelsted.co.uk
www.theswanatfelsted.co.uk

Looks can be deceiving and The Swan is no exception. The imposing redbrick and timber pub dates from the 1900s, when the original Tudor building burnt down, and for years it was a rough local boozer. Jono and Jane Clarke took the Ridley's lease in 2002 and the transformation has been remarkable. Step inside to find a spacious, beautifully designed interior, featuring smart wooden floors, mustard yellow walls hung with attractive works of art, leather sofas in the bar, and a high-ceilinged dining area filled with chunky tables and high-backed dining chairs. Food is sourced locally and the imaginative menus offer a good choice of dishes, from lunchtime salads and sandwiches to main-menu classics such as shepherd's pie, the Swan burger and steak, ale and mussel suet pudding, both made with Barnston beef. Alternatively, go for one of the daily specials, perhaps Thaxted duck breast with raspberry jus. Wines are well chosen (13 by the glass).

Prices: Restaurant main course from £9.50. Main course bar/snack from £5.50. House wine £10.95.
Last orders: Bar: lunch 15.00 (Sunday 18.00); dinner 23.00 (Sunday dinner 22.30). Food: lunch 14.30 (Sunday 16.00); dinner 21.30 (no food Sunday evening).
Closed: Never.
Food: Modern British.
Other points: No-smoking area in the restaurant. Children welcome. Dogs welcome in the bar. Garden. Car park. Wheelchair access.
Directions: Exit 8/M11. Take the A120 and then the B1256 towards Colchester, turn right onto the B1417 to Felsted. (Map 10, E6)

Stansted

Oak Lodge

Jacks Lane, Takeley, near Stansted, Essex CM22 6NT
Telephone: +44(0)1279 871667
oaklodgebb@aol.com
www.oaklodgebb.com

If you are flying from Stansted or just want a quiet break in a tranquil setting, head for this character bed and breakfast deep in the Essex countryside. This classic Tudor building dates from the 16th-century and is set in two acres of attractive gardens with fish ponds, and parking. You can leave your car if flying from the airport two miles away, and proprietor Ron Griffith will take and pick you up. Inside, the house is a wealth of Tudor style and character. There are oak beams throughout and marvellous fireplaces, but you'll also find all the modern facilities you'll need. The en suite bedrooms are tastefully decorated and comfortable, and have TV, coffee-making facilities and a hairdryer. In addition, there is an attractive sitting room for guests' use and an area to sit in the garden. Jan Griffith prides herself on the quality of her home-cooked breakfasts, served in the quaint breakfast room. Her English breakfasts are made using locally sourced ingredients, and include fantastic sausages, bacon and eggs from local farms. It's easy to relax here as Ron and Jan are friendly hosts and the wonderful setting is inspiring.

Rooms: 3. Double/twin from £55, single from £45. Family from £65.
Prices: Restaurant main course from £9.
Closed: Never.
Food: Modern British.
Other points: Totally no smoking. Garden. Credit cards not accepted (cash or cheque only). Car park. Children welcome. No wheelchair access.
Directions: Exit 8/M11. Follow the B1256 to Takeley. After the second set of traffic lights, take the first left. The second right turn is onto Jacks Lane, and Oak Lodge is at the end. (Map 10, E6)

Cirencester

The Organic Farm Shop Café

Abbey Home Farm, Burford Road, Cirencester,
Gloucestershire GL7 5HF
Telephone: +44(0)1285 640441
info@theorganicfarmshop.co.uk
www.theorganicfarmshop.co.uk

Hilary Chester-Master opened her Organic Farm Shop in June 1999 with the objective of establishling a market garden offering fresh local organic produce, including eggs, beef, lamb and pork from Abbey Home Farm, direct to the local community. And her expanding business continues to go from strength to strength. The highly labour-intensive, 15-acre vegetable growing area surrounding the shop produces more than 230 varieties of vegetable, herbs, soft fruits and cut flowers, which you can buy in the shop and sample in the café. Her organic café is one of no more than a dozen in the country that has been awarded a Soil Association certificate. Tuck into a vegetarian menu that takes its lead from what's in season. In the summer you can look foward to delicious fresh salads, such as broad bean, feta and mint, homemade soups, quiches and pasties, alongside a good range of cakes and generously filled rolls and sandwiches. Hilary also offers a take-away menu. The café is adjacent to her well-stocked organic shop and education centre, the Green Room, where seminars and cooking demonstrations are held.

Prices: Main course from £5 to £8.
Last orders: 16.00. Saturday 15.30.
Closed: Sunday and Monday.
Food: 100% organic. Vegetarian and vegan/special diets.
Other points: Totally no smoking. Children welcome. Garden. Car park. Wheelchair access.
Directions: Two miles north of Cirencester just off the A417.
(Map 4, A7)

Cirencester

Wild Duck Inn

Ewen, Cirencester, Gloucestershire GL7 6BY
Telephone: +44(0)1285 770310
wduckinn@aol.com
www.thewildduckinn.co.uk

Creeper-clad with well-tended gardens, this fine Elizabethan inn creates a favourable first impression. The bar is brimming with character and atmosphere, with its backdrop of rich burgundy walls, covered with old portraits and hunting trophies, and large comfortable armchairs creating a warm atmosphere. The restaurant's labyrinth of small rooms features dark beams, more burgundy walls and wooden tables and chairs; the same printed menu is available throughout, along with blackboard specials. The lively repertoire draws the crowds with its modern take and realistic pricing, perhaps a one-course lunch of fresh tuna burger, chicken Caesar salad or a classic fish pie. Dinner could run to roast duck with port and redcurrant sauce, slow-roast belly pork with cider gravy, and fresh Brixham fish. The globetrotting wine list offers some 30 by the glass, and the bar has five real ales. There are 12 individually decorated en suite bedrooms for those not wanting to drive home.

Rooms: 12. Double room from £95, single from £70.
Prices: Main course from £6.95. House wine £11.
Last orders: Bar: 23.00. Food: lunch 14.00; dinner 22.00 (Saturday and Sunday all day until 21.30).
Closed: 25 December.
Food: Modern British.
Other points: Smoking by request, not in the restaurant. Children welcome. Dogs welcome overnight. Garden.
Directions: J15 or 17/M4. From Cirencester, take the A429 towards Malmesbury. On reaching Kemble turn left to Ewen.
(Map 4, B7)

Fairford

Allium

No 1 London Street, Market Place, Fairford,
Gloucestershire GL7 4AH
Telephone: +44(0)1285 712200
restaurant@allium.uk.net
www.allium.uk.net

In the pretty Cotswold village of Fairford, this restaurant is smartly contemporary. The white walls
and modern art fit well with the linen-clad tables and
interesting sculptures. An uncluttered yet sophisticated dining experience with attention to detail is of
the utmost importance to proprietors James and Erica
Graham and Nick Bartimote. Before going through
to the dining area, there is the option of relaxing
for a pre-dinnner drink. Comfortable sofas are an
inviting proposition before the culinary delights
that await, especially with a fire roaring away in the
winter months. The immaculate dining area lives up
to their motto of 'relaxed fine dining' and it becomes
obvious from the menu that the true focus is on the
food. Everything is locally sourced where possible.
An excellent set course table d'hôte is offered on
Wednesday, Thursday and Sunday nights, while the
magnificent carte runs all week and offers delights
such as smoked haddock risotto and pan-fried foie
gras to start, followed by red-wine poached brill or
pan-fried fillet of zander. Puddings of crème caramel
with rum and raisin ice cream and apricot soufflé are
highly recommended. The set Sunday lunch includes
interesting dishes at good-value prices.

Prices: Set lunch £17.50 and dinner £29.50. Gourmand meal £42.
Last orders: Food: 22.00.
Closed: Two weeks at the beginning January.
Food: Modern British/French.
Other points: No smoking in the restaurant, smoking in the bar.
Children welcome. Wheelchair access (no WC).
Directions: J13/M5 and J15/M4. Between Cirencester and
Lechlade on the A417. On the market place in Fairford.
(Map 5, B3)

Frampton Mansell

White Horse

Cirencester Road, Frampton Mansell,
Gloucestershire GL6 8HZ
Telephone: +44(0)1285 760960
www.cotswoldwhitehorse.com

Shaun and Emma Davies' White Horse is a welcome
beacon along the busy A419. The pair have revived
the pub's fortunes with a smart makeover but, more
importantly, with their excellent food and drink.
Brightly painted walls, modern art and chunky
tables provide a fitting setting for the modern menu
built around fresh produce from quality local suppliers. Meat comes from Butts Farm butchers near
Cirencester, game is from local shoots, and fish is
delivered twice-weekly from Cornwall. Seafood has
become quite a focus, especially since a large lobster
tank was installed. As with other seafood, the lobster
is simply served as the quality speaks for itself. Fine
dining begins with pan-fried foie gras, sweet-potato
pancake, crisp pancetta and a muscat butter or rock
oysters, then moves on to mains of halibut saffron
and a chive cream sauce or venison with red wine and
ginger jus. Puddings are an equally delectable bunch.
A global wine list focuses on smaller growers.

Prices: Restaurant main course from £8.95. Bar main course
from £4.95. House wine £11.75.
Last orders: Bar: lunch 15.00; dinner 23.00. Food: lunch 14.30;
dinner 21.45 (Sunday 15.00).
Closed: Sunday evening.
Food: Modern British.
Other points: No smoking in the restaurant. Children welcome.
Dogs welcome in the bar. Garden. Car park.
Directions: J15/M4 and J13//M5. Between Cirencester and Stroud
on the A419. On the main road, not in the village of Frampton
Mansell itself. (Map 4, A7)

Northleach

The Wheatsheaf Inn

West End, Northleach, Gloucestershire GL54 3EZ
Telephone: +44 (0)1451 860244
info@wsan.co.uk
www.wsan.co.uk

Quietly situated in this celebrated Cotswold wool town, the pretty, stone-built, 300-year-old coaching inn has been revamped by brothers Caspar and Gavin Harvard-Walls. Expect classic period features – worn flagstone floors, big oak beams, blazing log fires and chunky wooden furnishings – throughout the three, light and airy and connecting front rooms. The rustic bar deals in Hook Norton with changing guest ales and a blackboard menu. The classy, understated dining room is marginally more formal. Modern British favourites are inspired by what is available locally, Gloucester Old Spot pork tenderloin with parsnip mash and cabbage, for example, or Bibury trout with watercress and bacon. Treacle tart, or apple crumble with custard are classic desserts, with local cheeses making a savoury alternative. There are some impeccable choices on a globally inspired wine list. All eight en suite bedrooms have been refurbished along cool, white Scandinavian lines. There is a lovely garden for alfresco dining.

Rooms: 8. Double/twin room from £60, single from £50, family room from £70.
Prices: Main course from £7. Bar/snack from £4. House wine £10.75.
Last orders: Bar 23.00. Food: lunch 15.00; dinner 22.00 (Sunday 21.00).
Closed: Never.
Food: Modern British.
Other points: No smoking in the restaurant. Children welcome. Dogs welcome in the bar. Garden. Car park. Licence for civil weddings. Wheelchair access.
Directions: Exit 15/M4. The village is just off the A429 between Stow-on-the-Wold and Cirencester. (Map 4, A8)

Painswick

The Falcon Inn

New Street, Painswick, Gloucestershire GL6 6UN
Telephone: +44(0)1452 814222
bleninns@clara.net
www.falconinn.com

Standing opposite the parish church, the Falcon is a handsome, stone-built, 16th-century coaching inn with a colourful history, including a period as the village courthouse. It is also the unlikely setting in which to find the world's oldest bowling green. Interconnecting bar and dining areas are full of traditional character, the scene set by stone, tiled and carpeted floors, wood panelling, open log fires, and an eclectic mix of furnishings. Jonny Johnston's careful sourcing of local produce, notably game from nearby shoots, locally grown vegetables, and butchers' meats, including belted Galloway beef, is evident on changing menus and the list of daily chalkboard dishes. Expect the likes of organic pork loin with cider and honey and braised venison with root vegetables, and fish dishes such as organic Cockleford trout with red pesto. Twelve individually decorated bedrooms are split between the main building and the converted coach house. The Cotswold Way passes the door.

Rooms: 12. Double room from £68, single from £45.
Prices: Set lunch £12 and dinner £16. Restaurant main course £7.50. Bar snack from £4. House wine £8.95.
Last orders: Bar: 23.00. Food: lunch 14.30 (Sunday 15.00); dinner 21.30 (Saturday 22.00).
Closed: Never.
Food: Modern and traditional British and European.
Other points: No-smoking area. Children welcome. Dogs welcome overnight. Garden. Car park. Wheelchair access (no WC), fully equipped bedroom available.
Directions: J11a/M5. Painswick is on the A46 between Cheltenham and Stroud. (Map 4, A7)

Winchcombe

Juri's The Olde Bakery Tea Shoppe

High Street, Winchcombe, Cheltenham, Gloucestershire GL54 5LJ
Telephone: +44(0)1242 602469
miyawaki@ma.kew.net
www.Juris-Tearoom.co.uk

This quaint 18th-century Grade ll-listed building has been a teashop for more than 25 years. The Miyawaki family took it on over a year ago and have firmly established themselves as quality bakers. Their traditional cakes, particularly their scones, will have you swooning; enjoy them as part of the astonishingly good-value cream tea. Juri's success stems from her insistence on using quality ingredients. She learned her trade at Raymond Blanc's Le Manoir aux Quat' Saisons. Her luscious chocolate cake incorporates the best Belgian chocolate, and most of the ingredients for the other seven cakes are organic. The menu kicks off with an English breakfast, scrummy things on toast, before moving on to snacks and substantial mains. The good choice of tea is set to expand, while coffee options include a mashmallow and cream-topped special. Juri's parents run the front of house efficiently, and here, light lunches such as Japanese-style beef curry, creamy fish pie and Sheepdrove organic sausages are on offer. A licence means lunch can be accompanied by a glass of wine, sherry or saké.

Prices: Daily lunch specials from £7. Toasted sandwiches from £4. Cream tea £3.90. House wine £10.
Last orders: Food: 16.30.
Closed: Monday (except Bank Holiday Mondays), Tuesday and January.
Food: Modern European with Japanese influences. Homemade patisserie and scones.
Other points: No-smoking area. Garden. Conservatory. Children welcome.
Directions: Exit 9/M5. Take the A46, B4077, B4632 signposted to Winchcombe. From Cheltenham and the South take the B4632 towards Broadway which takes you directly into Winchcombe. (Map 5, B2)

Crondall

The Hampshire Arms

Pankridge Street, Crondall, Farnham,
Hampshire GU10 5QU
Telephone: +44(0)1252 850418
dining@thehampshirearms.co.uk
www.thehampshirearms.co.uk

Alan Piesse and Tim Dyer took over this 18th-century village pub in January 2005. It was a courthouse and then a bakery before becoming a pub to serve the community. Behind the unpretentious exterior, Alan and Tim have succeeded in sweeping away the expectations that existed with regard to the atmosphere and style. Chef Colin McCavana produces fresh, well-presented food and now includes a lighter lunch menu in the bar featuring classic pub favourites, in addition to an imaginative carte. Typically, starters include mussels with white wine, shallots and herb butter or home-cured salmon with lime and honey dressing. Mains may offer whole bass with lemon balm, ginger and fennel, or lamb with coriander and apricot couscous. Leather sofas front the log fire in the informal bar area, which draws local drinkers in, while there's more formal dining in the newly refurbished restaurant. There's also a private room and a terrace for summer alfresco dining.

Prices: Restaurant main course from £10.50. Bar main course from £7.50. House wine £12.50.
Last orders: Bar: lunch 14.30; dinner 23.00. Food: lunch 14.00; dinner 21.15. No carte menu Monday evening.
Closed: Sunday nights.
Food: Modern British.
Other points: No smoking in the restaurant. Garden. Children welcome. Car park. Wheelchair access.
Directions: Exit 5/M3. Take the A287 for Farnham, and turn off at Crondall. (Map 5, C4)

Littleton

The Running Horse

88 Main Road, Littleton, Winchester,
Hampshire SO22 6QS
Telephone: +44(0)1962 880218
christineabrams@btconnect.com
www.therunninghorsepubrestaurant.co.uk

Considerable investment over the past two years has transformed this once run-down village pub into a stylish dining venue, but one that hasn't lost sight of its roots as a village local. Expect a smart interior featuring opulent Italian sofas, a marble-topped bar, plenty of stainless steel, slate floors and trendy wooden blinds, but the original fireplace and wooden floor remain. Light lunch in the bar may take in crab cakes with tartare sauce and seared scallops with caper dressing. In the evening, sit in the bar or restaurant to experience Joe Cathers' inventive cooking. 'Quality ingredients, well cooked – food the way it should be' is his philosophy and his freshly prepared dishes may include scallops, artichoke and grapefruit with truffle oil for starters, followed by roast Minstead duck with pak choi, broad beans and pink peppercorn sauce, and chilled vanilla rice pudding. There are also excellent wines and local Ringwood ale, and en suite rooms planned for 2006.

Rooms: 8. Double/twin from £85, family from £110.
Prices: Restaurant main course £15.50. Bar main course £9.95. House wine £12.95.
Last orders: Bar: lunch 14.00 (Saturday 16.00); dinner 21.30. Food: lunch 14.00 (Saturday 16.00); dinner 21.30.
Closed: Rarely.
Food: Modern British.
Other points: No-smoking area. Dogs welcome. Garden. Car park. Wheelchair access.
Directions: M3. Take fourth exit to the A34. At the first junction, turn left to Salisbury, then take the third exit to Littleton. Turn left at the junction, and The Running Horse is half a mile further on the left. (Map 5, D3)

www.routiers.co.uk

Petersfield

Langrish House

Langrish, Petersfield, Hampshire GU32 1RN
Telephone: +44(0)1730 266941
frontdesk@langrishhouse.co.uk
www.langrishhouse.co.uk

Apart from a 26-year gap, Langrish House has been in the Talbot-Ponsonby family since 1842. Now owned by Nigel and Robina Talbot-Ponsonby, it's all that a country-house hotel should be: elegant, but not pompous. All 13 spacious rooms are individually decorated to a high standard, and have lovely garden views. Frederick's Restaurant, named after a larger-than-life family member born in the 19th-century, is newly refurbished and intimate, or dine in the Old Vaults, which were dug by prisoners of war. Frederick's serves a variety of dishes, with fresh produce carefully prepared by head chef Duncan Wilson. Start with scallops with pancetta salad and herb butter sauce or chicken and mango roulade with pickled plums, then follow with an updated classic, say, fillet of lamb with apricot and port stuffing. Desserts are a dream selection, or there's a fine selection of cheeses served with grape chutney and homebaked black olive bread. A well-selected, interesting wine list complements the menu. This is a beautiful location for a wedding or special event. In the spring, 27,000 daffodils come into bloom in the gardens.

Rooms: 13. Doubles from £95.50, single from £72, family from £120.
Prices: Set lunch £12.50. Set dinner £27.95. House wine £15.95.
Last orders: Bar: lunch 14.00; dinner 23.00. Food: lunch 14.00; dinner 21.00.
Closed: Rarely
Food: Modern British.
Other points: No-smoking area. Children welcome. Dogs welcome. Garden. Car park. Wheelchair access.
Directions: Follow the A272 and Langrish House is signposted. (Map 5, D4)

Southampton

The White Star Tavern & Dining Rooms

28 Oxford Street, Southampton, Hampshire SO14 3DJ
Telephone: +44(0)2380 821990
manager@whitestartavern.co.uk
www.whitestartavern.co.uk

Southampton's first gastropub, in a former seafarers' hotel in up-and-coming Oxford Street close to Ocean Village and West Quay, has proved a great success, drawing both a lively drinking crowd and discerning diners. Smart front-bar lounge areas sport modern brown-leather banquettes and cream walls are adorned with shipping photographs and retro mirrors, yet retain the original flagstone floors and the period open fireplaces. Beyond lies the spacious, wood-floored and panelled dining rooms. Good use of fresh produce from Hampshire suppliers can be seen in light bites such as chicken rillette and homemade piccalilli, or a classic Caesar salad, and in the lunchtime carte with smoked haddock and grain mustard cream. In the evening, steamed mussels in black bean sauce, and pork loin with confit of root vegetables and mustard jus, show style, as do the homemade breads and puddings, say, warm chocolate fondant with pistachio ice cream. There is also an impressive list of cocktails, Champagnes, vodkas and wines by the glass.

Prices: Restaurant main course dinner from £11.50, lunch from £4. House wine £11.50.
Last orders: Bar: lunch 15.00; dinner 23.00 (Friday to Sunday open all day, April to October open all day). Food: lunch 15.00; dinner 21.30 (Friday and Saturday 22.00, Sunday 21.00).
Closed: Rarely.
Food: Modern British.
Other points: No-smoking area. Children welcome during the day at weekends. Outside seating. Wheelchair access.
Directions: Exit 14/M3. Take the A33 to Southampton and head towards the Ocean Village and Marina. (Map 5, D3)

Hoarwithy

Aspen House

Hoarwithy, Hereford, Herefordshire HR2 6QP
Telephone: +44(0)1432 840353
sallyandrob@aspenhouse.net
www.aspenhouse.net

Robert Elliot and Sally Lawrance wanted their guest house to be friendly and to offer great food. They have achieved just that at their 18th-century farmhouse in a get-away-from-it-all location. The most important thing is the ethos. The pair are against everything mass-manufactured, industrial and unseasonal and for everything which is handmade, organic and personal. Every aspect of Aspen House reflects this; they have made a real feature out of the garden, which has been terraced to provide a number of secluded loggias and lawns, and the coach house at the back has been converted into a self-contained unit. The sitting room and dining room are quite simply furnished, but everything is good quality and there is an emphasis on comfort and service. Their culinary inspiration comes from Robert's Polish mother, but there are also Mediterranean, North African and Indian influences to their fine cooking. The daily menu could include cream of sorrel and potato soup or mezze to start, followed by a hearty slow-roasted beef hussar or lamb tagine with couscous. The short wine list is an interesting selection.

Rooms: 4. Double/twin from £56, single room from £35.
Prices: Set dinner £20. Aspen House 'Special' £50 for 2 people.
Closed: Rarely.
Food: Eclectic. Mediterranean, Polish, Middle Eastern.
Other points: Totally no smoking. Children welcome. Dogs welcome by arrangement. Garden. Wheelchair access.
Directions: J4/M50. Take the A49 towards Ross-on-Wye to Hereford. Hoarwithy is signposted from the A49. Aspen House is on the T-junction in the centre of the village. (Map 8, D5)

Walterstone

Allt-yr-Ynys Hotel

Walterstone, Abergavenny, Herefordshire HR2 0DU
Telephone: +44(0)1873 890307
allthotel@compuserve.com
www.allthotel.co.uk

Accommodation and food at Allt-yr-Ynys is top-class. The beautifully preserved 16th-century manor house has 19 en suite bedrooms, a fine restaurant, an indoor heated and spa pools and beautiful gardens. The house was once owned by William Cecil, chief minister to Elizabeth I, and many of its original features have been preserved. In the comfortable sitting room, there is fine oak panelling. The Jacobean suite also retains its original oak panelling and 16th-century four-poster bed. The bedrooms are split between the main house and converted stables and outbuildings; most have views over the mountains and woodlands. They have canopied beds, tasteful fabrics and furnishings, and offer every modern convenience. The kitchen is loyal to regional and local produce, offering Welsh lamb, beef and cheeses in starters such as pan-fried whole Greenland Bay prawns with a lime-butter and herb sauce. Mains could take in roasted rack of local lamb with a herb crust or baked aubergine with courgette and pepper ratatouille topped with Welsh cheddar. Equally appealing are puds such as bread and butter pudding and vanilla crème brulée.

Rooms: 21. Double room from £85, single from £65.
Prices: Set lunch £16.95 and dinner £25. Main course from £11. House wine £14.75.
Last orders: Food: lunch 15.00; dinner 21.30.
Closed: Rarely.
Food: Modern British.
Other points: No-smoking area. Children welcome. Garden. Car park. Licence for civil weddings. Swimming pool, spa and sauna. Clay-pigeon shooting.
Directions: A465 Abergavenny to Hereford road. Turn off five miles north of Abergavenny at Old Pandy Inn; After 400m, turn right at Green Barn. (Map 8, E5)

Flaunden

The Bricklayers Arms

Hog Pits Bottom, Flaunden, Hertfordshire HP3 0PH
Telephone: +44 (0)1442 833322
goodfood@bricklayersarms.com
www.bricklayersarms.com

Cloaked in Virginia creeper, Flaunden's low-roofed cottagey pub is a peaceful, inviting spot, especially in summer when its country-style garden becomes the perfect place to enjoy an alfresco pint of ale. On cooler days, the refurbished, timbered and low-ceilinged bar, replete with blazing log fires, old prints and comfortable traditional furnishings, is popular with both local diners and walkers for its modern take on pub food. Alvin and Sally Michaels have smartened up the place and offer a good range of menus to suit all who visit. In the bar, follow a country stroll with thick-cut sandwiches or tuck into steak and kidney pie or lamb shank with red wine and shallot sauce. In the evening, come for home-smoked fish with lemon coriander butter and tomato chutney, then follow with roast sea bass with sweet-pepper cream sauce, and finish with hot chocolate pudding. Don't miss the summer Sunday barbecues and live jazz in the garden.

Prices: Restaurant and bar main course from £9.95.
House wine £10.95.
Last orders: Bar: 23.00.
Food: lunch 15.00 (Sunday 16.00); dinner 21.30 (Sunday 21.00)
Closed: Rarely.
Food: Modern British and French.
Other points: No smoking in the restaurant. Children welcome. Dogs welcome in the bar. Garden. Car park.
Directions: 10 minutes from Exit18/M25. Three miles south west of Hemel Hempstead. (Map 5, B4)

East Cowes

Coasters Coffee Shop

1 Clarence Road, East Cowes, Isle of Wight PO32 6EP
Telephone: +44(0)1983 200009
medinamews@wight365.net
www.coasterscoffeeshop.com

Standing proudly on the corner of Clarence Road in East Cowes, Coasters is a magnet for those who want good coffee and a baguette or sandwich which is a cut above the norm. In summer, outdoor seating extends the options. Close to the ferry port, it's an excellent place to stop pre- or post-crossing. You can even phone in your order in advance and it will be ready waiting for you. Its special blend of Segafredo coffee beans is freshly ground every hour and attracts customers from all over the Isle of Wight, as does its fresh range of sandwiches, baguettes, wraps and paninis, which are filled with a tempting array of locally sourced ingredients – the ripest, freshest tomatoes and crispiest lettuce, meats and local vegetables. Chef/patron Kevin Dullaghan bakes the baguettes on site throughout the day. He swapped the rigours of the House of Commons to open Coasters and, with his team, can provide a varied catering service for private and corporate functions. As well as baguettes, they serve hot snacks such as pasties and homemade soups. A drinks licence means you can enjoy beer or wine with your meal.

Prices: House wine £7.
Last orders: Food: Lunch 13.45 (in the winter) and 15.30 (in the Summer).
Closed: Rarely.
Food: Modern British.
Other points: Totally no smoking. Well-behaved children welcome. Wheelchair access.
Directions: Two minutes from Cowes floating bridge. (Map 5, E3)

Dover

Wallett's Court Country House Hotel and Spa

Westcliffe, St Margaret's-at-Cliffe, Dover, Kent CT15 6EW
Telephone: +44(0)1304 852424
stay@wallettscourt.com
www.wallettscourt.com

The Oakley family purchased what was a rundown Jacobean farmhouse over a quarter of a century ago and have developed it over the years to its full potential. They have a good restaurant and, more recently, separate spa facilities in the grounds. The house retains many period features. The sitting room is filled with sofas, armchairs, coffee tables and candles, and service is relaxed but professional and lacks pretention. Main house bedrooms range from small but comfortable standard rooms to vaulted beamed ceilings and antique four-poster beds. Other cosy rooms are in conversions in the grounds. Additional farm outbuildings now house a state-of-the-art gym, indoor swimming pool, sauna, mineral steam room and hydrotherapy spa, plus there's an all-weather tennis court. Stephen Harvey delivers food with a broadly English character, derived mainly from carefully sourced ingredients, many of which are local and in seasonal. Brochettes of Rye Bay scallops and medallions of monkfish with a truffled balsamic reduction, and St Margaret's Bay lobster, Dover sole and Kentish asparagus and broad beans could make up a typical summer meal.

Rooms: 16. Double room from £90, single from £75.
Prices: Set lunch £17.50, set dinner £35. House wine £14.95.
Last orders: Food: lunch 14.00; dinner 21.00.
Closed: Monday and Saturday lunch.
Food: Modern British.
Other points: No-smoking area. Children welcome. Garden. Car park.
Directions: From Dover, follow the signs for A258 Deal. Once on the road, take the first right to St Margaret's-at-Cliffe; the hotel is one mile down on the right. (Map 6, C7)

Maidstone

Who'd A Thought It

Headcorn Road, Grafty Green, Maidstone,
Kent ME17 2AR
Telephone: +44(0)1622 858951
joe@whodathoughtit.com
www.whodathoughtit.com

You'll find plenty of glitz and glamour at this cosy country inn, built in the reign of Henry Vlll. Whether you want a flute of Cristal or a pint of ale, you'll find your every whim catered for here. This inn is a fascinating mix of pub, champagne and oyster bar, tasteful restaurant and luxury accommodation. The rooms are finished to a very high standard; many have four-posters, DVDs and stereos. Downstairs, be it in the bar, brasserie, restaurant or on the attractive outside terrace, you will find food options to match your every mood. Colchester oysters and seafood are on offer in the brasserie. Start with king scallops with black pudding and Parma ham, then follow with wild sea bass with pak choi or garlic lobster, or opt for a gourmet meat dish such as chateaubriand. Balsamic strawberry mille feuille makes for an indulgent finish. The extensive wine list extends to a fine choice of cognacs and cigars.

Rooms: 9. Double/twin from £60, four-poster with double spa pool from £160.
Prices: Restaurant main course from £13. Bar/snack from £8. House wine £11.
Last orders: Bar: lunch 15.00 (open all day Sunday); dinner 23.00. Food: lunch 14.30 (Sunday 16.00); dinner 21.30 (no food Sunday evening).
Closed: Rarely.
Food: Modern British.
Other points: No-smoking area. Garden. Children welcome. Car park.
Directions: Exit 8/M20. (Map 6, C6)

Whitstable

The Crab & Winkle Restaurant

South Quay, The Harbour, Whitstable, Kent CT5 1AB
Telephone: +44(0)1227 779377
dine@seafood-restaurant-uk.com
www.seafood-restaurant-uk.com

This harbourside restaurant, a pebble's throw from the sea, is named after the first passenger railway that ran from Whitstable to Canterbury. Andrew Bennett has recently taken over from his parents and made a number of subtle changes to the décor and the menu. He owns the fish market below so has no shortage of fresh produce. The menu stays broadly the same throughout the day, although the buzzy lunchtime atmosphere winds down to more cosy and intimate dining at night. Starters include the local speciality, native oysters, as well as crab and Waldorf salad or potted brown shrimps. Mains offer an extensive seafood platter, crab and winkle paella and Whitstable Bay organic ale-battered cod and chips. Although predominantly fish, the daily specials allow for carnivore and vegetarian tastes. Traditional bread and butter pudding, Eton mess and Cartmel Village sticky toffee puddings are indulgent ways to round off. With bustling harbour views and balcony seats in summer, this is a charming place to relax over a locally sourced bottle of wine or one from the Old World collection. Diners receive a discount in the downstairs fish market.

Prices: Restaurant main course from £9.95. House wine £10.95.
Last orders: Food: lunch 16.00; dinner 21.00 (Friday and Saturday 21.30).
Closed: Rarely.
Food: Seafood.
Other points: No smoking in the restaurant. Children welcome. Free parking after 18.00. Wheelchair access.
Directions: Go through the town centre of Whitstable towards the harbour entrance which is on the left just as you exit the one-way system. (Map 6, C7)

Whitstable

Wheelers Oyster Bar ⭐

8 High Street, Whitstable, Kent CT5 1BQ
Telephone: +44(0)1227 273311
www.whitstable-shellfish.co.uk

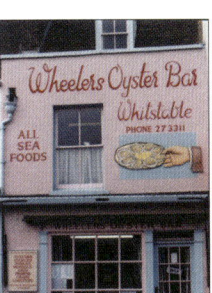

Whitstable is the oyster capital of Kent, and Wheelers is a most winsome place to sample the fine local catch. Originally a simple oyster bar when it opened in 1856, the restaurant has long since branched out to become a mini seafood paradise, serving everything from cockles and crab to lobster, with plenty inbetween. It's essential to book, as demand far outstrips the number of tables in the small dining room. Chef Mark Stubbs's talent for cooking seafood speaks for itself. He cooks with the freshest seafood, but is not afraid to introduce intense and interesting flavours to his dishes. Each is carefully considered, such as the salad of pan-fried langoustines and queen scallops with baby leeks and local asparagus, or the combination of pan-fried John Dory with prawns, coriander, butter beans and chorizo. But the simple native oysters unadorned are equally thrilling. A cold menu to eat in or take away is offered in the tiny Victorian front oyster bar (four stools): delicate tarts of crab, prawns and butter sauce, hot-smoked salmon fillets, crab sandwiches, oysters, eels, prawns, mussels, and baby octopus. There's no licence, but no charge for corkage either.

Prices: Main course from £10.00. Unlicenced.
Last orders: Food: 19.30.
Closed: Wednesday, and the last two weeks of January.
Food: Seafood.
Other points: Totally no smoking. Credit cards not accepted. BYO. Wheelchair access.
Directions: Exit 7/M2. Turn off the Thanet Way at the roundabout to Whitstable and follow road through town. The restaurant is at the end of High Street. (Map 6, C7)

Wingham

The Dog Inn

Canterbury Road, Wingham, near Canterbury, Kent CT3 1BB
Telephone: +44(0)1227 720339
thedoginn@netbreeze.co.uk

Realising that there was plenty of life in the 'old Dog', Richard and Sherry Martin took on this ancient village hostelry and have begun scraping away years of black paint and grime to expose the impressive features of the original building, which dates back to the 13th-century. Superb heavy beams and panelling blend well with the antique oak floors throughout the character bars, and there's a historic function room and renovated en suite bedrooms under the eaves. It's early days and there's still plenty to do, but it's a promising start and the building has huge potential. Beers come from Adnams, Greene King and Shepherd Neame and upgraded menus feature game from Godmersham Estate, organic meats from Chandler and Dunn in Ash and fish from Whitstable. This translates as Romney Marsh lamb with rosemary jus, rib-eye steak with pepper sauce, baked trout with parsley butter, and upmarket lunchtime bar snacks. One to watch!

Rooms: 9. Double/twin from £69, single from £40. Family from £89.
Prices: Set lunch £15. Set dinner £20. Restaurant main course from £8.95. Bar main course from £6.95. House wine £12.95.
Last orders: Bar: Open all day until 23.00. Food: Lunch 15.00 (open all day Saturday and Sunday); Dinner 22.00.
Closed: Never.
Food: British. Eclectic.
Other points: Totally no smoking. Dogs welcome. Garden and BBQ. Children welcome. Car park. Licence for civil weddings.
Directions: M2/A2 to Barham. Four miles from Canterbury on the A257. (Map 6, C7)

Cardium Shellfish
South Quay, The Harbour, Whitstable
Tel: 01227 264769

Mark buys Cardium's plump, sweet cockles, which are gathered from the Thames Estuary when they're a juicy three years old. Their flavour is so good that they can be enjoyed with just a little vinegar and brown bread and butter – often the simplest ideas are the best. Mark also recommends eating cockles with just a chilled glass of Chablis – one to try at home.

Mallards Farm
Waterham Road, Hernhill
Tel: 01227 751245

The farm supplies fresh fruit and vegetables to Wheeler's Oyster Bar all year round. You can buy direct from its farm shop that is open daily.

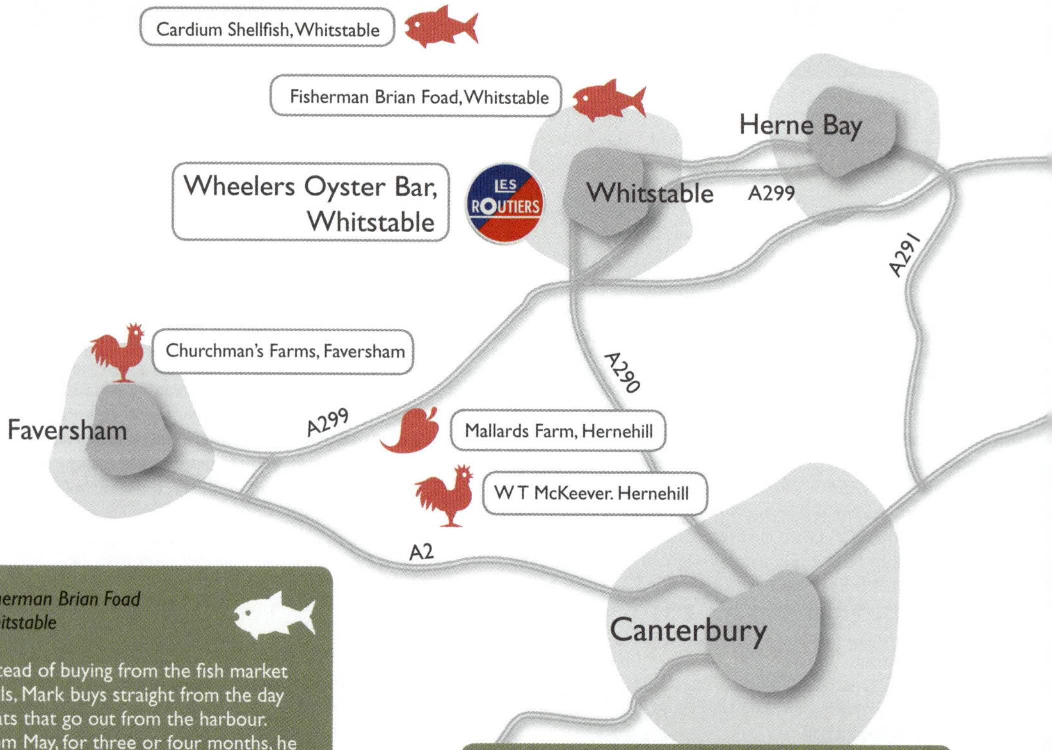

Cardium Shellfish, Whitstable

Fisherman Brian Foad, Whitstable

Herne Bay

Wheelers Oyster Bar, Whitstable

Whitstable   A299

A291

Churchman's Farms, Faversham

A290

Faversham   A299

Mallards Farm, Hernehill

W T McKeever. Hernehill

A2

Canterbury

Fisherman Brian Foad
Whitstable

Instead of buying from the fish market stalls, Mark buys straight from the day boats that go out from the harbour. From May, for three or four months, he buys his lobsters direct from Brian Foad, and his sea bass, skate and crabs from Ian Brook.

A28

Churchman's Farms
Kennaways, Ospringe, Faversham
Tel: 01795 531124

The farm's free-range eggs are used to make Mark's light and airy smoked-eel soufflé.

Wheelers Oyster Bar, Whitstable

Just a stone's throw from the seafront, the cheery pink-coloured Wheelers on Whitstable High Street is in the enviable position of having the pick of the local fish and shellfish catch. The famous Whitstable native oysters, available from Whitstable's oyster beds from September to April, are a star attraction at the restaurant. Head chef Mark Stubbs also uses other local ingredients in his superb menu, and shares a few suppliers from his address book that help make it special.

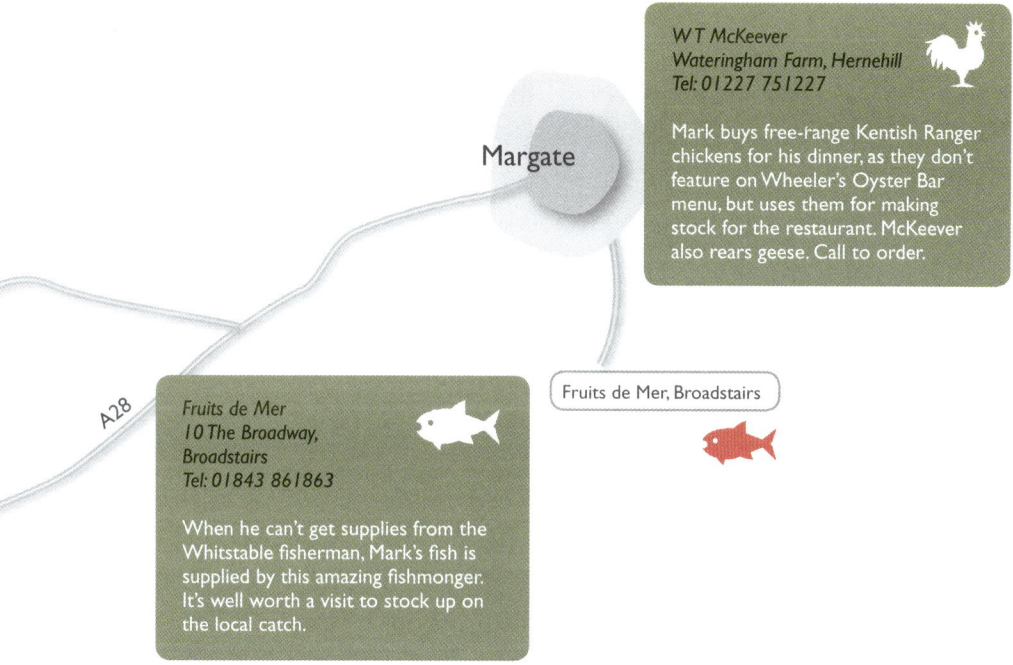

W T McKeever
Wateringham Farm, Hernehill
Tel: 01227 751227

Mark buys free-range Kentish Ranger chickens for his dinner, as they don't feature on Wheeler's Oyster Bar menu, but uses them for making stock for the restaurant. McKeever also rears geese. Call to order.

Margate

A28

Fruits de Mer
10 The Broadway,
Broadstairs
Tel: 01843 861863

When he can't get supplies from the Whitstable fisherman, Mark's fish is supplied by this amazing fishmonger. It's well worth a visit to stock up on the local catch.

Fruits de Mer, Broadstairs

Oysters delivered to your home

Treat yourself to the decadence of Whitstable oysters by having them delivered direct to your home. Order them online at www.whitstable-shellfish.co.uk, or by calling 01227 282375. Prices start at £17.42 for a dozen, excluding delivery, or there are cultivated Scottish rock oysters, from £11.42 for a dozen.

Visit the Oyster Festival

Whitstable's nine-day annual Oyster Festival in July celebrates the start of the oyster season and coincides with the town's regatta and carnival. Those keen to sample seafood will be in their element at South Quay, where you can try cockles, whelks, shrimps and oysters. For more information and this year's dates, call the Festival Office on 01227 275482 or visit www.whitstableoysterfestival.co.uk.

Blackpool

Raffles Hotel and Tea Rooms

73-77 Hornby Road, Blackpool, Lancashire FY1 4QJ
Telephone: +44(0)1253 294713
enquiries@raffleshotelblackpool.fsworld.co.uk
www.raffleshotelblackpool.co.uk

This exceptional B&B-hotel just minutes from Blackpool's Tower is ideal for a traditional seaside break. The owners Graham Poole and Ian Balmforth have a real passion for their spick-and-span little gem. The standard of décor is high, the housekeeping exemplary. The atmosphere is relaxed from the moment you step over the doorstep and are served a welcoming coffee or tea in your room. At other times, morning coffees and evening drinks are served in the comfortable lounge. All the bedrooms are compact, but not small, and meticulously decorated with flair. A do-it-yourself tea tray, TV and quality towels are standard issue in bedrooms. There's a fabulous, oriental-themed room with Thai furniture and Chinese bedspread and rooms inspired by north Africa, Egypt and India. In addition, there are two bedrooms on the ground floor for guests who are not so nimble on their feet. And, it is worth noting that the recently acquired premises next door have been converted into a tea room where meals, as well as fluffy cakes and scones, are served.

Rooms: 17. From £26 per person.
Prices: Main course from £4.95. Starters and sweets from £1.50.
Last orders: Food: 18.00.
Closed: Rarely.
Food: Traditional and Modern British.
Other points: No smoking in the restaurant. Children welcome. Dogs welcome overnight. Car park. Wheelchair access.
Directions: Take the M55 towards Blackpool and follow the red signs for the central car park. Leave the car park for the one-way system, Central Drive. Turn left and Hornby Road is the first immediate right. (Map 11, E4)

Bolton-le-Sands

Packet Bridge Village Fish and Chip Shop

30 Main Street, Bolton-le-Sands, Carnforth,
Lancashire LA5 8DL
Telephone: +44(0)1524 822791
john.wild@ukonline.co.uk
www.packetbridge.com

People travel from miles around for John and Hilary Wild's renowned traditional fish and chips. Testament to the couple's continued success is the fact they feature in the top 100 of the Seafish Friers' Quality Award scheme. Although they don't offer an eat-in option, the Wilds (above) are happy to point you in the direction of several local beauty spots where you can park and enjoy stunning views over Morecambe Bay, while eating your chip lunch or supper. They'll even supply serviettes and wipes. Their good, honest food is cooked to perfection, and as well as the wide fish selection, there is also a good range of Hollands pies or homemade chilli or beef curry, all with chips, of course. Those with bigger appetites will appreciate the Moby Dick, a large cod. If you're eating here around Christmas and not worried about your calorie intake, try John's famous battered Christmas pudding. Also worth looking out for are the shop's state-of-the-art frying range and the Art Deco Frank Ford range clock.

Prices: Fish and chips from £3.20. Soft drinks from 60p.
Last orders: Food: lunch 13.00 (Saturday until 13.30); dinner 20.00 (Friday until 21.00 in the summer).
Closed: Sunday and Monday.
Food: Traditional British.
Directions: Exit 35/M6. (Map 11, E4)

Clitheroe

Weezos @ The Old Tollhouse

1-5 Parson Lane, Clitheroe, Lancashire BB7 2JP
Telephone: +44(0)1200 424478
weezos@btconnect.com
www.weezos.co.uk

At the foot of Clitheroe's ancient castle, Weezos is housed in an old character cottage. This charming restaurant has quaint old beams and original corner stonework, but what grabs your attention are the classic and professional table settings – crisp white linen, sparkling cutlery and tall Schott Zwiesel glasses. The vast experience of Stosie and her partner shows in all areas – style, service, wine and, above all, the pair show a real understanding of good ingredients and how make the best of them. Stosie's cooking talent is evident from her superb gazpacho starter, which has lovely fresh flavours and good bite, and is enhanced by an avocado and fresh crab cake, through to her pan-roasted scallops over a broad bean, pecorino and parmesan mash served on toasted Staffordshire oatcakes. The Goosnargh corn-fed duck livers come lightly pan-fried over rocket with a Gambian hibiscus honey vinaigrette – again a lightness of cooking touch to show off the ingredients, with the vinaigrette lifting the dish into something quite special. The wine list offers plenty of interest and good value.

Prices: Set meal plus wine on Friday and Saturdays £25. Set lunch (Sundays only) £15 (2 courses), £18 for 3 courses. Restaurant main course from £12.20. House wine £11.95.
Last orders: Lunch; 15.00 (Friday and Saturday). Dinner; Tuesday-Saturday 19.00, Sunday 18.00.
Closed: Monday and Sunday evening.
Food: Modern European.
Other points: No-smoking area. Wheelchair access. Children welcome.
Directions: A59. Follow signs to the town centre and the castle. Travel down Parson Hill and Weezos is 50m from the castles main gate. (Map 11, E4)

Poulton-le-Fylde

Monsieurs

12d Blackpool Old Road, Poulton-le-Fylde,
Lancashire FY6 7DH
Telephone: +44(0)1253 896400

Monsieurs is a one-stop dinner solution, offering takeaways with a difference. Now concentrating on its evening trade, this upmarket eaterie dispenses fine homemade French and British 'ready' meals. The brainchild of Guy and Anita Jenkinson, it is a welcome addition to the many Chinese and Indian takeaways that are the high-street norm, and is well placed in the middle of town. Waiting for your order is a pleasant experience as Monsieurs has a Mediterranean café atmosphere, where you can sit in comfortable chairs and read glossy magazines instead of copies of the day's tabloids. The French-style and British dishes are made from quality ingredients and are a far cry from the supermarket equivalent. Here you can tuck into a hearty coq au vin, navarin of lamb, Basque chicken and pork Dijon, with side orders of garlic sautéed potatoes, Vichy carrots and ratatouille. Pasta and vegetarian dishes and popular British desserts of fruit crumbles, and sticky toffee and bread and butter puds extend the range.

Prices: Main course from £8. Snacks from £5.
Last orders: Food: 17.00-21.00.
Closed: Lunchtimes, all day Monday and the last two weeks of July and first week of August.
Food: Traditional French and English. Takeaway.
Other points: Totally no smoking. Children welcome. Car park. Credit cards not accepted.
Directions: Exit 3/M55, then the A585 to Fleetwood. Turn left at first traffic lights, then left at the second lights onto the A586, and into Poulton's one-way system. Monsieurs is situated opposite the library. (Map 11, E4)

Whitewell

Inn at Whitewell

Forest of Bowland, Whitewell, Clitheroe,
Lancashire BB7 3AT
Telephone: +44(0)1200 448222

Standing next to the church overlooking the River Hodder, in the wild beauty of north Lancashire, this magnificent inn is far from the hustle and bustle of town life. The atmosphere is unique, thanks to Richard Bowman and his staff, who imbue this ancient hostelry with warmth and personality. Inside, the ambience is relaxed with a haphazard arrangement of furnishings, bric-a-brac, open log fires, heavy ceiling beams and colourful rugs throughout the stone-floored taproom, rambling dining areas and library. The bar supper choice may include pork medallions with mustard sauce, with salads and substantial sandwiches featuring at lunchtime. The evening carte majors on quality local ingredients, perhaps breast of Goosnargh duck with tomato and bean cassoulet, fantastic puddings and British and Irish cheeses. Individually styled bedrooms are furnished with antique furniture, peat fires and Victorian baths. Eight miles of fishing, a superlative wine list (and wine merchant), art gallery and shop selling homemade foods completes the picture.

Rooms: 23. Double/twin room from £89.
Prices: Restaurant main course from £12. Bar main course from £7.50. House wine £9.50.
Last orders: Bar: lunch 15.00; dinner 23.00. Food: lunch 14.00; dinner 21.30.
Closed: Never.
Food: Modern British.
Other points: No-smoking area. Children welcome. Dogs welcome overnight. Garden. Car park. Licence for civil weddings. Fishing. Wheelchair access throughout.
Directions: Exit 32/M6 to Longridge. From the centre of Longridge follow signs to Whitewell. (Map 11, E4)

Leicester

San Carlo Restaurant

38-40 Granby Street, Leicester, Leicestershire LE1 1DE
Telephone: +44(0)116 251 9332
www.sancarlo.co.uk

Part of a small chain of city-centre restaurants, San Carlo serves good Italian food that puts many chains in the shade. It majors in good-value pizza and pasta. The décor is contemporary, simple and the same across the chain, which has outlets in Birmingham, Bristol and Manchester. The light and airy feel is helped by mirror-lined walls and white-tiled floors that create a sleek Mediterranean look softened by lots of potted plants and trees. This branch ranges over three floors, and has a great atmosphere. The look inside may be modern but the food is traditional, with an extensive range of pizza and pasta, and classic trattoria dishes such as pollo sorpresa and saltimbocca alla Romana. Seafood is delivered once, sometimes twice daily, and the seafood specials board is updated accordingly. Sardines, dressed crab, lobster tagliolini, grilled Dover sole, and king prawn and monkfish kebab are typical examples. The wine list covers an extensive selection of Italian and French wines, with just a couple from the New World, and a dozen served by the glass.

Prices: Main course from £9. House wine £11.20.
Last orders: Food: 23.00.
Closed: Rarely.
Food: Italian.
Other points: No-smoking area. Children welcome.
Directions: Situated in Leicester city centre just outside the busy shopping area. (Map 9, C3)

Nether Broughton

The Red House

23 Main Street, Nether Broughton, Melton Mowbray, Leicestershire LE14 3HB
Telephone: +44(0)1664 822429
bookings@the-redhouse.com
www.the-redhouse.com

This impressive, revamped early-Victorian house now functions as a modern and very individual pub-restaurant with rooms, and successfully combines a relaxed atmosphere with contemporary luxury. The bar has a traditional feel, where chalkboards offer the day's bar menu. The line-up takes in tuna and salmon fishcakes with creamed spinach, bangers and mash, and a steak and red onion sandwich. The restaurant has a more contemporary feel with its bar made of a pine wood frame filled with books. Alternatively, head for the adjoining dining room that's filled with light from patio doors that look on to the teak-decked courtyard. Here you can choose pan-roasted scallops with chorizo, roast suckling pig with Calvados jus, and iced white-Malteser parfait from a seasonally inspired menu. The global wine list is expansive and keenly priced. Eight en suite bedrooms are imaginatively designed and feature a DVD player and a host of goodies. Old Stables houses both the Garden Bar and Grill.

Rooms: 8. Twin/double room from £50 per person.
Prices: Restaurant main course from £9.95. Bar snacks from £5. House wine £12.
Last orders: Bar: 23.00 (Sunday 22.30). Food: lunch 15.00 (Sunday 17.00); dinner 22.00 (Sunday 18.00).
Closed: Rarely.
Food: Modern British.
Other points: No smoking in the restaurant. Children welcome. Dogs welcome in the bar. Car park. Outside garden bar and open kitchen. Meeting room. Marquee facility. Wheelchair access to the restaurant/bar.
Directions: Exit 25/M1. Take the A52, then the A606 to Melton Mowbray. The Red House is situated on the A606 between Nottingham and Melton Mowbray. (Map 9, C4)

Lincoln

The Farmers Arms

Market Rosen Road, Welton Hill, Lincoln,
Lincolnshire LN2 3RD
Telephone: +44(0)1673 885671
farmersarmsuk@yahoo.co.uk
www.farmers-arms.co.uk

For this imposing, 18th-century pub to have survived and thrived on the wind-blown and flat farmlands north of Lincoln is testament to the hard work and genuine hospitality of Andrew Bennett and Vicky Herring. Customers are drawn to this hamlet on the A46 for the pub's quirky interior, the impressive range of micro-brewery beers, freshly prepared food that favours produce from quality local suppliers, and the mind-boggling list of wines. The latter offers good tasting notes, 35 wines by the glass, and you can buy a case or two from Andrew's wine shop next door. Come for lunch and tuck into a baguette filled with Lincolnshire sausage and red-onion jam, or opt for the lamb casserole or bacon chops with mustard cream. Evening diners could start with scallops with lemon beurre blanc, then follow with Lincoln Red sirloin with sautéed mushrooms, and finish with the impressive cheeseboard – try the Lincolnshire Yellow Belly, made by a local farmer.

Prices: Set lunch £15. Set dinner £23. Restaurant main course from £10.95. Bar main course from £4.95. House wine £9.95.
Last orders: Bar: Lunch 15.00; dinner 21.00. Food: lunch 14.00; dinner 21.00.
Closed: Mondays and Sunday evening.
Food: Modern British.
Other points: Totally no smoking. Garden. Children welcome. Car park. Wheelchair access. Wine shop on the premises.
Directions: A1. Travel on the A46 to Lincoln for 10 minutes, heading towards Market Rasen. (Map 9, B4)

Lincoln

Hillcrest Hotel

15 Lindum Terrace, Lincoln, Lincolnshire LN2 5RT
Telephone: +44(0)1522 510182
reservations@hillcrest-hotel.com
www.hillcrest-hotel.com

It's easy to relax in the quiet grounds of this town house, formerly a rectory. Set in the middle of Lincoln, all the town's highlights are on the doorstep, including the cathedral and the arboretum. Host Jennifer Bennett makes you feel immediately at home and can provide information about local events, from race meetings to recitals. The bedrooms are spread over four floors and are all individually designed; the best is a spacious four-poster bedroom decked out in pretty lace and florals. In the public rooms, the décor is a mix of the bold and the traditional. The food is hearty homecooking using meats from the local butcher and local fresh produce. Popular choices include pork with an apple and marmalade gravy made with apples from the hotel garden, and duck with an orange and redcurrant sauce, and both are served with generous helpings of fresh vegetables. They barely leave room for a pudding, but it's hard to resist the locally made ice cream. A short list of mainly New World wines provides good drinking at reasonable prices.

Rooms: 14. Double room from £85, single from £65.
Prices: Set dinner £20. Main course from £13.75.
House wine £11.75.
Last orders: Food: lunch 14.00; dinner 20.30. No food Saturday lunch and all day Sunday..
Closed: 21 December to 6 January.
Food: Modern European.
Other points: No smoking in the restaurant. Children welcome. Dogs welcome overnight. Garden. Car park. Internet.
Directions: From Wragby Road/Lindum Hill (A15), take a very small road – Upper Lindum Street. Go to the bottom of the road, then turn left into Lindum Terrace. The hotel is 200m on the right. (Map 9, B4)

Lincoln

Jocasta's Restaurant

Moor Lane, Thorpe on the Hill, Lincolnshire LN6 9DA
Telephone: +44(0)1522 686314
enquiries@jocastas.co.uk
www.jocastas.co.uk

Its stunning lakeside location in The Whisby Water Park has put Jocasta's very much on the map. It's no surprise that this beautiful situation is popular with wedding parties, as well as for more intimate dining. The setting has a Hellenic ambience with its pillars, drapes and palms. Apart from a Caesar salad though, the food leans towards international with an emphasis on using the best local produce. The week's meat suppliers are chalked up on a blackboard. Head chef David Witlea has taken a very good menu and improved it even further, offering a broad range of dishes, from the rustically simple to the fantastically complex. On the carte menu, you will find beluga caviar or terrine of honey-roast ham, with mains of Ashbourne Farm beef, Lincolnshire sausages, monkfish wrapped in Parma ham or John Dory with olive-crushed potatoes. For unbeatable value, come for the set-lunch menu. An extensive wine list offers a distinctly European flavour, firmly centred around France, but with numerous New World entries.

Prices: Set lunch £11.50. Restaurant main course from £12.95. House wine £10.50.
Last orders: Food: lunch 14.00 (Sunday 15.00); dinner 21.00 (Friday and Saturday 22.30).
Closed: Sunday evening and all day Monday.
Food: International.
Other points: Totally no smoking. Garden. Car park. Licenced for civil weddings. Wheelchair access.
Directions: Follow the A46 from the A1 towards Lincoln. Follow the brown signs for Whisby Nature Park. Jocasta's is opposite the golf course. (Map 9, B4)

Lincoln

The Kitchen

Sleaford Road, Nocton Heath, Lincoln, Lincolnshire LN4 2AN
Telephone: +44(0)1522 811299
davidmat@tesco.com
www.thekitchenatnoctonheath.co.uk

Since taking over the business, chef/proprietor David Mathers has succeeded in rejuvenating this former RAF mess hall, turning it into a thoroughly modern British restaurant. The Kitchen is a prime stop-off for travellers and tourists, but is a service station like no other. Expect to see upmarket motors alongside the clutch of lorries in the car park, which is testament to its broad appeal. The menu focuses on local produce, most notably Lincolnshire sausages and Lincoln Red beef, as well as fresh vegetables, eggs and cheese. The main dishes are traditional and hearty and include chicken cobbler, liver and onions, prime steaks and warming vegetable casseroles. Sunday lunch is quite an event and is how The Kitchen's reputation for good food began. And it's not just the food that has been overhauled; the interiors have been gutted and rebuilt to create a bright and modern space. The two dining rooms have tiled floors, local-limestone walls and neutral colours. Service is eager and friendly, and worked from a long hot counter. With new chef Andrew Sloan on board, expect even more dishes to be added to the already excellent repertoire.

Prices: Set dinner from £7.25. Restaurant main course from £5.50. Breakfast from £3.
Last orders: Food: 22.00 (Friday 22.30, Saturday 23.00, Sunday 18.00)
Closed: Rarely.
Food: Modern British
Other points: No-smoking area. Garden. Children welcome. car park. Wheelchair access.
Directions: A15. Five miles south of Lincoln and seven miles north of Sleaford. (Map 9, B4)

Lincoln

The Lincoln Hotel

Eastgate, Lincoln, Lincolnshire LN2 1PN
Telephone: +44(0)1522 520348
sales@thelincolnhotel.com
www.thelincolnhotel.com

This 72-bedroom city-centre hotel has undergone something of a renaissance since it became independently owned three years ago. Its anonymous corporate look has been replaced, following a stylish makeover. Bedrooms are contemporary-chic with an emphasis on quality beds and bed linen and have all the creature comforts. The modern bar and lounge is a pleasant setting for an evening drink and a light snack or afternoon tea, while the smart restaurant offers a comprehensive table d'hôte, carte and wine list. Dishes are modern European with a distinct Italian slant. Start with cannellini bean and parsley soup or crab and prawn fritters with caviar salsa, followed by mains of wild mushroom risotto with slow-roasted garlic or something more traditional such as grilled prime Lincolnshire rump steak with thyme-roasted tomato and flat mushrooms. This is a great location for exploring Lincoln – in fact, part of the Roman remains of Eastgate are in the front car park and gardens, and many rooms have views of the cathedral.

Rooms: 72. Double from £89.
Prices: Brasserie main course from £7.25. Main course bar/snack from £4.75. House wine £11.95.
Last orders: Food: 21.30.
Closed: Rarely.
Food: Modern European.
Other points: No smoking in the restaurant. Garden. Children welcome. Car park. Licence for civil weddings. Conference facilities. Wheelchair access.
Directions: From the A46 follow the signs for Lincoln North. At the roundabout turn right onto Riseholme Road and continue to follow this road to the junction, turn right and the hotel is on the right. (Map 9, B4)

London

Adria Hotel

44 Glenthorne Road, Hammersmith, London W6 0LS
Telephone: +44(0)20 7602 6386
info@adria-hotel.co.uk
www.adria-hotel.co.uk

This family-run hotel in a large smart house has bags of character and has the edge over the more anonymous chain hotels in Hammersmith. It's conveniently located only a few minutes walk from Hammersmith tube, while drivers can park opposite in a multistorey car park (although the hotel does have some limited parking of its own). You are also just a short stroll from Hammersmith's main shopping street and near the concert venue of Hammersmith Apollo. This attractive house is big on kerb appeal: smart wrought-iron gates open into a tidy paved front courtyard and polished stone steps lead up to an entrance porch surrounded by coloured marble tiles with video-entry intercom. The interiors are just as neat and well looked after. Up-to-date bright, modern bedrooms, some with three beds are available, each have compact, modern shower rooms. Tea and coffee-making facilities and a TV are also provided in the room. You breakfast in the south-facing basement room, and this is where you can also relax at other times of the day on sofas to watch TV. Cold drinks are available from a vending machine in the hall.

Rooms: 16. Double room from £69, single from £49.
Closed: Rarely.
Food: Traditional British.
Other points: No-smoking area. Children welcome. Garden.
Directions: Nearest Tube Station: Hammersmith.
(Map 1, see inset)

London

Café in the Crypt

Crypt of St Martin-in-the-Fields, Duncannon Street,
London WC2N 4JJ
Telephone: +44(0)207 839 4342
www.smitf.org

Just a few steps away from Trafalgar Square and the West End, this café is a welcome escape from the crowds. The landmark church crypt, with its brick-vaulted ceilings, pillars, and gravestones on the floor makes for a dramatic and airy setting in which to tuck into the good-value wholesome food. It's relaxed atmosphere is ideal for an inexpensive meal pre- or post-theatre, or before catching a train from nearby Charing Cross station. The extensive self-service offers an appealing array of pick-and-mix salads, soup and daily-changing meat and fish dishes. Popular choices include avocado and tuna mayonnaise or papaya filled with salt beef, peach and buffalo mozzarella salads, and stuffed peppers. For something more substantial, look to mains of roast leg of lamb steak with a rosemary sauce and minted apricots with fresh vegetables or wild-mushroom pasta bake with a Stilton glaze. But you can also just relax with a hearty sandwich and pot of tea. Generous portions and the fact tables are spaced well apart are other plus points. The short, well-chosen wine list is clearly annotated and reasonably priced. Allow yourself extra time to explore the gallery in the vault or to book for one of the many classical concerts.

Prices: Main course from £5.95. House wine £11.50.
Last orders: Food: Monday-Wednesday 20.00 (Thursday-Saturday 23.00, Sunday 20.00).
Closed: Rarely.
Food: Traditional English.
Other points: No-smoking area. Children welcome.
Directions: Nearest Tube Stations: Charing Cross, Leicester Square, Embankment. (Map 2, C7)

London

Food for Thought

31 Neal Street, Covent Garden, London WC2H 9PR
Telephone: +44(0)20 7836 9072/0239

On a street better known for trendy clothes shops, this friendly restaurant continues to serve reassuringly wholesome vegetarian food on its daily-changing menu. The chefs cook in the ground-floor kitchen, where take-out meals are dispensed, while eat-in customers head to the snug white-washed basement. It's small and you'll probably have to share a table, but the food makes up for these inconveniences. Customers are happy to queue to partake in Vanessa Garrett's seasonal, homemade dishes made from fresh fruit and vegetables from Borough and New Covent Garden markets. A day's offering may include a warming country-vegetable soup with poppy-seed bread or a savoury scone flavoured with sage, tomato and red onion; deep-filled broccoli and red-pepper quiche; warming Jamaican stew of sweet potatoes, spinach and green pepper with black-eye beans with a coconut sauce; and aubergine and cauliflower Toscano. Strawberry and banana scrunch or apple, pear and plum crumble double as puddings or afternoon tea treats. The restaurant is unlicenced, but you can bring your own wine and there's no corkage charge.

Prices: Set lunch and dinner £9.90. Main course from £4.
Unlicenced, BYO's welcome, no corkage charged.
Last orders: Food: eat in 19.50 (Sunday 16.50); take-away 20.30 (Sunday 17.00).
Closed: Easter Sunday.
Food: Vegetarian.
Other points: Totally no smoking. Children welcome.
Directions: Nearest Tube Station: Covent Garden. Head north from the exit and the restaurant is approximately three minutes walk down Neal Street on the left. (Map 2, C7)

London

Fung Shing

15 Lisle Street, London WC2H 7BE
Telephone: +44(0)20 7437 1539
www.fungshing.co.uk

Rest assured, this restaurant may look like the new kid on the block, but the old timer remains among the best Chinese restaurants in the area. The Cantonese food is top of its class, and the extensive menu caters for all budgets and tastes. Starters range from the modestly priced vegetarian spring rolls to the more lavish and daring braised shark's fin and jellyfish served with shredded chicken. The same applies to the main courses, with the more unusual ingredients available at a price. But you can keep within a moderate budget by choosing sweet-and-sour prawns or chicken, or go some way to blowing it with the lobster with black-bean sauce or braised fresh carp with ginger and spring onion. Specials of the day add plenty of interest – try clay-pot duck with plum sauce or stir-fried eel with coriander. But you won't feel shortchanged if you opt for one of the mainstream dishes, which are thoughtfully prepared. They also put plenty of effort into the homemade puddings. Mango pudding is a dome of golden mousse with a lightly spiced cream, and is tropical and refreshing. The wine list covers most bases, and includes a fine wine selection.

Prices: Set menu £17. Main course from £8. House wine £14.50.
Last orders: Food: 23.00.
Closed: Rarely.
Food: Traditional Cantonese.
Other points: Smoking throughout. Children welcome. Two private rooms available.
Directions: Nearest Tube Station: Leicester Square. The restaurant is behind the Empire cinema. (Map 2, C4)

London

Hanoi Café

98 Kingsland Road, London E2 8DP
Telephone: +44(0)20 7729 5610
hanoicafe@hotmail.com

It looks basic and unassuming, but don't be fooled by its understated décor, as it serves exceptionally good, authentic Vietnamese food. The interiors may not be fancy, but nice touches, such as fresh flowers on each of the wooden tables and oriental pictures on the walls help create a pleasant vibe. Hai Nguyen has built this business into a friendly neighbourhood restaurant whose welcome extends to children. The menu is a comprehensive collection of Vietnamese favourites and some less well-known dishes. New and interesting recipes are added periodically. The noodles are much noted, especially the Vietnamese wonton noodle and chicken glass-noodle soups. Among the most well-known dishes are stir fries, such as beef with oyster sauce, cashew chicken and ginger and spring-onion chicken. The more adventurous might opt for the roll-your-own summer rolls of grilled pork belly, the crispy aromatic lamb, or the enticing choice of claypot dishes. Among the list of light bites, the spare ribs are excellent, as are the crisp-wrap prawns, fried crab claws and vegetable tempura. Towards the end of the evening, it gets quite buzzy as a livelier crowd makes the most of the late opening.

Prices: Set lunch £3.80 and dinner £10. Main course from £4.60. House wine £8.90.
Last orders: Food: 23.30 (Friday and Saturday 24.00).
Closed: Rarely.
Food: Vietnamese.
Other points: Children welcome.
Directions: 15 minutes walk towards Shoreditch from Liverpool Street Station or a short walk from Old Street station. (Map 1, see inset)

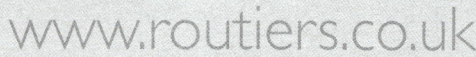

London

The Harlingford

61-63 Cartwright Gardens, London WC1H 9EL
Telephone: +44(0)20 7387 1551
book@harlingfordhotel.com
www.harlingfordhotel.com

It's boutiquey and contemporary, but the Harlingford does modern while retaining the mood of a smart Georgian townhouse. The elegant surroundings provide the perfect backdrop for the vibrant furnishings and bold colour schemes. The high standard of refurbishment by interiors specialist Nathalie O'Donohoe, coupled with its central location, makes the Harlingford outstanding value. The all-white foyer creates a sense of calm, while the smart lilac sitting room that shows off Victorian paintings in a setting of modern fabrics and textures, or the hotel's private garden, are the perfect place to flop after sightseeing. Like many well-priced central London hotels, the rooms are not huge, but are perfectly formed. The bedrooms are decorated in one of five themes, and several can accommodate three or four. The rooms are spread over five floors, so older or infirm guests should request ground-floor accommodation. The breakfast room is dominated by an Art Deco stained-glass mural, while modern vases form centrepieces on tables, and splashes of colour complement the clean lines of the light design.

Rooms: 43. Double room from £99, single from £79, family room from £110.
Closed: Never.
Other points: Smoking throughout. NCP car park nearby. Access to tennis courts and garden.
Directions: Few minutes walk from Kings Cross, Euston and St Pancras stations. Turn into Mabledon Place which turns into Cartwright Gardens. The hotel is at the bottom of the crescent. (Map 2, B7)

London

Justin James Hotel

43 Worple Road, Wimbledon, London SW19 4JZ
Telephone: +44(0)20 8947 4271
info@justinjameshotel.com
www.justinjameshotel.com

Conveniently located to make the most of Wimbledon's highlights, this attractive late-Victorian hotel was originally built in the 1890s as a doctor's surgery. It's close to town-centre shops and the railway station for trains into central London, and just a leisurely uphill stroll away from pretty Wimbledon Village and the many shopping and eating and drinking opportunites that has to offer. Tennis fans will be able to walk to the the All England Tennis Club which is just over a mile away, although, during the two-week tournament, buses run from the town centre to the Club. The house is smart, homely, friendly and efficiently run. All the well-maintained bedrooms are en suite and have cable TV, tea- and coffee-making facilities, as well as the extra perks of a hairdryer and IT connection. There is no lounge or bar, but there is a neat, small ground-floor breakfast room where you can enjoy a traditional English breakfast. This hotel makes a welcome change from the impersonal middle-market chains and compares favourably on price. Consequently, it has many returning guests, so you will need to book at least a month in advance.

Rooms: 20, 1 not en suite. Double room from £80, single from £45, family room from £95.
Closed: Rarely.
Food: Traditional British.
Other points: No-smoking area. Garden. Children welcome. Car park.
Directions: Follow the A219 to Wimbledon. The hotel is a few minutes walk from Wimbledon Station. (Map 1, see inset)

London

Langorf Hotel & Apartments

20 Frognal Lane, Hampstead, London NW3 6AG
Telephone: +44(0)20 7794 4483
langorf@aol.com
www.langorfhotel.com

Housed in a handsome red-brick Edwardian building in fashionable Hampstead, the Langorf is the perfect location for exploring the village as well as for getting into the West End. Finchley Road Tube Station is a five-minute walk, so the highlights of central London are just a 10-minute tube ride away. The hotel has 31 en suite bedrooms, all furnished to high standards, which range from singles to triples and studio, one and two-bedroomed apartments, which are available for a minimum of three nights and a maximum of three-month stays. The attractive and spacious bedrooms are well-equipped and come with TV, satellite, hairdryer and coffee tea and coffee-making facilities. Studios and apartments are equally spacious and have DVD players. Their small kitchens are well-equipped and you can pre-order a starter food pack for your stay. Continental breakfast is served in the restaurant, which looks out over a leafy walled garden, and light snacks are available throughout the day. This level of comfort and space at these prices would be hard to find elsewhere.

Rooms: 31 plus 5 apartments and 10 studios. Double/twin room from £80, single from £70. Studios from £100, apartments from £115 (1 bedroom) and £130 (2 bedrooms).
Closed: Never.
Food: Light meals.
Other points: No smoking in the restaurant. Children welcome.
Directions: Three miles north of Oxford Street. Three miles south of J1/M1. Off the A41 Finchley Road. (Map 1, see inset)

London

Mamma

2 Rocks Lane, Barnes, London SW13 0DB
Telephone: +44(0)20 8878 2824
caffemamma@hotmail.com
www.caffemamma.co.uk

This traditional and friendly restaurant is now happily ensconced at its new location in Barnes after a move from its former premises at Richmond. It has successfully recreated its friendly and welcoming Mediterranean atmosphere and the overall ambience is bright and fresh, with small wooden tables set for twos and fours and bright place settings adding a cheery note. The centrepiece is an eye-catching bar, which dispenses cocktails such as the Godfather, a potent mix of whisky and amaretto, and mid-priced Italian wines such as Frascati and Pinot Grigio leading the whites and the swiggable Montepulciano d'Abruzzo leading the reds. The menu is a comprehensive selection of Italian favourites that are all reasonably priced, starting with an extensive line-up of antipasti, from bread and marinated olives to sautéed prawns. Pastas, from carbonara to vongole, and seconds of popular meat and fish dishes form the backbone of the choice, and there are several pizza options. The desserts continue along classic lines with tiramisù and ice creams, and there's excellent coffee to finish.

Prices: Set lunch and dinner £15.95. Restaurant main course from £5.65. House wine £11.95.
Last orders: Food: 23.30.
Closed: Rarely.
Food: Italian.
Other points: Totally no smoking. Children welcome. Wheelchair access. Private room.
Directions: Opposite the London Wetland Centre and Barn Elms Sports Centre. (Map 1, see inset)

London

No 77 Wine Bar

77 Mill Lane, West Hampstead, London NW6 1NB
Telephone: +44(0)20 7435 7787

London

Le Truc Vert

42 North Audley Street, London W1K 6ZR
Telephone: +44(0)20 7491 9988
info@trucvert.co.uk

This long-standing, friendly neighbourhood wine bar hasn't changed much since it opened in the early 1980s, but it continues to update its wine collection and adapt its menu. Every two months, its wine list is spruced up with new bottles added to an already comprehensive list, and new recipes crop up just as often. Its ever-popular, proper beefburger that comes with melted smoked cheese and a homemade relish of braised onions and capsicums remains a favourite, and its daily fish special, such as roast salmon with sautéed potatoes and French beans, plus a small selection of meat dishes, such as chicken schnitzel, find favour, too. At lunch, there are some light options that include Spanish tapas and Mediterranean snacks such as houmous and flatbreads. Dine alfresco in summer, or cosy up inside around one of the small polished pine tables scattered throughout a maze of tiny quarry-tiled rooms. A good degree of intimacy is guaranteed, though do beware, the atmosphere can become quite smoky unless you happen on a section devoid of puffers. What keeps this place in the popularity stakes is simple but wholesome food and its wide choice of good-value wines.

Prices: Main course from £7.95. House wine £11.45.
Last orders: Food: lunch 15.00; dinner 23.30.
Closed: Rarely.
Food: Modern British and pan-Pacific.
Other points: No-smoking area. Children welcome. Dogs welcome in the bar. Alfresco seating.
Directions: Nearest Tube Station: West Hampstead. Ten minutes' drive from the foot of the M1. (Map 1, see inset)

If only all London neighbourhoods had a quality deli and restaurant like Le Truc Vert. It is a feast for the senses and a haven of civility, just a short walk from Oxford Street. Throughout the day, there is much to tempt in the shape of home-baked croissants, Danish pastries, cakes, quiches, and savoury vegetarian pasties. Early risers will be pleased to note that breakfast kicks off at 7.30am, including Saturdays. You can order from the menu, or make up your own selection from the shop's supplies, including stacks of pestos, salsas, sun-dried tomatoes, and delicacies such as artichoke cream, as well as a range of French honey, and top-quality cheeses. Free-range organic eggs and natural yogurts are also for sale, as are pâtés, an astonishing range of fruit juices, and an array of vegetables, which add a bright splash of colour. In the early evening, Le Truc undergoes a slick and seamless transformation into a smart restaurant. The wooden tables sport crisp white linen and the lighting is lowered for intimate dining. The menu delivers the likes of seafood and sausage gumbo to start, followed by chargrilled veal escalope with roast broccoli, roast fig, watercress and blue-cheese dressing, with raspberry crème brûlée to finish, and you can eat well here for less than £20 a head. A good range of French wines complete the picture.

Prices: House wine £8.
Last orders: Food: 21.00 (Sunday 16.00).
Closed: Public holidays.
Food: Modern European.
Other points: Totally no smoking. Children welcome.
Directions: Nearest Tube Station: Bond Street. Between Oxford Street and Grosvenor Square. (Map 2, C5)

Manchester

Dimitris Tapas Bar and Taverna

Campfield Arcade, Tonman Street, Deansgate,
Manchester M3 4FN
Telephone: +44 (0)161 839 3319
manchester@dimitris.co.uk
www.dimitris.co.uk

Good-value dining with dishes made for sharing and cheery surroundings has been a winning formula for owner Dimitris, who has since expanded the idea into a chain. The vibe is strongly Mediterranean, and at weekends, the atmosphere has a lively holiday feel. The restaurant, with its brightly painted walls is warm and inviting; wooden floors and check table-cloths make for an informal atmosphere. Outside, the large heated dining area is perfect for alfresco dining, plus there's a separate bar and cellar bar. The menu has something for everyone, from lunch mezzes to hearty tapas in the evening, which includes Greek taverna favourites such as houmous and taramasa-lata and Spanish specialities. In the mains section, Loukanika pork sausages or octopus slowly cooked with onions in red wine vie for attention with salt-and-pepper spare ribs and chorizo sausage and salsa, and so on through salads, vegetables, pasta and cous-cous. Popular dishes such as the kalamata platas and the mega mezzes are set menus for two or more people and are exceptional value. The wine list takes a popular global view and includes some Greek wines.

Prices: Set lunch from £10.95, set dinner from £16.35. House wine £11.35.
Last orders: Food: 23.30.
Closed: Rarely.
Food: Mediterranean.
Other points: Children welcome. Dogs welcome in the bar. Wheelchair access. Heated arcade.
Directions: At the end of Deansgate, near GMEX and Castlefield just off the main road in the arcade. (Map 12, F5)

Manchester

San Carlo Restaurant

40-42 King Street West, Manchester M3 2WY
Telephone: +44(0)161 834 6226
www.sancarlo.co.uk

This is one of those restaurants that pulls off the double whammy of buzzy atmosphere and great food. With outlets in Bristol, Leicester and Birmingham, the expanding San Carlo chain could easily fall into being formulaic, but each restaurant has its own individual menu and vibe. This smart city-centre Manchester branch majors in fish and puts its fine catch to good use in its specials and menu. The main menu focuses on popular Italian favourites using excellent ingredients, many from Italy, mixed with quality fish. The chef has a good eye, so everything from the antipasti to the mains comes pleasingly presented and in generous portions. Antipasti of carpaccio tascanoal, porcini and fresh mussels in either a Provençal or meunière sauce are a cut above the norm. Moving on to mains, you can choose from a wide selection of pasta dishes, which are also strong in the fish department. Tonna arrabbiata is nicely hot and the chilli marries well with the tuna, while spaghetti shellfish is a veritable extravaganza. There is much else besides fish to tempt, from mushroom risotto to the Italian connoisseur's breast of chicken with spicy Italian sausage, or the classic ham-wrapped veal saltimbocco.

Prices: Restaurant main course from £12. House wine £12.50.
Last orders: Food: 23.00.
Closed: Rarely.
Food: Italian.
Other points: No-smoking area. Children welcome.
Directions: Just off Deansgate. (Map 9, B2)

Ramsbottom

Ramson's

16-18 Market Place, Ramsbottom, Bury,
Greater Manchester BL0 9HT
Telephone: +44(0)1706 825070
chris@ramsons.org.uk
www.ramsons.org.uk

Chris Johnson brings Italian flair and flavour to his well-thought-out menu. Ramson's is cosy and compact with three small ground-floor rooms decorated in a smart, timeless style. Come for Italian breakfast, brunch or lunch when they offer tremendously good-value dishes. At dinner, the dishes step up a gear and you can look forward to wild-boar salami with rocket and parmesan shavings and steamed fillet of salmon with roast fennel and champagne sauce. Dishes are built around prime ingredients, impeccably sourced and simply but superbly cooked, as can be seen in a classic roast sirloin of beef with baby potatoes and red-wine sauce served for Sunday lunch. Seasonality is the key to the impressive repertoire, and flavours work well, whether it's a starter of wild-nettle soup with basil infusion, or a pudding of rhubarb crumble and Jersey cream. The wine list is concise but inspiring, and is accompanied by excellent tasting notes. A retail discount for those wanting to take some home is a novel touch. You are also invited to check the cellar for the many wines that are stocked but not on the list. The basement café is modelled on an Italian enoteca and has a good menu of light dishes.

Prices: 'Everyday' lunch £18 (3 courses). 'Everyday' dinner £20 (3 courses). Tasting menu £39.50 (8 courses). Main course from £9.50 to £27.50. House wine £13.50.
Last orders: Food: lunch 14.30 (Sunday 15.30); dinner 22.00.
Closed: All day Monday, Tuesday and Sunday evening.
Food: Italian influenced.
Other points: Totally no smoking.
Directions: From the M66 take exit 1 northbound. Turn right at the traffic lights and left at the next lights. Take a right at the third lights and Ramson's is on the right. (Map 9, A2)

Norfolk

The terroir garden
Cley next the Sea

A few minutes walk from the restaurant, this supplies a good proportion of the vegetables all year round. Along with herbs and all the usual suspects, it grows an interesting selection of salad leaves, yellow and purple French beans, Jerusalem artichokes, borlotti and haricot beans, Italian greens such as cavalo nero, cime di rapa and several varieties of courgette chicory and pumpkin.

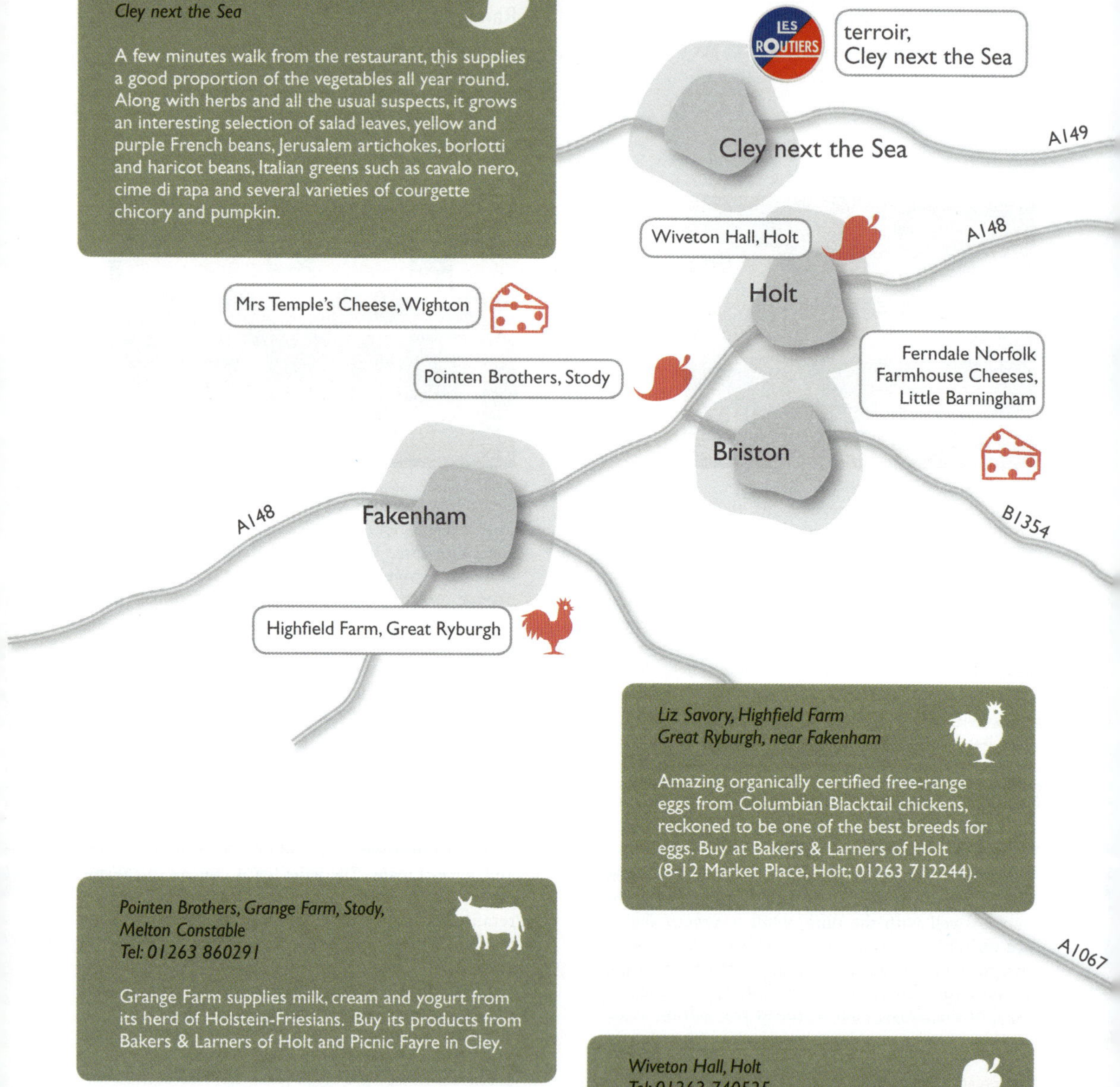

terroir,
Cley next the Sea

Cley next the Sea

A149

Wiveton Hall, Holt

A148

Holt

Mrs Temple's Cheese, Wighton

Ferndale Norfolk Farmhouse Cheeses, Little Barningham

Pointen Brothers, Stody

Briston

Fakenham

A148

B1354

Highfield Farm, Great Ryburgh

Liz Savory, Highfield Farm
Great Ryburgh, near Fakenham

Amazing organically certified free-range eggs from Columbian Blacktail chickens, reckoned to be one of the best breeds for eggs. Buy at Bakers & Larners of Holt (8-12 Market Place, Holt; 01263 712244).

A1067

Pointen Brothers, Grange Farm, Stody,
Melton Constable
Tel: 01263 860291

Grange Farm supplies milk, cream and yogurt from its herd of Holstein-Friesians. Buy its products from Bakers & Larners of Holt and Picnic Fayre in Cley.

Wiveton Hall, Holt
Tel: 01263 740525
Off the A149 between
Cley and Blakeney

The farm grows small quantities of superb strawberries and raspberries, plus blackcurrants and redcurrants. Its asparagus is also highly prized. Pick your own or pick up a punnet at the farm shop.

terroir, Cley next the Sea

Kalba Meadows and John Curtis describe their restaurant as one that serves vegetable-based dishes as opposed to being vegetarian, saying that they cook for passion rather than for political reasons. The pair are as keen about finding good ingredients as they are about cooking them, and use mainly seasonal produce from local, small-scale producers. The result is not only fabulous food at terroir, but an enviable, well-stocked address book of suppliers in the area, whose produce supplements the ingredients from their well-tended, organic kitchen garden. Here they share a few.

Cromer

A140

Groveland Fruit Farms, Roughton

Aylsham

Norwich

Visit the local Farmers' Market

Farmers' markets are held at Aylsham on the first Saturday of the month and Fakenham on the fourth Saturday of the month. Contact Hazel Stringer on 01263 734580 for information on Aylsham and Ann Chapel on 01328 850104 for information about the Fakenham market. The Norfolk farmers' market is held at the Norfolk Showground on the second Saturday and fourth Sunday monthly, 9am to 1pm.

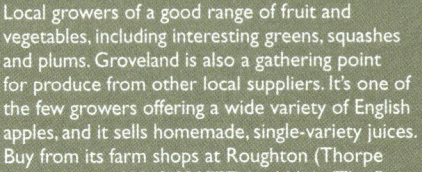

Groveland Fruit Farms
Roughton

Local growers of a good range of fruit and vegetables, including interesting greens, squashes and plums. Groveland is also a gathering point for produce from other local suppliers. It's one of the few growers offering a wide variety of English apples, and it sells homemade, single-variety juices. Buy from its farm shops at Roughton (Thorpe Market Road, 01263 833777), and Holt (The Barn, Feathers Yard, Market Place, 01263 711411).

Ferndale Norfolk Farmhouse Cheeses
Little Barningham, near Itteringham

Ellie Betts only recently set up her cheese business, but is already making a name for herself on local cheese boards. Dapple is an unpasteurised, hard cheese with a delicate, grassy flavour; Norfolk Tawny a creamy, young and lively cheese washed in Men of Norfolk Ale from the Iceni Brewery. Buy at the Picnic Fayre, The Old Forge, High Street, Cley next the Sea, 01263 740587.

Mrs Temple's Cheese
Copys Green Farm, Wighton

Catherine Temple makes several cheeses using milk from the award-winning Chalk Farm Herd; terroir takes her Binham Blue, a full-flavoured, semi-hard blue cheese that sits in style somewhere between a Cashel Blue and a Stilton, and Wighton, a soft fresh ricotta-type cheese that makes great torte or polpettoni. You can buy them at Picnic Fayre, Larners', or Fakenham or Aylsham farmers' markets.

Brancaster Staithe

The White Horse

Brancaster Staithe, King's Lynn, Norfolk PE31 8BY
Telephone: +44(0)1485 210262
reception@whitehorsebrancaster.co.uk
www.whitehorsebrancaster.co.uk

The evocative call of the curlew and memorable views across breezy salt marsh are among the magical treats that await you at this stylishly refurbished inn on the North Norfolk coast. Drinkers will find a welcoming atmosphere within the light and airy bar, kitted out with scrubbed pine. The conservatory dining room, with its adjoining summer sun deck and one of the finest views in Norfolk, is the place to linger over dinner. Reflecting the view, colours throughout are muted and natural, and Nick Parker's modern menus focus on fresh local fish and seafood. Start, perhaps, with salad of confit duck with balsamic dressing, move on to black bream with tomato dressing, or lamb rump with sweet onion and creamed leek tartlet. Sandwiches, salads and chargrilled rib-eye steak are available for lunch. Original bedrooms are in the grass-roofed extension facing the marsh. Those upstairs feature handsome modern furniture, simple clean lines, and soft colours.

Rooms: 15. Double room from £90, single supplement £20 per night.
Prices: Main course from £9.50. House wine £10.80.
Last orders: Bar: 23.00. Food: lunch 14.00; dinner 21.15.
Closed: Rarely.
Food: Modern British.
Other points: No smoking in the restaurant. Children welcome. Dogs welcome overnight. Garden. Car park. Wheelchair access.
Directions: Midway between Hunstanton and Wells-next-the-Sea on the A149 coast road. (Map 10, C6)

Cley next the Sea

terroir

High Street, Cley next the Sea, Norfolk NR25 7RN
Telephone: +44(0)1263 740336
terroir.restaurant@virgin.net
www.terroir.org.uk

It may be one of the smallest restaurants, but the effort put into sourcing ingredients puts this menu in the superleague. Kalba Meadows and John Curtis cook with mainly home-grown, local ingredients with a few specials from farther afield, such as Neal's Yard Dairy cheeses from London. Their menu reads like a Who's Who of Norfolk's top producers. Dinner starts at 7.30pm and is intended to be a relaxed affair. Set dinner menus run to three or four courses, with the first two courses of a similar size. Start with trofie with pesto Genovese, green and yellow beans and potatoes or a tart Tatin of caramelised beetroot, with poached Great Ryburgh organic egg. Next up could be a bouillabaisse of Rosewal and Spunta potatoes, rouille and wilted sprouting broccoli. Course three is cheese, then four fab desserts. The one super-deluxe suite has all the extras.

Rooms: One suite. Minimum two-night stay. Two nights for two people from £260 for dinner, bed and breakfast.
Prices: Set dinner £23.50 (four courses). Wines from £13.
Last orders: Dinner served Tuesday to Sunday 19.30 for 20.00. Booking essential.
Closed: Lunchtime, all day Monday, two weeks in September/October and December to February.
Food: Seasonal vegetable cooking – Modern British/Southern European.
Other points: Totally no smoking. Credit cards not accepted. Wheelchair access to the restaurant (no access to WC).
Directions: On the A149 coast road midway between Cromer and Wells-next-the-Sea. (Map 10, C7)

Norwich

The Wig & Pen

6 St. Martin's Palace Plain, Norwich, Norfolk NR3 1RN
Telephone: +44(0)1603 625891
info@thewigandpen.com
www.thewigandpen.com

Arrive early, bag a window seat, or a table on the sunny front terrace, and savour the fabulous cathedral views over lunch at this old beamed pub opposite the cathedral close. Log fires crackle in the original bar, where legal-related prints adorn the walls, and the welcoming atmosphere extends through to the modern dining extension. Expect to find lawyers and locals supping pints of ale at the bar, shoppers and tourists popping in for lunch and, in the evenings, a young, lively crowd, here for the beer and live sport on the TV. Real-ale enthusiasts are spoilt rotten. Brewery badges on the six hand-pumps may feature Oulton Ales Wet and Windy and Adnams Old Ale. All are kept in tip-top condition, great beer to wash down some hearty, traditional pub food – sandwiches, ham, egg and chips, or a home-cooked special such as steak and kidney pie or fresh battered fish.

Prices: Restaurant main course from £7.50. Bar main course from £3. House wine from £8.95.
Last orders: Bar: 23.00. Food: lunch 14.30; dinner 21.00.
Closed: Sunday evening. Christmas Day, New Year's Day.
Food: Traditional and Modern British.
Other points: No-smoking area. Children over 14 welcome. Garden. Wheelchair access (not WC).
Directions: Adjacent to Norwich Cathedral. 100 yards from Maid's Head Hotel in Tombland. Walking distance from the River Wensum. (Map 10, C7)

Swaffham

Strattons

4 Ash Close, Swaffham, Norfolk PE37 7NH
Telephone: +44(0)1760 723845
enquiries@strattonshotel.com
www.strattons-hotel.co.uk

This Queen Anne Palladian villa has been transformed into a luxurious hotel-restaurant. Strattons is just minutes from the marketplace in Swaffham, but manages to transport you away from the every day. Owners Les and Vanessa Scott have restored the villa to its former glory, but treated each guest room to an individual look, from a plush red bedroom to a grand blue-and-gilt Venetian room. And they pay as much attention to the food as they do to the furnishings. The couple pride themselves on using local, seasonal and, where possible organic, ingredients. The cooking style is modern British using the best local game, fish and meat. Starters include pan-fried Castle Acre chicken livers on garlic crôutes or Cromer crab with avocado and sesame-filo wafers. Mains are also a delectable bunch and include roasted Castle Acre lamb cannelloni or roasted scallops with asparagus and parsnip sauce. Puddings are just as plush – bread and butter pudding with cinnamon ice cream or blood-orange tart, or a well-chosen cheeseboard. The extensive range of fine wines is pitched at fair prices. Prepare to be pampered in all departments.

Rooms: 8. Double from £50, single from £85, family from £180. Prices per person.
Prices: Set dinner from £37.50. A set tapas menu is available to residents on Sunday for £14.50.
Last orders: Food: 21.00. (Dinner only, closed Sunday though tapas is available to residents).
Closed: Rarely.
Food: Modern European.
Other points: Totally no smoking. Garden. Children welcome. Dogs welcome overnight. Car park.
Directions: At the north end of the market place, tucked behind the shop fronts. (Map 10, C6)

Strattons, Swaffham

This luxurious hotel appeals to all the senses, and eating here is a real pleasure. The menu has a strong regional identity, and includes many organic products. Based in The Brecks, the hotel is well placed to source good ingredients grown in this rich and diverse area, which has long been associated with agriculture and food production. The fertile countryside is covered with swathes of wheat, barley, oil-seed rape and sugar beet. Game and other reared meats are also plentiful.

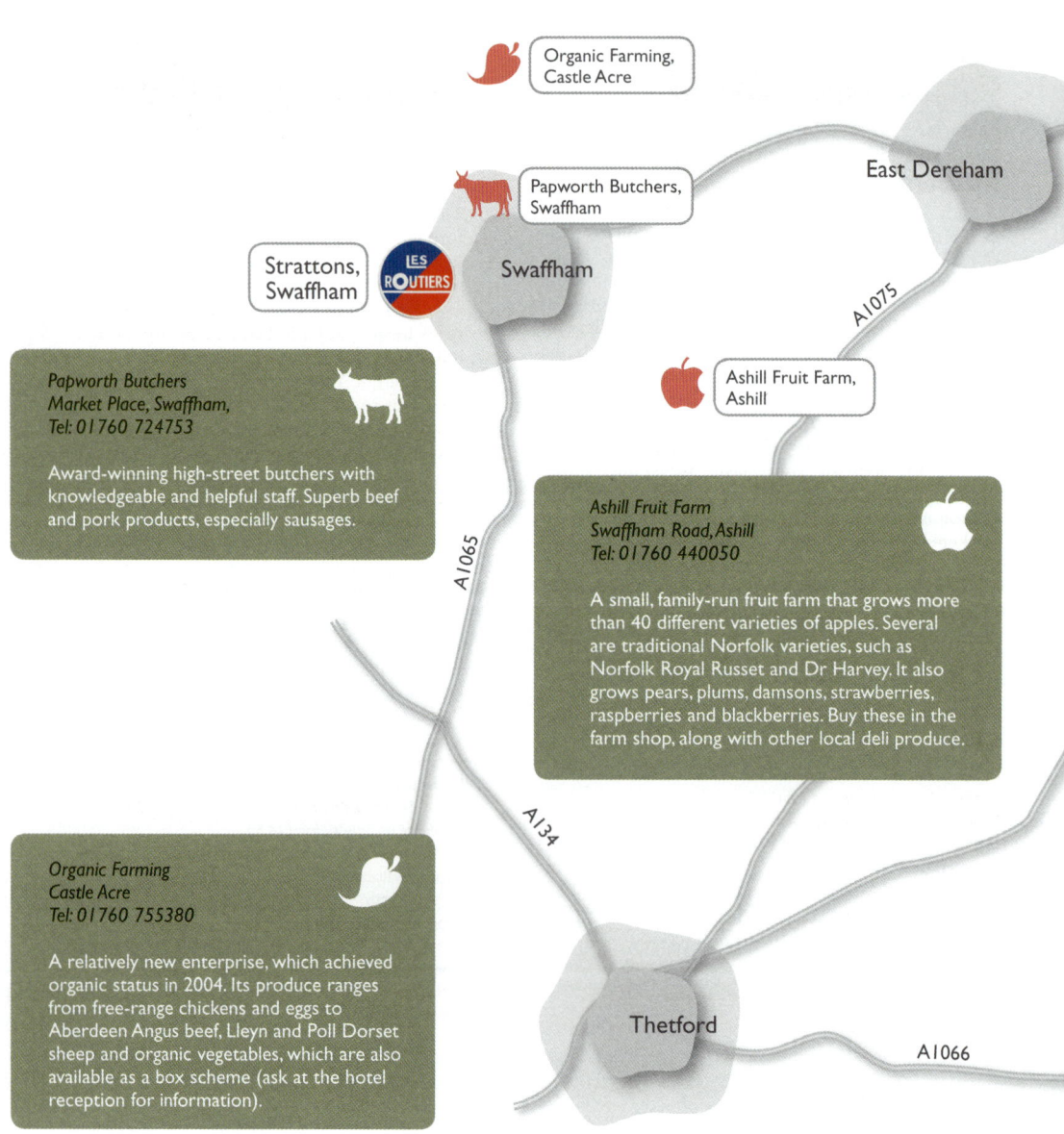

Organic Farming, Castle Acre

Papworth Butchers, Swaffham

Strattons, Swaffham

LES ROUTIERS

Swaffham

East Dereham

A1075

Ashill Fruit Farm, Ashill

Papworth Butchers
Market Place, Swaffham,
Tel: 01760 724753

Award-winning high-street butchers with knowledgeable and helpful staff. Superb beef and pork products, especially sausages.

A1065

Ashill Fruit Farm
Swaffham Road, Ashill
Tel: 01760 440050

A small, family-run fruit farm that grows more than 40 different varieties of apples. Several are traditional Norfolk varieties, such as Norfolk Royal Russet and Dr Harvey. It also grows pears, plums, damsons, strawberries, raspberries and blackberries. Buy these in the farm shop, along with other local deli produce.

A134

Organic Farming
Castle Acre
Tel: 01760 755380

A relatively new enterprise, which achieved organic status in 2004. Its produce ranges from free-range chickens and eggs to Aberdeen Angus beef, Lleyn and Poll Dorset sheep and organic vegetables, which are also available as a box scheme (ask at the hotel reception for information).

Thetford

A1066

A47

Norwich

Burrage & Associates
Rose Cottage, Hempnall Road,
Woodton, Bungay, Suffolk
Tel: 01508 483814

Venison and woodland consultants with a licence to
cull deer in the nearby forests. The produce is available at Swaffham Farmers' Market or by mail order.

A11

Burrage & Associates,
Bungay

A140

Visit the local Farmers' Market

The Swaffham farmers' market is held on the
first Wednesday of the month at Swaffham
War Memorial. Call 01760 722 922 for
more details.

Simon Cattermole,
New Buckenham

Simon Cattermole
King Street, New Buckenham
Tel: 01953 860264

A good source of organic meat and specialist products such as pancetta from local
pork. It can deliver for larger quantities.

Belllingham

Riverdale Hall Hotel

Bellingham, Northumberland NE48 2JT
Telephone: +44(0)1434 220254
iben@riverdalehall.demon.co.uk
www.riverdalehall.demon.co.uk

Run by the Cocker family for 27 years, this country-house hotel is also a popular local with a good reputation for food. The cricket field in the grounds explains much of the décor, as trophies and cricketing photos adorn many of the walls, clashing merrily with the rural-chic stencilling. The proximity and opportunity to fish from the River Tyne explains why the restaurant fish is so good and fresh. The kitchen draws on many top-notch local ingredients for its daily-changing menu. This may include succulent Northumbrian lamb, rich Kielder venison and tasty locally made pork and leek sausages. A selection of local cheeses is an alternative to more fancy puds such as white chocolate panna cotta. For a less formal experience, you can eat in the bar, where the menu consists of sandwiches, jacket potatoes and steaks, or there's an extremely good-value set menu that expands the choice to include slow-cooked lamb on root mash with wine gravy, Cajun-spiced sea bass or a simply cooked fillet steak with chips. Puddings are just as good, with garden-fresh rhubarb crumble or local Northumbrian cheeses completing the picture.

***

Rooms: 22. Double room from £88, single from £49.
Prices: Set lunch £10.95 (2 course), set dinner £16.90 (two courses). House wine £9.40.
Last orders: Food: lunch 14.30; dinner 21.30.
Closed: Never.
Food: Traditional English.
Other points: No-smoking area. Children welcome. Dogs welcome overnight. Garden. Car park. Indoor swimming pool. Licence for civil weddings.
Directions: From the A69 take the B6320 to Bellingham. After the bridge in Bellingham, turn left. The hotel is 150 yards along on the left. (Map 12, B5)

Langley-on-Tyne

Langley Castle Hotel

Langley-on-Tyne, Hexham, Northumberland NE47 5LU
Telephone: +44(0)1434 688888
manager@langleycastle.com
www.langleycastle.com

If you want a fairytale setting, then this handsome medieval fortified castle is just the place. Castellated towers and mullioned windows, coupled with a tasteful makeover, create a fantastically romantic setting. Bedrooms have been lavishly decorated and each comes with a canopied or four-poster bed, and a luxurious bathroom. You can't fail but be won over by the drama of it all, especially as the medieval feel has been captured in the huge public rooms and in the Josephine Restaurant. The exposed stone and arched doorways provide the ideal setting for Andrew Smith's classic Anglo-French cooking. The set-price table d'hôte menus use locally and regionally sourced ingredients, and are complemented by a separate menu offering dishes at a supplement. The choices are exquisite, with salmon and pimento ravioli or Northumbrian three-cheese tartlet to start, then a variety of local game with homemade herb dumplings and vegetables, and lemon sponge topped with vanilla ice cream and drizzled with a lemon and rosemary sauce to finish. The wine list offers a good choice of Old and New World wines.

***

Rooms: 18. Double rooms from £115, single from £99.50. Family room supplement £20.
Prices: Set lunch £18.50. Set dinner £29.50. Restaurant main course from £12.50. Bar main course from £7.50. House wine £12.75.
Last orders: Food: lunch 14.00; dinner 21.00.
Closed: Rarely.
Food: Modern British and French.
Other points: No-smoking area. Children welcome. Garden. Car park. Licence for civil weddings.
Directions: M6. Situated between Newcastle and Carlisle, two miles south on the A686 from Haydon Bridge. (Map 12, C5)

Longframlington

The Anglers Arms

Weldon Bridge, Longframlington, Morpeth,
Northumberland NE65 8AX
Telephone: +44(0)1665 570271
johnyoung@anglersarms.fsnet.co.uk
www.anglersarms.com

Set in an idyllic spot beside the old stone bridge over the River Coquet, this grand 18th-century coaching inn is perfectly located for fishing and wonderful walking in the Cheviot Hills. Bar and lounges are spacious and handsomely appointed, with wood panelling, log fires, antique ornaments and some fine old prints. Cosy up with a pint and a good old-fashioned bar meal, perhaps cod and chips and steak-and-ale pie, prepared from quality local ingredients. For quite a different dining experience, book into The Carriage restaurant, where fine foods are served in a refurbished Pullman train carriage. Starters takes in French onion soup and Thai-style fish cakes, while mains may include fillet of pork stuffed with apricot-and-prune and wrapped in prosciutto. Puddings are the hard-to-resist variety such as hot-chocolate fudge cake, while cheese lovers will appreciate the fine selection of Shropshire blues. Pleasant en suite bedrooms have lovely rural views.

Rooms: 5. Double room from £60, single from £40, family from £90.
Prices: Restaurant main course from £14.95. Bar main course from £7.95. Set menu on request. House wine £12.50.
Last orders: Bar: lunch 14.00 (Sunday 14.30); dinner 21.30 (Sunday 21.00). Food: lunch 14.30; dinner 21.30.
Closed: Rarely.
Food: Traditional British.
Other points: No smoking in the restaurant. Children welcome. Dogs welcome in overnight. Garden. Car park. Licence for civil weddings. Wheelchair access to the restaurant/pub.
Directions: From the A1 take the A697 to Wollder & Coldstream, carry on to Weldon Bridge and follow signposts. (Map 12, B5)

Otterburn

Otterburn Tower

Otterburn, Northumberland NE19 1NS
Telephone: +44(0)1830 520620
reservations@otterburntower.com
www.otterburntower.com

It used to protect armies in turbulent times, but now all the action at Otterburn Tower is on providing a relaxing stay for guests in its effortlessly luxurious surroundings. The historic Tower is set in extensive grounds and has an evocative atmosphere created by its thick walls, large fireplaces and oak panelling. The 17 comfortable bedrooms come with their quota of period features. The Library Room with log fire and four-poster bed is the most distinctive. This remote part of Northumberland is rich in fine food products, used superbly in the Tower's menu. The farm and Tower kitchen garden provide vegetables and herbs, while local ingredients, from River Rede wild trout to Doddington luxury ice creams, make for an exquisite dinner, whether that's the good-value Fireside or table d'hôte set menus or the carte. They excel with their homemade pâtés, marinated Longwitton lamb and tender beef dishes. There is much else besides to tempt, from local game, free-range chicken and pork to Northumbrian cheeses. Even the mineral water comes from the Tower's own well. After dinner, retire to the elegant bar or the drawing room.

Rooms: 17. Double from £65, single from £80 per person. Children £30 each.
Prices: Set dinner £25. Restaurant main course from £14.50. Bar snack from £6. House wine £12.50.
Last orders: Food: lunch 17.00; dinner 21.30.
Closed: Never.
Food: Modern British.
Other points: No smoking in the restaurant. Garden. Children welcome. Dogs welcome overnight. Car park. Licence for civil weddings. Wheelchair access.
Directions: Take the A1, Newcastle airport exit, then follow the A696 until you reach Otterburn. (Map 12, B5)

Seahouses

The Olde Ship Hotel

9 Main Street, Seahouses, Northumberland NE68 7RD
Telephone: +44(0)1665 720200
theoldeship@seahouses.co.uk
www.seahouses.co.uk

Run by the Glen family for more than 100 years, this character inn is decked out with nautical memorabilia. The bar offers superb views over the harbour and across to the Farne Islands and the famous Longstone Lighthouse, where Grace Darling heroically rowed out to save people from the ship wrecked Forfarshire. Food is local and hearty from a well-honed menu of around six starters, six mains and a range of puds and cheese. Homemade soups, a salmon medley, followed by Bosun's fish stew or roast leg of lamb, with saucy lemon pudding or clootie dumpling to finish make for a formidably satisfying meal. Well-priced wines, in the main European, add up to excellent value all round. The hotel's other trump card is its accommodation that comes in all shapes and sizes; from the single with a built-in bunk like a captain's cabin to the beautifully decorated four-poster room with original stone fireplace and period furnishings. A self-contained bungalow provides two comfortable bedrooms for those seeking ground-floor access. There are also apartments overlooking the harbour. Alnwick Castle and Howick Gardens are nearby, while inland, the Cheviot Hills roll up to the Scottish border.

Rooms: 18. Double/twin from £90, single from £45.
Prices: Set lunch £11. Set dinner £19. Restaurant main course from £8.75. Bar main course from £6.75. House wine £9.95.
Last orders: Bar: 23.00. Food: lunch 14.00; dinner 20.30.
Closed: Mid December to end of January.
Food: Traditional British.
Other points: No-smoking areas. Garden. Children over 10 welcome. Car park.
Directions: Take the B1340 off the A1 eight miles north of Alnwick. The Hotel is above the harbour. (Map 12, A6)

Warkworth

Warkworth House Hotel

16 Bridge Street, Warkworth,
Northumberland NE65 0XB
Telephone: +44(0)1665 711276
stay@warkworthhousehotel.co.uk
www.warkworthhousehotel.co.uk

A fine example of a provincial former coaching inn, the ambience of this smart hotel is traditional and relaxing. Warkworth village is enclosed by a loop of the River Coquet and has a magnificent castle as a centrepiece; the hotel is near the old stone bridge. Enjoy a morning coffee as you sink into a comfortable leather sofa in the lounge, or a pre-lunch or dinner drink in the bar, remembering on your way in to check out the magnificent stairway originally made for Brandenberg House in London. The individually designed bedrooms are spacious. Two on the ground floor are suited to those with mobility difficulties. Dinner is served in the dining room, overlooking the courtyard. The kitchen team takes great pride in preparing everything, from breads to puddings. Start with smoked salmon roulade with cream cheese and move onto duck breast with creamed apple tarte Tatin. You can also eat in the bar. As with its sister establishment, the Brackenbrigg Inn, wines are well chosen and there's a good selection by the glass.

Rooms: 15. Double/twin from £79, single from £49 and family rooms from £95.
Prices: Set lunch £11.95 (Sunday only). Set dinner £24.95. Restaurant main course from £8.50. Bar snack from £6.25. House wine £10.95.
Last orders: Bar: lunch 15.00; dinner 23.00. Food: lunch 14.00; dinner 21.00. Open all day for food during the summer.
Closed: Never.
Food: Modern British.
Other points: No-smoking area in restaurant. Children welcome. Dogs welcome in the bar. Car park. Wheelchair access all areas.
Directions: A1(M). From the A1(M) take the B6345 for Amble and Felton. Follow the signs for Warkworth Castle and the hotel is down the main street. (Map 12, B6)

Newark

The Curio Café

57/59 Castle Gate, Newark, Nottingham,
Nottinghamshire NG24 1BE
Telephone: +44(0)1636 700716
info@thecuriocafe.com
www.thecuriocafe.com

If you like cakes and culinary delights with your collectables, then this café/restaurant should be a number one destination. Behind its 16th-century façade, lie the two modern dining rooms of The Curio Café, while upstairs a warren of small rooms showcases an array of antiques, plus there's a shop and exhibitions. By day, the downstairs and adjoining patio is a bustling café serving delicious light meals, sandwiches, cakes and top-notch Williamson's teas and fair trade coffee. In the evening, chef/proprietor John Partridge cuts free to present his eclectic mix of seasonally inspired dishes that lean towards modern-European with touches of the pan-Asian, and he often prepares sushi. Every effort is made to use the best regional produce, from vegetables to game. Fresh asparagus with gorgonzola gratin or ravioli filled with sage and butternut squash are typical starters, while the main courses include an array of well-priced meat and vegetarian specials. The short wine list majors in good-value New World wines. Hearty eaters not tempted by the puddings, will find a savoury treat in the baked camembert. Gourmet wines and food evenings are in the pipeline.

Prices: Restaurant main course from £7.95. Bar/snack from £3.95.
House wine £9.75.
Last orders: Food: lunch 16.30 (Sunday 16.00); dinner 21.30.
Closed: Sunday to Wednesday evening.
Food: Modern European.
Other points: Totally no smoking. Children welcome.
Dogs welcome. Garden. Wheelchair access.
Directions: A1. Follow signs from the A1 to Newark Castle. The Curio Café is 200 yards from the entrance to the castle on Castle Gate. (Map 8, B8)

Nottingham

Saagar Tandoori Restaurant

473 Mansfield Road, Sherwood, Nottingham,
Nottinghamshire NG5 2DR
Telephone: +44(0)115 962 2014

In Urdu, 'saagar' means ocean, and its name reflects the far-reaching Indian influences on its menu. Its upmarket menu encompasses Punjabi, Balti and Kashmiri dishes, and much more besides, and without stinting on quality. Now in its 25th year under charismatic owner Mr Khizer, the food and atmosphere attract a discerning crowd. Dining, though, is a relaxed affair in elegant surroundings. Indecisive diners should plunder the five set menus, which are ensembles of well-matched dishes, while vegetarians get a fair look-in with two vegetable thali specials. The selection of individual dishes is immense, from the list of two dozen starters to the popular favourite mains of korma, bhona and Bangalore dishes to a mouth-tingling array of specials. There is something for all tastes, from the gentle green masala, Kashmiri and begum bahar dishes with yogurt, cream, nuts and herbs to the more fiery and challenging house specialities, such as chilli chicken tikka masala and dilkush dishes. Prices look dear at first, but mains include rice, poppadums and chutney. It's best to book, as the restaurant is one of the town's top foodie destinations, popular with the post-theatre crowd.

Prices: Restaurant main course from £10 (including rice, papadums and chutney). House wine from £12 a litre.
Last orders: Food: lunch 14.00; dinner 24.00.
Closed: Rarely.
Food: Traditional Indian.
Other points: Totally no smoking. Children over 5 welcome.
Private room.
Directions: Exit 26/M1. Follow the ring road to Sherwood and Saagar Tandoori is on Mansfield Road opposite the County Library. (Map 9, C3)

Tuxford

Mussel and Crab

Sibthorpe Hill, Tuxford, Newark,
Nottinghamshire NG22 0PJ
Telephone: +44(0)1777 870491
musselandcrab1@hotmail.com
www.musselandcrab.com

Pubs and restaurants in land-locked Nottinghamshire are not renowned for offering great seafood, but this busy, energetic country pub is clearly bucking the trend. They aim to provide the freshest fish, whether native or exotic, with much of it delivered daily from Brixham. Choose from starters of crab bisque or oysters with chilli relish. Main courses might be grilled sea bass and salmon with avocado, pineapple and mango salsa, or baked swordfish with pesto sauce. Meat eaters will not be disappointed with the huge mixed grill or game from local shoots. The stylishly refurbished interior offers various eating areas, a couple of bars with welcoming log fires, a mass of specials blackboards, and the complete wine list out on display. Then there are two distinct restaurant areas, one is sheer vibrant Mediterranean, with terracotta and ochre hues. Gents – note the live goldfish in the plastic cistern above the urinals in the 'buoys' room.

Prices: Main course from £11. House wine £10.50.
Last orders: Bar: lunch 14.30 (Sunday 14.45); dinner 22.00 (Sunday 21.30). Food: lunch 14.30 (Sunday 14.45); dinner 22.00 (Sunday 21.00).
Closed: Rarely.
Food: Modern British.
Other points: No smoking in the restaurant. Children welcome. Dogs welcome in the bar. Garden. Car park. Wheelchair access.
Directions: From JA57/A1 (Markham Moor), take the B1164 to Ollerton/Tuxford; the pub is 800 yards on the right. (Map 9, B4)

Witney

The Fleece

11 Church Green, Witney, Oxfordshire OX28 4AZ
Telephone: +44(0)1993 892270
fleece@peachpubs.com
www.peachpubs.com

The Witney outpost of the hugely successful Peach Pub Company is a stylish, 10-bedroomed inn overlooking the church green in this upmarket little town. Refurbishment is ongoing but the company's unique and stylish formula has been replicated here. The trademark leather sofas around low tables, individual mirrors and modern artwork on warm, earthy-coloured walls, a laid-back atmosphere, and a continental-style opening time of 8am for coffee and breakfast sandwiches have certainly proved a hit among Witney residents. Equally popular is the all-day sandwich, salad and deli-board menu, the latter offering starters or nibbles of charcuterie, cheese, fish and unusual antipasti. Modern main menu dishes range from smoked salmon fishcake with caper sauce and sea bream with lemon peas and fennel chips to lamb noisette with roasted vegetables and pesto, and stone-baked pizzas. En suite bedrooms have warm, vibrant colours, chic mirrors, fabrics and furnishings. There's a private dining room in the converted stables.

Rooms: 10 Double/twin from £75, single from £65 and family from £85.
Prices: Restaurant main course from £7.50. Bar main course from £1.35. House wine £10.50.
Last orders: Bar: 23.00.
Closed: Rarely
Food: Modern European.
Other points: Children welcome. Dogs welcome. Garden. Car park. Wheelchair access to the restaurant/pub and one bedroom.
Directions: Witney is just off the A40 Oxford to Cheltenham road. The Fleece is in the town centre. (Map 5, B3)

Witney

Greens Restaurant

Witney Lakes Resort, Downs Road, Witney, Oxfordshire OX29 0SY
Telephone: +44(0)1993 893012
resort@witney-lakes.co.uk
www.witney-lakes.co.uk

Greens adds up to more than a restaurant, as it combines an 18-hole golf course, a Scandinavian chalet-style private health club and conference centre. Dining at the restaurant is a pleasure as, besides the good food, it has a peaceful lakeside setting with views across fairways to the 18th hole. Light and airy with a central bar area and a splendid summer dining terrace – the perfect place to enjoy good-quality brasserie-style food. Sean Parker is passionate about local produce and sources all meats, free-range eggs and soft fruits from local farms as well as using quality small suppliers associated with the Oxfordshire Food Group. Nearly everything is freshly made on the premises, including the bread. The menu has an international flavour that leans towards the Mediterranean. Start with roast asparagus and Parma ham on bruschetta, tomato confit, red pepper and sweet soy dressing, and follow with Oxfordshire loin of pork saltimbocca with celeriac mash and sticky Madeira and sage jus. There's much to tempt on the puddings menu, too: bitter chocolate tart, chocolate ice cream and strawberry compôte or British farmhouse cheeses.

Prices: Restaurant main course from £9.50. Bar main course from £6. House wine £10.95.
Last orders: Food: lunch 15.00; dinner 22.00.
Closed: Saturday lunch, Sunday evening.
Food: Modern British.
Other points: Totally no smoking. Garden and terrace. Children welcome. Car park. Private dining. Golf course. Business centre.
Directions: Exit 9/M40. From Oxford take the second turning on the A4 towards Witney and turn right at the roundabout following the signs to Witney Lakes Resort. (Map 9, F3)

Ludlow

The Feathers Hotel

Bull Ring, Ludlow, Shropshire SY8 1AA
Telephone: +44(0)1584 875261
feathers.ludlow@btconnect.com
www.feathersatludlow.co.uk

This stunning 400-year-old black-and-white landmark has been described as 'that prodigy of timber-framed houses and the most handsome inn in the world' by the *New York Times*. It's certainly one of Ludlow's best-known and most photographed buildings. Admirers of its Jacobean architecture will find much to please inside. The lounge rooms are comfortable and relaxing, while the 40 bedrooms are stuffed with creature comforts. There are either standard or four-poster rooms plus there's a luxury four-poster suite. The kitchen concentrates on cooking with locally sourced ingredients. The short dinner menu can be two or three courses and head chef Stuart Leggett uses the quality produce imaginatively, but without fuss and gimmicks. Start with a vine-tomato soup or grilled mackerel fillet with olive mash and lemon beurre blanc, before moving on to seared organic salmon fillet, Clun Valley lamb or pan-fried duck breast. Vanilla panna cotta or a selection of British cheeses continue the quality theme. An astute selection of wines offers an international selection

Rooms: 40. Double room from £90, single from £70, luxury from £140.
Prices: Set lunch £16.50 and dinner £27.50. Main course from £12. House wine £12.
Last orders: Food: lunch 14.30; dinner 21.30 (Friday and Saturday 22.00).
Closed: Rarely.
Food: Modern British.
Other points: No smoking in the restaurant. Children welcome. Dogs welcome overnight. Car park. Licence for civil weddings. Wheelchair access.
Directions: From Hereford take the A49 towards Leominster and on to Ludlow. (Map 8, D5)

Exford

Exmoor White Horse Inn

Exford, Exmoor National Park, Somerset TA24 7PY
Telephone: +44(0)1643 831229
linda@exmoorwhitehorse.demon.co.uk
www.devon-hotels.co.uk

A lovely creeper-clad 16th-century building, this coaching inn stands opposite the River Exe in the heart of a small village in the Exmoor National Park. Close to Tarr Steps, the picture-postcard villages of Dunster, Selworthy and Porlock, and the dramatic north Somerset/Devon coast, the White Horse has long been a favoured pit-stop on the tourist trail. It is also popular among walkers as a base for exploring Exmoor. Downstairs in the comfortable, beamed and carpeted bar there are country-themed prints adorning the walls, open log fires, Exmoor ale on tap, and an extensive menu listing traditional pub meals. Look out for the inn's specialities, namely venison, pheasant and partridge from the surrounding moors, locally caught lobster and fresh fish, and the platter of Somerset cheeses – all from select local suppliers. There is also a Sunday lunch carvery. The inn offers en suite accommodation in cottagey bedrooms that reflect the character of the inn.

Rooms: 28. Double/twin room from £80, single from £40.
Prices: Set dinner £30 (3 courses). Main course from £12. Bar snack menu from £6. House wine £9.50.
Last orders: Bar: 23.00. Food: lunch 14.30; dinner 21.30.
Closed: Never.
Food: Traditional British.
Other points: No smoking in the restaurant and food bar. Children welcome. Dogs welcome overnight. Garden. Car park. Wheelchair access to the ground floor.
Directions: On the B3224 midway between Simonsbath and Wheddon Cross (A396) south of Minehead. (Map 4, C5)

Highbridge

Battleborough Grange Country Hotel

Bristol Road (A38), Brent Knoll, Highbridge, Somerset TA9 4HJ
Telephone: +44(0)1278 760208
info@battleboroughhotel.co.uk
www.battleboroughhotel.co.uk

An extension means there are more bedrooms at the popular Battleborough Grange Hotel. Set in beautiful countryside, the hotel has Brent Knoll, an Iron-Age fort on one side and clear views over the Somerset Levels to Glastonbury Tor on other. Add in its smart facilities and it's easy to see why it's in demand for holidays, conferences, wedding ceremonies, lunch and evening meals. The former farmhouse, with beautifully landscaped gardens, has been sympathetically updated over the years. There are 15 bedrooms in the main building, some with four-posters and spa baths, and with luxurious modern bathrooms. The lively bar and a spacious conservatory restaurant are the focal point in the evenings. The set and carte menus offer traditional dishes that focus on local ingredients. Start with avocado and crab salad or eggs Benedict, before moving on to duck with an orange and Grand Marnier sauce, or beef medallions with a mushroom, onion and red wine sauce. The global wine list is sensibly priced. Battleborough Grange is coveniently just one mile from the M5.

Rooms: 15. Double room from £77, single from £57.
Prices: Set menu £18.75. House wine from £10.25. Lunch from £5.95 Monday-Saturday. Sunday lunch is available.
Last orders: Lunch 14.00; dinner 21.00.
Closed: One week over Christmas.
Food: Modern British.
Other points: No smoking in the restaurant. Children welcome. Garden. Car park. Licence for civil weddings. Wheelchair access.
Directions: Exit 22/M5. Turn right at the roundabout towards Weston-super-Mare (A38). Highbridge is one mile on the left of the A38, after passing the garden centre which is on the right of the A38. (Map 4, C6)

South Cadbury

The Camelot

Chapel Road, South Cadbury, Yeovil, Somerset BA22 7EX
Telephone: +44(0)1963 440448
enquiries@thecamelot.co.uk
www.thecamelot.co.uk

Formerly known as the Red Lion, this pub has undergone a major refurbishment to re-emerge as the jazzier and more magnificent Camelot. Zizi Montgomery and her business partner Alexandra have created a fantastic setting in which to showcase their amazing, well-sourced and wide-ranging menu. The Montgomery family has long been involved in food and produce the much-acclaimed Montgomery Cheddar on its farm in North Cadbury, and supply game in season. The friendly bar with flagstones, wooden tables or the relaxing lounge with comfortable leather sofas are ideal places for wining and dining. Enjoy a pint of local ale – Butcombe Bitter is the house ale and there are often up to four other well-kept real ales available – with a ploughman's, or something more international, culinary and wine wise. A house speciality is zakuski – Russian-style tapas starters, such as spiced lentils and chorizo, mushrooms and crème fraîche, or seafood – while the bar and carte menus offer an extensive line-up of favourites from bangers and mash to lamb shank. A lovely beer garden extends the dining area options. There is a fine B&B across the road.

Prices: Set lunch £13. Set dinner £19. Restaurant main course from £7.50. Main course bar/snack from £4.50. House wine £11.
Last orders: Bar: lunch 14.30; dinner 22.00 (open all day Saturday and Sunday). Food: lunch 14.30; dinner 21.30.
Closed: Rarely.
Food: Modern British and Russian.
Other points: No-smoking area. Children welcome. Dogs welcome in the bar. Garden. Wheelchair access. Skittle alley.
Directions: A303. Half a mile off the A303, between Wincanton and Yeovil. (Map 4, C5)

Stoke-sub-Hamdon

The Priory House Restaurant

1 High Street, Stoke-sub-Hamdon, Somerset TA14 6PP
Telephone: +44(0)1935 822826
reservations@theprioryhouserestaurant.co.uk
www.theprioryhouserestaurant.co.uk

This dual-aspect restaurant has a lovely bright and airy feel, and is decorated in blues and creams. Diners can be assured of attentive service by proprietor Sonia Brooks, while husband Peter prepares the fine food. His beautifully executed menu focuses on English food with hints of the Mediterranean. Dishes are made using what's best in season from the local area. Peter's signature dish is available for all to try – as it's a complimentary amuse-bouche of lobster with chopped shallot, caviar and crème fraîche, delicately topped with a soft poached quail's egg. The menu changes frequently. In late-spring, try asparagus and white truffle mousse or seared hand-dived scallops with smoked bacon and baby capers. Main courses offer fillet of Somerset beef with confit shallots, seared foie gras or baked Brixham turbot fillet with spinach and pine nuts, mushroom duxelle and hollandaise sauce. Desserts of hot vanilla soufflé or panna cotta with strawberries in red-wine caramel are both fabulously indulgent. Alternatively, sample the cheeseboard, which features local varieties. This small restaurant also offers a remarkable wine list, with plenty by the glass and half bottle, or there's potent Somerset cider.

Prices: Restaurant main course from £15.50. House wine £15.
Last orders: Food: lunch 14.00 (Saturday only); dinner 21.00.
Closed: The first week in May, first two weeks of November and all day Sunday and Monday.
Food: Modern British and Mediterranean.
Other points: Totally no smoking. Children over 10 welcome. Garden. No car park. Wheelchair access.
Directions: Exit 25/M5. Half a mile off the A303 in the centre of Stoke-sub-Hamdon. (Map 5, A1)

Wedmore

Table 8

Church Street, Wedmore, Somerset BS28 4AB
Telephone: +44(0)1934 710232
table8restaurant@aol.com

It's hard to believe that this house was derelict just two years ago. Mike and Chrissie McKenzie have worked wonders to restore its traditional elements and introduce a Mediterranean feel to this now chic bistro and restaurant. The simple but stylish décor sets off the original features of this traditional Wedmore stone house. In keeping with the individual look, food on the bistro and à la carte menus is not run-of-the-mill either, but an interesting array of dishes using good seasonal, local ingredients. The bistro menu features modern European dishes with an Italian bent. Start with sun-dried tomato and basil soup and move on to a main of Mules (mussels with a kick), or orecchiette Genovese. Wedmore lamb, local fillet of beef and free-range chicken are used in the mouth-watering and inventive dinner mains, and there is always a good supply of fresh, dayboat-caught Cornish fish. If you don't have room for one of the gorgeous puds, opt for the luscious sorbets. Much thought has gone into the wine list, which focuses on single-estate wines from a top supplier.

Prices: Set lunch and dinner £18. Restaurant main course from £15. House wine £10.95.
Last orders: Food: lunch 14.00; dinner 21.30
Closed: Saturday lunch, Sunday evening and all day Monday.
Food: Modern European.
Other points: No-smoking area. Children welcome.
Directions: Exit 22/M5. Take the Weston Road and turn right at the Fox and Goose. Follow the road to the B3139 and turn left to Wedmore and Cheddar for approximately six miles. (Map 5, C1)

Wells

The Crown at Wells and Anton's Bistrot

Market Place, Wells, Somerset BA5 2RP
Telephone: +44(0)1749 673457
eat@crownatwells.co.uk
www.crownatwells.co.uk

Quaker William Penn, founder of Philadelphia, preached from an upper window of the historic Crown. Built in 1450 within sight of the Gothic cathedral and Bishop's Palace, this 15th-century inn retains many of its original features. For a traditional pub atmosphere head for the Penn Bar where popular bar meals are served, and, for a more contemporary dining experience head to Anton's, a wine-bar-cum-bistrot, where the dark-wood beams are offset by half pitch-pine walls with cartoons by local artist Anton (Antonia Yeoman). The dining is informal and stripped-pine tables, and candles by night, set a relaxed scene. Anton's menu offers dishes that don't stint on quality. Start with, say, wok-steamed mussels with a creamy saffron sauce before moving on to beef fillet with roasted garlic mash and roasted vegetables. At lunchtime and early evening Sunday to Thursday, there is a Les Routiers menu, which includes good-value mains of pan-fried salmon, rib-eye steaks or an asparagus and Swiss cheese tart. A 30-plus wine list offers 12 by the glass. Bedrooms are all en suite and are decorated in keeping with the traditional inn.

Rooms: 15. Double room from £85, single from £55. Family room from £100.
Prices: Set lunch from £11.95. House wine £11.50.
Last orders: Bar: lunch 15.00; dinner 23.00. Food: lunch 14.30; dinner 21.30 (Sunday 21.00).
Closed: Never.
Food: Mediterranean.
Other points: No smoking in the restaurant and bedrooms. Children welcome. Dogs welcome overnight. Courtyard. Car park. Wheelchair access to the restaurant.
Directions: Centre of Wells, in the Market Place. Follow signs for hotels and deliveries to take you to Market Place. (Map 4, C6)

The Camelot, South Cadbury

The Camelot opened in July 2004 after an extensive six-month refurbishment programme by the owners, the Montgomery family, who farm the surrounding countryside as well as making award-winning handmade cheese. The result has been the creation of a great local pub, in a fantastic location, with fabulous food. Head Chef Sasha Matkevich first became interested in cooking when inspired by his grandmother in his home in southern Russia. There is a good deal of Spanish/Italian/Mediterranean influence in his cooking. He is a great believer in cooking with local fresh produce, organic where possible.

Visit the local Farmers' Market

The Wincanton farmers' market, offering a range of fresh produce, is held at the Memorial Hall in the town centre on the first Friday of every month, from 9am to 1pm.

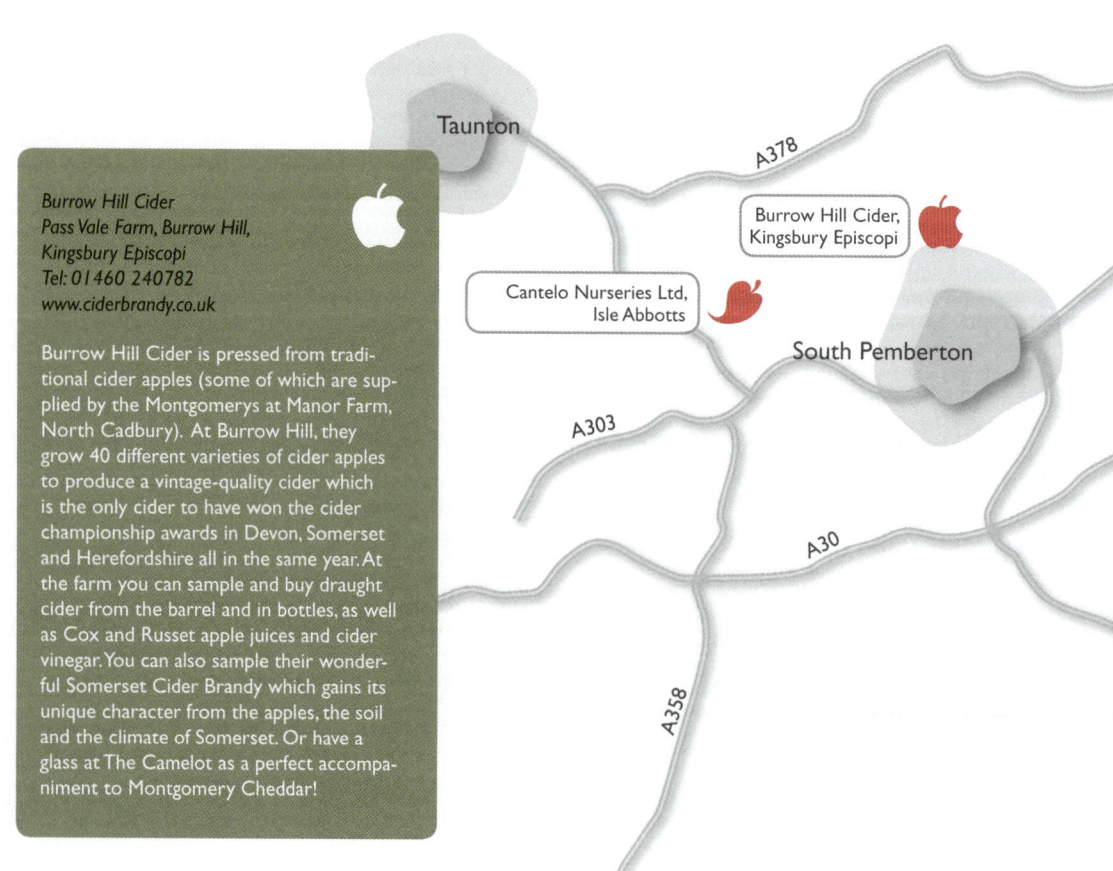

Burrow Hill Cider
Pass Vale Farm, Burrow Hill,
Kingsbury Episcopi
Tel: 01460 240782
www.ciderbrandy.co.uk

Burrow Hill Cider is pressed from traditional cider apples (some of which are supplied by the Montgomerys at Manor Farm, North Cadbury). At Burrow Hill, they grow 40 different varieties of cider apples to produce a vintage-quality cider which is the only cider to have won the cider championship awards in Devon, Somerset and Herefordshire all in the same year. At the farm you can sample and buy draught cider from the barrel and in bottles, as well as Cox and Russet apple juices and cider vinegar. You can also sample their wonderful Somerset Cider Brandy which gains its unique character from the apples, the soil and the climate of Somerset. Or have a glass at The Camelot as a perfect accompaniment to Montgomery Cheddar!

Taunton

A378

Burrow Hill Cider,
Kingsbury Episcopi

Cantelo Nurseries Ltd,
Isle Abbotts

South Pemberton

A303

A30

A358

Cantelo Nurseries Ltd
Bradon Farm, Isle Abbotts, Taunton
Tel: 01935 851041

Supplies organic vegetables which Sasha chooses for their superb flavour. He particularly rates their red peppers, which he fills with couscous and feta. He also serves their cucumbers in his duck salad with spring onions and plum sauce.

Gilcombe Farm Shop & Somerset Organics
Bruton
Tel: 01749 813825

Buy its wonderful organic smoked, dry-cured bacon. It's worth visiting to stock up on its wide range of organic products.

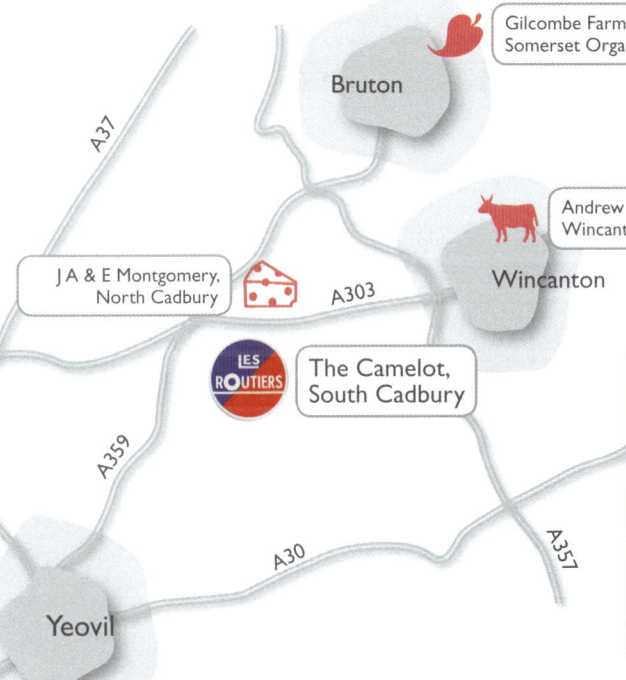

Gilcombe Farm Shop & Somerset Organics, Bruton

Bruton

A37

Andrew Barclay, Wincanton

Wincanton

J A & E Montgomery, North Cadbury

A303

LES ROUTIERS

The Camelot, South Cadbury

A359

A30

A357

Yeovil

Andrew Barclay
45 High Street, Wincanton
Tel: 01963 34880

This long-established family butcher supplies The Camelot's meat. This includes lamb from James Tabor (Home Farm, Sutton Montis) and succulent Gloucester Old Spot pork, from Guy Mason (Sutton Farm, Sutton Montis) which Sasha cooks with local cider-and-sage sauce and caramelised apples.

J A & E Montgomery
Manor Farm, North Cadbury
Tel: 01963 440243

The Montgomerys have been farming in North and South Cadbury since 1911, and Jamie is the third generation to continue to hand-make traditional unpasteurised cheeses. The Camelot is a showcase for the award-winning Montgomery Cheddar (Supreme Champion, British Cheese Awards, September 2004), Ogle Shield (Best English Cheese at the same), and Montgomery Butter. All are made from the milk of the Montgomerys' own herd of cows — Freisian milk for the cheddar and milk from the beauiful Jersey cows for the Ogle Shield, which is a creamier, softer cheese. You can try both of these on The Camelot cheese plate.

129

Leek

Number 64

64 St Edward Street, Leek, Staffordshire ST13 5DL
Telephone: +44(0)1538 381900

Tasteful refurbishment has transformed this Grade II-listed Georgian town house. It has plenty more to offer besides smart bedrooms and a fine restaurant, as it has a speciality food shop and patisserie. There's also a coffee lounge, serving an all-day menu, plus a vaulted basement wine bar that's good for a simple snack and a glass of wine, or the pretty restaurant. In the kitchen, they cook with regional ingredients to create modern British dishes. Lunch includes stroganoff of Aberdeenshire beef and escalope of Cornish cod with a puy lentil and bacon ragoût. For a truly gastronomic experience, try the evening signature menu of four courses. This starts with tian of hot-roasted West Coast salmon, then moves on to pavé of Devon lamb with a creamed leek, apple and baby-spinach suet pudding. The chocolate delight 64 is just as its name suggests, delightful. The wine list opens with two pages of global house wines; prices, even at the finer end, are reasonable. There are three well-appointed bedrooms.

Rooms: 3. From £65 per night (continental breakfast included, cooked breakfast £5 supplement).
Prices: Sunday lunch from £15 (two courses). Main course lunch from £7.95. Main course dinner from £12. House wine £12.
Last orders: Food: snacks 17.00; lunch 14.00 (15.00 on Sunday); dinner 21.00 (22.00 on Saturday).
Closed: Sunday evening.
Food: Modern British.
Other points: No-smoking area. Garden. Licence for civil weddings.
Directions: In the centre of Leek. (Map 9, B2)

Stafford

The Holly Bush

Salt, Stafford, Staffordshire ST18 0BX
Telephone: +44(0)1889 508234
geoff@hollybushinn.co.uk
www.hollybushinn.co.uk

The origins of this pretty thatched 14th-century pub are thought to reach back to 1190 – it is reputedly Staffordshire's oldest licenced premises. It maintains its historic charm throughout the cosy interior, with carved heavy beams, a planked ceiling, exposed brick walls, old oak furnishings, open fires and intimate alcoves characterising the main bar. Landlord Geoff Holland is passionate about using fresh local produce, and sources meat from W M Perry, an Eccleshall butcher with his own abbatoir, and game from local shoots. Among the good-value dishes on offer you will find homemade soups or grilled black pudding on spinach with poached egg for starters, followed by grouse casserole, slow-cooked lamb-and-barley stew and steak-and-kidney pudding. Alternatives include monkfish with fennel, shallots and morels, and prime steaks, including a 20oz T-bone. Expect good lunchtime sandwiches and daily seafood specials. Round off with a traditional pudding or a plate of Staffordshire cheeses.

Prices: Main course from £6.95. House wine £7.25.
Last orders: Bar: lunch 14.30; dinner 23.00. Food: lunch 14.00 (all day Friday, Saturday and Sunday); dinner 21.30.
Closed: Rarely.
Food: Modern and traditional British.
Other points: No-smoking area. Children welcome. Garden. Car park. Wheelchair access.
Directions: J14/M6. Four miles along the A51 Stone to Lichfield road, or half a mile from the A518 Stafford to Uttoxeter road. (Map 9, C2)

Bungay

Earsham Street Café

11-13 Earsham Street, Bungay, Suffolk NR35 1AE
Telephone: +44(0)1986 893103
earshamst@aol.co.uk

Despite its name, Rebecca Mackenzie and Stephen David's stylish café has evolved into a restaurant. Moving their deli to new premises has freed up more space. The three-storey restaurant's unfussy, rustic-chic makeover is in keeping with the age of the building, a 17th-century terrace. At lunchtime, an extensive menu offers inspired Mediterranean-style dishes such as fricasée of monkfish and shellfish, saffron, fennel and linguine to the more local, venison sausage with olive mash, honey-roast parsnips and onion gravy. Mornings and afternoons bring pots of tea, cakes and snacks. The restaurant comes into play on the last Friday and Saturday of each month, offering a pleasing set menu in the evening. Start with a crayfish cocktail with caviar, crème fraîche and chargrilled bread or chicken-liver parfait with brioche toast and onion chutney, then move on to mains of tortellini with ricotta and walnuts, sautéed oyster mushrooms and sprouting broccoli or magret of duck with pan-fried foie gras. Puds are a treat, from the warm chocolate brownie with clotted cream to pear and frangipane tart with vanilla ice cream. The expanded wine list offers a good-value selection, and 10 by the half bottle.

Prices: Restaurant main course from £7.95. Snack from £3. House wine £11.50.
Last orders: Food: lunch 14.00; dinner 21.00.
Closed: Sunday and evenings except for the last Friday and Saturday of every month.
Food: Modern British and Mediterranean.
Other points: Totally no smoking. Children welcome. Garden. Wheelchair access.
Directions: In the centre of Bungay. (Map 10, D7)

Southwold

The Crown

High Street, Southwold, Suffolk IP18 6DP
Telephone: +44(0)1502 722275
crown.hotel@adnams.co.uk

Celebrated brewer and wine merchant, Adnams, can take the credit for the stylish restoration of Southwold's central Georgian inn. From the outside the Crown looks stately, all white paintwork, with a flag flying and a wrought-iron sign hanging over the pavement. Inside, the town's martime past is echoed in a magnificent ship's binnacle, marine paintings and glazed screen in the Back Bar, while at the front, the Parlour is a buzzing mix of contemporary wine bar, brasserie and English village pub, and the centre of local life. Here you will find prime-condition Adnams beers, excellent wines (20 by the glass), and daily menus offering, perhaps, crab spring roll with Mersea oyster and seared scallop, as a precursor to crisp bass with pickled cucumber and sauce vierge. However, seared livers with celeriac remoulade and braised lamb shank with pease pudding should assuage alternative appetites. The restaurant menu, two or three courses, adds a further dimension, while imaginatively selected wines and beautifully refurbished and maintained en suite bedrooms simply underline the thread of quality that runs throughout.

Rooms: 14, 1 with private bathroom. Double/twin from £116.
Prices: Set lunch £21.50 and £18.50 (2 courses) and dinner £29 and £24 (2 courses). House wine £13.75.
Last orders: Bar: 23.00. Bar food: lunch 14.30; dinner 21.30. Restaurant food: lunch 14.30; dinner 21.00.
Closed: Never.
Food: Modern British.
Other points: Totally no smoking. Children welcome. Dogs welcome in the back bar. Car park. Wheelchair access to the restaurant/pub.
Directions: Take the A1095 off the A12, 14 miles south of Lowestoft, for Southwold. (Map 10, D8)

Thornham Magna

Thornham Hall & Restaurant

Thornham Magna, Eye, Suffolk IP23 8HA
Telephone: +44(0)1379 783314/788136
hallrestaurant@aol.com
www.thornhamhallandrestaurant.com

It's been the family home for the Henniker-Majors since the 1750s, but Lady Lesley Henniker-Major is happy to share what she modestly calls her 'restaurant with rooms'. The grand old house was destroyed by fire in the 1940s, leaving only the clock tower, and a stylish new barn-style replacement building now stands in the amble acres of fields and woods. The spacious restaurant is housed in the Old Coach House, which has an extensive courtyard area for alfresco dining. Chef David Pickles' lunch and dinner menus focus on traditional British favourites using local ingredients, many from the estate. Set and carte menus offer simple homemade dishes. Start with soups and salads then tuck into braised Thornham partridge (from the estate) on sweet-potato purée with a game sauce and lamb leg steak on mash with a mint and raspberry gravy. Old-fashioned desserts, such as bread and butter pud and crumbles, hit the sweet spot. The small, well-priced wine list has much to offer. The three rooms to rent in the main house are roomy and excellent value.

Rooms: 3. Double room from £85, single from £55. Prices include breakfast.
Prices: Set lunch £15. Restaurant main course from £10. House wine £13.
Last orders: Food: lunch 14.00: dinner 21.30.
Closed: Rarely.
Food: Traditional and modern British.
Other points: Totally no smoking in the bar. Children welcome. Dogs welcome overnight. Garden. Car park. Licence for civil weddings.
Directions: Halfway between Ipswich and Norwich. From the A140 turn left at Stoke Ash White Horse Pub. Turn right at Thornham Magna, past the church and turn in at Hall Drive. (Map 10, D7)

Alfold Crossways

The Alfold Barn

Horsham Road, Alfold Crossways, Cranleigh,
Surrey GU6 8JE
Telephone: +44(0)1403 752288
maguirescott@hotmail.com

A handsomely converted 16th-century barn with vast beamed ceilings, this striking pub is split into two areas separated by an adjoining bar, the latter the domain of local drinkers. A further spacious bar has deep leather sofas and armchairs, old church pews, flagstone floors, and cream-painted walls adorned with quotes from Shakespeare, while the spacious dining area is decorated with old gardening tools. Daily-changing menus are extensive, and do come with an appetite, as portions are generous. A basket of warm bread rolls could precede a starter of garlic and chilli mushrooms, followed by an enormous whole sea bass grilled in herb butter and accompanied by a dish of fresh vegetables. Alternatives may include carrot, potato and coriander soup or fillet steak with béarnaise sauce. If you've room, try a pudding, perhaps Eton Mess. Expect few frills, just good homecooked food using quality ingredients.

Prices: Restaurant main course from £8. Snacks from £4.95.
House wine £10.95. Pensioners special Tuesday-Friday morning
£3.95 for main course plus coffee/tea.
Last orders: Food: lunch 14.00; dinner: 21.00 (Friday and Saturday
21.30) No food all day Monday or Sunday evening.
Closed: Sunday evening and all day Monday.
Food: Modern British – but will make almost anything
on request!
Other points: No smoking in the restaurant. Garden with play
area and animal corner. Children welcome. Car park.
Directions: Exit11/M23 and Exit10/M25. Mid way between
Guilford and Horsham on the A281. Three miles from Cranleigh
at the Alfold Crossways. (Map 5, D4)

Chiddingfold

The Swan Inn

Petworth Road, Chiddingfold, Guilford, Surrey GU8 4TY
Telephone: +44(0)1428 682073
the-swan-inn@btconnect.com
www.theswaninn.biz

A hip hotel meets gastropub concept has breathed new life into this expertly reincarnated 14th-century inn, providing all the charm of the country with modern, chic Manhattan-style rooms and suites, all of which are superbly appointed. A drink in the welcoming bar is a pleasant precursor to a meal in the rustic-meets-contemporary open-plan bar area or the more formal restaurant. Chef Darren Tidd, formerly of Cliveden Hotel, offers classic European dishes in the bar – calves' liver and bacon, moules, fishcakes, fresh sardines or a delectable duck confit. The carte may list poached haddock on a fricasée of broad beans, tomato, pancetta and mash, or roasted partridge with fondant potato and glazed figs. Desserts include homemade ice creams, as well as classics such as crèpes and brulée. The comprehensive wine list includes 15 house choices by the glass or bottle. In summer, there's a lovely terraced area to make the most of the attractive garden.

Rooms: 10. Double room from £90, single from £70,
family from £120.
Prices: Restaurant main course from £14.95. Bar main course
from £9.95. House wine £9.95.
Last orders: Bar: lunch 15.00; dinner 23.00. Food: lunch 14.30;
dinner 22.00 (all day at the weekend).
Closed: Accommodation closed 24 and 25 December.
Food: Traditional and modern British and European.
Other points: No-smoking area. Children welcome. Dogs
welcome in the bar. Garden. Car park.
Directions: A3. From the south take the Elstead, Milford and
Petworth Jand from London take the Guilford Jfor Milford and
Petworth. (Map 5, C4)

Cobham

La Capanna

48 High Street, Cobham, Surrey KT11 3EF
Telephone: +44(0)1932 862121
reservations@lacapanna.co.uk
www.lacapanna.co.uk

This traditional Italian restaurant is set in an unusual building: behind its 17th-century cottage façade is a rebuilt 16th-century farmhouse. Take time out to enjoy an apéritif in the comfortable bar while you choose from the menu and before dining in the main restaurant with its abundance of beams and brickwork. In summer, you can dine in the bright and airy conservatory, which leads through onto a Italian patio garden. At lunchtimes and weekday evenings, the table d'hôte menu offers good value and an excellent choice of dishes, with Italian favourites and more global starters. The carte menu majors on the house specials, including an antipasto selection or individual choices such as asparagus wrapped in Parma ham grilled with white wine. Mains include hearty dishes: venison with red wine and a girolle risotto, or halibut wrapped with pancetta on lemon-roasted fennel, caperberries and black butter, as well as a selection of pasta dishes. Italian puddings are chosen from the trolley. La Capanna looks to its homeland for top wines and offers the best of Tuscany and Umbria, Veneto and Piedmont. A three-course Sunday lunch is another popular option.

Prices: Set lunch and dinner £19.95. Restaurant menu £29.95. House wine £14.
Last orders: Food: lunch 14.30; dinner: 23.00.
Closed: 27-28 December and 1 January.
Food: Italian.
Other points: No-smoking area. Children welcome. Dogs welcome in the bar. Garden. Car park. Al fresco dining in the summer.
Directions: From London exit the M25 onto the A3. Leave the A3 at the next exit and follow the signs to Cobham. Take the A245 to the far side of Cobham. (Map 6, C4)

Esher

The Albert Arms

82 High Street, Esher, Surrey KT10 9QS
Telephone: +44(0)1372 465290
enquiries@albertarms.com
www.albertarms.com

Money has been lavished on this impressive, white-painted pub on the corner of Park Street and Esher's busy High Street. Swing open the doors and you are immediately hit by style, be it the sleek mahogany bar, the polished oak flooring, or the large plasma TV screen in the lively bar area. A mind-boggling range of drinks takes in 36 wines by the glass, six cask ales and a raft of spirits. If you're here to eat, you'll find the dining-room décor and furnishings equally impressive. Vast menus offer an eclectic choice, from traditional favourites such as rack of lamb and Dover sole, to veal Milanese, fish stew, and fillet steak Rossini. Good-value 'executive' lunch and set Sunday lunch menus. Style and flair extends to the five luxury bedrooms. Expect air conditioning, tasteful furnishings, mini hi-fi systems, 30-channel TV, internet access, and magnificent en suite 'wet-rooms'. Live jazz at weekends and wine schools add to the appeal.

Rooms: 6. Double/twin from £100.
Prices: Set lunch £13. Restaurant main course from £10.50. Bar main course from £6. House wine £11.50.
Last orders: Bar: 23.00. Food: lunch 14.45; dinner: 21.45. (No food Sunday evening).
Closed: 25 26 December, 1 January.
Food: Modern British with Italian influence.
Other points: Smoking throughout. Children welcome.
Directions: A3, at the junction of the A244. Follow the signs to Esher, and as you come into the town, the Albert Arms is in the middle of the High Street. (Map 6, C5)

Farnham

The Pride of the Valley Hotel

Tilford Road, Churt, Farnham, Surrey GU10 2LH
Telephone: +44(0)1428 605799
email@theprideofthevalley.co.uk
www.theprideofthevalley.com

This smart inn, dating back to 1868, is one of those places you always hope you'll come across as you wind your way down country lanes. A lovely country garden, cosy interiors and a good choice of food are just a few of its draws. Bedrooms are wonderfully spacious yet cosy, with all en suite rooms having different themes, from Moroccan to Far Eastern. The dining options are also extensive, with a wide choice of dishes, from steak and kidney pie, Thai green curry and paella to light bites and fish specials. You can eat in the bar, where comfy sofas, scrubbed pine tables and real fires create a warm, friendly ambience, or in the grand, baronial-style, oak-panelled restaurant. Candlelit at night, this is a very special place. There are also stunning walks from the inn – an excellent prelude to a delicious Sunday lunch and a pint of Hog's Back ale.

Rooms: 16. Double/twin from £115, single from £95, family from £125.
Prices: Restaurant main course from £12.95.
Bar meal from £4.95. House wine £12.95.
Last orders: Bar: 23.00. Food: lunch 14.30; dinner 21.00 (Friday to Sunday 21.30).
Closed: Never.
Food: Traditional British and modern European.
Other points: No-smoking area. Garden. Children welcome. Car park.
Directions: Exit 10/M25. Four miles from Farnham on the outskirts of Churt village; two miles from the A3. (Map 5, C4)

Hampton Wick

Chase Lodge Hotel

10 Park Road, Hampton Wick, Kingston-upon-Thames, Surrey KT1 4AS
Telephone: +44(0)20 89431862
www.chaselodgehotel.com

This cosy and intimate family-run hotel is wonderfully positioned to make the most of the tranquillity of Bushey or Richmond Park, the historical palace of Hampton Court and the extensive shopping opportunities at Kingston. It's also only a short train journey into the centre of London. You will be greeted with a warm welcome by Denise Dove before being shown to your tastefully decorated en suite bedroom, which has all the creature comforts, including internet access. Downstairs there is a charming sitting room and a patio where you can enjoy a pre-dinner drink. Dinner in the hotel's Wickers restaurant takes in traditional favourites and modern classics. Start with pan-fried camembert with a raspberry coulis or tomato, avocado and mozzarella salad then follow with braised lamb shank or salmon and spinach in a tarragon and white wine sauce. There are plans to open for lunch soon, and the restaurant is also a good place for private parties and functions.

Rooms: 12. Double/twin £98.
Prices: Restaurant main course from £9.50. House wine £9.99.
Last orders: Bar: 23.00. Food: 21.00
Closed: Never.
Food: Modern British.
Other points: No smoking in the restaurant. Children welcome. Courtyard.
Directions: A3 Kingston. Go over Kingston Bridge towards Hampton Wick. (Map 6, C5)

Lingfield

The Hare & Hounds

Common Road, Lingfield, Surrey RH7 6BZ
Telephone: +44(0)1342 832351
hare.hounds@tiscali.co.uk

It might not dazzle from the outside, but this pub has reserved all its best features for inside. The old-fashioned, traditional look – old settles or Chesterfields strewn with plump cushions – is individualised by the slightly eccentric air created by a collection of old posters and art for sale. There's an ever-rolling, wide choice of exciting dishes to choose from, with specials chalked up on the giant board. Chef-patron Fergus Greer creates unusual and interesting dishes; Siberian ravioli filled with mince beef, and pork with soured cream, caraway and tomato sauce, followed, perhaps, by rack of lamb with butternut squash and mushroom tarte Tatin and a spinach and caper salsa. Chocolate, orange and chilli panna cotta is a fitting way to finish. The wine list includes French classics at good prices. Fergus and his wife have created a convivial setting and certainly made their mark in the kitchen and brought personality to this pub.

Prices: Set lunch £18.95, set dinner £23.95. Restaurant main course from £11.50. Bar snack from £7.50. House wine £10.95.
Last orders: Bar: 23.00 (Sunday until 20.00). Food: lunch 14.30 (Sunday 15.30); dinner: 21.00 (Friday and Saturday 21.30, no food served Sunday evening).
Closed: Never.
Food: Modern European.
Other points: No-smoking area. Dogs welcome in the bar. Garden. Children welcome. Car park.
Directions: Exit 6/M25. From the A22, follow the signs to Lingfield racecourse. (Map 6, D5)

Battle

Fairacres

Udimore Road, Broadoak, near Battle,
East Sussex TN31 6DG
Telephone: +44(0)1424 883236
John-Shelagh@fairacres.fsworld.co.uk
www.smoothhound.co.uk/hotels/fairacres.html

Eighteen months into their B&B business and John Smith and Shelagh Franklin have turned their beautiful home into an extremely comfortable and relaxed environment. You can't miss the bright pink exterior of Fairacres as you approach from either Battle or Rye. Grade II-listed and built around 1680, the house has been extended and modernised while retaining great character and charm. Inside, it has more than its fair share of beams and attractive inglenook fireplaces – this is really like staying in your very own country cottage. The three rooms – two twins with showers and one four-poster with an en suite bath – are charmingly decorated and the personal touches are done to a very high standard. There is a shared but comfortable sitting room and the extensive breakfast is served at the huge dining table; don't miss your very own soldiers with the boiled eggs. The surrounding area is steeped in history, and your well-travelled hosts are more than happy to supply local knowledge. The gardens are well maintained and are the ideal spot to relax in the summer.

Rooms: 3. Double/twin from £75.
Closed: Rarely.
Food: Local produce.
Other points: Totally no smoking. Dogs welcome overnight. Garden. Children welcome. Car park.
Directions: Exit 10/M20. A21 from London turn left on to the B2089 to Broadoak and Rye. (Map 6, D6)

Brighton

The Coach House Restaurant and Bar

59 Middle Street, Brighton, East Sussex BN1 1AL
Telephone: +44(0)1273 719000
info@coachhousebrighton.com
www.coachhousebrighton.com

It's good to see a chain-free original emerge and wow us in Brighton, as many of its fun cafés and bars have disappeared. The Coach House is approached through a pretty sun-trap courtyard garden, which is a lovely place to while away the time with a cool drink in the summer months, then it's into the bar area with its high glass roof and selection of plants hanging from the rafters. The wide choice of drinks extends to cocktails, bottled and draft beers, and seven wines by the glass. The attractive adjoining restaurant has stone walls, plenty of character and a giant octagonal fire in the middle; to the front there are huge windows for people-watching. The cutting-edge menus are well priced and offer plenty of choice. At one end, you have wraps, pastas and bangers and mash (Toulouse or vegetarian), or there are buttered tiger prawn starters, dolcelatte and herb salad or Thai mussels cooked with lemon grass, ginger and coconut cream. Steaks came in every shape and size, and other hearty meals take in lamb gigot and roasts on Sunday. The Coach House is all about choice, and with occasional live music and good service, it's a fun place to visit.

Prices: Restaurant main course from £8.95. Bar/snack from £5.75. House wine £10.95.
Last orders: Bar: 23.00. Food: lunch 17.00; dinner 22.00 (Sunday all day to 21.30).
Closed: Rarely.
Food: Modern British.
Other points: No-smoking area. Garden. Children welcome. Wheelchair access.
Directions: M23. Head towards Brighton seafront and turn right at the pier into the Lanes. (Map 6, D5)

Brighton

Terre à Terre

71 East Street, Brighton, East Sussex BN1 1HQ
Telephone: +44(0)1273 729051
mail@terreaterre.co.uk

Philip Taylor and Amanda Powley's groundbreaking vegetarian restaurant continues to go from strength to strength. It's truly a one-off that thinks about food in a way that other restaurants don't. The cooking style is truly international, with ideas drawn right across the Mediterranean to Central and Eastern Europe, the Far East and America, backed up by a kitchen confident enough to break culinary boundaries. Thus, a pâté brik is filled with minted cracked wheat, pressed sheep's cheese and preserved lemon and served with saffron-scented fennel, buttered string beans, and pickled apricots finished with tiger-nut pesto. The house tapas plate is a great introduction to this unusual style – a starter for two to share or a satisfying lunch dish where myriad textures and culinary styles gives each mouthful an unpredictability that keeps interest buoyant. Right from the word go you notice the flavours, picking up on mint, cardamom, coriander, wasabi and tamarind. Other ingredients bolster strength: roast Jerusalem artichoke risotto served with truffled seasons mushrooms, a Madeira and balsamic reduction and sage and rootie chippers. The enthusiasts' wine list is totally organic; it is worth checking the board for the week's recommendations.

Prices: Restaurant main course from £11.95. Organic wine list from £15.
Last orders: Food: 22.30.
Closed: Monday.
Food: International and Vegetarian.
Other points: No-smoking area. Patio. Children welcome.
Directions: M23. Just off the seafront, close to Palace Pier. (Map 6, D5)

Hove

Coriander Restaurant & Deli

4/5 Hove Manor Parade, Hove Street, Hove,
East Sussex BN3 2DF
Telephone: +44(0)1273 730850
info@corianderbrighton.com
www.corianderbrighton.com

Deli by day, restaurant by night, foodies will find much to please at this neighbourhood gem that is strong on organic produce. You could easily do a one-stop shop, as the well-stocked deli sells vegetables, groceries, and spices ground to order, as well as all the classic French and Italian offerings. At lunchtime, enjoy a chorizo-and-manchego sandwich with a coffee, and in the evening, treat your taste buds to a quite different carte experience in the restaurant next door. An exotic and eclectic menu has been created by chef-patrons South African David Smale and his half-German, half-Russian wife, Katrin, for their modern restaurant with a bohemian air. North African and Latin influences make for interesting combinations. Start with lobster aranchi with a creamy chowder and avocado salsa fresca. Mains take in barramundi fillet with Persian rice, chermoula and tarrator, ostrich steak with wattleseed carrots, or marinated tofu steak on butternut squash with pistachio, herb and argan oil pesto. Chocolate ravioli and a chocolate-croissant pudding with Indian chai ice cream hold their own for originality in the puds section. The extensive wine list is mainly organic, and there's a fun range of beers.

Prices: Set lunch £15.20. Set dinner £25.30. Restaurant main course from £12.20. House wine £13.25.
Last orders: Food: lunch 16.00; dinner 20.30.
Closed: Sunday and Monday evening.
Food: North African with Latin influence.
Other points: Totally no smoking. Children welcome. Wheelchair access.
Directions: M23. In the centre of Hove on Hove Street, the A2023. (Map 6, D5)

Rye

Jeake's House Hotel

Mermaid Street, Rye, East Sussex TN31 7ET
Telephone: +44(0)1797 222828
stay@jeakeshouse.com
www.jeakeshouse.com

Built by merchant Samuel Jeake as a storehouse, 17th-century Jeake's House is steeped in history. Its most recent famous owner of the last-century was American poet, novelist and Pulitzer Prize winner Conrad Aiken, who has a suite named after him. Owner Jenny Hadfield has decorated each room individually to create an opulent feel that mixes bold floral prints and striking colours with beams and standing timbers and many period pieces. An open fire may greet you (as well as Jenny's two cats), as you come down to breakfast in the galleried hall. The breakfasts are legendary and can be enjoyed by non-residents. Tuck into award-winning sausages, natural oak-smoked kippers and haddock from Rye Harbour, devilled kidneys, scrambled free-range egg with smoked salmon, and bread and croissants from the local baker. An honesty bar operates in the library. Bedrooms are splendid, with brass mahogany beds and four-posters. If you really want to spoil yourself, stay at the Aiken Suite. A private car park is a real boon as parking in Rye can be difficult.

Rooms: 11, one not en suite. Double room from £43 per person, single from £39.
Prices: Full breakfast menu £9.50. House wine from the bar £12.
Closed: Rarely.
Other points: No smoking in the restaurant. Dogs welcome overnight. Car park.
Directions: Exit 10/M20 and follow signs for Brenzett, then follow directions for Hastings and Rye. Parking in Rye is restricted, but Jeake's House has its own private car park. (Map 6, D6)

Rye

Oaklands

Udimore Road, Rye, East Sussex TN31 6AB
Telephone: +44(0)1797 229734
info@oaklands-rye.co.uk
www.oaklands-rye.co.uk

If you want to get away from it all without being in a remote location, head to tranquil and secluded Oaklands. Set in extensive and secluded grounds, this Edwardian house offers the best of both worlds. It's set in an Area of Outstanding Natural Beauty, but the historic towns of Rye and Battle and their many interesting diversions, cafés and inns are close by. Use the house as a base for exploring the area all-year round, or, in summer, simply unwind in the grounds, join in a game of croquet or even have your own barbecue. All three of the comfortably furnished bedrooms make the most of the all-round views. They have showers, TV, small fridge, hospitality tray, hairdryer, and reception are happy to supply emergency supplies of toiletries you may have left at home. After a hearty traditional or continental breakfast in the elegant dining room or on the terrace, head to the medieval, Tudor and Georgian buildings of Rye or Rye Harbour Nature Reserve, which are just over a mile away. While dinner is not served at Oaklands, they do prepare packed lunches and picnics on request, and can recommend local restaurants and inns.

Rooms: 3. Double/twin room from £70. Single supplement from £10.
Closed: Rarely.
Food: Homemade afternoon teas.
Other points: Totally no smoking. Garden. Children welcome. Car park. Croquet.
Directions: Exit 10/M20. Follow the signs for Brenzett, then Hastings and Rye. From Rye take the B2089 to Broad Oak and Battle. Oaklands is on the right, just past the fire beacon, approximately one mile from Rye. (Map 6, D6)

Chichester

The Anglesey Arms at Halnaker

Stane Street, Halnaker, Chichester,
West Sussex PO18 0NQ
Telephone: +44(0)1243 773474
angleseyarms@aol.com
www.angleseyarms.co.uk

An unpretentious Georgian brick-built pub that has seen its reputation for quality food grow since Roger and Jools Jackson took over two years ago. Stripped pine, flagstones, beams and panelling, and crackling log fires draw walkers from the South Downs, Goodwood and Fontwell race goers, and well-informed locals for pints of Adnams Bitter and interesting menus that use top-notch local and organic produce. Come for mouth-watering Sunday roasts, lunchtime classics such as home-baked ham, free-range eggs and bubble-and-squeak, pasta meals and ploughman's, or book an evening table and tuck into one of their renowned 21-day hung steaks. Local fishermen supply the rope-grown mussels and the fish listed on the daily-changing chalkboard. A hearty and robust alternative may include venison stew with polenta. Game comes from the Goodwood Estate and vegetables from the Organic Farm Shop in Chichester. The sheltered, south-facing garden with petanque pitch is the perfect setting for the memorable 'Moules and Boules' evenings in summer.

Prices: Restaurant main course from £9.95. Bar main course/snack from £4.95. House wine £11.
Last orders: Bar: lunch 15.00 (Saturday and Sunday 17.00); dinner 23.00. Food: lunch 14.30; dinner 21.30.
Closed: Rarely.
Food: Traditional British and modern European.
Other points: No-smoking area. Dogs welcome in the bar. Garden. Car park. Wheelchair access (no WC).
Directions: On the A285, Chichester to Petworth road. From the A27, take the Boxgrove exit at Tangmere and turn right at the A285. (Map 5, D4)

Chichester

The Royal Oak

Pook Lane, East Lavant, Chichester,
West Sussex PO18 0AX
Telephone: +44(0)1243 527434
nickroyaloak@aol.com
www.sussexlive.co.uk/royaloakinn

Flint-built 200 years ago and accessed via a pretty raised terrace, this thriving gastro-pub-with-rooms comprises an open-plan bar and dining area with crackling log fires, leather sofas, fat cream candles on scrubbed tables, and Sussex ales tapped from the cask. Classy modern British food draws the discerning, the main menu and daily blackboard additions featuring quality fish and meats from London markets and vegetables from local organic farms. Typically, begin with crispy duck salad with honey, sesame, ginger and alfalfa, followed by lamb steak with rosemary mash, or whole skate with prosciutto and potato salad. Lunchtime brings sandwiches, home-cooked ham, eggs and bubble-and-squeak, and there are good homemade puddings, such as crisp lemon tart with raspberry sauce. Decent wines include some interesting French classics, 12 by the glass. Six stylish bedrooms feature pastel décor, smart, contemporary furnishings, high-spec CD players and flat-screen televisions, and quality tiled bathrooms with power showers.

Rooms: 6. Double/twin from £70.
Prices: Restaurant main course from £11. House wine £9.95.
Last orders: Bar: 23.00. Food: lunch 14.30; dinner 21.30.
Closed: Rarely.
Food: Modern British.
Other points: No smoking in the bedrooms. Garden and terrace. Car park. Wheelchair access to the restaurant/pub (no WC).
Directions: Village signposted off A286 Midhurst road a mile north of Chichester. (Map 5, D4)

Chichester

The Ship Inn

The Street, Itchenor, Chichester,
West Sussex PO20 7AH
Telephone: +44(0)1243 512284

Built on the site of the original 18th-century inn, the exterior of this 1930s reincarnation belies its nicely nautical interiors and the excellent seafood to boot. Just 150 yards away from Chichester Harbour, it's decked out in ship décor; with old wood panelling with portholes, wonderfully scrubbed tables and a weather station. Apart from the appealing atmosphere – cosy fires in winter and a relaxed buzz in summer – the good local fish is the big draw. At lunch, you can have a simple filled baguette or melon with smoked salmon and prawns to start, with mains of beer-battered cod or steak and kidney pie. At dinner, dishes step up a gear to include large crevettes with garlic mayonnaise, followed by pot-roasted pheasant or lemon sole stuffed with salmon with a lobster sauce. Add in four locally brewed ales, decent wines, plus excellent walks and boat trips nearby, and this becomes a day-trip destination in itself.

Prices: Restaurant main course from £6.95. Bar snack from £4.75. House wine £11.
Last orders: Bar: 23.00. Food: lunch 14.30; dinner 21.15 (Sunday 21.00).
Closed: Afternoons of 25-26 December and 1 January.
Food: Traditional British and French.
Other points: No-smoking area in restaurant. Dogs welcome in the bar. Patio. Car park. Wheelchair access. Separate function room.
Directions: Six miles south of Chichester on the A286 towards West Wittering. Turn right at the sign for Itchenor, and The Ship is one and a half miles further, on the left. (Map 5, D4)

Fontwell

Denmans Garden

Denmans Lane, Fontwell, West Sussex BN18 0SU
Telephone: +44(0)1243 542808
denmans@denmans-garden.co.uk
www.denmans-garden.co.uk

Set in the four-acre garden owned and designed by renowned landscape designer and writer John Brookes, the Garden Café is a lovely place to enjoy morning teas and lunches after exploring the stimulating gardens. There is an admission charge to see the gardens, but you can head straight to the café for which there is no admission charge. The relaxing room is tastefully decked out with garden-style furniture covered with pretty check tablecloths, with stunning plants dotted about. Improvements over the last year include an all-weather cover to the original terrace so the café can be open all year round, an outside terrace with tables and umbrellas for alfresco dining in summer, and a drinks licence, so you can have wine with your meal. The menu takes in morning coffee, lunches and cream teas. Choose from homemade quiches, paninis and sandwiches, or the popular higgidy pie, which comes with a choice of fillings such as chicken, baked ham, sweetcorn and leek. Within the café is a charming gift shop selling an array of souvenirs, chutneys and jams, while in the plant sales area, there are over 1,500 varieties of perennials, shrubs and herbs.

Prices: Bar main course from £4.50. House wine £8.99.
Last orders: Food: Lunch 16.45.
Closed: Rarely.
Food: Modern British.
Other points: Totally no smoking. Garden. Children welcome. Car park. Wheelchair access.
Directions: A27. Five miles from Chichester, five miles from Arundel. (Map 5, D4)

Henfield

The Gallops Restaurant

Wheatsheaf Road, Woodmancote, near Henfield,
West Sussex BN5 9BD
Telephone: +44(0)1273 492077
info@the-gallops.co.uk
www.the-gallops.co.uk

Richard Holmes and Cara Bexton have transformed The Wheatsheaf pub, once renowned as one of the first purveyors of chicken in the basket, into a sophisticated and modern setting with fine menus to match. Before you enter the elegant restaurant with tables set with crisp tablecloths and sparkling glasses, there's a seating area furnished with comfortable sofas, which is the perfect place for an apéritif and for choosing from the fabulous carte. As well as a range of lighter lunch options, such as smoked haddock and chive fishcakes or salad Niçoise, the main menu is a delectable line-up of dishes made using well-sourced ingredients. Start with asparagus soup served with sautéed white asparagus and morel tortellini or roasted pear and camembert filo tart, then choose from the mains, which take in free-range breast of chicken, seared fresh sea-trout fillets and English spring lamb. The dessert menu is the sort that's hard to resist and tempts with hot mocha soufflé with a banana parfait and caramelised bananas and Baileys panna cotta. A broad range of sensibly priced wines from around the world offers many by the glass and half bottle.

Prices: Restaurant main course from £12.95. House wine £11.95.
Last orders: Bar: Lunch 14.30; Dinner 21.30.
Closed: Rarely. All day Monday and Sunday evenings.
Food: Modern European.
Other points: Totally no smoking in the restaurant. Garden. Car park. Wheelchair access (not WC).
Directions: Situated on the B2116 between Henfield and Albourne. The Gallops is close to the A23 at Hickstead. (Map 6, D5)

Petworth

Halfway Bridge Inn

Halfway Bridge, Petworth, West Sussex GU28 9BP
Telephone: +44(0)1798 861281
hwb@thesussexpub.co.uk
www.thesussexpub.co.uk

Nick and Lisa Sutherland, owners of the hugely successful Royal Oak near Chichester (see entry), have worked their magic once again on this attractive old coaching inn. Although spruced up with style and panache, it's not a clone of the Oak, and you'll find a warren of charming little rooms decorated with a relaxed, contemporary feel. A272 travellers, local diners and the polo set are drawn here for first-class modern pub food, tip-top local ales on handpump, and the decent list of wines. Snack in the bar on a poached-salmon open sandwich or smoked-chicken Caesar salad, or look to the chalkboard in the dining area for scallops with tomato salsa, steak and kidney pudding or fresh fish (Dover sole) from Billingsgate Market. Across the lane, in a beautifully converted barn, are six stunning en suite rooms. All have been given the Sutherland treatment – old exposed beams, luxury bathrooms, DVD/CD systems, and plasma-screen TVs. A super Sussex base.

Rooms: 6. Double/twin room from £90, single from £60. Family/Suite from £120.
Prices: Restaurant main course from £8.75. Bar main course from £4.95. House wine £11.50.
Last orders: Bar: 23.00. Food: Lunch 14.00; Dinner 21.30 (20.30 on Sundays).
Closed: Never.
Food: Modern British.
Other points: No smoking in the restaurant. Children welcome. Dogs welcome in the bar. Garden areas. Car park. Wheelchair access (Disabled Bedroom Suite).
Directions: A3. Take the A272 from Midhurst to Petworth. Continue past the left turn to Lodsworth, and the Halfway Bridge is just after this on the left. (Map 5, D4)

Steyning

Springwells Bed and Breakfast Hotel

9 High Street, Steyning, West Sussex BN44 3GG
Telephone: +44(0)1903 812446
contact@springwells.co.uk
www.springwells.co.uk

This handsome creeper-clad Georgian merchant's house is an excellent base for touring the South Downs, and is also close to Brighton, Horsham and Gatwick Airport. Downstairs there is a comfortable lounge and an attractive breakfast room where you can tuck into delicious porridge with whisky, brown sugar and cream. There's also a bar at the back of the ground floor that incorporates a further lounge-cum-conservatory area, looking out over a neat walled garden. Bedrooms, whether they are on the first or second floor, are well appointed, well maintained and generously sized. For the biggest, request the first-floor rooms with the high ceilings, and for the best views, ask for bedrooms at the back, which look out over the garden and have a sunnier aspect. The bedroom furnishings are in keeping with the building's character, and two rooms have four-posters. On the top floor, a couple of rooms share a bathroom. As well as tea- and coffee-making facilities and biscuits, a bowl of fresh fruit stands at the bottom of the stairs, and there's a fridge with fresh milk and beers at the end of the first-floor corridor. Springwells also has a heated swimming pool.

Rooms: 11, 2 not en suite. Double room from £61, single from £37.
Closed: Two weeks over Christmas and New Year.
Other points: Children welcome. Dogs welcome overnight in one room. Garden. Car park.
Directions: Take the road signposted to Steyning from the A283 and Springwells is situated on the main street opposite the Methodist church. (Map 6, D5)

Coventry

Turmeric Gold

166 Medieval Spon Street, Coventry,
Warwickshire CV1 1BB
Telephone: +44(0)2476 226603
info@turmericgold.co.uk
www.turmericgold.co.uk

Set on the otherwise less-than-attractive Coventry Inner Ring, Turmeric Gold is a vibrant place in many senses. It serves Indian food with a modern twist in an exotically coloured setting. The building, on a medieval street, has kept its original charm, but its revamped interiors complement its spicy food. There is even a special private lounging area, which is covered in silk and can be draped over for privacy, under which you can eat and drink like a Maharaja. The rest of the restaurant has exposed brick, beams and timber framework, which works well with the vibrant colours and oriental antiques. The upstairs dining room has a particularly romantic feel, with lots of hidden features and private dining areas. The menu has the popular line-up of baltis and tandoori dishes and a wide choice of specials such as chicken jalfrazi, chicken moglai, lamb khatta massala, duck and fish specials. A good choice of breads, vegetarian sides and set menus complete the offering. What distinguishes the cooking, however, are the fresh-tasting flavours and lightness of touch to the dishes which are made using the minimum of oil. The set price lunch courses are excellent value.

Prices: Set lunch £7.50-£8.50 and dinner £15-£20. Restaurant main course from £10. House wine £9.95.
Last orders: Food: lunch 14.00; dinner 23.30.
Closed: Sunday lunch.
Food: Modern Indian.
Other points: No-smoking area. Car park. Large private room.
Directions: Situated off the city ring road on J9, going towards Upper Well Street. Turn right at the second traffic lights onto Corporation Street. At the top of the street, turn right at the roundabout onto Medieval Spon Street. Turmeric Gold is situated opposite Bonds night club. (Map 9, D3)

Knowle

Cafe Saffron

1679 High Street, Knowle, Solihull,
Warwickshire B98 ORL
Telephone: +44(0)1564 772190

This evening-only Indian in well-heeled Knowle is a cut above your average curry house. Just one mile from junction 5 of the M42, it is easy to find, thanks not only to a prominent High Street location, but to its bright outside lights. Inside, the minimalist contemporary décor, with modern prints and warm orange-plastered walls, is a refreshing change from that of the more traditional curry house. The owners have also set high standards with their menu, as the kitchen pays much attention to detail, preparation, and the look of the dishes. Good-quality meat and poultry are sourced from local butchers, and many herbs and spices imported directly from Calcutta and then freshly ground on site. All the favourites recipes from India, Pakistan and Bangladesh are here. Start with a classic chicken shashlick or prawn pathia puri, for example, and move on to tandoori grills, and curries such as bhuna, korma, dopiaza, passanda, jalfrezi and rogan josh. The wide menu provides a comforting, something-for-everyone choice, but look to the list of specialities for a more varied selection.

Prices: Main course from £8. House wine £7.95.
Last orders: Food: 23.30.
Closed: Lunch.
Food: Indian.
Other points: Children welcome. Car park.
Directions: Two miles south east of Solihull. Exit5/M42. (Map 9, D3)

Birmingham

San Carlo

4 Temple Street, Birmingham B2 5BN
Telephone: +44(0)121 633 0251
www.sancarlo.co.uk

This popular restaurant in a narrow street off the city centre has a lively and friendly buzz. It was the first in what is now a chain with three other branches in the Midlands area and Manchester. Its modern Mediterranean look has a façade of marble and glass, which leads into a spacious light and bright dining area with mirrored walls, white ceramic floor tiles, potted plants and small trees creating a fresh and airy contemporary look. Classic flavoursome dishes are the order of the day, and prices are very fair for cooking that's above the norm for a city-centre eaterie majoring in pizzas and pasta. There's plenty to tempt in the way of soups, salads and risottos, as well as trattoria classic mains, such as pollo sorpresa, scallopa Milanese, and saltimboca alla Romana. Blackboard specials extend an already wide choice, offering some very good fresh fish dishes; look out for excellent lobster Thermidor, crevettes in garlic butter, and spaghetti shellfish. There's a selection of well-priced Italian wines, with a good selection by the glass, but with France and New World wines also making a splash.

Prices: Main course from £11. House wine £11.20.
Last orders: Food: 23.00.
Closed: Rarely.
Food: Italian.
Other points: No-smoking area. Children welcome.
Directions: In the centre of the city. (Map 9, D2)

Chippenham

Revolutions Cafe Bar and Restaurant

66 New Road, Chippenham, Wiltshire SN15 1ES
Telephone: +44(0)1249 447500
sanddwebb@aol.com

Contemporary in style, this town-centre brasserie-style restaurant is classically good looking and serves excellent seasonal food. Sandie and Doug Webb are passionate about buying produce from local suppliers, so much so that menus credit their beef and organic egg producers. Despite using top-notch ingredients, you can eat very well here at reasonable prices. Lunch dishes produce wonderful Wiltshire ham and eggs with sautéed potatoes and salad or roasted green pepper, mushroom and pimento risotto. There's also a good choice of salad and filled jacket potatoes. The evening menu offers a selection of imaginative starters, such as pan-fried duck breast with an almond and apricot sauce and mushrooms with a creamed garlic and Marsala sauce. The mains include a strong line-up of steaks plus other meat and vegetarian meals. Although licensed, a bring-your-own-wine policy with a small corkage charge has proved popular and is encouraged, but if you forget, there's always the house Australian, and a selection of lagers, beers and spirits.

Prices: Lunch menu from £2.95. Set dinner £14.95.
House wine £7.95.
Last orders: Food: 21.00.
Closed: Sunday and Monday evening.
Food: Modern British.
Other points: No-smoking area. Children welcome.
Directions: Exit17/M4. Take the dual carriageway towards Chippenham and follow the signs to the town centre. Turn left through the railway arches and just before the first crossing Revolutions is on the right. (Map 5, C2)

Teffont Evias

Howard's House Hotel

Teffont Evias, Salisbury, Wiltshire SP3 5RJ
Telephone: +44(0)1722 716392 or 716821
enq@howardshousehotel.com
www.howardshousehotel.com

Howard's House Hotel looks as if its straight out of a Merchant Ivory production. This quaint country house dates back to 1623 and has been in the same family since 1692. The Mayne family crest proudly hangs in the hall. It has been smartly furnished in an understated way that steers clear of over-fussy swags and tails. The beautiful garden with well-tended lawns and pretty cottage-garden flowers is just as tasteful. Large comfortable sofas in the sitting room are the perfect spot for relaxing, and in winter, a log fire is lit in the large stone fireplace. Upstairs are luxuriously decorated en suite bedrooms, some have four-poster beds, all have bathrobes, and are spacious and comfortable with good views. Chef Boyd McIntosh heads the kitchen and delivers sophisticated, ambitious cooking. He insists on quality, fresh local ingredients such as Dennay Farm bacon, Fundamentally Fungus mushrooms and Sealy game, backed up by home-grown vegetables and herbs from the garden. The table d'hôte is equally enticing, while an extensive wine list ranges from well-priced house wines to a spoil-yourself selection.

Rooms: 9. Double room from £145, single from £95. Four-poster £165.
Prices: Set lunch £23.50 and dinner £25.95. Main course from £19.95. House wine £13.50.
Last orders: Food: lunch 14.00; dinner 21.00. Reservations only.
Closed: Closed Monday and Friday lunch.
Food: Modern British.
Other points: No smoking in the restaurant. Children welcome. Dogs welcome overnight. Garden. Car park. Wheelchair access to the restaurant.
Directions: Head due west from Salisbury towards Wilton and Chilmark, off the B3089 towards Hindon and the A303. (Map 5, D2)

Tenbury Wells

The Fountain Inn

Oldwood, St Michael's, Tenbury Wells,
Worcestershire WR15 8TB
Telephone: +44 (0)1584 810701
enquiries@fountain-hotel.co.uk
www.fountain-hotel.co.uk

There aren't many pubs, if any, in Britain that can boast of having a 1,000-gallon aquarium complete with a leopard shark in the bar, but then the Fountain Inn is no ordinary pub. The real attractions in this striking, black-and-white 17th-century inn are the smart wood-beamed bar and the nautically styled restaurant serving fresh food using quality local ingredients. Seafood is, of course, big business, with fish bought direct from Birmingham market, but other produce is sourced more locally. Chef Paul Smith also has the pick of the pub's organic herb and vegetable garden. Diners come from miles around to see the shark and tuck into homemade soup, garlic mushrooms or terrine of the day, or mains of steak-and-ale pie, lamb Wellington and fine Herefordshire steaks, as well as the many fish options. There are smart en suite rooms, and The Oldwood Suite is ideal for wedding functions. Beer lovers will appreciate the award-winning Fountain Ale.

Rooms: 11. Double/twin room from £49.95.
Disabled suite available.
Prices: Main course from £6.95. Sunday lunch £9.95.
House wine £9.95.
Last orders: Bar: 23.00. Food: 21.00 (later for bookings).
Closed: Never.
Food: Traditional British with Continental influences.
Other points: No smoking in the restaurant. Children welcome.
Garden. Car park. Shark aquarium. Wheelchair access.
Directions: J5/M5. One mile from Tenbury Wells on the A4112
Leominster road. (Map 8, D5)

Pain de Campagne
Organic crusty white from Flour Power.
£2.10

Butterm
Soft loaf made with
whit flour, butter
sugar from C
£1.5

The Fountain Inn, Tenbury Wells

Purchased by Russell Allen and his family in 1999, a series of developments have seen an ageing alehouse transformed into an award-winning establishment. The Fountain's newest addition, a silver-star award-winning 11 en suite bedroom hotel, has already won awards for food, beer and service, not to mention a Four-Diamond Rating. The use of fresh, local produce is the key to the quality menu, which earned the Fountain the title British Catering Pub of the Year 2004.

Birmingham Market
50 Edgbaston Street
Tel: 0121 622 0200
www.bullring.co.uk

Part of the first phase of the £400-million redevelopment of the Bullring, this vast indoor market houses almost 100 traders. It's foodie heaven; more than half the stalls sell fresh produce such as fish, seafood, poultry, meat and game, and the remainder offering fruit and vegetables, deli lines and Caribbean foods. You will find plenty of bargains and choice. In addition, there are clothes, haberdashery, florists, hairdressers and cafés. There's also ample parking.

Ludlow

A49

Leominster

Hereford

Visit the local Farmers' Market

The post office car park in Tenbury Wells is the location for the town's farmers' market on the fourth Saturday of the month, from 9am to 2pm.

Birmingham Market

Fish from the River Tay, Scotland

Although not strictly local to The Fountain, some of the country's finest available fish finds its way onto the menu courtesy of owner Russell Allen's father, Doug. A keen fisherman, Doug fishes the Tay and some of Scotland's other salmon and trout rivers regularly and his catches are some of The Fountain's best-selling dishes.

The Fountain Inn, Tenbury Wells

A456

Tenbury Wells

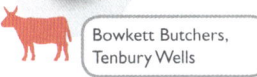

Bowkett Butchers, Tenbury Wells

Bowkett Butchers
Market Square, Tenbury Wells
Tel: 01584 810351

Roger Bowkett and his dedicated team of butchers are renowned throughout the area for their quality meat. Situated within the GH Bowkett supermarket in Tenbury, the butchers counter supplies The Fountain with all of its fresh meat, including the incomparable Herefordshire beef. A trip to the area is considered incomplete without taking some of Bowketts' produce home.

A44

Worcester

Wye Valley Brewery, Stoke Lacy

A417

A465

Wye Valley Brewery
Stoke Lacey, Herefordshire
Tel: 01885 490505

This is the leading cask-ale brewery in the county. Get together with a group of 10 or more beer fans and you can book a guided tour of the brewery to see the ale being made. The latest addition to the line-up is Butty Bach, a burnished-gold full-bodied beer. Its popular Dorothy Goodbody selection includes ales for every season, plus a wholesome stout. You can order drinks and memorabilia from its online shop at www.wyevalleybrewery.co.uk.

Bridlington

Georgian Tea Rooms

56 High Street, Old Town, Bridlington,
East Yorkshire YO16 4QA
Telephone: +44(0)1262 608600
gadandy@aol.com

Brother and sister David and Diane Davison's traditional tea rooms are part of one the most complete Georgian high streets in Britain. This historic quarter of Bridlington is a source of pride and tourism for the old town, tucked a mile inland from the better-known bustling seaside resort. The tea rooms are on the ground floor of a fine Grade II-listed building, forming part of a three-floored antique emporium. The spacious rooms have a welcoming glow, with walls painted in striking yellows and greens and highly polished wooden tables. There's a separate room for smokers, plus a fantastic patio and garden dominated by a central fountain. What you get are reassuringly British favourites. Breakfast starts the day, a full English perhaps, vegetarian medley or a breakfast bap filled with sausage or bacon, then the menu moves on to snacks of filled jacket potatoes, salads, toasted sandwiches and creamed mushrooms on toast as well as those teashop stalwarts of toasted teacakes, homemade scones and other irresistible cakes and pastries. The coffee and tea selection is wide and includes flavoured milks and coffees. The tea rooms also cater for private functions.

Prices: Main course from £3.45. House wine £8.99.
Last orders: Food: 17.00 (Sunday 15.00).
Closed: Closed for two weeks over Christmas and New Year.
Food: Traditional English.
Other points: No-smoking area. Children welcome. Garden.
Directions: In Bridlington's Old Town. (Map 12, E8)

Bridlington

Marton Grange

Flamborough Road, Sewerby, Bridlington,
East Yorkshire YO15 1DU
Telephone: +44(0)1262 602034
www.marton-grange.co.uk

Formerly a Georgian farmhouse, this Grade II-listed building has been immaculately restored into a smart and comfortable hotel. Proprietor Stuart Nelson has transformed the house, keeping its Georgian elegance but bringing a fresh, cheery contemporary feel to the rooms. Downstairs, two fine dining rooms look out on to the south-facing, well-tended grounds. The terrace that leads out from french windows is a lovely place to enjoy a drink and the beautiful surroundings. Breakast is served in two interconnecting drawing rooms that are also sunny in look and feel. There are two choices of bedrooms: large premier en suite rooms in the older part of the house, or classic rooms in the newer extension. The full English breakfasts are quite an event, and come with their own freshly laid fresh eggs, with all the other ingredients coming from local suppliers. Explorers should head to nearby Flamborough Head, an outstanding stretch of coastline, which is famed for its colonies of nesting seabirds.

Rooms: 11. Double from £30 per person, single from £36.
Closed: December, January and February.
Food: Traditional British.
Other points: Totally no smoking. Garden. Car park. Dogs welcome overnight. Wheelchair access.
Directions: Exit 37/M62. Take the B1255 Bridlington to Flamborough road and Marton Grange is on the left, up the last drive-way off the lay-by. (Map 12, E8)

Burnsall

The Red Lion Hotel

By the Bridge, Burnsall, Skipton,
North Yorkshire BD23 6BU
Telephone: +44(0)1756 720204
info@redlion.co.uk
www.redlion.co.uk

Traditional charm and hospitality abound at this stone-built 16th-century inn, which stands beside an ancient arched bridge in the pretty Dales village of Burnsall. Cosy and rambling, with lovely gardens running down to the River Wharfe, and stylish en suite bedrooms, it has long been a favoured base for exploring the Dales. In the rustic, stone-flagged bar, with its roaring fires, relaxing sofas and handpulled pints of Theakston ale, you can tuck into some hearty home-cooked food. Local ingredients play a big part on seasonal menus, for example, daily specials of Wharfedale lamb stew, roast grouse (from Bolton Abbey estate), and locally smoked haddock with egg, spinach and hollandaise. Light lunch options include decent sandwiches and salad Niçoise with quails eggs, while dinner in the restaurant could feature Whitby crab and avocado, followed by steamed steak-and-kidney pudding or roast cod with tomato and courgette chutney, with chocolate bread and butter pudding to finish. There are wonderful local walks.

Rooms: 15 (plus 3 cottages by the river). Double/twin from £60, single from £60 per person.
Prices: Set lunch £29.95. Set dinner £29.95. Restaurant main course from £12.50. Bar main course from £3.95.
House wine £12.50.
Last orders: Bar: 23.00. Food: Lunch 14.30, Dinner 21.30.
Closed: Rarely.
Food: Modern British.
Other points: No-smoking areas. Children welcome.
Dogs welcome. Garden. Car park. Licence for civil weddings.
Wheelchair access in the restaurant. Residents' lounge.
Conference facilities.
Directions: A65. From Leeds to Ilkley, turning towards Bolton Abbey, the hotel is situated just throught the town. (Map 12, E5)

Filey

The Downcliffe House Hotel

The Beach, Filey, North Yorkshire YO14 9LA
Telephone: +44(0)1723 513310
info@downcliffehouse.co.uk
www.downcliffehouse.co.uk

Sit in the restaurant overlooking the beach and you'll immediately feel in holiday mode at The Downcliffe. The hotel is right on the beach and most of its rooms have picture-postcard views of Filey's six miles of golden sands. The hotel has recently come under new ownership, but it continues to provide a homely welcome in stylish surroundings. In winter, a real fire roars in the bar and the restaurant. All the bedrooms are en suite and generously proportioned, some have four-poster beds, and all are decorated in the Victorian style that runs through the house. True to its location, the menu includes fresh fish, but also acknowledges the farms that surround Filey. The strongly modern British menu may offer seafood hors d'oeuvres or a homemade soup to start, followed by its popular platter of fruits de mer or Whitby creel prawns, plus there's an extensive choice of meat dishes. A suitably indulgent finish would be hot fudgy chocolate gateau with cream or banana ice-cream cake. The wine collection offers much under £15, plus a number of treats. Coffee with mints or a liqueur coffee are fitting finishes for a meal at this traditional English seaside-town hotel.

Rooms: 12. Double room from £96, single from £48, family room from £144.
Prices: Set dinner £20. Main course from £10. House wine £10.
Last orders: Food: lunch 14.00; dinner 20.00.
Closed: January.
Food: Modern British and Seafood.
Other points: Totally no smoking. Children welcome. Dogs welcome overnight. Car park.
Directions: Leave the A165 taking the A1039 and follow it to the centre of Filey. Drive through the centre and down Cargate Hill and turn right along the sea front. (Map 12, D8)

Harrogate

Ascot House

53 Kings Road, Harrogate, North Yorkshire HG1 5HJ
Telephone: +44(0)1423 531005
admin@ascothouse.com
www.ascothouse.com

Luxuriate in the laid-back elegance of this conveniently placed hotel that is just a 10-minute stroll from the shops, attractions and conference and exhibition centre. Lovely gardens give it a peaceful feel. It has a relaxed and friendly atmosphere throughout, from the lounge furnished with comfortable and inviting sofas and armchairs overlooking the garden to the attractive bar, which has views on to a pretty patio balcony. The well-kept en suite bedrooms are individually styled. The good sound cooking, which caters for a wide range of tastes and offers value for money, is another excellent reason to stay here. The set-dinner menu covers good British cooking with a twist: grilled lamb chops with a warm red-onion marmalade, and chicken breast wrapped in smoked bacon and served with Madeira sauce. A typical meal from the carte could include chargrilled vegetable terrine with a balsamic dressing, and roasted pork fillet with apple-and-onion chutney, and Marsala wine sauce. The wine list is strong on French classics. Private car parking is another plus.

Rooms: 19. Double room from £87, single from £59.
Prices: Set dinner £17.50. House wine £10.95.
Last orders: Food: dinner 20.30.
Closed: 22 January-6 February.
Food: Traditional and modern English.
Other points: No smoking in the restaurant and bedrooms. Children welcome. Small garden. Car park. Licence for civil weddings.
Directions: Follow signs for the town centre/conference and exhibition centre of Harrogate. This will bring you to Kings Road. Drive past the exhibition centre and the hotel is on the left, immediately after the open park area as you drive up the hill. (Map 12, E6)

Helmsley

Pheasant Hotel

Harome, Helmsley, North Yorkshire YO62 5JG
Telephone: +44(0)1439 771241

Two former cottages and the village blacksmith's shop have been merged for the best of both worlds – country pub meets hotel. Overlooking a duck pond, the location and look of this country hotel is quintessentially English. The flagstoned and beamed bar is cottagey, while the restaurant and lounge is smartly chintzy and comfortable. The small heated swimming pool in one of courtyard buildings is a pleasant addition, and great for a few leisurely lengths before a hearty breakfast or dinner. The neatly decorated bedrooms mirror the rest of the décor are cottagey in style, quite roomy and well equipped, and all overlook the pond. With its open lounge fire and peaceful village position, you will find this an easy place to relax and slow the pace. The restaurant, partly set in a conservatory, serves a daily-changing menu of traditional British food, such as cream of asparagus soup, roast breast of Gressingham duckling with apple sauce and onion stuffing, or poached fillet of fresh Scarborough sole with parsley sauce, and blackberry-and-apple pie to finish. There is also plenty of seating outside in summer.

Rooms: 12. Double room from £150, single from £75 dinner, bed and breakfast.
Prices: Set dinner £22.50. House wine £9.50.
Last orders: Food: lunch 14.00; dinner 20.30.
Closed: December, January and February.
Food: Traditional British.
Other points: No smoking in the restaurant. Dogs welcome overnight. Garden. Car park. Indoor heated swimming pool. Wheelchair access.
Directions: Take the A170 from Helmsley towards Scarborough. After 0.25 miles turn right for Harome. The hotel is opposite the church. (Map 12, D7)

www.routiers.co.uk

Hunmanby

Wrangham House Hotel

10 Stonegate, Hunmanby, Filey,
North Yorkshire YO14 0NS
Telephone: +44(0)1723 891333
info@wranghamhouse.co.uk
www.wranghamhouse.co.uk

This elegant, well-designed 18th-century Georgian house has seamlessly made the transition from former vicarage to comfortable country-house hotel. Two acres of secluded woodland provide plenty of leisurely walks, or there are the coastal paths and 13 top golf courses nearby for the more energetic. The majority of the renovations and extensions to the house were planned by Francis Wrangham, a correspondent of William Wordsworth. In the grand dining room, you can dine on traditional and updated dishes, made from fresh local ingredients. Starters include smoked trout with avocado-and-shrimp mousse, and mains might be roasted rack of lamb with redcurrant coulis or breast of Barbary duck in a red wine, button-onion and mushroom sauce. The wine list has something for most tastes, and prices rarely top £15. The day rooms are tastefully furnished and have log fires and lovely views on to the grounds. Four of the bedrooms are in an adjacent converted coach house, and one on the ground floor is equipped for guests with disabilities. They all are well appointed and come with TV, hairdryer and tea- and coffee-making facilities.

Rooms: 12. Double room from £75, single from £60.
Prices: Set dinner £19.50 and £16 (2 course). Bar/snack from £5.95. House wine £11.75.
Last orders: Food: dinner 21.30.
Closed: Never.
Food: Modern British.
Other points: No smoking in the restaurant. Children welcome. Dogs welcome overnight. Garden. Car park. Licence for civil weddings. Wheelchair access.
Directions: Nine miles south of Scarborough via the A165, then the A1039. (Map 12, D8)

Lastingham

Lastingham Grange

Lastingham, Kirkbymoorside, York,
North Yorkshire YO62 6TH
Telephone: +44(0)1751 417345
reservations@lastinghamgrange.com
www.lastinghamgrange.com

The Grange is located in a rural setting. Built of stone and set around a central courtyard in 10 acres of gardens, it has a timeless elegance. The former farmhouse, dating from the 16th century, is well maintained, from its gardens down to its flower baskets. The Wood family has lived here for nearly 60 years and make visitors feel at home. The public areas and bedrooms are spacious and furnished in soft colours with antiques. Bedrooms and en suite bathrooms are pristine and comfortable. Local produce features prominently on the menu; all meat comes from S Waind & Sons in Kirkbymoorside, fish from Whitby and ice cream and cheeses from Wensleydale. Lunches include homemade pâté, followed by vegetable lasagne or fish of the day. Set dinners are a more grand affair and could start with dressed crab or Blue Wensleydale and leek tart before moving on to venison Madeira or baked skate wings with a basil-and-caper sauce.

Rooms: 12. Double room from £189, single from £99, dinner, bed & breakfast.
Prices: Set lunch £18.75 (four courses) and dinner £37.50 (five courses). Main course from £12.50. House wine £8.75.
Last orders: Food: lunch 13.45; dinner 20.30 (Sunday 20.00).
Closed: December to the beginning of March.
Food: Traditional British.
Other points: No smoking in the restaurant. Children welcome. Dogs welcome overnight. Garden. Car park.
Directions: From Pickering take the A170 towards Kirkbymoorside for five miles. Turn off right towards Appleton-le-Moors and Lastingham; follow the road for two miles turning right by the church. After 75 yards turn left up the no-through road for 400 yards. (Map 12, D7)

...for topical features

Pheasant Hotel, Helmsley

Two generations of family run this established smart hotel that was once a blacksmiths. Mr Binks senior and his wife, Patricia, have been joined by their eldest son Ken Binks and his wife. Susan is in charge of the kitchen and is a big believer in using local suppliers, including for fish, meat and game, a few of which she shares here.

Visit the local Farmers' Market

Farmers' markets are held at Malton in the sheep sheds that flank two sides of Market Square. The sheds are still used on Tuesdays and Fridays, for the cattle sales. The farmers' market is held on the last Saturday of each month, apart from the months of August and December. For more information, call the Market Office on 01653 694905.

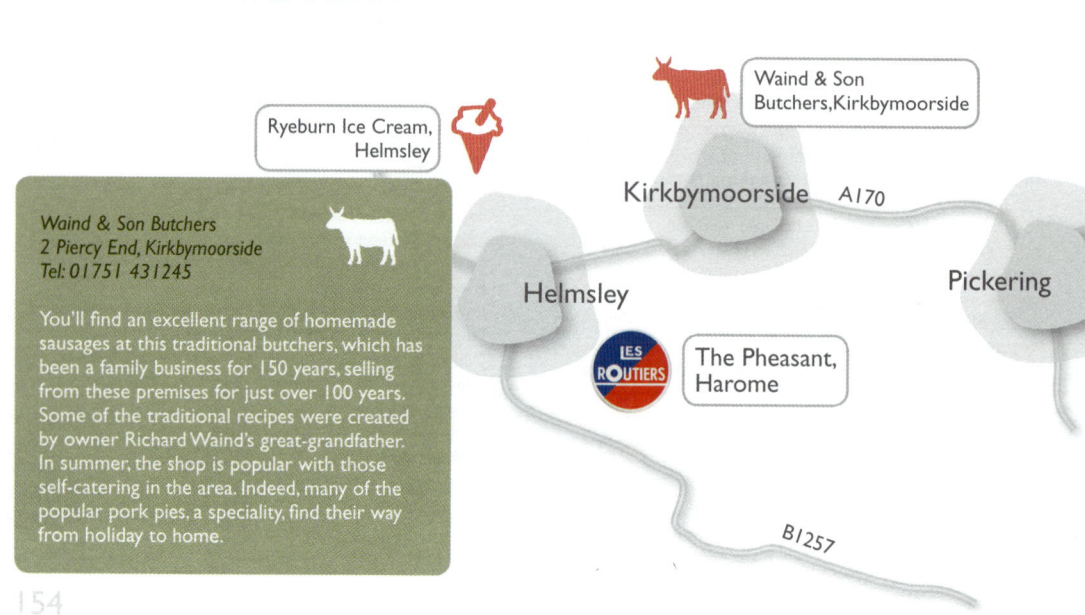

Ryeburn Ice Cream, Helmsley

Waind & Son Butchers, Kirkbymoorside

Kirkbymoorside   A170

Helmsley

Pickering

The Pheasant, Harome

B1257

Waind & Son Butchers
2 Piercy End, Kirkbymoorside
Tel: 01751 431245

You'll find an excellent range of homemade sausages at this traditional butchers, which has been a family business for 150 years, selling from these premises for just over 100 years. Some of the traditional recipes were created by owner Richard Waind's great-grandfather. In summer, the shop is popular with those self-catering in the area. Indeed, many of the popular pork pies, a speciality, find their way from holiday to home.

Hodgsons Fresh Fish
Hartlepool
Tel: 01429 263698

This shop sells fish at its freshest caught off the local coastline. Make a point of buying cod here, as it is fished from sustainable stocks. Other delights include sea bass, John Dory and langoustines. This is also the place to buy lobsters, which are kept live in a tank.

Radfords Butchers
18 Coach Road, Sleights, Whitby
Tel: 01947 810229

This traditional family butchers is run by Andrew and Sue Radford. Andrew's mother is the brains behind its renowned steak pies and pork pies. The lamb and beef they sell is from a local farm that specialises in rare-breed meats. In season, they also have plentiful supplies of game – pheasant, venison, guinea fowl – from local estates.

 Hodgsons Fresh Fish, Hartlepool

Whitby

Radfords Butchers, South Whitby

A169

Alliance Fish
West Pier, Scarborough
Tel: 01723 350400

Ocean's Pantry on the harbour is run by Alliance Fish and is one of the best wet-fish shops in the north. Between them, the owners have almost a dozen day boats, which ensures plentiful supplies. Their fresh crabs are magnificent, and feature on The Pheasant's menu as whole dressed crabmeat in the shell. Also worth sampling are the shop's sea bass, turbot, squid and lobster.

A171

Alliance Fish, Scarborough

Scarborough

A170

A165

Ryeburn Ice Cream
Church Farm, Helmsley
Tel: 01439 770331

Former farmers David Otterburn and his parents Richard and Christine started making ice cream to use up milk surplus to their quota. Twelve years ago, the family closed the farm and opened a tea room and ice-cream parlour. Since 1995, David has won more than 50 awards for his ice cream, which comes in 46 different flavours, including a dozen sorbets and his personal favourite, bilberry yogurt ice cream. The Pheasant serves a wide choice, from raspberry, coffee and butterscotch ice creams to Champagne and lime & lychee and mango sorbets.

North Yorkshire

Northallerton

Lovesome Hill Farm

Lovesome Hill, Northallerton, North Yorkshire DL6 2PB
Telephone: +44(0)1609 772311
pearson1hf@care4free.net

Mary and John Pearson's 156-acre working farm deep in the Yorkshire Dales of James Heriott's *All Creatures Great and Small* and *Heartbeat*'s North Yorkshire Moors offers tranquillity and plenty of walking opportunities. It is just 200 yards from Wainright's Coast to Coast walk. You can expect a warm welcome and to be well fed, from the moment Mary ushers you into the lounge with a tray of tea and homemade biscuits on arrival. Breakfast is a hearty affair with eggs from the farm, local honey, sausages and bacon, homemade marmalade and lemon curd. Dinner is cooked around local supplies, too. Homemade soups, chicken in tarragon or pork with apricots, served with locally grown vegetables, and raspberry Pavlova to finish are some of the dishes you can expect to tuck into. There is one bedroom in the main house; the rest are in a barn conversion; however, this is attached to the main house, so has easy access without going outside. A neat cottage style with floral prints, some canopied beds, and delicate touches distinguish the rooms, which are all en suite. Gate Cottage sleeps two and offers the flexibility of bed and breakfast or self-catering.

Rooms: 6. Double room from £56, single from £30-£40, family room £86.
Prices: Set dinner £20.
Closed: Rarely.
Food: Traditional English.
Other points: Totally no smoking. Children welcome. Garden. Car park. Wheelchair access.
Directions: Four miles north of Northallerton on the A167 towards Darlington, on the right hand side. (Map 12, D6)

Whitby

Magpie Café

14 Pier Road, Whitby, North Yorkshire YO21 3PU
Telephone: +44(0)1947 602058
ian@magpiecafe.co.uk
www.magpiecafe.co.uk

You'd hope to find a good fish restaurant in a fishing port, and the Magpie Café satisfies on all levels. The building has long been associated with fishing, and the Café moved to this site in 1937. Its quality fish is legendary, so much so that queues have to make way for the daily deliveries of halibut, salmon or boxes of lobster that are delivered daily, fresh off the boats in the quayside. Its traditional fish and chips, either haddock or cod, are renowned and come in small, regular or large sizes. Dieters needn't feel excluded as there are plenty of grilled and poached options, and much else to tempt besides. Owner Ian Robson has an extensive repertoire, taking in fish pies and speciality recipes such as haddock and prawns in a creamy leek sauce, salmon with lime crème fraîche, and whole oven-baked sea bass, served plain or with a garlic or lemon butter. The meat dishes, such as local pork, sausage, egg and chips, or own-boiled ham with homemade coleslaw, and steak pie, are equally good and are made using locally sourced ingredients. In contrast, the wine list is small but offers good value and an international choice, and there's a wide selection of beers, too. If you have room after the generous Yorkshire portions, the nursery puds, such as jam roly-poly, won't disappoint.

Prices: Main course from £5.95. House wine £9.95.
Last orders: Food: 21.00.
Closed: Mid January-early February.
Food: Seafood.
Other points: Totally no smoking. Children welcome.
Directions: Directly opposite the fishmarket on Whitby's historic harbourside. (Map 12, D7)

Whitby

Quayside ⭐

7 Pier Road, Whitby, North Yorkshire YO21 3PU
Telephone: +44(0)1947 602059
carol@fusco123.wanadoo.co.uk
www.fuscowhitby.com

With the fish market on its doorstep, Quayside is in the enviable position of having the pick of the local catch for its traditionally cooked fare. The freshest fish supplies are cooked in the Fusco family's special batter and accompanied by its special crinkle-cut chips, and the popularity of this menu continues to grow. Whitby cod, wholetail scampi, seafood platter and homemade fishcakes are just a few of the piscine favourites on offer, but those looking for meat and vegetarian dishes are well catered for, too, with home-made steak pie and cream cheese and broccoli bake. The three-storey building, once changing facilities for returning fishermen, is open-plan and airy, helped not only by air conditioning but a good eye for décor. The tiled floors are offset with dark green timbered walls, attractive lighting and cast-iron tables. It is claimed Bram Stoker wrote some of his Dracula stories in the first-floor library. Before dining, enjoy a drink in the contemporary upstairs bar that has fantastic harbour views.

Prices: Restaurant main course from £6.75. House wine £8.
Last orders: Food: 20.00.
Closed: December and January, excluding Boxing Day and school holidays.
Food: Traditional British.
Other points: Totally no smoking. Children welcome.
Directions: (Map 12, D7)

Leeds

Hazlewood Castle Hotel  ⭐

Paradise Lane, Hazlewood, Tadcaster,
West Yorkshire LS24 9NJ
Telephone: +44 (0)1937 535353
info@hazlewood-castle.co.uk
www.hazlewood-castle.co.uk

This centuries-old castle is the place to luxuriate in the finer things of life. You arrive through mature park-land and the grandness continues inside. Bedrooms in the main castle or the courtyard wing are sumptu-ously appointed. Food is another source of indul-gence. Celebrity chef John Benson-Smith showcases his fine cooking at restaurant 1086, named after the date the castle was first mentioned in the Domesday Book. The room is beautifully designed with tall french windows opening on to a terrace overlooking the lawns. The stylish black-and-white colour scheme sets the right mood for the sophisticated dishes that follow. From the lunch menu you could start with ham hock and parsley terrine with puy lentil dressing, and follow with fillet of beef grand mere with a red wine sauce. Early evening, there's a good-value big-idea set menu before the carte starts at 7.30pm. The latter is stuffed with treats such as foie gras, truffles and mouth-watering recipes. As well as the extensive wine list, there is a long modern bar offering a selec-tion of drinks. For more casual dining, head to the Castle's Prickly Pear bistro.

Rooms: 21. Doubles from £155, suites from £260.
Prices: Restaurant 1086 set lunch £29.50 and dinner £19.95.
Restaurant 1086 main course from £17. Prickly Pear Pizzeria main course from £4. Prickly Pear house wine £10.95.
Last orders: Food: 21.30.
Closed: Never.
Food: Modern French.
Other points: No-smoking area. Garden. Children welcome. Car park. Licence for civil weddings. Wheelchair access.
Directions: A64 JA1M, take the A64 towards York then the first left, A659, towards Tadcaster and follow the information signs to Hazlewood Castle Hotel. (Map 12, E6)

SCOTLAND

Lochs full of fresh salmon, oysters and mussels, heather to make fragrant honey, oats for the heartiest porridge, and the beefiest Angus steaks - no wonder the well-fed Scots were able to keep the English at bay.

The country is rightly proud of its natural culinary resources. While North Sea oil is the country's biggest export, its fantastic food and drink and stunning scenery continue to draw its biggest import, the tourists.

Les Routiers' membership in Scotland is particularly strong and covers the spectrum from castles to smaller cottage-style bed and breakfasts. Armed with our guide, you can stay in hotels and restaurants in the busy city centres of Glasgow and Edinburgh or places as far-flung as Balicanich in the Western Isles.

The food on offer covers the traditional and the modern, offering old favourites such as haggis, neeps 'n' tatties, cullen skink soup (a smoked-haddock soup) and cranachan (oat-and-raspberry pudding), alongside modern European delights, and Mexican, Italian, Indian and Thai dishes. If you are so inclined, you can also go out and shoot your own supper if game is your dish of choice. Scotland is a place to indulge in every sense of the word.

Ballater

The Glen Lui Hotel

Invercauld Road, Ballater, Aberdeenshire AB35 5RP
Telephone: +44(0)13397 55402
info@glen-lui-hotel.co.uk
www.glen-lui-hotel.co.uk

This smart hotel, surrounded by the Cairngorm mountains, is set in countryside favoured by royals. When you're not taking a leisurely walk in the extensive grounds or honing your handicap on Ballater golf course, lounge in the attractively refurbished public rooms. The en suite bedrooms, some of which are in nearby pine lodges, are comfortably spacious and decorated in neutral colours. Beds are tastefully accessorised with tartan rugs. On the menu, you'll find locally sourced ingredients, many from the same producers who supply the Queen at Balmoral. Head chef Watson McNeill uses prime local game, fish from Aberdeen and local seasonal soft fruits. Start with the chef's special of fresh asparagus with smoked salmon gravadlax style, or the daring haggis, neeps 'n' tattie samosas, before moving on to a main course of tender roast best end of Scotch lamb set on black pudding mash with an Arran mustard-and-whisky sauce or pan-seared sea bass fillets. Fans of sticky toffee pudding will appreciate the generous lashings of caramel sauce on McNeill's version. The wine list takes an international view, and offers many by the half bottle. From November to March, the hotel's holds wine tastings and gourmet five-course meals.

Rooms: 19. Double from £43.33 per person per night, single from £53. Seasonal price variations.
Prices: Restaurant main course from £11.50. House wine £9.99.
Last orders: Food: lunch 14.00; dinner 21.00.
Closed: Never.
Food: Modern Scottish.
Other points: No-smoking area. Children welcome. Dogs welcome overnight. Car park.
Directions: Off the A93 in Ballater. (Map 14, A7)

Ballater

The Station Restaurant

Station Square, Ballater, Aberdeenshire AB35 5RB
Telephone: +44(0)13397 55050

You can't fail to be bowled over by the tasteful regeneration of this once almost derelict station, which was the arrival point for visiting royals from the 1860s until its closure in 1966. After major structural restoration, hotelier and railway enthusiast Nigel Franks revamped these refreshment rooms, transforming them into an informal restaurant, but staying true to the spirit of the place. The setting has a period, film-set feel thanks to the fact many of the original features, such as stunning wood panelling and a smoked glass ceiling, are still in place. These are tastefully offset by Lloyd Loom wicker chairs and marble tables. The food, mainly locally sourced ingredients, puts your average station snacks well and truly into the sidings. Breakfasts offer real indulgences, either Scottish porridge with honey and cream, French toast with cinnamon sugar, banana, maple syrup and mascarpone or the full Scottish monty. Later in the day, eat like a king on the home-made cakes, scones and caramel shortbread. Lighter dishes of soup, sweetcorn fritters with bacon, roasted tomatoes and rocket and specials are a delight. Make time to visit the Station Museum next door, with its interesting exhibits about the history of the royal train, Balmoral Castle six miles away, and the miles of beautiful Highland countryside.

Prices: Restaurant main course from £6. House wine £12.
Last orders: Food: lunch 17.00; dinner 21.00. Seasonal variations.
Closed: Rarely.
Food: Traditional and Modern Scottish.
Other points: Totally no smoking. Children welcome. Car park.
Directions: In central Ballater, the old royal station. (Map 16, F7)

Auchmithie

The But 'n' Ben

Auchmithie, by Arbroath, Angus DD11 5SQ
Telephone: +44(0)1241 877223

If you want to sample the flavours of Scotland, just one meal here would give you a taster of what's so good about the indigenous ingredients. Margaret Horn's menu is unpretentious and she presents her dishes beautifully. The restaurant in the village of Auchmithie is in two fisherman's cottages knocked into one to form a lounge bar and dining area. As you enter directly from the street at Number 2, you are struck by the cosy and friendly atmosphere, which could be straight out of a Bill Forsyth film. Linger in the lounge over the menu before heading through to dine, where the ambience is just as welcoming. There's a real wood fire at one end and the furniture is rustic country-pine style. Lunch focuses on the excellent local seafood of lobster, crabs, prawns and langoustines, supplemented by game and Aberdeen Angus beef. At dinner, dishes become more lavish with chicken with prawns flambéed in brandy and served in a cream sauce or medallions of venison pan-fried with red rowan jelly and juniper berries. After dinner, sample whiskies from the 45-strong collection. Margaret also serves a mean homebaked afternoon tea, which is a real treat.

Prices: Restaurant main course from £8. House wine £10.
Last orders: Food: lunch 14.30; dinner 21.30. High teas served between 16.00 and 17.30.
Closed: Never.
Food: Traditional Scottish.
Other points: Totally no smoking. Children welcome. Car park.
Directions: From Arbroath, head north towards Montrose on the A92. Approaching Arbroath, look for signs to Authmithie on the right. The But 'n' Ben is on the left in the middle of the village. (Map 14, B8)

Arrochar

Greenbank Guest House

Arrochar, Argyll & Bute G83 7AL
Telephone: +44(0)1301 702305
shirleyandsam@cluer101.freeserve.co.uk

This compact 19th-century house makes for a cosy and comfortable stay. Set in the centre of Arrochar, it positions you right in the middle of the action, which amounts to a bustling trade in summer and a more peaceful and sedate pace in winter. You can't fault the bedrooms, which are well maintained. The four en suite rooms are comfortable and homely, and the views from some are wonderful, taking in the famous Cobbler Mountain as well as Loch Long. Downstairs it's a pleasure to linger in the welcoming lounge and bar areas. Food is available all day in the dining room, with a series of menus ranging from snacks and light lunches to a full carte. Scotch broth, mussels from the Isle of Mull, and fried Loch Fyne herring in oatmeal, and haggis and neeps are among the typical choices, and showcase the wealth of ingredients available locally.

Rooms: 4. Double room from £37, single from £22 including breakfast.
Prices: Set lunch and dinner £10.95. Main course from £7. House wine £9.95.
Last orders: Food: 20.00 November-March (22.00 March-November).
Closed: Rarely.
Food: Traditional Scottish and seafood.
Other points: No-smoking area. Children welcome. Garden. Car park. Licence for civil weddings.
Directions: On the A83, opposite Cobbler Mountain. (Map 14, C5)

Cardross

Ardardan Estate Farm Shop & Nursery

Cardross, Argyll & Bute G82 5HD
Telephone: +44(0)1389 849188
enquiries@ardardan.co.uk
www.ardardan.co.uk

This nursery and farm shop occupies a beautiful spot on the west coast of Scotland, just 10 miles west of Glasgow, and it's worth visiting for this reason alone, even before you take into consideration the stunning array of produce they sell. It's run by the Montgomery family (above), who stock the shop with a bountiful selection of fresh produce from their farm's 120 acres, plus homemade cakes and breads and much more besides. Aberdeen Angus beef and wonderful grocery lines, from cheeses to preserves, make up a delicious array of Scottish produce. By popular demand, the family has opened a teashop that showcases its homemade soups and light lunches, as well its wonderful home-baking. After refreshments, head out to the nursery set in a walled garden with a plant house where they stock a comprehensive array of plants. There are experienced staff on hand to help with garden and planting advice, who are also specialists on hardy perennials.

Last orders: Teashop 16.00, shop 17.00.
Closed: Rarely.
Food: Light lunches and home-baking.
Other points: Totally no smoking. Children welcome. Garden. Car park. Wheelchair access.
Directions: On the M8, head over the Erskine Bridge. Two miles from Cardross on the A814 towards Helensburgh. (Map 14, C5)

Isle of Bute

Russian Tavern at The Port Royal Hotel

37 Marine Road, Kames Bay, Port Bannatynne,
Argyll & Bute PA20 0LW
Telephone: +44(0)1700 505073
stay@butehotel.com
www.russiantavern.co.uk

Norwegian-born landlord Dag Crawford and his Russian wife Olga have won much deserved praise for their 'Russian Tsarist tavern' in the pretty village of Port Bannatyne. The stone-built Georgian building overlooks the stunning Kames Bay, where fishermen catch the fish and langoustines that feature on the menu. Dag cooks a Russian-style brasserie menu, after researching recipes from the Tsarist kitchen archives in St Petersburg, but using local fish, beef from Orkney and vegetables and salad from his garden. His beef stroganoff is outstanding, but gets strong competition from blinis with marinated herring, and spicy Russian sausage served with apple, latkas, red cabbage and sauerkraut. Dinner is remarkably good value, consisting of, say, langoustine soup, then halibut steak in cream and white wine sauce with accompaniments, followed by Russian Pavlova. They excel in real ales, and won CAMRA Scottish pub of the Year 2005, or there's Russian stout. There are five unpretentious, good-value bedrooms.

Rooms: 5, 3 not en suite. Room from £22 per person, £26 for an en suite.
Prices: Set lunch and dinner £20. Main course £18. Bar main course from £5.50. House wine £5 per pint.
Last orders: Bar: 01.00 (Saturday 02.00).
Closed: 1-28 November.
Food: Traditional Russian.
Other points: Totally no smoking. Children welcome. Dogs welcome in the bar. Car park. Five free yacht moorings. Beach. Golf course at the rear. Wheelchair access.
Directions: Three miles north along the coast road from the Rothesay ferry on the Isle of Bute and six miles south on the coast road from the ferry at Colintraive, Argyll. (Map 13, C4)

Luss

Coach House Coffee Shop

Loch Lomond Trading Co Ltd, Luss, Loch Lomond,
Loch Lomond Trossachs National Park,
Argyll & Bute G83 8NN
Telephone: +44(0)1436 860341
enquiries@lochlomondtrading.com
www.lochlomondtrading.com

Set in the centre of one of the most visited villages on the banks of Loch Lomond, this shop and coffee shop draws the crowds all day, but manages the high demand efficiently. Although it looks like an old-style coaching house, this is, in fact, a new building with traditional-style exposed beams and a rustic stone fireplace. It's a friendly stop-off, offering light refreshments and substantial meals along the regional speciality line. The kilted Gary Grove and his wife Rowena (above) make you feel welcome and ensure an ever-revolving line-up of treats. The bedrocks of the menu include scones, caramel apple granny or Skeachan fruit cakes, light lunches of homebaked quiche with coleslaw, salad and fresh bread, or stokies (traditional soft bread rolls) filled with egg mayonnaise from their own free-range Black Rock hens. Haggis, neeps and tatties, and bacon and courgette pasta are the more filling lunch dishes, and they don't stint on the portions. The choice of beverages such as cappuccinos and lattes, speciality teas and smoothies is long enough to require a separate menu, although you won't find any whisky-liqueur coffees here, as they don't have a licence. If you don't get a chance to try their fruity whisky cakes, buy some from the well-stocked shop to take home.

Prices: Meals from £6.
Last orders: Food: 17.00.
Closed: 25 December.
Food: Modern Scottish.
Other points: Totally no smoking. Children welcome. Garden. Wheelchair access.
Directions: From the A82, follow the signs for Luss. The café is next to the church in the centre of the village. (Map 14, C5)

Rothesay

Brechin's Brasserie

2 Bridgend Street, Rothesay, Isle of Bute,
Argyll & Bute PA20 0HU
Telephone: +44(0)1700 502922
info@brechins-bute.com
www.brechins-bute.com

Owners Tim Saul and Ann Council spotted a gap in the market for an upmarket brasserie in this bustling town, and have not looked back since opening Brechin's. Their brightly coloured lemon-and-blue brasserie is a cheery addition to the Rothesay landscape. Much of the success of their popular menus is down to the quality local ingredients used in the breakfast, snacks and hot meals available throughout the day. On Fridays and Saturdays, they also offer an evening restaurant menu. Ann is in charge of the kitchen, while Tim sees to front of house. Lattes, cappuccinos and Americanos make great accompaniments for the luscious French pastries and puds, while filled ciabatta, salads and hot dishes such as steak and Guinness pie, vegetable lasagne and a curry bowl are ideal for lunch. At dinner, the menu features smoked trout and salmon from Ritchie's of Rothesay, Isle of Bute lamb, steak and beef from Richard H McIntyre of Rothesay and Isle of Bute cream and milk. These ingredients translate into seafood bisque or king prawns, followed by tournedos Highlander, with crème brulée to finish. The short wine list has classics at reasonable prices.

Prices: Restaurant evening main course from £7.95. Lunchtime snack from £4.95. House wine £9.95.
Last orders: Food: lunch 15.00; dinner 21.00
(Fridays and Saturdays only).
Closed: Sunday, Monday all day. Tuesday to Thursday evening.
Food: Traditional Scottish, English and continental dishes.
Other points: Totally no smoking. Children welcome.
Wheelchair access.
Directions: By road to Wemyss Bay and by Calmac Ferry to Rothesay. Situated in the town centre 400m from the ferry terminal and marina. (Map 13, C4)

Tobermory

Fisherman's Pier Fish and Chip Van

Raraig House, Tobermory, Argyll & Bute PA75 6PU
Telephone: +44(0)1688 302390
jeanette@scotshop.biz
www.silverswift.co.uk/van.htm

Jeanette Gallagher and Jane MacLean's smart black-and-gold takeaway fish and chip van on Fisherman's Pier serves stupendously good fish and chips in a superb location. Their takeaway occupies an amazing position overlooking Tobermory Bay, a spot famous for the sinking of a galleon from the Spanish Armada in 1588. After sightseeing round the island or visiting the nearby Tobermory Distillery, this is the perfect place to stop for lunch or supper. The two friends are into their second decade of trading and have built up a loyal following of regular customers who come from miles around. Park up at the Clock Tower or on the lobster/prawn creels on the Pier before ordering your meal, which is freshly prepared in no time. Fish comes straight off the boats and into the van, where it is cooked to order. Haddock, for example, is supplied by Taste of Argyll, Oban, while the freshest local scallops are supplied by Grampian Seafood off its fishing vessel Western Belle, which is skippered by Jeanette's son Geoffrey. Come rain or shine, the queues are long, but always good humoured, there's plenty of banter from the double act. Fish and chunky-cut chips have never tasted so good.

Prices: From £3.80.
Last orders: Food: 21.00.
Closed: Sundays and January-March.
Food: Seafood.
Directions: On the Fisherman's Pier in Tobermory. (Map 13, B3)

Tobermory

Highland Cottage

Breadalbane Street, Tobermory, Argyll & Bute PA75 6PD
Telephone: +44(0)1688 302030
davidandjo@highlandcottage.co.uk
www.highlandcottage.co.uk

It may be set in a cottage, but this Highland accommodation has the feel of a luxury hotel. The cream-painted terrace is distinctive from the entrance, a black-timber canopy over the door with Victorian coach lights either side, and its period charm continues inside. A comfortable lounge in a conservatory is great for relaxing, while dinner is served in the attractive dining room, where the smartly dressed tables are set with cut-glass crystal and linen tablecloths. Dishes include local specialities and start with, say, Tobermory smoked salmon and trout roulade or Croig crab cakes with a tomato and chilli sauce before moving on to mains of pan-fried fillet of salmon or roast saddle of Ardnamurchan venison. Puddings are the hearty sort; crumble and pies. David and Jo Currie have a table licence and dispense other drinks on an honesty basis from an oak dresser. The level of accommodation is excellent and the six en suite rooms have superior beds, hospitality trays, DVD players and white fluffy robes. The Curries have an excellent eye for detail, which, coupled with their hospitality, makes staying here pleasure and a treat.

Rooms: 6. Double/twin from £120, single from £96.
Prices: Set dinner £35 (five courses). House wine £14.50.
Last orders: Bar: Dinner 21.00.
Closed: November-February.
Food: Modern Scottish with an international twist.
Other points: Totally no-smoking. Children over 10 welcome. Dogs welcome. Garden. Car park. Wheelchair access.
Directions: From the main ferry port of Craignure, head for Tobermory (approx 25 minutes). On approaching Tobermory, at the mini roundabout, go straight across the narrow stone bridge and immediately turn right. Keep going until you see Highland Cottage opposite the Fire Station. (Map 13, B3)

...for special offers

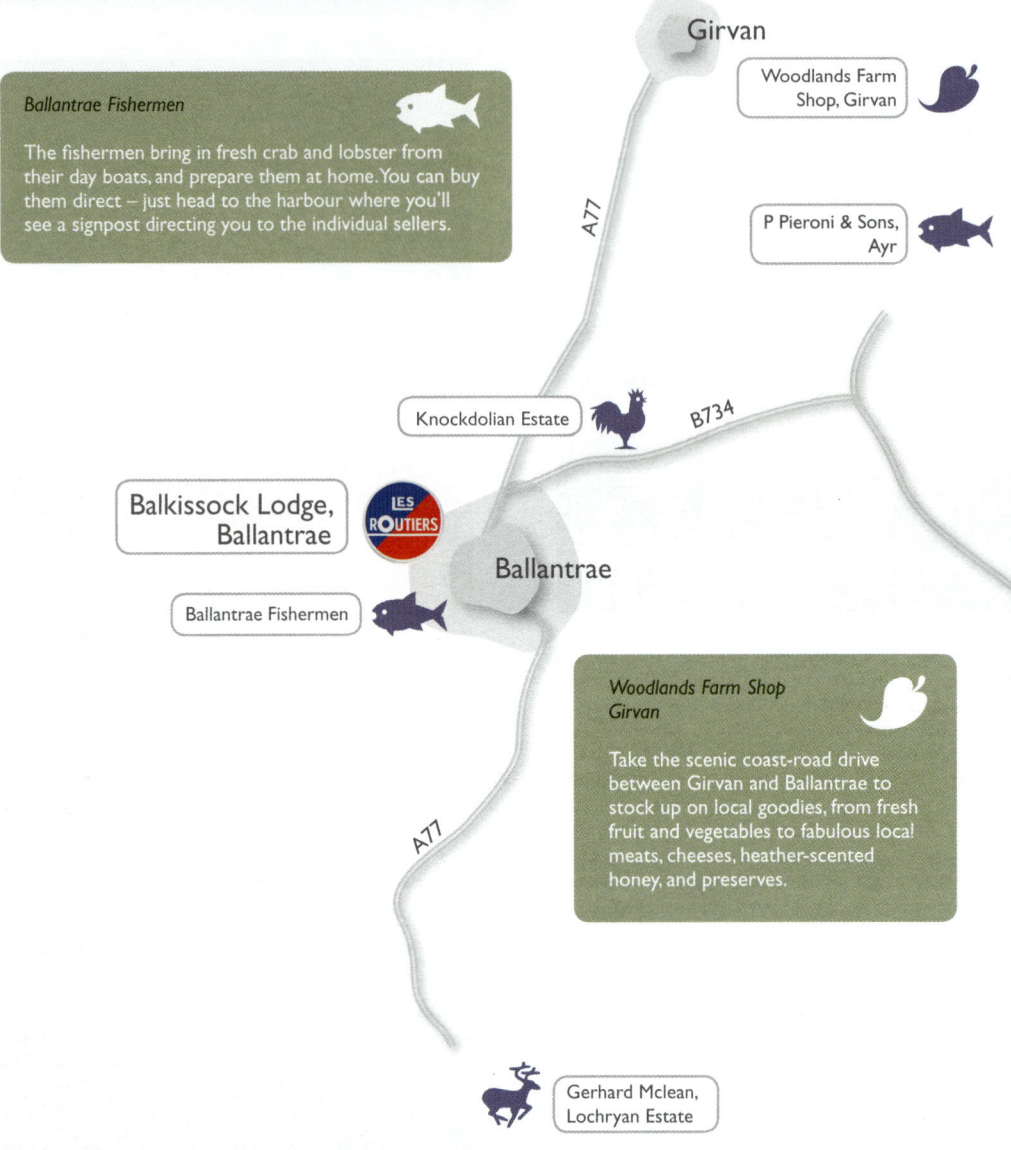

Girvan

Ballantrae Fishermen

The fishermen bring in fresh crab and lobster from their day boats, and prepare them at home. You can buy them direct – just head to the harbour where you'll see a signpost directing you to the individual sellers.

A77

Woodlands Farm Shop, Girvan

P Pieroni & Sons, Ayr

Knockdolian Estate

B734

Balkissock Lodge, Ballantrae

LES ROUTIERS

Ballantrae

Ballantrae Fishermen

Woodlands Farm Shop Girvan

Take the scenic coast-road drive between Girvan and Ballantrae to stock up on local goodies, from fresh fruit and vegetables to fabulous local meats, cheeses, heather-scented honey, and preserves.

A77

Gerhard Mclean, Lochryan Estate

Balkissock Lodge, Ballantrae

Fran Sweeney serves traditional Scottish dishes at her bed and breakfast. As well as devising her own recipes, Fran sources some top-notch local ingredients, and her fabulous cheeseboard is a prime example. It features cheeses made at Kinfauns Farm, which include Bishop Kennedy, a whisky-washed brie-style cheese, and a soft, creamy and wonderfully ripe Scottish camembert. Both are rich, so Fran serves them without butter and with her homemade oatcakes.

Visit the local Farmers' Market

Ayr farmers' market is held on the first Saturday of the month at River St, Ayr. Stallholders offer an array of local produce, including meat, fish, cheeses, honey, preserves, fruits, home-baking, confectionery, Hebridean whisky liqueurs and plants. For details, call 01655 770217, or visit www.scottishfarmersmarkets.co.uk.

Kinfauns Farm, Perth & Kinross

Kinfauns Farm
Perth & Kinross

Franpiles her cheeseboard high with Kinfauns' fabulous cheeses, notably Bishop Kennedy, Howgate Camembert, and Ayrshire blue cheeses. You can buy these from The Tryst Farm Shop (26 West High Street, Crieff or online at www.the-tryst.co.uk).

A714

B7027

Newton Stewart

Galloway Smokehouse
Carsluith, Newton Stewart
Tel: 01671 820354

Apart from its popular smoked Scottish salmon, trout, seafood and game are first salted and then gently smoked with whisky-cask sawdust at Galloway Smokehouse for a gentle, yet distinctive flavour. Both hot-and-cold smoked foods are available at the smokehouse shop. The company also offers free delivery on hampers to within the UK.

 Galloway Smokehouse, Newton Stewart

A75

Ballantrae

Balkissock Lodge

Ballantrae, Girvan, South Ayrshire KA26 0LP
Telephone: +44(0)1465 831537
franaden@aol.com
www.balkissocklodge.co.uk

In its other guises, Balkissock has been a shooting lodge and farm, but it now more than fulfills its remit as an attractive guest house. Fresh country air and peaceful contemplation in comfortable surroundings, plus a warm welcome from hospitable hosts Denis and Fran Sweeney, are guaranteed. The lounge is stylishly decorated in cream with comfy sofas, cushions and throws, and a real fire creates a warm glow in winter. Fran has designed the three bedrooms to the same high standards. The largest has an adjoining room and is perfect for families, while the other two are in the adjoining barn. Each has en suite facilities and comes with extras such as TV, hairdryer, beverage tray and mini fridge. Breakfast in the separate dining room offers the best of Scottish fare, including porridge and smoked salmon and scrambled eggs. At dinner, the Sweeneys share the cooking, for which they have a real flair. Fran makes the starters and puddings, which may include king scallops with a hazelnut-and-herb butter, and sticky apple cake with an elderflower cream, while Denis cooks the mains using local ingredients, for example, pheasant in a cider-apple cream sauce and wild mushrooms.

_____

Rooms: 4. Double room from £29, single from £39 and family from £85. Prices are per person.
Prices: Set dinner £20.
Last orders: Dinner served at 19.00.
Closed: Rarely.
Food: Modern British.
Other points: Totally no smoking. Garden. Car park.
Directions: Three miles off the A77 near Ballantrae. On the south side of Ballantrae, take the turn signposted to the camp site. At the T-junction turn right, bear left at the fork and continue for one mile. The Lodge is on the right. (Map 13, E4)

www.routiers.co.uk

Castle Douglas

Craigadam

Castle Douglas, Dumfries and Galloway DG7 3HU
Telephone: +44(0)1556 650233
enquiry@craigadam.com
www.craigadam.com

Surrounded by its country estate of 25,000 acres of farmland, woodland and moorland, there are plenty of shooting, stalking and fishing opportunities at this 300-year-old farmhouse. Cecilia Pickup runs Craigadam as a charming guesthouse, but with the space, style and service of a country-house hotel, while husband Richard runs the farm along organic lines and organises shooting parties. The dedication they bring to their farm business is extended to the welcome they afford guests, who benefit from the attention to detail from the dinner table to the bedrooms. Dinner is served house-party style around a massive communal table in the oak-panelled dining room, which has an honesty bar and snooker table. Locally smoked salmon, home-reared lamb, or estate game, with home-grown vegetables, homebaked bread and regional cheeses make for a fine meal. All seven en suite bedrooms are decorated in different themes, are generously proportioned and beautifully furnished; many have french doors opening onto a gravelled courtyard. There is also a three-bedroom self-catering cottage.

Rooms: 7. Double/twin room from £76, single from £45 per person.
Prices: Set dinner £19 served at 19.00. House wine £9.95.
Closed: 24 December-2 January.
Food: Scottish.
Other points: No-smoking area. Children welcome. Dogs welcome. Garden. Car park.
Directions: M74. Leave the motorway on the A75 to Dumfries. Follow the signs to Castle Douglas, then, after nine miles go through the village of Crocketford and turn right on the A712. Craigadam is two miles along on the right. (Map 14, F6)

Gretna

Garden House Hotel

Sarkfoot Road, Gretna,
Dumfries and Galloway DG16 5EP
Telephone: +44(0)1461 337621
enquiries@gardenhouse.co.uk

The Garden House is firmly on the Gretna weddings map. Its elegant setting, lovely grounds with a Japanese water garden and stylish suites make it an appealing choice for wedding parties and honeymooners. However, its spacious, well-equipped bedrooms, offering good value for money and the Sark Leisure Club with a state-of-the-art 15-metre swimming pool, sauna and steam room, will appeal just as much to travellers in general. Families, in particular, will find the hotel a useful stopping-off point on a journey north or south. As well as large honeymoon suites with super-king size beds, there are 38 spacious en suite bedrooms with satellite TV, hairdryers and coffee-making facilities. The lounge and dining room are bright and open plan. In the latter, a traditional country-house menu delivers something for everyone. Meals range from salads, such as Waldorf and Caesar, to meats from the chargrill, fillet steak with crushed black peppercorn sauce, rack of lamb with redcurrant sauce. Fish dishes include lemon sole with basil and herb butter and Solway salmon steak with a lemon-and-herb crust. Around 80 or so wines offer a good choice and at good prices.

Rooms: 38. Rooms from £42.50 per person.
Prices: Main course from £11. House wine £8.25.
Last orders: Food: lunch 14.00; dinner 21.00.
Closed: Rarely.
Food: Modern British
Other points: Children welcome. Garden. Car park. Licence for civil weddings.
Directions: On the A74, just across the Scottish border. (Map 14, F7)

...for the latest news

Edinburgh

40a Heriot Row

40a Heriot Row, Edinburgh EH3 6ES
Telephone: +44 (0)131 226 2068
diane@heriotrow.com
www.heriotrow.com

Rooms in this Georgian garden flat B&B are on a par with smart upmarket hotels. It's conveniently placed just minutes from Princes Street, so you have the city centre on the doorstep. The attention to detail and style is exemplary throughout, and the accommodation over two light and airy levels is spacious and tastefully done. The long, light hallway leads to a large beautifully furnished drawing room with wall-to-wall bookcases and antiques. This is the ideal place to relax in the evening over a complimentary glass of whisky. One bedroom, a twin, is on this floor, which is a lovely cosy room with an en suite shower room, and the second en suite bedroom is on the lower-ground floor. Both rooms have tea trays, mineral water and a little decanter of whisky. The dining room is also on the lower level, making use of the old cellar. It is decorated with painted stone walls, bookcases covering one wall, light cream paintwork, an antique dining table and sideboard. Here, Diane Rae serves breakfast, using as much homemade produce as possible; the local butcher and fishmonger supply sausages, bacon, and kippers. There's a tiny patio filled with exotic and unusual plants and across the road is the 3-4 acre private Queen Street Garden, to which guests have access. This B&B is a real gem, and cat lovers will be enchanted by the resident felines.

Rooms: 2. Double room from £50 per person, single from £60.
Closed: Rarely.
Food: Traditional Scottish.
Other points: No-smoking area. Garden. Children welcome.
Directions: From Princes Street, turn left at Frederick Street and then left after the gardens. 40a is at the end of the block on the right. (Map 14, C7)

Edinburgh

The Blue Parrot Cantina

49 St Stephen Street, Edinburgh EH3 5AH
Telephone: +44(0)131 225 2941
blueparrot@blueyonder.co.uk

In the bustling Stockbridge area of the city, this small, colourful and exotic restaurant is as popular as ever. With only nine tables in the basement, the dining room is either intimate and cosy – usually midweek – or absolutely buzzing at weekends. It's attractively decorated with dark blue and red walls, wooden floors, chunky wooden tables and chairs and iron wall-candle sconces. This is Mexican food at its best. And the clientele obviously think so as, by popular demand, the menu rarely changes. Fiona Macrae doesn't serve the usual suspects, such as chilli con carne or tacos, but offers starters of homemade bean and vegetable soup or seafood ceviche marinated with lime and orange juice with cold avocado, chilli and coriander. Mains include steak fajitas, burritos and enchiladas. To finish, it's hard to resist the chocolate fudge cake or pecan pie. Drinks are a colourful collection of Mexican beers, margaritas, of course, an impressive range of tequila, plus a tasty bunch of New and Old World wines.

Prices: Main course from £8.05. House wine £10.15.
Last orders: Food: 22.30 (Friday and Saturday 23.00).
Closed: Monday-Friday lunch, Sunday lunch and all day Tuesday apart from August and December.
Food: Modern Mexican.
Other points: Smoking throughout.
Directions: In the centre of Edinburgh. (Map 14, C7)

Edinburgh

Britannia Spice

150 Commercial Street, Britannia Way, Leith,
Edinburgh EH6 6LB
Telephone: +44(0)131 5552255
info@britanniaspice.co.uk
www.britanniaspice.co.uk

Its contemporary interiors, a trendy Leith Docks address and an ever-evolving menu puts this exotic restaurant in a league of its own. The royal yacht Britannia is docked nearby, hence the name of this restaurant set in an attractive converted whisky bond. Due to its lofty proportions, the dining room is open plan, yet offers an intimate feel at the same time. The nautically themed room combines blond wood tables, dark blue chairs, with sunken ceiling spots, creating a sense of light and space. The restaurant has many supporters, and this could be down to its varied menu, which explores northern Indian, Bangladeshi, Nepalese and Thai cuisines. It is constantly changing, with new dishes added every few weeks. From Nepal comes spicy trout roasted with fried mushrooms, tomatoes, green chilli, mustard seeds and fresh herbs, with its counterpart from Bangladesh of freshwater fish marinated in spices and herbs. Thailand supplies a popular green curry of chicken or there's chicken kebab with hot spices and a ginger-based sauce with fresh coriander from North India. There's also tikka masala in chicken, lamb and prawn versions, as well as biryanis, and a decent selection of vegetarian dishes. The wine list offers a balanced variety from European vineyards and the New World.

Prices: Main course from £6.95.
Last orders: Food: lunch 14.15; dinner 23.45.
No food Sunday lunch.
Closed: Rarely.
Food: Indian and Thai.
Other points: No-smoking area. Children welcome. Car park.
Directions: In Leith, follow signs for the ocean terminal or the royal yacht Britannia. (Map 14, C7)

Edinburgh

Merchants

17 Merchant Street, Edinburgh EH1 2QD
Telephone: +44(0)131 225 4009
www.merchantsrestaurant.co.uk

Just off the main street, it's well worth the short detour to this welcoming and cheery restaurant. The attractive setting of stone walls painted bright red, a low-beamed ceiling, varnished floors, clever lighting with well-placed mirrors diffusing the light, create a cosy and intimate atmosphere. The white linen, cream napkins, white crockery and fine glassware are a sophisticated contrast, and an indication that they take their dining seriously. The set lunch and dinner menus change weekly and local and seasonal produce features prominently in the classic Scottish dishes. For dinner, you could start with an imaginative Catherine Wheel of Angus beef with an Arran mustard dressing or a more traditional salmon gravadlax. Mains offer some of the best Scottish produce, with tenderloin of Border lamb filled with a lemon farce and a garlic jus, or there's gnocchi scented with sun-dried tomatoes and red pesto for those wanting something more Mediterranean. The short wine list opens with well-priced house French wines, and prices remain under £20 throughout for most of its varied international selection.

Prices: Set lunch £12.95 and dinner £24.95.
House wine from £10.95.
Last orders: Food: lunch 14.00; dinner 22.00.
Closed: Saturday lunch and all day Sunday and 2-3 January.
Food: Modern Scottish.
Other points: Smoking throughout. Children welcome.
Wheelchair access.
Directions: In Edinburgh old town; just off the Grassmarket.
(Map 14, C7)

Edinburgh

Teviotdale House

53 Grange Loan, Edinburgh EH9 2ER
Telephone: +44(0)131 667 4376
eliza@teviotdalehouse.com
www.teviotdalehouse.com

Together Elizabeth and Willy Thiebaud (she is Scottish, he is French) have created a charming and friendly hotel, which is an excellent base for exploring the city on foot. The spacious terraced house is just 10 minutes from the city centre and provides a quiet and restful base close to the action. All the bedrooms are individually decorated and show great attention to detail. The bathrooms of the five en suites have recently been enlarged and renovated. All the rooms have co-ordinated soft furnishings, which provide an attractive finish, hot drinks trays, TVs, hairdryers, and fluffy towels. The dining room looks out of a picture window onto the back garden and is a lovely spot to start the day with a hearty Scottish breakfast. The couple provide an excellent choice of teas or herbal infusions, porridge, compote of dried fruits, prunes in nectar, free-range eggs, Ayrshire-cured bacon, homemade sausages from the local butcher, oatcakes, and homemade scones. Golfing pictures and memorabilia adorn the walls, a reminder that your hosts are happy to book golfing lessons and rounds at 20 different courses.

Rooms: 7, 2 not en suite but private facilities. Double/twin room from £31 per person, single from £41, family from £28 per person.
Closed: Rarely.
Other points: Totally no smoking. Children welcome.
Directions: A720. Leave the city bypass at Straiton junction and head towards the city centre for 2.1 miles. Fork left, down Mayfield Road for one mile. Cross the traffic lights at Mayfield church and then take the first left. (Map 14, C7)

Anstruther

The Anstruther Fish Bar

42-44 Shore Street, Anstruther, Fife KY10 3AQ
Telephone: +44(0)1333 310518
ansterfishbar@btconnect.com
www.anstrutherfishbar.co.uk

It seems fitting that two fishermen's cottages have been turned into one of the finest fish bars in Scotland. The Anstruther Fish Bar occupies the ground floor, overlooking the picturesque harbour. Its popularity with locals and tourists is down to its consistently good fish and chips, and two years running it has won a Best Fish and Chip Shop in Scotland award. The owners have their own fish-processing business in the nearby fishing village of St Monans, so have access to the freshest and best-quality seafood. People travel from miles around for its fare and, in summer months, queues outside stretch right along the street. The interiors are designed for maximum efficiency. A brass rail maintains an orderly queue for takeaways or you can sit in at two restaurant areas. Service keeps up with demand, and despite the hussle and bustle, you don't feel rushed. The star of the show is haddock, battered or breadcrumbed, but there are plenty of alternative fish. The catch-of-the-day board can include tuna, monkfish, halibut, trout, salmon, lemon sole, prawns or dressed crab. A popular non-fish choice is white pudding, a delicious mixture of oatmeal, onion and seasoning. A licence means you can also enjoy wine or beer with eat-in meals.

Prices: Set lunch £6.30. Restaurant main course from £4.50. House wine £7.50.
Last orders: Food: 22.00.
Closed: Rarely.
Food: Traditional fish and chips.
Other points: Totally no smoking. Children welcome. Public car park opposite. Wheelchair access to the restaurant.
Directions: M90. Nine miles south of St Andrews, B9131. Next to the Scottish Fisheries Museum. (Map 14, C7)

Anstruther

The Spindrift

Pittenweem Road, Anstruther, Fife KY10 3DT
Telephone: +44(0)1333 310573
info@thespindrift.co.uk
www.thespindrift.co.uk

Ken and Christine Lawson have refurbished this former sea captain's house beautifully, but have kept its nautical charm, including a large captain's cabin-style bedroom at the top of the house. As you might expect, it has lovely views of the sea over Anstruther harbour. The décor maximises the relaxed elegance of the rooms, from the comfortable lounge with honesty bar to the dining room. Eight en suite bedrooms, excluding the large cabin room, make up this well-run guesthouse. Each has TV, telephone and internet connection and tea tray. Breakfast is served buffet style, and the porridge is a top choice as Ken is a champion porridge maker. Set dinners revolve around locally sourced meat, fish and vegetables and speciality smoked products. Starters include cullen skink or smoked duck pâté with oatcakes, and are followed by mustard and honey salmon steaks or sweet pepper and gruyere lasagne. Desserts revolve around local specialities; Orkney ice cream, fruits of the forest crème brulée and Pittenweem oatcakes with cheese. There is also the opportunity to try beers from small local brewers, whiskies and Scottish liqueurs.

Rooms: 8. Double/twin room from £27.50 per person, single from £35.
Prices: Set dinner £18. House wine £10.
Closed: Christmas.
Food: Traditional Scottish.
Other points: Totally no smoking. Children over 10 welcome. Dogs welcome overnight. Car park.
Directions: Exit2A/M90. Approaching Anstruther from St Andrews, turn right at the roundabout onto Pittenweem Road, Spindrift is the last house on the right leaving the village. (Map 14, C7)

Anstruther

The Waterfront Restaurant

18-20 Shore Street, Anstruther, Fife KY10 3EA
Telephone: +44(0)1333 312200
enquiries@anstruther-waterfront.co.uk
www.anstruther-waterfront.co.uk

Just a few steps from Anstruther harbour, The Waterfront wouldn't look out of place in a city location. Its modern glass-and-timber frontage adds a stylish note to the traditional buildings on this attractive street. The contemporary theme continues inside, where the bar and restaurant décor is dark chocolate, with oak panelling and plants. Head for a table at the front for harbour views. In keeping with its location, the menu includes Scottish favourites, but also stars international choices. You can start with cullen skink or sweet chilli tiger prawns. Mains are an equally eclectic mix: calves' liver or fajitas, but it's the seafood selection that impresses the most; stuffed trout cooked in a parcel or 'canoe', king scallops, maple salmon fillet and Australian shark stand out from the comprehensive choice. Carnivores are equally spoilt with three Angus beef options – sirloin, fillet and popeseye – with a choice of sauces. The nursery puds are a treat. A short wine list keeps things simple, but caters for most tastes. Cool and contemporary guesthouse rooms and self-catering apartments complete the picture.

Rooms: 8. Double/twin from £25 per person per night.
Prices: Restaurant main course from £6.50. Snacks from £4.95. House wine £9.95.
Last orders: Food: 22.00.
Closed: Never.
Food: Modern British.
Other points: Totally no smoking. Children welcome.
Directions: Exit 3/A90(M). Take the A92 to Glenrothes and then the A911 signed to Leven, then the A917 and B942 to Pittenweem and on to Anstruther. In Anstruther, turn right at the roundabout and go down to the harbour. The Waterfront is on the left. (Map 14, C7)

Kincardine

Seasons Coffee Shop

7 Kirk Street, Kincardine-on-Forth, Fife FK10 4PT
Telephone: +44(0)1259 730720

Leslie Mitch's cosy bistro-cum-coffee shop has a friendly, homely feel. Inside this pretty whitewashed old terrace, you'll find an inviting ground-floor shop that is traditionally decorated with dark wood furniture, with seating for 24 and plenty of local crafts for sale. Home-cooked, hearty fare to eat in or take away is the mainstay of the menu. At lunchtime, Leslie and her team are kept busy dispensing coffees, of which there are many styles, and snacks to the local ladies who lunch. The menu may be somewhat limited, but what they serve, they do exceptionally well: soup, perhaps an excellent carrot and ginger, followed by a generous prawn sandwich made with chunky brown bread, or a hot panini filled with mixed salad and melted brie or hot crispy bacon, or a bacon roll or filled baguette. Cakes and homemade scones from the tempting display cabinet are irresistible, none more so than the sweet crumbly cream and fruit meringues. Wines come by the small bottle, or there are plenty of refreshing soft drinks and herbal teas.

Prices: Light snacks from £2.40.
Last orders: Food: 16.00.
Closed: Sunday, 1-4 January.
Food: Coffee shop fare, sandwiches and homemade cakes.
Other points: Totally no smoking.
Directions: In the centre of Kincardine. (Map 14, C6)

St Andrews

Inn at Lathones

By Largoward, St Andrews, Fife KY9 1JE
Telephone: +44(0)1334 840494
lathones@theinn.co.uk
www.theinn.co.uk

The ancient and modern blend perfectly at this 400-year-old former coaching inn, which is the oldest hostelry in St Andrews. Beautifully restored and extended by Nick and Jocelyn White, the inn has built up a sound reputation for fine modern food, first-class wines and stylish bedrooms. The reception has an old-fashioned shop-fronted bow windowed room that houses Nick's extensive wine cellar, while the large lounge has stone walls, a mix of leather and upholstered chairs. The dining room blends elegance with informality. Here, chef Marc Guibert offers a carte menu built around Fife's finest produce – first-class meats, fresh seafood and organic fruits and vegetables. Dinner could open with tartar of local smoked salmon and home-cured salmon, go on to canon of Highland venison, and finish with one of Marc's outstanding desserts such as crème brulée or pistachio ice cream. At lunchtimes, the good-value menu includes soup, followed by fish and chips or a pasta dish. The refurbished rooms focus on personal comfort and have goose-down duvets, entertainment systems, internet access and sparkling en suites.

Prices: Set lunch £20 and dinner from £25. Main course from £17. House wine £12.95.
Last orders: Food: lunch 14.30; dinner 21.30.
Closed: Two weeks in January.
Food: Modern European.
Other points: No smoking in the restaurant. Children welcome. Dogs welcome overnight. Garden. Car park. Licence for civil weddings. Wheelchair access (not WC).
Directions: On the A915 midway between St Andrews and Leven, 5 miles south of St Andrews. (Map 14, B7)

Glasgow

City Merchant

97-99 Candleriggs, Glasgow G1 1NP
Telephone: +44(0)141 5531577
citymerchant@btinternet.com
www.citymerchant.co.uk

There is plenty to please discerning tastes at affordable prices at this restaurant set in the part of town where wealthy merchants used to work and live. Owner Tony Matteo has perfected his Scottish-themed menus and focuses on quality fish. Langoustines, mussels and oysters all come from local suppliers and are either simply cooked or feature in more sophisticated dishes. On the daily fixed-price set menu, available until 6.30pm, you'll find scallop and crayfish bisque, and prawn and smoked salmon timbales to start, with mains of pan-seared hake with Thai green curry sauce or braised lamb shoulder. Meat is supplied by Macbeths of Forres, which comes with the stamp of approval of Quality Meat Scotland, so you get enjoy steak on both the set and carte menus. The latter delivers the fancier fare: fish soup, seared king scallops and a magnificent Scottish seafood platter. Scottish stalwart haggis, neeps and tatties is also a fixture, and game is served in season. Scottish puds of Cranachan ice cream with Atoll brose served with homemade shortbread or a clootie dumpling with whisky-and-oatmeal ice cream are real treats. The extensive wine list offers classics at fair prices.

Prices: Set lunch £13. Main course £7.50. House wine £12.75.
Last orders: Food: 22.30.
Closed: Sunday.
Food: Modern Scottish and seafood.
Other points: No-smoking area. Children welcome.
Wheelchair access.
Directions: Take exit 15, east- or west-bound on the M8 and follow signs for Glasgow Cross. Turn right into Ingram Street, then second left into Candleriggs. Number 97 is situated on the right, opposite City Halls. (Map 14, C5)

Glasgow

La Parmigiana

447 Great Western Road, Glasgow G12 8HH
Telephone: +44(0)141 334 0686
s.giovanazzi@btclick.com
www.laparmigiana.co.uk

This popular and elegant restaurant near Glasgow's West End has a well-earned reputation for fine food. In fact, they do everything well here, from the purple leather-bound menus to the impeccable service. Given the small size of the kitchen, the menu is sensibly pared down and changes quarterly, drawing on what's in season. Regulars prefer that Sandro Giovanazzi sticks to favourite dishes and they resist too much change on the menu. Popular favourites to start include lobster ravioli with cream and basil, beef carpaccio with parmesan shavings and rocket salad, or chargrilled Minch scallops with lemon and olive oil. The excellent mains include escalope of veal with Parma ham, mozzarella and tomato, or risotto with porcini mushrooms, Parmesan and cream. Fish is also a reliable bet, perhaps zuppa of mixed fish and shellfish with bruschetta. Finish with crème brûlée with Calvados and caramelised apples or a traditional tiramisù. Set-price menus at lunch and dinner are very good value. The wine list offers a good selection of Italian favourites, from a prosecco aperitivo to Tuscan vin santo for dessert, with much to tempt in between.

Prices: Set lunch £9.50 and dinner £12.50. Restaurant main course from £13.50. House wine £12.50.
Last orders: Food: lunch 14.30; dinner 23.00.
Closed: Easter Monday.
Food: Italian
Other points: Totally no smoking. Children welcome.
Directions: Exit18/M8. Follow signs for West End along Great Western Road and over Kelvinbridge and La Parmigiana is on the left. (Map 14, C5)

Altnaharra

Altnaharra Hotel

By Lairg, Altnaharra, Highland IV27 4UE
Telephone: +44(0)1549 411222
altnaharra@btinternet.com
www.altnaharra.com

The remoteness of this hotel makes it ideal as a Highland retreat. While it's fabulous to sit back and admire the surrounding views of spectacular mountains and lochs, Altnaharra has another trump card up its sleeve. It is regarded as one of the best-located hotels for salmon and trout fishing in the Highlands, and it is one of the oldest. It offers a truly comprehensive range of fishing options, but there's as much of a welcome for locals and non-sporting visitors as there is for those who come mainly to fly fish and shoot game on neighbouring estates. The several public areas, bar, lounge and library are welcoming, with open fires, comfortable seating, flowers, plants, and fishing memorabilia. The hotel is open throughout the day and will happily provide light refreshments or meals, and the superb daily-changing limited-choice dinner menu features locally sourced meat and game. Start with partridge breast with a redcurrant and port jus or smoked salmon with crispy salad and capers, then enjoy fillet of Aberdeen Angus or seared scallops, and finish Scottish style with an orange-and-whisky cheesecake. The spacious bedrooms are en suite and freshly decorated.

Rooms: 15. Rooms from £45 per person.
Prices: Set dinner £40 (5 courses). House wine £14.50.
Last orders: Food: 21.30 (flexible).
Closed: Rarely.
Food: Modern Scottish.
Other points: No-smoking area. Children welcome.
Dogs welcome overnight. Garden. Car park.
Directions: From Inverness, take the A9 for Wick. At Bonar Bridge, follow the A836 towards Tongue. The hotel is situated between Lairg and Tongue. (Map 16, C5)

Boat of Garten

Old Ferryman's House

Nethy Bridge Road, Boat of Garten, Highland PH24 3BY
Telephone: +44(0)1479 831370

It may be one of the smallest establishments in Les Routiers, but you'll enjoy a big, friendly welcome at this B&B, run with some style by Elizabeth Matthews. The traditional stone-built former ferryman's cottage is just across the River Spey from Boat of Garten and is a relaxing setting. The cottage has a homely feel throughout. There's a comfortable sitting room filled with flowers, books and magazines and warmed by a wood-burning stove, three pine-furnished bedrooms and a large bathroom. The dining room backs on to a lovely enclosed garden of cottage-garden flowers. No TV is a bonus for those wanting a quiet, getaway-from-it-all break, as are flexible breakfast times, which are a hearty traditional Scottish affair of grill-up with homemade bread, kippers, Scotch pancakes or kedgeree. Another bonus is the afternoon tea of bran tea breads, shortbread and flapjacks included in the B&B price. Residents also eat well at dinner, starting with, say, smoked venison and homemade mayonnaise, or cullen skink, followed by wild venison stroganoff, or organic Gloucester Old spot pork, with herbs, vegetable and salad leaves from the garden in season. Fabulous puds include rhubarb-and-banana crumble and baked apples with heather honey.

Rooms: 4. 2 double/twin rooms from £46, 2 singles from £23.
Prices: Set-price dinner £17.50.
Closed: Ring to check.
Food: Modern Scottish.
Other points: Totally no smoking. Children welcome. Dogs welcome overnight. Garden. Car park. Credit cards not accepted.
Directions: Follow the main road through Boat of Garten and across the River Spey; the house is immediately on the right. (Map 16, F6)

Glencoe

The Clachaig Inn

Glencoe, Highland PH49 4HX
Telephone: +44(0)1855 811252
inn@clachaig.com
www.clachaig.com

Set in the heart of Glencoe, this 300-year-old inn is a favourite haunt of mountaineers and walkers. It has a lively atmosphere and is an activity centre in itself, offering mountain-bike hire, mountaineering courses and live folk music on Saturdays. Huge log fires provide a roaring welcome in the cosy, wood-floored lounge bar, and in the rustic, stone-flagged Boots Bar. In the latter, booted walkers can take refuge and enjoy refreshments at a bar dispensing six Highland micro-brewery ales and 120 malt whiskies. The traditional pub food served in generous portions is perfect following a bracing walk, and can be enjoyed in the three bars or restaurant. The choice ranges from filled baguettes and pasta dishes to venison casserole and chargrilled steaks. If you want to sample something local, make room for the homemade ecclefechan tart. Refurbished bedrooms are split between the main house and chalet-style rooms to the rear.

Rooms: 23. Double room from £30, prices per person per night.
Prices: Main course from £5.85.
House wine from £8.25.
Last orders: Bar: 23.00 (Friday 24.00, Saturday 23.30).
Food: 21.00.
Closed: Rarely.
Food: Scottish, American and Mexican.
Other points: No-smoking area. Children welcome.
Dogs welcome overnight. Garden. Car park. Bike shed.
Wheelchair access to the restaurant/pub.
Directions: Located in the heart of Glencoe, just off the A82 Glasgow to Fort William Road. (Map 13, A4)

Grantown-on-Spey

Tigh-na-Sgiath Country House Hotel

Skye of Curr, Dulnain Bridge, By Grantown on Spey, Highland PH26 3PA
Telephone: +44(0)1479 851345
iain@tigh-na-sgiath.co.uk
www.tigh-na-sgiath.co.uk

This elegant house has an interesting history. Built by a rich shipping family in 1902, it was bought by the Lipton tea family, who owned it until the 1940s before it passed to the Hartley jam family, eventually becoming a hotel in 1969. While its exterior is baronial Victorian, inside it is more evocative of the 1920s. The many original features, from stone fireplaces and oak panelling to a fine staircase, create a stylish and comfortable atmosphere. The six bedrooms are tastefully decorated and well appointed. Only one is not en suite, but has its own Art Deco bathroom across the corridor. Owners Mr and Mrs MacDonald-Coulter provide genteel hospitality and superb Scottish cuisine. Elaine MacDonald-Coulter leads the kitchen, offering classic dishes from home-produced ingredients, such as Shetland salmon, Highland lamb, beef and game. The four-course set menu offers cream of apple and parsley soup, oven-roasted leg of lamb, pan-fried Aberdeen Angus sirloin and an indulgent array of puddings. The wine list picks off interesting choices from Mexico and New Zealand. Head to the bar to sample one of the 90 malt whiskies on offer.

Rooms: 7. Double/twin from £40 (one not ensuite).
Prices: Set dinner £29.50 (four courses). House wine £16.50.
Last orders: Bar: 23.00. Food: 21.30.
Closed: December and January.
Food: Traditional Scottish with a modern style.
Other points: No-smoking area. Children welcome.
Dogs welcome. Garden. Car park. Wheelchair access.
Directions: A9. From Carr Bridge, follow the A938 to Dulnain. Turn right at the post office to Syke or Curr, turn second right into Skye of Curr Road. Tigh-na-Sgiath is 400m further along on the right. (Map 16, F6)

Onich

Allt-nan-Ros

Onich, Fort William, Highland PH33 6RY
Telephone: +44(0)1855 821210
lr@allt-nan-ros.co.uk
www.allt-nan-ros.co.uk

It's not only in an enviable spot overlooking Loch Linnhie, but this smart family-run hotel also has panoramic views to the mountains beyond. The peaceful setting is perfect for a relaxing break, or if you're feeling energetic, there's riding, fishing, golfing, watersports and walking available nearby. All the spacious bedrooms, bar one, offer amazing views; five on the ground floor offer disabled access and two have bathrooms fully equipped for people with disabilities. Each room varies in style, but all are decorated to a high standard. The converted stables house two light, cottagey bedrooms. James and Fiona Macleod provide friendly and efficient service. On colder days, a welcoming fire roars in the bar and lounge. The Macleods are meticulous about the ingredients for their small but carefully drawn dinner menu. They source prime local foods and supplement these with their own home-grown produce. On the menu are locally smoked salmon, Letterfinlay game, the Macleods' own smoked venison and local seafood such as Mallaig cod served with wilted spinach and a homemade wholegrain mustard sauce. Their home-grown herbs provide the fresh flavourings.

Rooms: 20. Double room from £150, single from £75, dinner, bed and breakfast.
Prices: Set lunch £15 and dinner £30. House wine £12.95.
Last orders: Food: lunch 13.30; dinner 20.30.
Closed: Rarely.
Food: French and Scottish.
Other points: No-smoking area. Children welcome.
Dogs welcome overnight (but not in the bar). Garden. Car park. Wheelchair access.
Directions: Ten miles south of Fort William on the A82.
(Map 13, A4)

Tain

Glenmorangie, The Highland Home at Cadboll

Cadboll Fearn, Tain, Highland IV20 1XP
Telephone: +44(0)1862 871671
relax@glenmorangie.co.uk
www.glenmorangie.com

Owned by the Glenmorangie Distillery, this luxurious country-house hotel is top of its class, and superbly run by Helen McKenzie-Smith. Built in 1710, the house makes for a spacious and comfortable hotel. The whisky connection is evident in the artefacts on the walls and the complimentary decanter of whisky in your well-appointed bedroom. There are nine rooms in the main house, three in lodges, and all are individually decorated and named after the nine counties that can be seen from the hotel. Extras include Molton Brown lotions, fluffy towels and bathrobes, and flat-screen TVs. You'll even find green wellies for walking by the back door. The dining room offers a nightly treat of modern Scottish classics, care of head chef David Graham. The four-course set menu offers Rossshire beef and lamb, fish from the coast and salmon from Loch Fyne. Each menu comes with recommended wines from an extensive list. Retire to the Buffalo Room for a post-dinner Scotch.

Rooms: 9. Double/twin from £140, master suite from £185.
Prices: Set lunch £18. Set dinner £42.50 (four courses).
House wine £12.50.
Last orders: Food: Dinner 20.00.
Closed: 3-24 January.
Food: Modern Scottish.
Other points: No-smoking area. Children over 12 welcome.
Dogs welcome. Garden. Car park. Licence for civil weddings.
Wheelchair access for restaurant and some ground-floor bedrooms. Two Lounges.
Directions: A9. 33 miles north from Inverness. Take the B9175 to Nigg from the roundabout. Over the railway crossing, stay on this road for one and a half miles, then turn left to Glenmorangie. Continue for five miles on the top road until the primary school on the left. Half a mile later, turn right to the hotel. (Map 16, E5)

Ullapool

Brae Guest House

Shore Street, Ullapool, Highland IV26 2UJ
Telephone: +44(0)1854 612421

The longest-established guesthouse in Ullapool is run by Mr and Mrs Ross, who have been in residence for more than 45 years. And they have made it into one of the nicest and friendliest in Scotland. The seafront Victorian property was originally two houses and two shops. Now combined, everything is of a very high standard, from the genuinely warm welcome on arrival to the homely, comfortable bedrooms and the excellent traditional breakfast in the morning. Its setting on the front, overlooking Loch Broom, is splendid and Brae House is within easy walking distance of the village centre and the Stornoway ferry. Although the Rosses no longer offer evening meals, there are several restaurants in Ullapool that they would be happy to recommend. The guesthouse is open from May to September only.

Rooms: 11, 2 not en suite. Double room from £26 per person, single from £24.
Closed: October to May.
Food: Traditional Scottish.
Other points: No-smoking area. Children welcome. Car park.
Directions: In the centre of Ullapool. (Map 15, D4)

Ullapool

The Seaforth Inn

Quay Street, Ullapool, Highland IV26 2UE
Telephone: +44(0)1854 612122
drink@theseaforth.com
www.theseaforth.com

Right on the quayside, with stunning views of Loch Broom, the Seaforth has developed from a basic bar and chippy to an award-winning pub and seafood restaurant since Harry and Brigitte MacRae took over in 1995. The extended and modernised 18th-century building takes in a huge ground-floor bar with oak floors and large picture windows, an upstairs bistro for more intimate dining, and 'The Chippy', a traditional fish-and-chip takeaway. In fact, menus throughout the pub are overwhelmingly (and unashamedly) biased towards locally caught seafood. In the bar, snack on fresh oysters, steamed mussels or sweet pickled herrings, or feast on the amazing seafood platters. Linger longer in the bistro over seafood soup, fresh lobster or sea bream with tarragon and Pernod. Carnivores can tuck into Highland steaks. The Chippy menu is equally impressive – where else can you 'take away' scallops and chips, mussels by the kilo, and the best haddock and chips for miles?

Prices: Restaurant main course from £8. Bar/snack from £3.50. House wine from £9.50.
Last orders: Bar: 01.00. Food: 22.00. Times vary according to season.
Closed: New Year's Day.
Food: Seafood and traditional Scottish.
Other points: No-smoking area. Garden and patio. Children welcome. Car park. Air-conditioning. Wheelchair access.
Directions: Take the A835 from Inverness to Ullapool. (Map 15, D4)

Inverness

Westbourne Guest House

50 Huntly Street, Inverness IV3 5HS
Telephone: +44(0)1463 220700
richard@westbourne.org.uk
www.westbourne.org.uk

The Paxton family has lived on this site with lovely river views for generations, and in 1998, Richard Paxton decided to rebuild the house to create an up-to-date, purpose-built guesthouse. The result is this spick-and-span modern house that maintains a character feel. The bedrooms are individually styled with a tartan scheme and offer an exceptional level of accommodation. All the rooms have colour TV, hairdryer, beverage tray and sweeties, fluffy towels and safes. Superior beds make for a very comfortable stay. Downstairs is a cosy residents' lounge with internet access, books and games. The spacious breakfast room is light and bright and furnished with cheerful bistro-style furniture, with scenes of Inverness decorating the walls. The hearty Highlander breakfast is prepared from fresh local ingredients and will set you up for the day, whatever your outdoor pursuits. Richard has a vast knowledge of the area and can suggest tours that take in beautiful scenery and distilleries, as well as suggest wildlife excursions and walks.

Rooms: 10. Double/twin £25 per person per night.
Last orders: Breakfast: 08.30 (Monday to Friday); 09.00 (Saturday and Sunday), or by arrangement.
Closed: Rarely.
Other points: Totally no smoking. Children welcome. Dogs welcome overnight. Car park.
Directions: Take the A9 to Kessock Bridge roundabout and follow the signs to Inverness. Go straight over three roundabouts and, at the fourth, take the first exit onto Wells Street, which becomes Huntly Street. (Map 16, E5)

Sleat

Hotel Eilean Iarmain

Eilean Iarmain, Isle Ornsay, Sleat, Isle of Skye IV43 8QR
Telephone: +44(0)1471 833332
hotel@eilean-iarmain.co.uk
www.eileaniarmain.co.uk

Built in 1888, this handsome inn is attractively sited beside the fishing harbour. Rural chic sums up the traditional interiors that combine simplicity and style. The 16 bedrooms are all smartly individual – one even has a canopy bed from nearby Armadale Castle – and there are four suites in the converted stables with bedrooms upstairs and sitting rooms below. The bustling timber-clad An Pranban bar is a relaxing place to enjoy a wee dram and there are 30 local malt whiskies to try, including their own blend, Te Bheag. Their bar food is first rate. At lunch-times, tuck into sandwiches and homemade soups, hearty casseroles, steaks and local seafood. The dining room has a refined air and head chef Graham Smith serves fine food. Local seafood includes oysters from the hotel's own beds and shellfish from its private stone pier. Game, especially venison, is from the estate. A typical dinner might include Ord Estates rich game terrine, parsnip crisps and apple chutney, followed by cappuccino of smoked haddock and potato, then a medley of seafood poached in Chablis and saffron. Finish with a decadent dessert or some superb Scottish cheese.

Rooms: 12. Double/twin room from £60 per person, single occupancy £90. 4 suites in restored stables at £200.
Prices: Set lunch £16.50, set dinner £31. House wine £15.85.
Last orders: Bar: 23.00. Food: lunch 14.30; dinner 21.00.
Closed: Rarely.
Food: Modern Scottish.
Other points: No-smoking area. Children welcome. Garden. Car park.
Directions: 40 miles from Portree and seven miles from Broadford on the A851. (Map 15, F3)

Blair Atholl

Atholl Arms Hotel

Old North Road, Blair Atholl, Perth & Kinross PH18 5SG
Telephone: +44(0)1796 481205
enquiries@athollarmshotel.co.uk
www.athollarmshotel.co.uk

If you want a taste of the high life in the Highlands, head for this stunning, grand Victorian house that is now a smart hotel. In a commanding position and commanding attention, this fine old gabled Victorian granite-stone building was until recently owned by the Atholl Estate and home to the Duke of Atholl. The interiors reflect the house's Victorian and Scottish heritage, and rooms are sumptuously decorated in deep burgundies and greens, with walls covered in baronial-style accessories of weaponry and stags' heads, with tartan making tasteful appearances throughout. The bedrooms are smartly attired as are the Bothy Bar and Baronial Dining Room, where you can sample the best of local produce from on-the-doorstep Blair Atholl estate game to Tombuie Smokehouse meats and cheeses, and fish from Kerrachers, not to mention the superb shellfish from Skye. The hospitality and atmosphere are amazing. And if you want more than relaxation, shooting and fishing trips can be organised

---

Rooms: 31. Double/twin from £50, single from £35.
Family from £50.
Prices: Set lunch from £12. Set dinner from £20. Restaurant main course from £10. Bar/snack from £6.45. House wine £10.50.
Last orders: Bar: 23.00 (Friday and Saturday 23.45). Food: 21.30.
Closed: Rarely.
Food: Modern Scottish.
Other points: No-smoking area. Children welcome.
Dogs welcome in the bar. Garden. Car park.
Directions: A9 Inverness. Six miles north of Pitlochry on the A9, turn right at the T-junction and follow signs for Blair Castle. The Atholl Arms is 200 yards past the main gate on the left.
(Map 14, A6)

Bridge of Cally

Bridge of Cally Hotel

Bridge of Cally, Blairgowrie, Perth & Kinross PH10 7JJ
Telephone: +44(0)1250 886231
enquiries@bridgeofcallyhotel.com
www.bridgeofcallyhotel.com

The grounds of this old drover's inn extend over many acres along the banks of the River Ardle. It's an attractive wooded spot and has become an increasingly popular choice because of the sports available in the area. The hotel has expanded to meet demand, and its bedroom count has increased from nine to 18, the dining room has been remodelled, a conservatory added and new furniture installed throughout. Thanks to the refurbishments, it exudes a fresh feel throughout. The conservatory makes the most of the riverside location, plus there's a comfortable sitting room to unwind after a hard day's hunting and fishing. The bar is warm and inviting – a fun, friendly place used by locals, and a perfect place for a pint of Speckled Hen or one of a magnificent selection of single malts. Food is served in the bar or the dining room, with menus built around the likes of local venison sausages, wild venison, local lamb, and locally smoked trout, and offering garlic mushrooms in a cream sauce to start, followed by confit of duck. Good-value bedrooms are bright, and comfortable, with light wood furniture, modern bathrooms, and all the usual extras, except room phones.

Rooms: 18. Room from £35 per person.
Prices: Restaurant main course from £8.95. Bar main course from £6.95. Snack from £2.50. House wine £9.95.
Last orders: Bar: 23.00 (Friday and Saturday 23.45). Food: 21.00.
Closed: Never.
Food: Traditional Scottish, specialising in game.
Other points: No-smoking area. Children welcome. Dogs welcome. Garden. Car park.
Directions: Six miles north of Blairgowrie on the A93 heading for Braemar. (Map 14, B6)

Comrie

The Royal Hotel

Melville Square, Comrie, Perth & Kinross PH6 2DN
Telephone: +44(0)1764 679200
reception@royalhotel.co.uk
www.royalhotel.co.uk

Finely restored in 1995, this 18th-century coaching inn exudes a country-house atmosphere, with period antiques, paintings and stylish soft furnishings complemented by the Milsom family and their staff's cheerful, helpful hospitality. The cosy lounge bar, along with the wood and stone public bar, are the focus of the local community, offering an informal atmosphere and a warm welcome to all comers. Here, and in the conservatory-style brasserie, homemade venison and leek burgers, fishcakes with hot tomato sauce or haggis hash brown and whisky sauce may be washed down with a glass of Deuchar's IPA or one of 170 Highland malts. Dinner in the intimate Royal Restaurant can be a fixed-price, three-course affair or taken from a seasonal carte that makes full use of the seasonal produce from fresh fish, meats and game to Tobermory cheddar and local farm fruit and vegetables. The beautifully appointed bedrooms and suites feature furniture by local craftsmen and some stunning fabrics.

Rooms: 11. Double/twin £60 per person, single £75. Four-poster suite from £80 per person.
Prices: Set dinner £27.50. Restaurant main course from £9.95. Bar main course from £6.95. House wine £9.50.
Last orders: Bar: 23.00 (Friday and Saturday 23.45). Food: lunch 14.00; dinner 21.00.
Closed: Rarely.
Food: Modern and Traditional British.
Other points: No smoking in the restaurant. Garden. Children welcome. Dogs welcome overnight. Car park. Wheelchair access to the restaurant.
Directions: From the A9 at Greenloaning, take the A822 heading for Crieff, then the B827 to Comrie. (Map 14, B6)

Dunkeld

The Pend

5 Brae Street, Dunkeld, Perth & Kinross PH8 OBA
Telephone: +44(0)1350 727586
molly@thepend.sol.co.uk
www.thepend.com

With its classic good looks and leisure options, this hotel, set in the attractive Perthshire village of Dunkeld on the banks of the River Tay, offers quite an itinerary of activities. Hunting, fishing and shooting on local estates, picturesque walks and the use of sporting facilities at a nearby hotel are all available. The hotel has an appealing lack of pretentiousness and its small scale allows for genuine friendliness and a homely feel. All the bedrooms are beautifully decorated, with antique furniture here as well as in the lounge-dining room. The traditional cooking is based around quality ingredients from local suppliers – the smoked salmon comes from the Dunkeld smokery just across the road, then there's local Bestwick game, soft fruits from nearby farms, home-grown vegetables and exquisite local cheeses. From the daily-changing table d'hôte comes mains of pan-fried Orkney salmon, Balemund Farm organic lamb chops or rib-eye steak. There is no bar, but a fully stocked drinks cabinet runs on an honesty basis. In the bedrooms, drinks trays come with a selection of tea and fresh milk. In the past, the whole house has been taken over for small weddings or fishing and shooting parties.

Rooms: 3. £35 per person bed and breakfast. £60 per person dinner, bed and breakfast.
Prices: Set dinner (four courses) from £25.
Closed: Rarely.
Food: Traditional Scottish with French and Italian influences.
Other points: No smoking in the restaurant. Children welcome. Dogs welcome overnight. Car park.
Directions: 12 miles north of Perth on the A9. Cross the river into Dunkeld and take the second right into Brae Street. (Map 14, B6)

Perth

The Famous Bein Inn

Glen Farg, Perth, Perth & Kinross PH2 9PY
Telephone: +44(0)1577 830216
stay@beininn.com
www.beininn.com

An institution and local landmark, this old drovers' inn stands alone in a deep-wooded glen, five minutes drive from the M90 (junction 9). Since David Mundell has been at the helm, the Bein has become famous for live-music sessions, attracting some top recording artists. Rock music fans travel miles to experience David's Rock Bar, a basement museum filled with rock memorabilia. Décor is a tad more traditional in the MacGregor Bar, with its tartan carpet and comfortable sofas and armchairs, and in the more formal Balvaird Restaurant. Food is home-cooked, with the simple menus appealing to a loyal local clientele and passing travellers. Expect lunchtime sandwiches and light meals and heartier fare such as classic beefburger, haggis, neeps and tatties and pan-fried lamb's liver. House specialities are chosen on a daily basis and take in dishes such as grilled Shetland salmon with herb and prawn butter. En suite bedrooms in the modern extension are clean, tidy and unpretentious.

Rooms: 12. Double from £70, single from £45, family from £65. Prices include breakfast.
Prices: Set lunch £14, set dinner £18. Restaurant main course from £10.95. Bar main course from £5.95. House wine £10.50.
Last orders: Bar: lunch 14.00; dinner 23.00 (open all day at the weekend). Food: lunch 14.00; dinner 21.00 (food served all day Sunday).
Closed: Rarely.
Food: Traditional Scottish.
Other points: No-smoking area. Children welcome. Car park.
Directions: Exit 9/M90. Exit for Glen Farg and drive through the village, Famous Bein Inn is one and a half miles into the wooded glen. (Map 14, B6)

Perth

Let's Eat

77-79 Kinnoull Street, Perth, Perth & Kinross PH1 5EZ
Telephone: +44(0)1738 643377
enquiries@letseatperth.co.uk
www.letseatperth.co.uk

Combine local ingredients and two owners who are passionate about food and you are on to a culinary winner. Tony Heath and Shona Drysdale have built up a much-deserved fan club for their delightful cooking in a smart venue that was built in 1822 as Perth's Theatre Royal. Their seasonal-changing menu is packed with quality Scottish produce, with venison from the Rannoch Moors, asparagus and sea kale from Eassie Farm, and deer from the Glenisla Estates. The quality and quantity of local riches makes choosing from the menu a pleasurable dilemma. Starters include seared dived Mallaig scallops with a parsnip purée, white truffle oil and parsnip crisps or Isle of Skye mussels with a creamy white wine sauce, followed by pan-roasted fillet of West Coast halibut with Skye queen scallops and prawns on thyme-roasted potatoes or grilled pavé of Scotch beef on the bone with a puff-pastry casket. Puddings are equally impressive, especially the honey, whisky and oatmeal parfait with local strawberries. The wine list is extensive and well priced, with a number offered by the half bottle. The restaurant's cheery red and grey décor creates a relaxing, contemporary setting.

Prices: Lunch main course from £9.50. Dinner main course £13.95. House wine £11.
Last orders: Food: lunch 14.00; dinner 21.45.
Closed: Sunday, Monday, two weeks in January and last two weeks in July.
Food: Modern British.
Other points: No smoking in the restaurant. Children welcome. Wheelchair access.
Directions: In the centre of Perth on the junction of Atholl Street and Kinnoull Street. (Map 14, B6)

Tyndrum

Green Welly Stop Restaurant

Tyndrum, Crianlarich, Perth & Kinross FK20 8RY
Telephone: +44(0)1838 400271
thegreenwellystop@tyndrum12.freeserve.co.uk
www.thegreenwellystop.co.uk

If you're en route to Oban or Fort William, stop off at this outdoor-equipment shop to sample some home-cooked Scottish dishes at its delicious all-day café-restaurant. This third-generation family business prides itself on making everything on the premises. Local supplies dictate what's on the menu, which offers fresh soups made daily, perhaps Scotch broth, curried apple and parsnip, cream of kale (a traditional winter vegetable soup) or cullen skink. The baking is excellent, with scones ranging from plain, through fruit, treacle, and cheese, with date and walnut slice, banana loaf, Border tart and Orkney broonie widening the tempting choice of cakes even further. Main courses include flavoursome haggis 'n' neeps, as well as crofter's stew (diced lamb with vegetables in a rich sauce) and Hebridean leek pie. Desserts include boozy bread and butter pudding or Atholl brose trifle. There's an amazing selection of whiskies, locally smoked salmon, haggis and Scottish preserves to buy in the shop, as well as snacks. With racks of water-proof gear, this is the place to stock up if the variable Scottish weather has caught you out – Barbours and green wellies are much in evidence.

Prices: Main course from £5. Snack from £2.95. House wine £2.70 for a small bottle.
Last orders: Food: 17.30.
Closed: Rarely.
Food: Traditional Scottish.
Other points: No-smoking area. Children welcome. Patio. Car park.
Directions: On the A82, in the centre of the village. (Map 14, B5)

www.routiers.co.uk

Hawick

Mansfield House Hotel

Weensland Road, Hawick, Scottish Borders TD9 8LB
Telephone: +44(0)1450 360400
ian@mansfield-house.com
www.mansfield-house.com

This Victorian mansion stands tall and proud, over-looking Hawick. The interiors match the grandeur of the exterior, but the traditional and lavish furnishings are combined with 21st-century amenities. The house has been in the MacKinnon family since 1985 and they have restored its character, successfully turning it into a comfortable hotel. The classic-styled sitting room features ornate cornicing, open fire and loungy sofas and chairs. A separate traditional bar is used for informal meals. The comforts extend to the bedrooms, which are spacious and well decorated and come with TVs. The restaurant offers up-to-date ideas using the best ingredients. Sheila MacKinnon uses seasonal local produce to ensure her menu offers only the freshest flavours. These ingredients are showcased in the regularly changing dinner menus that could take in new-season asparagus with crispy Cumbrian ham, capers and black olive balsamic dressing, or grilled new-season lamb chops with crushed new potatoes and mint. Rhubarb tart or coffee-date pudding make satisfying desserts. The wine list is a good mix of France and the New World at keen prices.

Rooms: 12. Double room from £70, single from £45, family room from £90.
Prices: Set lunch £19.50 and dinner £25. House wine £10.50.
Last orders: Lounge Bar: 21.00. Food: lunch 14.00; dinner 21.00 (Sunday 20.00).
Closed: Rarely.
Food: Traditional Scottish.
Other points: No smoking in the restaurant. Children welcome. Dogs welcome overnight. Garden. Car park. Licence for civil weddings. Wheelchair access.
Directions: Take the A7 to Hawick, then the A698 to Denholm/Jedburgh. The hotel is one mile ahead on the right. (Map 14, D7)

Kelso

Border Hotel

The Green, Kirk Yetholm, Kelso,
Scottish Borders TD5 8PQ
Telephone: +44(0)1573 420237
borderhotel@aol.com

Marking the end of the 268-mile-long Pennine Way walk, this old coaching inn is a welcoming and most hospitable place to revive after any journey, be it on foot or by car. Current owners, the Blackburns, have refurbished the inn, turning it into a comfortable place to wine, dine and stay. The hospitality starts in the stone-flagged bar with a blazing fire, where walkers who have completed the Pennine Way can claim a free ale. Quality local ingredients such as langoustines, crab, fresh fish, beef and game are used in traditional Scottish recipes, as well as international favourites, so, alongside starters of cullen skink and haggis are Thai fishcakes. Mains range from smoked Eyemouth haddock to Border curry of the day. Specials take in choice cuts of meat and game, all deftly cooked. Eat in either of the two dining areas in the bar, the conservatory or the dining room that looks out over the patio and beer garden.

Rooms: 5. Double/twin room from £40 per person. Single from £45 per person. Family room from £100.
Prices: Restaurant main course from £8. Bar snack from £3.50. House wine £10.
Last orders: Bar: 23.00. Food: lunch 14.00; dinner 21.00.
Closed: Rarely.
Food: Modern British.
Other points: No-smoking area. Children welcome. Dogs welcome in the bar. Garden. Car park. Games room. Wheelchair access to the restaurant/bar (no WC).
Directions: From Kelso, take the BB352. The Border Hotel is situated at the end of the Pennine Way. (Map 11, A4)

Falkirk

La Picardie

12 Union Road, Camelon, Falkirk, Stirlingshire FK1 4PG
Telephone: +44(0)1324 631666
info@lapicardie.co.uk
www.lapicardie.co.uk

For a flavour of France, look no further than this chic, rustic restaurant in the Stirlingshire town of Camelon. Its brasserie-style menu uses local ingredients to conjure up classic French dishes, and they've proved popular with locals and visitors alike. This friendly and informal restaurant is run by Brian Cochrane, with Ranald Davidson in charge of the cooking. The hearty food is offered at exceptionally keen prices that are not very much dearer than if you cooked them at home. You can enjoy an excellent value two-course lunch, choosing from homemade pâté or creamy leek and potato soup to start, followed by garlic roast chicken or seared salmon. The evening menu widens the choice with more French favourites. Start with soup or pâté and follow with fish, steak or pork. Simplicity is the key and, refreshingly, there are no hidden extras. Bread, chilled water and coffee are all included in the price. Brian sources all the easy-drinking wines from France and at £8.99, the house wine is a steal. The restaurant is cosy and the space is cleverly used; the tiny galley kitchen opens onto the dining rooms, so you can see Ranald in action. The atmosphere and good food make for a pleasant dining experience that won't break the bank.

Prices: Set dinner from £15. Restaurant main course from £7. House wine £8.99.
Last orders: Food: 21.00. Reservations required.
Closed: First two weeks of July.
Food: French.
Other points: Totally no smoking. Children welcome. Wheelchair access. Gourmet evening first Tuesday of each month.
Directions: M9 and M876. One mile from Falkirk Wheel. (Map 14, C6)

Killearn

The Black Bull Hotel

2 The Square, Killearn, Stirlingshire G63 9NG
Telephone: +44(0)1360 550215
sales@blackbullhotel.com
www.blackbullhotel.com

Traditional country charm with contemporary dining makes for a winning combination at this quiet village inn. The elegance extends from the reception to the bedrooms. The informal bistro is a popular choice with locals. Alternatively, dine in the smart, Poachers Restaurant in the conservatory overlooking the gardens. Its set menu features a good selection of dishes, and brings together quality Scottish ingredients cooked in the classic and modern style by award-winning chef Campbell Cameron. The choice takes in wild boar from Perthshire, venison from Pitlochry, Perthshire lamb, Aberdeen Angus beef, sea bass, salmon, oysters from Loch Fyne and Highland grouse. Start with an interesting seafood medley in a light saffron sauce, before moving onto a main of noisettes of lamb with a Champagne, grapefruit and mint sabayon. Finish with one of the fabulous chocolate desserts. All bedrooms are en suite and have been recently upgraded.

Rooms: 15. Double/twin room from £90, single from £65. Double/twin room dinner, bed and breakfast £65 per person.
Prices: Set lunch £12.95 and dinner £29.50. Restaurant main course from £9.95. House wine £14.95.
Last orders: Bar: 23.00. Food: 21.30 (Friday, Saturday and Sunday 22.00).
Closed: Never.
Food: Traditional and Modern Scottish.
Other points: No-smoking area. Children welcome. Dogs welcome in the bar. Garden. Car park. Licence for civil weddings.
Directions: Exit 16/M8. Head north on the A879 towards Milngavie and join the A81. Pass the Glengoyne Distillery and turn right on the A875 to Killearn. The Black Bull Hotel is on the left by the obelisk. (Map 14, C5)

Balivanich

Stepping Stone Restaurant

Benbecula, Balivanich, Western Isles H57 5DA
Telephone: +44(0)1870 603377
steppingstonehs7@tiscali.co.uk

If you arrive by air, you won't miss the Stepping Stone as it's one of the first places you'll see as you leave Benbecula airport. The restaurant gets its name from being the central island in the chain between North and South Uist. It was purpose built, but it's been stylishly designed and offers that much-needed warmth and welcome in these blustery parts. Inside, the wood and glass structure feels like a spacious, cheerful log cabin. It's split into two eating levels: the Food Base is an informal café where you enjoy get all-day snacks, sandwiches, takeaways and home-baked cakes, and more substantial meals such as fish and chips, while Sinteag, the no-smoking restaurant on the higher level, turns out scintillating food based around locally caught fish. The three or five-course menus are presented in a simple style, whether it's fillet of sole with a shrimp sauce, or scallops with bacon and cheese. Other specialities include Uist venison cooked in red wine. The restaurant is owned and managed by Ewen Maclead, whose family own the renowned town bakery that makes the famous oatcakes sold all over Scotland, and served here in the restaurant with delectable Scottish cheese.

Prices: Sunday lunch £11.95. Set dinner £21.75 (five courses). House wine £8.50.
Last orders: Food: 21.00.
Closed: Rarely.
Food: Traditional Scottish and seafood.
Other points: Totally no smoking. Children welcome. Garden. Car park.
Directions: On the island of Benbecula, on the airport over-road, 5 minutes from the ferry and the airport at Balivanich. (Map 15, E1)

WALES

Long renowned for its music, Wales may, in future, be renowned for its food. Every year, a fresh crop of eateries opens across the principality, ranging from renovated hotels in traditional seaside towns to ancient countryside barns converted into brasserie-style restaurants. These attract chefs eager to make the best use of locally grown, seasonal produce. Each year, there is a greater choice of produce being offered through a growing range of outlets. While the supermarkets lumber on, it's small, specialist farmers and farm shops, butchers, wine merchants and cheesemongers who ensure that the demand from kitchens for high-quality, seasonal, local produce is met.

Our members are keen to offer their customers the very best of saltmarsh lamb, Welsh Black beef, Pembrokeshire lobster, Gower cockles and laverbread and traditional Welsh cheeses, so, when you visit the establishments listed here, you can expect to sample not just proper Welsh hospitality but the true flavour of Wales as well.

COOKING UP A STORM IN MID-WALES

*The annual Abergavenny Food Festival, held in September, is the place to sample this area's stunning produce and excellent cooking. **Philip Moss** takes a taste tour of this culinary hot spot and highlights the temptations that are on offer all year round*

The festival attracts more than 25,000 visitors every year with its colourful mix of displays, demonstrations, talks, walks and tastings

Perched on the outskirts of the Brecon Beacons National Park, Abergavenny has long attracted walkers, cyclists and, more recently, motorcyclists. But in the mid-1990s, this quiet market town started to attract a new, slower-moving but altogether more stately type of visitor. The foodies had arrived, following in the wake of new chef/owners who, taking advantage of the relatively low property prices, began to renovate old eateries or open new ones in the area. Lured here initially by the range and quality of local produce, many wanted to follow the example of Franco Taruschio's Walnut Tree Inn Restaurant at Llandewi Skirrid, Abergavenny and produce capital-city food in the heart of the countryside.

According to one local chef, 'Monmouthshire is one of the few counties in the UK where you can pick samphire in the morning and bilberries in the afternoon.'

Katie Palmer, food officer of adventa, a publicly funded body that supports small food producers, is equally positive: 'Monmouthshire has become a "must-stay" destination for foodies. Consumer interest in how and where ingredients are grown has increased to the extent that we now publish a directory of Monmouthshire's specialist food producers and a series of local food-trail guides for visitors.'

The 100-plus stalls sell produce not only from mid-Wales, but the Med and Japan

'Monmouthshire has become a "must-stay" destination for foodies'

In 1998, the sea change was noted by Martin Orbach, Festival founder and owner of Shepherd's Sheep's Milk Ice Cream, and Chris Wardle, a local organic beef and lamb farmer, now Chairman of the Festival. 'It was in the aftermath of the BSE outbreak that we found a new enthusiasm among local food producers and consumers for small-volume, high-quality produce. Abergavenny, with its covered market hall and adjoining theatre, had the right venue for an event. We pitched the idea to Monmouthshire County Council which gave us its blessing, and, with Franco Taruschio's help, we got some celebrity names involved.'

The first Abergavenny Food Festival took place in 1999. It was a one-day event with a food market – before the era of farmers' markets – in the covered hall and a discussion in the theatre about the rights and wrongs of genetically modified food, chaired by newsreader Martyn Lewis. Three thousand people attended the event. The Festival has never looked back. In 2003, it won the Wales Tourist Board's Greatest Event in Wales award. In 2004, it welcomed around 25,000 visitors. There are usually more than a hundred stalls from Wales and the Borders, selling a wide array of produce – duck and chicken sausages from Madgett's Farm Poultry, single-variety apple juice from Gellirhyd Farm, Black Mountain Smokery's naturally smoked delicacies, organic vegetables from Ty Mawr, saltmarsh lamb from Palfreys, wild boar from Usk Castle Chase and Bacheldre Watermill Organic Flours to name a few. Local Monmouthshire vineyards and perry makers are also well represented.

There was also a wonderful mix of masterclasses, competitions, debates, displays, walks and talks in a variety of venues, including the Victorian market hall, local hotels and pubs, and the grounds of Abergavenny's ancient castle.

Apart from record foodie crowds, some of the brightest stars of the culinary world – celebrity chefs, food writers and journalists all find time to visit. Some are repeat attenders like Marguerite Patten; not only the UK's original TV chef, but also the first advocate for healthy school meals in the 1940s. She took part in the 1999 Festival. Gregg Wallace attended in 2004 as part of the 'Talking Vegetables' team and in 2005 wore his *Masterchef* hat. Antony Worrall Thompson, Jonathan Meades, Terry Durack and Jill Dupleix have all found time to take part in the event, supporting the view held by more than one national paper that Abergavenny is now one of the leading events of its kind in the UK. At the time of writing, rumours abound that the 2005 festival would see Times newspaper critic AA Gill, interviewing writer/chef Anthony Bourdain about his new book *Typhoid Mary*.

Hugh Fearnley-Whittingstall demonstrated some of the recipes from his *River Cottage Meat Book* at the 2004 festival. He says, 'It's a great event, with a really good atmosphere. There's a real devotion to the subject of local food production.' 'But', says Martin Orbach, 'as the event grows, so does the demand for accommodation and dining. So, if you want to come and celebrate good food and good eating with us at Abergavenny, remember to book early.'
To check the dates for the Abergavenny Food Festival 2006, visit its website at:
www.abergavennyfoodfestival.com.

Abergavenny's market hall is transformed into a theatre for demonstrations and talks by some of Britain's leading celebrity chefs

Local dining

There's plenty of opportunity to sample local food at Les Routiers members' restaurants, pubs and hotels in the area over the two-day festival season.
■ Kurt Fleming, chef at The Bell at Skenfrith (page 211), cooks local classics such as Welsh venison loin in juniper and thyme, a brioche and chestnut savoury Charlotte and a redcurrant soubise. The Bell also has one of the best wine lists in the country and often hosts a wine-tasting evening in the run up to the Festival.
■ Meanwhile, The Beaufort, in picturesque Crickhowell, provides a wonderful venue for James Lewis's exciting take on some French classics such as local pigeon served with Puy lentils, balsamic reduction and a magnificent pavé of turbot.

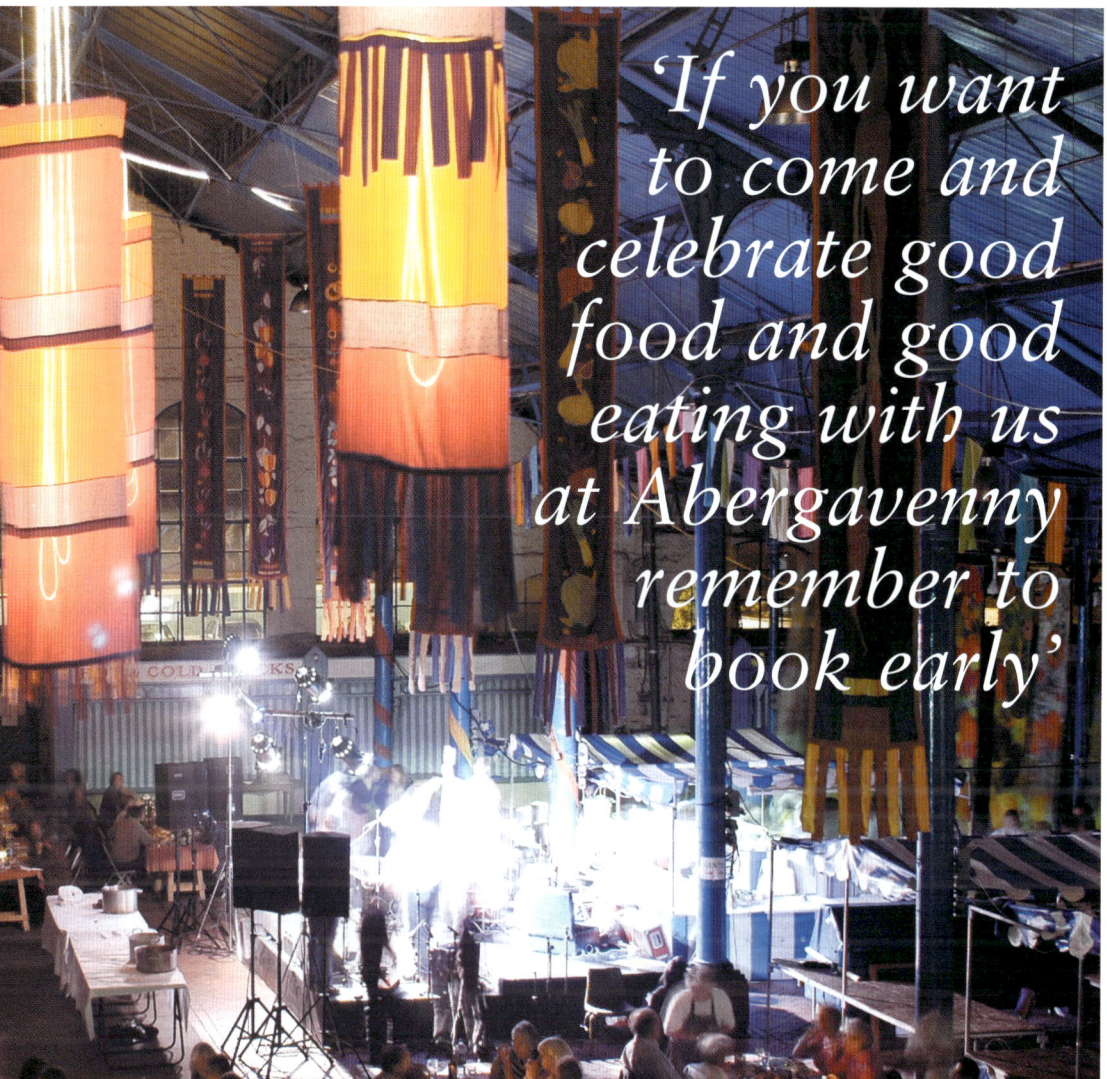

'If you want to come and celebrate good food and good eating with us at Abergavenny remember to book early'

■ Dan Vaughn, chef at The Stonemill restaurant in Rockfield (page 210), also likes to source his supplies close to home. Newhouse Farm (Dingestow) lamb with robust bubble-and-squeak and smoked local bacon is as good a taste of Monmouthshire as you will find anywhere.

■ Steve Molyneux buys his beef from the family butchers in nearby Raglan and cooks a really enjoyable short menu of hearty dishes at his dining pub, The Black Bear, at Bettws Newydd.

■ Pubs and good steaks seem to go together hereabouts. The Hunters Moon in Llangattock Lingoed serves Hereford steak from Mailes that is hung for 28 days for a full flavour.

■ For the full country-house hotel experience, visit The Llansantffraed Court Hotel (page 209) with its comfortable rooms and William and Mary revival architecture – a perfect setting for dishes such as fricassee of local rabbit with grain-mustard and chive cream, skilfully prepared by chef, Simon King.

■ Christina Jackson at Glangrwyney Court (page 215) offers a similarly opulent yet comfortable setting for those seeking B&B accommodation in between Abergavenny and Crickhowell.

■ Just over the Herefordshire border, Ian Jackson, chef at the Allt-yr-Ynys (page 91), cooks modern British food such as medallions of local pork with a Madeira sauce, braised cabbage and smoky bacon, caramelised apple and black pudding.

■ In Raglan, The Beaufort Arms (page 210) provides comfortable accommodation and a choice of bar and restaurant dining, which includes many favourite Welsh dishes.

Stock up on local specialities

Remember to take some local produce with you to enjoy at home. Either buy at one of the local farmers' markets (www.adventa.org.uk), or try local meat, sausages and award-winning pork pies from **J Edwards** (Abergavenny); rare-breed meats, such as Welsh Longhorn beef from **Neil James** (Raglan); prize-winning sausages from **Rawlings** (Abergavenny) and local bacon, lamb and game from **Hancock's** in Monmouth. Or buy direct from suppliers such as **Park Farm** (Llantilio Crossenny), **Brook's Farm** (Raglan) or **Little Mill Farm** (Newcastle). Local wild boar is available from **Castle Chase** (Usk) and a staggering array of local and other British cheeses from **McBlains** (Usk). **Richard Gaffney** (Abergavenny) supplies fresh seafood to local restaurants, as well as shoppers, through **Vin Sullivan** (Abergavenny). Try **Bower Farm Dairy**'s (Grosmont) rich Jersey cream, yogurt or crème fraîche or their Gloucester Old Spot pork, raised organically on whey. **Tredilion Farm**, **Glan Usk** and many others offer PYO or farm-gate sales of seasonal fruit and veg. For a local tipple, try apple and pear varietal juices or local cider and perry or local wines from either **Sugarloaf**, **Tintern Parva** or **Monnow Valley** vineyards.
Full details from adventa (01873 736035).

Markets in Wales

Part of the fun of eating out is trying new food. Years ago, restaurants kept their suppliers' details secret. Nowadays, markets play an increasingly important role in supplying not just the trade, but also the consumer with fresh, seasonal, local ingredients.

Cardiff has a large Victorian indoor market on St Mary Street, that was built in 1891. It continues to offer a wonderful mix of goods, including cheese and fish. Sample cockles or whelks or a hand-raised pork pie, followed by a pint of Brain's Dark. Upstairs in the café, tuck into a plate of hearty faggots and peas and a mug of strong tea.

Cardiff's Riverside Real Food Market (Fitzhamon Embankment, over the river from the Millennium Stadium) opens its doors for business between 10am and 2pm, providing a valuable city outlet for local, Welsh and organic producers. Prices are pitched to appeal to local pockets, and there's always some exotic snack to try from one of Cardiff's thriving ethnic communities. Visit www.riversidemarket.org.uk for more information.

Swansea indoor market looks very much as it did when it opened in 1961, but there has been a bustling market in the city centre for more than 1,000 years, although then it was near the castle, as opposed to on its current Oxford Street site. Today, it's a vibrant and busy arena, offering Welsh bacon, lamb and beef, cockles and laverbread from Penclawdd, local fruit and vegetables, Welshcakes, cheese, fish and flowers. Come in early October for the annual cockle festival and on 1 March for the St David's Day celebrations.

Carmarthen is famous for its weekly market, which was founded in 1180. It's now housed in a new hall, completed in 1981, on St Catherine Street. Here, you'll find range of local and regional specialities, including Carmathen ham, Welsh Black beef, farmhouse cheeses and a wide range of locally grown seasonal vegetables. Look out for Penclawdd cockles, laverbread from the Gower and homemade faggots. Visit www.carmathenmarket.co.uk for more details.

Fishguard farmers' market has been taking place on every other Saturday since July 2000, and is going from strength to strength. Known locally as *Shwd i chi heddi?* day (How are you today?), it takes place in Fishguard's old Market Hall and offers a great assortment of organic vegetables, meat and eggs, plants, flowers and herbs, savouries, breads, cakes, biscuits and preserves, supplied by nearby farms and the local Women's Institute.

In South East Wales, try Usk farmers' market, held at the town's Memorial Hall, for another great offering of quality local produce. There's a large selection of organics — lamb, beef, excellent chicken, seasonal fruit and veg, apple juice, cheeses and traditional breads. Don't leave without some wild-boar gammon, raised in nearby woodland.

Is it any wonder Abergavenny hosts one of the Greatest Events in Wales?

Abergavenny, the largest market town in Monmouthshire, has a history of producing food. Good food. Fresh food. Wholesome food.

The streets are lined with independent butchers, the market bustles with customers buying local fresh produce and the surrounding countryside is as stunning as the restaurants that you'll find here. It's a veritable land of milk and honey…

So no, it's no wonder, that the Abergavenny Food Festival won the Greatest Event in Wales 2003 in the National Tourism Awards. There is wonder here, however, and the wonder lies in the food.

If you're planning a visit, for the festival or at any time, why not spoil yourself in Green Dragon accredited accommodation*
www.greenbeds.adventa.org.uk

While you're here, you can also gorge yourself on the stunning scenery by taking a day trip around Monmouthshire
www.discovery.adventa.org.uk

If we've whetted your appetite, there is a selection of free brochures, with information on a wide range of subjects and places of interest in Monmouthshire, including local churches, gardens, and of course food. For more information email:
chepstow.tic@monmouthshire.gov.uk or call 01291 623772

For more information about Abergavenny Food Festival:
www.abergavennyfoodfestival.com

www.adventa.org.uk

Cardiff

The Thai House Restaurant

3-5 Guildford Crescent, Churchill Way,
Cardiff CF10 2HJ
Telephone: +44(0)2920 387 404
info@thaihouse.biz
www.thaihouse.biz

Noi Ramasut and his wife Arlene opened The Thai House in 1985, when there were only five other Thai restaurants in the country. They quickly found a loyal following for their fine cooking that brings together Thai flavourings with Welsh ingredients. Thanks to brisk trade, they moved to larger Georgian premises that have been transformed into a cutting-edge eating establishment by Welsh architect Huw Jones. The stunning reclaimed floor is from the capital's Philharmonic Hall. Difficulties sourcing Thai ingredients were solved when Noi set up his importing business to bring in produce weekly. Skilled staff cook these in the traditional way, so whether it's a larb (a Lao preparation of ground chicken or pork and chilli), or mild, creamy tom ga kai (chicken cooked in a coconut sauce), or starters of po pia tod (fried spring rolls), you know you are getting the real thing. Innovation is evident, as Cardigan Bay sea bass and mackerel, Welsh beef and lamb and Norfolk duck are used in the regional Thai dishes. The Welsh lamb in a southern Thai curry is particularly fine. The Chang beer and well-chosen wines are great matches for the spicy offerings.

Prices: Set lunch £10. Set dinner from £26. Restaurant main course from £11. House wine £11.50.
Last orders: Food: lunch 14.30; dinner 23.00.
Closed: Sunday and four days over Christmas.
Food: Thai.
Other points: No-smoking area. Children welcome.
Wheelchair access.
Directions: In the centre of Cardiff just off Churchill Way. The Thai House is next to the Ibis Hotel and opposite the stage door of Cardiff International Arena. (Map 4, 6B)

Brechfa

Ty Mawr Country Hotel

Brechfa, Carmarthen, Carmarthenshire SA32 7RA
Telephone: +44(0)1267 202332
info@wales-country-hotel.co.uk
www.wales-country-hotel.co.uk

It's been a small holding, grammar school, farmhouse and home to four families, but now this fine 15th-century house has come into its own as a small hotel. Steve Thomas and Annabel Viney have breathed new life into this wonderful house and extend a warm and friendly welcome to guests. Set in a peaceful location in the Cothi Valley, the hotel is well placed for exploring the south and west Wales countryside, Cardigan Bay and the Pembrokeshire Coastal Park, but is just 30 minutes from the M4. All the bedrooms have been newly decorated, and are well appointed and comfortable. Downstairs the character of the house has been maintained with open fires, tiled floors and beamed ceilings all beautifully restored. The food, sourced and cooked by Steve, is amazing. The set daily-changing menus feature starters of Penclawdd mussels in a white wine, garlic and cream sauce and cured ham set on Brynmelyn apple chutney, then mains of Cardigan Bay dressed crab and organic Fferm Tyllwyd Welsh black fillet steak with pink peppercorn sauce. Welsh cheeses or blackberry and apple tart are fine finishes. The wine list caters for all tastes and pockets.

Rooms: 5. Double/twin from £92. Single from £65. (4 en suite).
Prices: Set lunch £16.50. Set dinner £27.50. House wine £11.75.
Last orders: Food: Lunch 14.00 (Sunday only); dinner 2100.
Closed: Never.
Food: Modern British with emphasis on local,
seasonal ingredients.
Other points: No-smoking area. Children over 12 welcome. Dogs welcome. Garden. Car park. Bar area only open to residents and diners.
Directions: M4. From the A40/A48, take the B4310 North. Ty Mawr is in the centre of Brechfa on the left. (Map 7, E3)

Llanarthne

The Fig Tree

Dryslwyn Fawr, Llanarthne, Carmarthenshire SA32 8JQ
Telephone: +44(0)1558 668187
enquiries@thefigtreerestaurant.co.uk
www.thefigtreerestaurant.co.uk

Dryslwyn Fawr is a large, Grade II-listed farm, dating back to the 13th century, although much of the remaining structures are 17th century. The restaurant in the farm's courtyard joins the existing four self-catering holiday cottages. It is housed in a creeper-clad building and dining on three levels is brasserie-style. The décor makes the most of the original features, such as flagstone floors, stone walls and lots of natural wood. Under the skilful leadership of chef Tom French, the restaurant has built up an excellent reputation for fine food. His commitment to using local ingredients has paid off. At lunch, tuck into the menu of soups, salads and lighter dishes, plus fish and superb steaks. Specials are on offer at lunch and for the sophisticated dinner menus. There are six fish choices on the main menu alone. Succulent Welsh Black steaks come accompanied with a choice of well-made sauces. The hors d'oeuvres, including crayfish, smoked salmon and cream cheese, figs, smoked chicken and egg with curried mayonnaise are delightful, as are the irresistible puddings. Welsh nights, offering traditional recipes, and Sunday brunches are proving popular.

Rooms: 5. Double/twin from £50.
Prices: Set lunch £15. Set dinner £20. Restaurant main course from £10. House wine £9.50.
Last orders: Food: lunch 14.00; dinner: 21.00.
Closed: Sunday evening and all day Monday.
Food: Modern British and European.
Other points: No smoking in restaurant. Garden. Children welcome. Car park. Licenced for civil weddings. Wheelchair access throughout.
Directions: Exit 49/M4. Between Carmarthen and Llandeilo, just off the A40 by Dryslwyn Castle, signposted off the B4300. (Map 7, E3)

Aberaeron

Hive on the Quay

Cadwgan Place, Aberaeron, Ceredigion SA46 0BU
Telephone: +44(0)1545 570445
hiveon.thequay@btinternet.com
www.hiveonthequay.co.uk

Set on the seafront at Aberaeron's sheltered inner harbour, it comes as no surprise to find seafood features strongly at the Holgate family's bustling quayside café. Supplies are local and come via their harbourside fish shop, which is stocked with the freshest Cardigan Bay crabs and lobster. The other big draw is its honey ice cream made from locally farmed honey. The Hive offers a fairly compact lunch and dinner menu, but it's the sort of line-up where everything is delicious, from the Penclawdd cockle chowder to the local lobster salad. The daily specials menu features local meats, salads, vegetables, cheeses, yogurts and milk. Smaller portions of these specials are available to all ages, which gives the opportunity to sample more than one or two or their delicious recipes, such as the Welsh lamb chops or pasta with fresh broad beans, mint and ricotta. The drinks list is full of pleasant surprises such as the organic mead and lager, and a selection of organic wines. Sarah Holgate and her team make their bread and cakes, almost entirely from organic produce.

Prices: Main course from £7.50. Snack from £5. House wine £12.
Last orders: Café/Restaurant: 15.00 from Spring Bank holiday to mid-September; Dinner 21.00 in August.
Closed: From fourth week of September to Spring Bank Holiday.
Food: British (especially Welsh) and regional European.
Other points: Totally no smoking. Children welcome. Garden. Licence for civil weddings. Wheelchair access.
Directions: At the end of the M4. Continue to Carmarthen and Llandysul and take the A487 coast road to Aberaeron. Take the first left after the river bridge to the harbour and the Hive. Street parking available. (Map 7, D3)

Llandudno

Ambassador Hotel

Promenade, Llandudno, Conwy LL30 2NR
Telephone: +44(0)1492 876886
reception@ambasshotel.demon.co.uk

This efficiently run and spick-and-span Victorian listed hotel has been in the Williams family for three generations. It was started by Jim and Freda Williams in 1946, and is now run by Nigel Williams, who continues their good work and friendly hospitality. One of the most striking Victorian buildings in town, it is easy to lose yourself in the spacious lounges or soak up the rays in the plant-filled sun verandas. You'll enjoy a good Welsh welcome in the bar that has a convivial vibe in the evening. The restaurant serves good-value, set-price dinners that revolve around traditional fare. You can't fault the hearty ham or beef salads or roast salmon with a mustard and Welsh cheese crust, mushroom sauce and horseradish mash. There's also a good-value set menu at lunchtimes that's worth sampling, even if you aren't staying in the hotel. Bedrooms vary in size, but the best are spacious, and it's worth requesting one when you book. Rooms are light and decorated in soft colours, and have that all-important sea view.

Rooms: 57. Rooms from £31 per person.
Prices: Set lunch £8.25, set dinner £16. House wine £11.20.
Last orders: Food: lunch 13.45; dinner 19.30.
Closed: Never.
Food: British.
Other points: No smoking in the restaurant. Children welcome. Garden. Car park. Wheelchair access.
Directions: Leave the A55 and take the A470 to Llandudno. Follow to the Promenade, then turn left towards the pier. (Map 7, A3)

www.routiers.co.uk

Llandudno

Dunoon Hotel

Gloddaeth Street, Llandudno, Conwy LL30 2DW
Telephone: +44(0)1492 860787
reservations@dunoonhotel.co.uk
www.dunoonhotel.co.uk

Set a block or two back from the seafront, this splendid gable-ended mansion is one of many fine examples of Victorian architecture that define this traditional resort town. The charm of this old-fashioned seaside hotel has been maintained by new owners Rhys and Charlotte Williams, long-standing, second-generation friends of the previous owners. Young and enthusiastic, they have embraced a philosophy of 'if it ain't broke, don't fix it', retaining long-serving staff and an appreciation of what Llandudno did best in its Victorian heyday. Smart oak-panelled public rooms include the Welsh Dresser Bar, which sports a magnificent cooking range. There's a relaxing reading lounge and a panelled lounge with open fire and cosy corners. In the restaurant, chandeliers and draped windows make for elegant dining. Chef Mark Martin produces two five-course dinners. This may include a salad of beef tomatoes with feta and basil or chicken liver pâté, mains of Welsh chop with rosemary and redcurrant sauce or steak, kidney and mushroom pie cooked in ale, followed by steamed ginger and rhubarb sponge or delicious cheeses.

Rooms: 50. Double room from £72, single from £52.
Prices: Set Sunday lunch £12.75 (four courses + coffee) and set dinner £19.50 (5 courses + coffee). House wine £11.50.
Last orders: Food: lunch 14.00; dinner 20.00.
Closed: End of December–mid March.
Food: Traditional British.
Other points: No smoking in the restaurant. Children welcome. Dogs welcome overnight. Garden/patio. Car park. Wheelchair access.
Directions: Turn left off Llandudno Promenade near the pier. Continue straight on at the next two roundabouts. The hotel is 200 yards on the right. (Map 7, A3)

St George

The Kinmel Arms

St George, Abergele, Conwy LL22 9BP
Telephone: +44(0)1745 832207
info@thekinmelarms.co.uk
www.thekinmelarms.co.uk

Tucked away in the beautiful Elwy Valley, this refurbished 17th-century coaching inn marches on under the guiding hand of Lynn Cunnah-Watson and Tim Watson. Amid country furniture and polished wood floors, everything operates on clean, uncluttered lines around a slate-topped bar offering quality real ales and exceptional wines. Meals may be taken in the cosy lounge, a quieter segregated dining area or the sunny conservatory. A range of sandwiches and snacks, or 'boat-sinking battered cod' with tartare sauce make for a more-than-adequate lunch, with perhaps braised ham hock with white wine and herb sauce, or the award-winning dish of Welsh beef fillet with roast garlic and shallot jus as a mainstay of a full-blown evening feast. Look out for market-fresh fish and local meats on the boards. New for 2005 are four stunning, individually designed suites, each offering handmade beds, luxurious bathrooms, a balcony or patio, and views over the Kinmel Estate.

Rooms: 4 suites from £155.
Prices: Set lunch on Sunday £13.95. Restaurant main course from £9. Bar main course from £9. House wine £11.
Last orders: Bar: lunch 15.00 (Sunday 17.30); dinner 23.00. Food: lunch 14.00; dinner 21.30.
Closed: Monday.
Food: Traditional British, Welsh and French.
Other points: Totally no smoking. Children welcome. Dogs welcome in the bar on request. Garden. Car park. Wheelchair access.
Directions: Exit 16/M56. Take the A5517 and A550 to A55; St George is 2 miles south east of Abergele. (Map 7, A4)

Prestatyn

Nant Hall Restaurant & Bar

Nant Hall Road, Prestatyn, Denbighshire LL19 9LD
Telephone: +44(0)1745 886766
mail@nanthall.com
www.nanthall.co.uk

After much renovation, and now under new owners Peter Lavin and Graham Tinsley, Nant Hall shines inside and out like a newly polished button along the coast road. No expense has been spared on the airy open-plan interiors, which are split into different rooms and can cater for more than 200 covers. There are rooms for formal dining with expensive and eye-catching furniture and rooms with sofa seating by fires for relaxed pre-dinner drinks. Throughout, vivid wallpapers contrast nicely with polished wooden floors. The bar is imposing and well-lit and has tables with chairs and banquettes. Choose from a well-chosen and fairly priced selection of wine, or one of the two real ales from Conwy's micro brewery. Local dishes and ingredients also feature strongly on the menu and, alongside Caesar salad, Thai fishcakes and Mexican fajitas, you will find local specialities such as rump of Welsh Black beef or herb-crusted lamb shank and pork and leek sausages. A separate section is reserved for the fine local seafood; whole Anglesey lobster is offered at market price, and there are children's meals. Homemade puddings and excellent local cheeses rounds things off nicely. The choice here is staggering, but the waiting and kitchen staff pull of everything off with aplomb.

Prices: Restaurant main course from £8.95. House wine £12.85.
Last orders: Food: Dinner 21.30 (22.00 at weekends).
Closed: 25-26 December.
Food: Modern British and International.
Other points: No-smoking areas. Garden. Children welcome. Car park. Wheelchair access.
Directions: A55. Exit onto the A548 to Prestatyn. Nant Hill is on the Old Coast Road. (Map 7, A4)

St Asaph

Drapers Café-Bar

Tweedmill Factory Outlets, Llannerch Park, St Asaph, Denbighshire LL17 0UY
Telephone: +44(0)1745 731005
enquiries@tweedmill.co.uk

Once a mill weaving tweed, the Tweedmill Factory Outlets have been a star attraction by the Welsh Tourist Board. As well as plenty of shopping opportunities, the outlets offer the perfect spot for refuelling. The 100-seater Drapers Café-Bar is a bright and cheerful space filled with plants, pine furniture and a large, south-facing patio with beautiful views across a designated Area of Outstanding Natural Beauty. The menu changes daily and dishes are prepared using fresh local ingredients. Daily specials could take in leek and potato soup, or chicken liver pâté, grilled chicken breast filled with Welsh cheese wrapped in smoked bacon and served with a leek sauce, followed by meringue nest with fresh strawberries and cream. Snacks and light meals run to scrambled eggs with smoked salmon, cheese, chive and bacon bagel, chestnut and mixed-bean savoury loaf, and filled jacket potatoes. It's a popular place for tired shoppers, but big enough to accommodate quite a crowd without the service suffering.

Prices: Main course from £4.95. House wine £6.50.
Last orders: Food: 16.30 (Thursday 19.30, Sunday 16.00).
Closed: Never.
Food: Modern British.
Other points: No-smoking area. Children welcome. Patios. Car park.
Directions: Two miles south of St. Asaph on the A525 to Denbigh. Follow the tourist signs from the A55. (Map 7, A4)

Barmouth

Bae Abermaw

Panorama Road, Barmouth, Gwynedd LL42 1DQ
Telephone: +44(0)1341 280550
enquiries@baeabermaw.com
www.baeabermaw.com

Bae Abermaw combines the old and the new to great effect. Its imposing Victorian exterior hides a comfortable contemporary interior of polished-wood floors and log-burning marble and slate fire-places. Even the basement bar cuts a modern dash. White is the dominant colour in the well-presented bedrooms. Perched on Panorama Hill, most of the bedrooms have fabulous views, while others look onto Snowdonia National Park or are suites. Food is another compelling reason to visit Bae Abermaw. The chef is passionate about using local produce in a range of modern and traditional dishes, such as magnificent sewin from the Mawddach Estuary, Cardigan Bay lobster and Welsh Black beef. Many of the vegetables and herbs are grown in the hotel's own or local gardens. Puddings are sumptuous and range from the baked blueberry cheesecake to a tuille basket of seasonal fruits with coulis and cream. There is a good choice of Welsh cheeses served simply with crackers or grapes and celery. Richard Drinkwater is also a man with an eye for quality and price when it comes to his well-chosen wine list.

Rooms: 14. Double/twin from £110, single from £80.
Prices: Set dinner £23.50. Restaurant main course from £16. House wine from £11.50.
Last orders: Dinner: 21.00.
Closed: Rarely.
Food: Modern British.
Other points: Totally no smoking. Garden. Children welcome. Car park. Licence for civil weddings. Wheelchair access.
Directions: From the M54 at Shrewesbury, take the A458 to Welshpool then the A470 to Dolgellan. Bypass Dolgellan and at Llanelltyd roundabout take the A496 to Barmouth. (Map 7, C3)

Barmouth

The Bistro

Church Street, Barmouth, Gwynedd LL42 1EW
Telephone: +44(0)1341 281009
info@bistro-barmouth.co.uk
www.bistro-barmouth.co.uk

The cheery French-bistro style is perfect for this 18-seater restaurant that is big on atmosphere and friendliness. Its lively daytime vibe turns into a cosy-romantic atmosphere in the evenings. Owners Gareth Palmer and Rosemary Heath are keen on sourcing good ingredients, and this is evident in their flavour-some dishes. Conwy and North Sea fish is delivered from Llandudno, the local butcher provides spring lamb and aged beef, while the organic herbs and salad come from local growers. The food ranges from good old familiar field mushrooms stuffed with garlic and parsley butter and Hereford chicken breast topped with bacon and cheese and served with a creamy cider, chunky apple and rosemary sauce to Mediterranean dishes such as Spanish chicken with chorizo and red peppers. It is also worth exploring the fish specials, say, sea bass fillets with citrus butter and lemon and coriander sauce. Vegetarians are in for a treat with dishes such as mushroom tortellini with a creamy cheese sauce, sun-dried tomatoes and pesto. Puddings are exemplary and the homemade Cointreau and Merlin ice cream is always popular. The Bistro attracts a loyal clientele, so booking is a must, especially at weekends.

Prices: Restaurant main course from £10.95. Vegetarian main course from £8.95. Starter from £3.95. House wine £9.95. Special dietary requirements catered for with advance notice.
Last orders: Food: 21.30.
Closed: Wednesday all day.
Food: Modern British with Mediterranean influences.
Other points: Totally no smoking. Children welcome. Some street parking.
Directions: In the town centre. (Map 7, C3)

Abergavenny

Llansantffraed Court Hotel

Llanvihangel Gobion, Abergavenny,
Monmouthshire NP7 9BA
Telephone: +44(0)1873 840678
reception@llch.co.uk
www.llch.co.uk

Impressive in stature, this country-house hotel is making a name for itself with its fine dining. It has been a hotel since the 1920s and the present house has well-proportioned rooms with a sense of grandeur. Although some of the furnishings may be a little faded, this does not detract from its air of luxury. Comfortable en suite bedrooms are refurbished on a rolling basis, but the main glitz and gloss is saved for the food, which delivers exquisite flavours from the amuse-bouche and canapés through to the petits fours. After a fino sherry in the delightful bar, head through to the dining room; the chintzy look suits the spacious setting and sophisticated menu. Foie gras escalope with an orange salad is followed by Raglan Longhorn beef with oxtail ravioli and consommé. Puddings are formidably good – Granny Smith and Comice pear Tatin with Bower Farm clotted cream – plus there's a fine choice of mostly Welsh cheeses. The wine list focuses on accessibility with much in the fair-price bracket, but with blow-out options, too.

Rooms: 21. Double/twin from £97, single £86. Family room from £120.
Prices: Set lunch £16.50. Set dinner £29.50. Restaurant main course from £16. Bar snack from £7. House wine £15.
Last orders: Food: lunch 14.00; dinner 20.45.
Closed: Never.
Food: Modern Welsh.
Other points: No-smoking area. Children welcome. Dogs welcome. Garden. Car park. Licenced for civil weddings. Trout and salmon fishing.
Directions: Exit 24/M4. From the junction of the A40 and A465 at Abergavenny, follow the signs from the roundabout to Usk on the B4598. The hotel is four miles along on the right. (Map 8, 5E)

Abergavenny

Llanwenarth Hotel & Riverside Restaurant

Brecon Road, Abergavenny, Monmouthshire NP8 1EP
Telephone: +44(0)1873 810550
info@llanwenarthhotel.com
www.llanwenarthhotel.com

Under new ownership, this restaurant has shaken off its dowdy look of yesteryear and re-emerged as a serious culinary contender. As well as ditching its former Pantrhiwgoch name, the interiors have been transformed into a cheery-looking bistro and, more importantly, the menus have been given a new lease of life. The dishes are strong on local ingredients and on simple but effective presentation. Black pudding and boudin blanc on mash with a red-wine reduction or baked filo-pastry parcels of goat's cheese get things off to a flying start. The menu varies with the seasons, but avoids clichés, so rather than the ubiquitous Caesar salad, there's a delicious summer salad of guinea fowl. However it's hard to improve on local salmon served with a hollandaise sauce. Thoughtful vegetarian options include oyster mushroom fettucine with truffle oil and parmesan. An indulgent pudding menu might offer milk chocolate and orange mousse. The wine list offers a good house option and attractive half bottles. The well-appointed bedrooms are a tasteful addition to the main building.

Rooms: 17. Double/twin from £85, single from £65. Family room from £110.
Prices: Set lunch £12.95. Set dinner £14.25. Restaurant main course from £9.45. House wine £11.95.
Last orders: Food: lunch 14.00 (Sunday 15.00); dinner: 21.30 (Sunday 21.00).
Closed: Rarely.
Food: Modern British.
Other points: No-smoking area. Terrace. Children welcome. Car park. Wheelchair access.
Directions: Take the A40 out of Abergavenny, heading towards Brecon. The hotel is two miles out of Abergavenny on the left. (Map 8, E5)

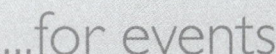

Monmouth

The Stonemill

Rockfield, Monmouth, Monmouthshire NP25 5SW
Telephone: +44(0)1600 716273
www.thestonemill.co.uk

Housed in a converted 16th-century farm cider barn, this restaurant is a stylish setting for some stunning food. Service is friendly and the enthusiastic team in the kitchen do justice to the excellent ingredients available locally. Thanks to its deepest Monmouthshire location, quality local produce features to great effect in the good-value set menu and a fairly priced carte. Starters of warm salad of foie gras, duck confit, green beans and truffle cream reduction or a crabmeat ravioli set the standards bar high, and the mains continue to showcase local glories to their best. Monmouthshire lamb is one of the foundations of this menu and this is joined by Hendre venison and pheasant in season, Monmouthshire beef and fish from Vin Sullivan in Abergavenny. Vegetarian interests are well looked after, with dishes changing regularly, but including aubergine with goat's cheese, spinach and chicory Tatin. Puddings are traditional with the occasional North American or even Afro-Italian flourish. A fine selection of Welsh cheeses with apple chutney is a fine alternative. There are a number of well-appointed suites at reasonable rates.

Rooms: 6. Double/twin from £40, single from £35.
Prices: Set lunch £11.95. Set dinner £15.95. Restaurant main course from £12.50. House wine £11.50.
Last orders: Food: lunch 14.00; dinner 21.30.
Closed: Sunday evening, all day Monday and two weeks in January.
Food: Modern British.
Other points: No-smoking area. Garden. Children welcome. Car park. Licenced for civil weddings. Wheelchair access to all areas.
Directions: M50 north and M4 south. From the centre of Monmouth, head out on the B4233 to Rockfield, Hendre and Abergavenny. The Stonemill is on the right after two and a half miles. (Map 8, 5E)

Raglan

The Beaufort Arms Coaching Inn and Restaurant

High Street, Raglan, Monmouthshire NP15 2DY
Telephone: +44(0)1291 690412
thebeauforthotel@hotmail.com
www.beaufortraglan.co.uk

This 16th-century coaching inn has some outstanding period features, including a huge fireplace taken from nearby Raglan Castle, Welsh slate floors and an impressive heavily carved oak bar in the lounge. Renovation by the Lewis family has introduced a modern feel, best exemplified in the restaurant, where contemporary colours complement heavy beams. Blazing log fires and a warm welcome have turned it into a vibrant community inn. Its team of talented chefs is committed to using first-class local ingredients. Bar menus comprise simple items such as rustic sandwiches of Welsh ham alongside inventive modern dishes listed on the daily specials board; and, overall, quality and presentation is well above average for an inn. In the restaurant, imaginative cooking produces highlights such as seared, marinated lamb with fine green beans, warm basil and mint oil on a red-wine glaze. All en suite bedrooms have been stylishly refurbished and kitted out with modern comforts.

Rooms: 15. Double/twin room from £55, single from £50.
Prices: Restaurant main course from £10.95. Bar main course from £5.75. House wine £8.95.
Last orders: Bar: 23.00. Food: lunch in the lounge bar served daily. Dinner: 21.00 (20.30 Sunday).
Closed: Never.
Food: Modern British.
Other points: No smoking in the restaurant. Garden. Car park. Wheelchair access.
Directions: One minute from the junction of the A40 from Abergavenny and the A449 to Monmouth. (Map 8, E5)

Skenfrith

The Bell at Skenfrith

Skenfrith, Abergavenny, Monmouthshire NP7 8UH
Telephone: +44(0)1600 750235
enquiries@skenfrith.co.uk
www.skenfrith.co.uk

This beautifully restored 17th-century coaching inn occupies a picturesque spot by a bridge spanning the River Monnow. It oozes all the charming allure of an old Welsh inn with its slate floors and old settles in the stylish open-plan bar and dining area, but it's the food and wine that really steal the show. A commitment to local produce in the kitchen, under the skilful hands of chef Kurt Fleming, produces seriously good cooking. Bar lunches bring Gloucester Old Spot pork open sandwiches, followed by apple tart with caramel sauce. The dining-room menu showcases local ingredients in dishes such as home-cured gravadlax with chive crème fraîche or ballotine of duck foie gras, followed by breast of roast duck. Carmamelised rhubarb and vanilla custard is a fitting finish. The owner, a big wine fan, has compiled the wine list of all wine lists, which must be one of the best in the UK, let alone Wales. En suite bedrooms are luxuriously appointed.

Rooms: 8. Double/twin from £95. Single from £75, family room from £145.
Prices: Sunday lunch £19.50. Restaurant main course from £10.20. Bar main course bar/snack from £5.50.
House wine from £10.
Last orders: Bar: 23.00. Food: lunch 14.30; dinner 21.30.
Closed: Two weeks end of January and early February. Monday from October to April.
Food: Modern British.
Other points: No smoking in the restaurant and bedrooms. Garden. Children welcome. Car park. Wheelchair access to the restaurant.
Directions: From the A40 at Monmouth, take the A466 towards Hereford. After 5 miles, turn left onto the B4521 towards Abergavenny. The Bell is straight ahead after two miles, on the banks of the River Monnow. (Map 8, E5)

Usk

Greyhound Inn Hotel

Llantrissant, Usk, Monmouthshire NP15 1LE
Telephone: +44(0)1291 672505
enquiry@greyhound-inn.com
www.greyhound-inn.com

£54·00   67325 5 Fox

This 17th-century Welsh longhouse, once a staging post for coaches, is surrounded by woodland and pasture in the beautiful Usk Valley and noted for its open fires and a comfortable atmosphere. Visitors can choose from a printed bar menu of traditional pub favourites alongside interesting home-cooked specials listed on a daily-changing chalkboard. Using fresh produce from well-sourced suppliers, including locally grown fruit and vegetables, venison from the Welsh Venison Centre, game and fish from Vin Sullivan in Abergavenny, and smoked products from Minola Smokery at nearby Triley Mill, top choices feature Usk salmon, venison-and-ale pie, local pheasant in season, and luxury fish pie. Conversion of the former stables has created 10 spacious en suite bedrooms, all decorated in a cottage style that suits the building's rural location. Ground-floor rooms open on to private patios in a garden setting and all rooms are well equipped with modern comforts. Summer alfresco drinking is a real treat among the colourful flower borders and hanging baskets of the Greyhound's garden, a regular Wales in Bloom Gold Award winner.

Rooms: 10. Double room from £74, single from £52.
Prices: Bar main course from £7. House wine from £12.
Last orders: Food: lunch 14.15 (Monday to Sunday); dinner 22.30.
Closed: No food Sunday evening (bar open 19.00-22.30).
Food: Traditional Welsh.
Other points: No smoking in the restaurant. Children welcome. Dogs welcome in the bar. Garden. Car park. Wheelchair access.
Directions: Exit 24/M4. Usk town square, second left, follow signs to Llantrissant for two and a half miles. (Map 8, E5)

The Greyhound Inn, Usk

Summer eating and drinking is a real treat at this 17th-century Welsh longhouse overlooking the Usk Valley, as the award-winning garden boasts colourful flower borders and attractive hanging baskets. Other than the stunning hillside position, the draw is the traditional Welsh cooking and comfortable accommodation in cottagey en suite rooms. Using fresh produce from well-sourced suppliers, food ranges from traditional pub favourites to imaginative chalkboard specials listing local venison, Usk salmon and Welsh lamb.

Visit the local Farmers' Market

The Memorial Hall in Usk is the venue for the local farmers' market on the first and third Saturday of the month from 10am to 1pm.

Brecon

A470

Merthyr Tydfil

Welsh Venison Centre
Middlewood Farm, Bwlch, Brecon
Tel: 01874 730929

Established and run by the Morgan family since 1985, the Welsh Venison Centre is located in the heart of the Brecon Beacons National Park and was the first to become accredited as both a farm and processing unit under the Quality Mark for Farmed Venison. The deer are raised in beautiful surroundings and importance is given to superb animal husbandry and the highest standards of animal welfare. The result is very tender meat that has a mild yet distinctive and succulent flavour, not at all like the tough gamey reputation venison often has, attributed to wild deer. Nick Davies at the Greyhound Inn in Usk uses their lean and healthy meat in his venison-and-ale pie.

Vin Sullivan Foods
Abergavenny and Blaenavon
Tel: 01495 792792

From humble beginnings at their shop in Abergavenny's High Street, which opened in 1960 and continues to thrive, Vin Sullivan Foods now produces, packages and distributes more than 5,000 products from Blaenavon. High-class gourmet products are supplied alongside more recognisable items in five main product areas – fresh fish, cheese, charcuterie, vegetables and dry provisions – some of which are not found in supermarkets.

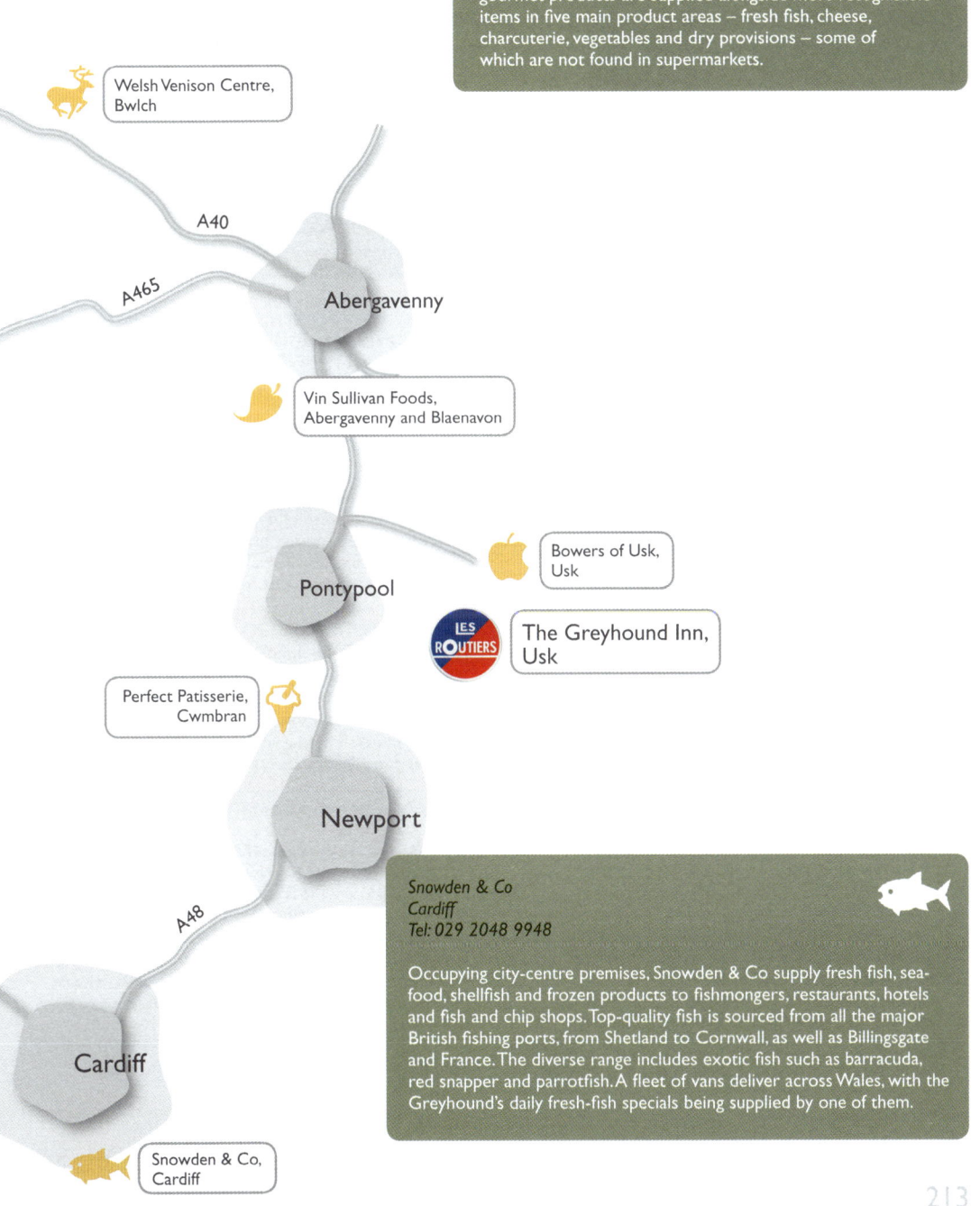

Welsh Venison Centre, Bwlch

A40

A465

Abergavenny

Vin Sullivan Foods, Abergavenny and Blaenavon

Pontypool

Bowers of Usk, Usk

The Greyhound Inn, Usk

Perfect Patisserie, Cwmbran

Newport

A48

Snowden & Co
Cardiff
Tel: 029 2048 9948

Occupying city-centre premises, Snowden & Co supply fresh fish, sea-food, shellfish and frozen products to fishmongers, restaurants, hotels and fish and chip shops. Top-quality fish is sourced from all the major British fishing ports, from Shetland to Cornwall, as well as Billingsgate and France. The diverse range includes exotic fish such as barracuda, red snapper and parrotfish. A fleet of vans deliver across Wales, with the Greyhound's daily fresh-fish specials being supplied by one of them.

Cardiff

Snowden & Co, Cardiff

Wolfscastle

Wolfscastle Country Hotel

Wolfscastle, Haverfordwest, Pembrokeshire SA62 5LZ
Telephone: +44(0)1437 741225
enquiries@wolfscastle.com
www.wolfscastle.com

This hotel is a perfect base for touring the rugged Pembrokeshire coastline and is a handy stopover en route to or from the Emerald Isle. Family run for more than 25 years, you are assured a friendly Welsh welcome and staff ensure everything runs like clockwork. The hotel's refurbishments keep it up to date, for example, the dining room has been transformed beautifully by a local designer. Bedrooms include three executive suites that are among the most spacious and agreeable in the area and they come with thoughtful extras – state-of-the-art TVs, videos and finger-touch bedside lighting make for a relaxing stay. The daily-changing menus follow an 'eat what you like, where you like' policy. Dishes incorporate fresh fish and seafood from nearby Milford Haven, local organic vegetables and herbs and Preseli lamb and beef. The scallops flambéed in Vermouth can't be faulted for freshness. The choice is extensive, with traditional lamb's liver and onions sitting alongside pan-fried fillet of Welsh beef on a baked croûte. These are offered in the clubby bar and elegant restaurant. As well as delicious desserts, there's always a superb choice of Welsh cheeses.

Rooms: 20. Double room from £79–£107, single from £55–£75.
Prices: Main course from £8.50. House wine £10.
Last orders: Food: lunch 14.00; dinner 21.00.
Closed: Never.
Food: International.
Other points: No-smoking area. Garden. Children welcome. Dogs welcome overnight. Car park. Licence for civil weddings. Wheelchair access to the restaurant/pub.
Directions: Signed off the A40, midway between Haverfordwest and Fishguard in the village of Wolfscastle. (Map 7, E2)

Brecon

The Felin Fach Griffin

Felin Fach, Brecon, Powys LD3 0UB
Telephone: +44(0)1874 620111
enquiries@eatdrinksleep.ltd.uk
www.eatdrinksleep.ltd.uk

Charles Inkin's smart, ochre-coloured inn has made a name for itself as one of the new breed of contemporary Welsh inns. Its innovative food brings together quality ingredients in mouth-watering combinations, while upstairs, you can stay in individually designed bedrooms that fall into the minimalist, rustic-charm category. Flagstone floors, open fireplaces, stripped-pine beams, and the Aga cooker retained in an inglenook create an inn with character and personality. With assorted dining and refectory tables and a glorious assortment of antique chairs, anticipation of exciting dining is raised. The ethos in the kitchen is to use fresh local ingredients and keep it simple to maintain freshness and flavours. Daily-updated chalkboard menus might list honey-roast parsnip soup followed by Welsh minute steak with béarnaise for lunch. Suppers consist of more adventurous dishes such as quail skewers, braised puy lentils and cep cappuccino with local venison with autumn fruits. There could be dark chocolate mousse or exemplary Welsh cheeses to finish.

Rooms: 7. Double room from £92.50, single from £67.50. Four-poster room £115.
Prices: Main course lunch from £7.95. Main course supper from £12.95. Starters from £4.50. House wine £11.95.
Last orders: Bar: lunch 15.00; dinner 23.00. Food: lunch 14.30; dinner 21.30 (Sunday 21.00).
Closed: Monday lunch (except Bank Holidays).
Food: Modern British.
Other points: No smoking in the restaurant. Children welcome. Dogs welcome overnight. Garden. Car park. Wheelchair access to the restaurant/pub.
Directions: Four miles north of Brecon on the A470. The Felin Fach Griffins large terracotta building on the left. (Map 7, D4)

Crickhowell

Glangrwyney Court

Glangrwyney, Crickhowell, Powys NP8 1ES
Telephone: +44(0)1873 811288
glangrwyney@aol.com
www.glancourt.com

Glangrwyney Court has all the elements of a fine B&B and more. It's set in an elegant Georgian house sympathetically refurbished by Christina Jackson, who is the perfect host. The wow factor starts at the gate of this lovely property, approached along an attractive tree-lined drive that runs through gorgeous gardens. Christina takes great pride in her home and in making you feel welcome. The lounges, with just the right amount of chintz, are supremely comfortable. These are complemented by five opulently decorated en suite bedrooms that are romantic in style and have lovely views over the grounds. Breakfast is quite an occasion, thanks to the sourcing of fabulous ingredients from the Black Mountain Smokery, local honey, vegetables and fruit. Christina doesn't cook other meals, but at lunch and in the evening, you can dine very well in nearby Crickhowell, which has plenty of pub and restaurant options. Glangrwyney Court does, however, have a residential drinks licence. Overall, this guesthouse offers excellent value for money for this level of comfort and outlook.

Rooms: 5, 1 with private bathroom. Double room from £60, single from £45. Family room £85.
Prices: Set dinner £23. Main course from £12.50. House wine £10.
Closed: Rarely.
Food: Traditional British.
Other points: Residents only. No-smoking area. Children welcome. Garden. Car park. Boules and croquet.
Directions: Two miles east of Crickhowell off the A40. (Map 8, E5)

Machynlleth

The Wynnstay Hotel & Restaurant

Heol Maengwyn, Machynlleth, Powys SY20 8AE
Telephone: +44(0)1654 702941
info@wynnstay-hotel.com
www.wynnstay-hotel.com

Since the arrival of Charles and Sheila Dark and chef Gareth Johns, this coaching inn has been moving effortlessly up the culinary ladder. Meals are fine affairs, and Johns' dishes never fail to engage. Lunches in bars and restaurant include plenty of local ingredients: juicy sewin served with samphire butter and Pembrokeshire new potatoes gives an idea of the quality and simplicity at work here. Barmouth lobster and monkfish from the Cambrian coast are some of the other piscine pleasures. Among the meat options, try the wonderful stuffed lamb shoulder with wild garlic mash and creamed leeks. A separate pizza menu widens the choice. The dinner menu resists the temptation of remaining stolidly traditional, so pink pigeon breast comes with a ginger purée. Puddings are awesome: bread and butter pudding with custard, or Welsh cheeses. The wine list has much for Italian fans, from prosecco to Brunello di Montalcino. En suite rooms are simply appointed and keenly priced.

Rooms: 23. Double/twin from £80, single from £55. Family from £80.
Prices: Set lunch £12.95 (Sundays only). Set dinner £25. Restaurant/Bar main course from £9.95. House wine £13.95.
Last orders: Bar: Lunch 14.00; Dinner 23.00. Food: Lunch 14.00; Dinner 21.00. Pizzeria: 21.30.
Closed: New Year's Day.
Food: Welsh with Italian influences. Real pizzas.
Other points: No smoking in the restaurant. Children welcome. Dogs welcome. Car park. Wheelchair access. Pizzeria on the premises with wood-fired oven.
Directions: M54/last exit. Follow signs to Newtown, continue on A470 to Machynlleth. Wynnstay is on the left as you approach the Clock Tower. Scenic route available on request. (Map 7, C3)

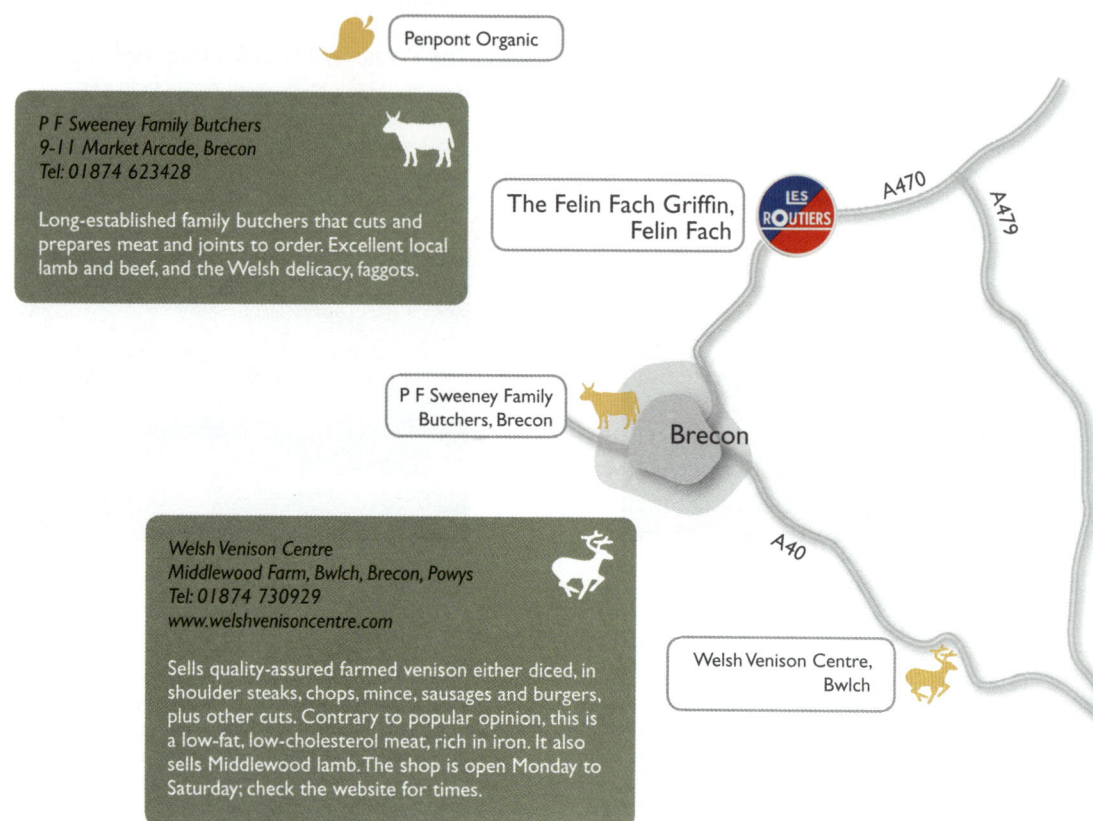

Penpont Organic

P F Sweeney Family Butchers
9-11 Market Arcade, Brecon
Tel: 01874 623428

Long-established family butchers that cuts and
prepares meat and joints to order. Excellent local
lamb and beef, and the Welsh delicacy, faggots.

The Felin Fach Griffin,
Felin Fach

P F Sweeney Family
Butchers, Brecon

Brecon

Welsh Venison Centre
Middlewood Farm, Bwlch, Brecon, Powys
Tel: 01874 730929
www.welshvenisoncentre.com

Sells quality-assured farmed venison either diced, in
shoulder steaks, chops, mince, sausages and burgers,
plus other cuts. Contrary to popular opinion, this is
a low-fat, low-cholesterol meat, rich in iron. It also
sells Middlewood lamb. The shop is open Monday to
Saturday; check the website for times.

Welsh Venison Centre,
Bwlch

The Felin Fach Griffin, Felin Fach

The Felin Fach is a contemporary gastropub full of rustic charm, whose owner Charles Inkin is a
big fan of the Slow Food philosophy of sourcing authentic, artisan foods, which, wherever possible,
are produced or grown locally. That's why you will find an array of supreme Welsh produce on the
menu, from fabulous meat and game to vegetables and cheeses. All these ingredients are simply,
but superbly, cooked and presented by head chef Ricardo Van Ede. Here, he shares a few of the
Felin Fach's top suppliers in this culinary hot spot of the Brecon Beacons.

Visit the local Farmers' Market

Abergavenny's farmers' market is held on the fourth Thursday of every month in Market Hall, Cross Street,
Abergavenny. There is plenty of organic produce among the fish, game, meat, fruit, vegetables, cheese, eggs
preserves, wines and crafts. For more information, visit www.abergavennymarket.co.uk.

Black
Mountains

Bower Farm Dairy,
Grosmont

A465

Bower Farm Dairy
Grosmont
Tel: 01981 240219

Victor and Val Collinson have developed a keen local market
for their dairy produce, with milk from a herd of pedigree
Jersey cows from which they make cream, clotted cream,
yogurt and crème fraîche. They sell to more than 80 local
hotels and restaurants, as well as several retail outlets. They
also produce rare-breed Gloucester Old Spot pork.

 Black Mountains Smokery,
Crickhowell

A485

Abergavenny

A40

A4042

Black Mountains Smokery
Unit 1, Leslie House, Elvitec Estate, Crickhowell
Tel: 01873 811566
www.smoked-foods.co.uk

Traditional smoking methods and hand-filleting and slicing from
quality ingredients make for a fine product collection. Wonderful
smoked salmon and duck and a range of gift packs, from fish or
meat party platters to the incredible 'Feast' collection of foods.
You can even order a monthly supply of salmon for a year.

CHANNEL ISLANDS

As they're surrounded by sea, it comes as no surprise that seafood is a big fixture on our exclusive band of members in Jersey, Guernsey and Sark. In fact from many of the restaurants, you can enjoy wonderful sea views as you tuck into the freshest lobster, oysters, langoustines and other seafood delights.

Quality is of the uttermost importance to these top-class hotels and restaurants, and the chefs source and cook with the best, whether that's the new season Jersey Royal potatoes or the most delicious Jersey cream.

You will find a host of country cuisines on Jersey and Guernsey and more than a nod to the French classics. What you will also be served in this area is plenty of fresh air, wonderful scenery and dollops of peace and tranquillity. These gems of islands are real get-away-from-it-all destinations, and our members provide discreet and quality places to stay. If you're looking to recharge and relax, then all of our Channel Island candidates fit the bill.

Herm Island

White House Hotel

Herm, via Guernsey, Herm GY1 3HR
Telephone: +44 (0)1481 722159
hotel@herm-island.com
www.herm-island.com

The White House Hotel is a breathtakingly picturesque holiday base and the perfect get-away-from-it all destination. The only hotel on Herm Island, a car-free zone, it sets dazzlingly high standards. Despite the island's peacefulness, there is plenty to do: walking, birdwatching, and exploring. The hotel was created from an old house in 1949 by Peter and Jenny Wood, and is now run by their daughter Penny and son-in-law Adrian. It has extensive lounges with open fires, a library, games cupboard, solar-heated swimming pool, tennis court and croquet lawn. The best bedrooms have sea views, and all rooms, by popular demand, have no TV or phone. With oyster beds visible from the dining room, local seafood is as fresh as you can get. Local shellfish – lobsters, crabs or scallops – is available as a supplement to the set evening menu. Alternatively, you could opt for set menu choices of salad of smoked chicken and mango, followed by roast rack of lamb and passion-fruit panna cotta. The wine list, offering a range of well-priced bottles, has France to the fore, but finds room for a wide selection of New World wines.

Rooms: 40. Rooms from £70 per person, half board.
Prices: Set menu £29.25 including boat fare. Main course lunch from £6. House wine £9.95.
Last orders: Bar: 23.00. Food: lunch 14.00; dinner 21.00.
Closed: Mid October to April.
Food: Modern and traditional British and French.
Other points: No smoking in the restaurant. Garden. Children welcome. No cars on Herm Island. Tennis court. Swimming pool. Croquet lawn.
Directions: Fly or take the boat from Guernsey. Regular 20-minute service by boat to Herm Island. (Map 4, E6)

St Brelade

Chateau Valeuse

Rue de la Valeuse, St Brelade's Bay, St Brelade, Jersey JE3 8EE
Telephone: +44(0)1534 746281
chatval@itl.net
www.user.super.net.uk/~chatval

With its large windows and impressive array of balconies and windows, Chateau Valeuse is more splendid Swiss chalet in style as opposed to traditional French pile. The design allows guests to enjoy the stunning coastal views across St Brelade's Bay, one of the most attractive in Jersey. The hotel has an excellent location in other ways as it's south-facing, set back from the road and surrounded by impeccably maintained gardens. Excellent-value bedrooms, many with sea-view balconies, are all comfortably furnished, well-maintained and have pristine bathrooms. A sun terrace overlooking the garden is the perfect place to enjoy a light lunch or early-evening apéritif, or you can relax in the Tudor Bar, while the more energetic can make the most of the outdoor swimming pool and putting green. In the restaurant, you can choose between the good four-course table d'hôte, perhaps moules marinière, or tiger prawns and mussels in garlic butter, followed by chargrilled pork fillets with tarragon and mustard cream or fresh grilled plaice. Choose your pudding from the trolley that's laden with delights.

Rooms: 34. Rooms from £34 per person.
Prices: Set dinner £19 (4 courses). House wine £7.
Last orders: Food: snacks 14.00; dinner 20.45.
Closed: Sunday and from November to March for non-residents.
Food: European.
Other points: No smoking in restaurant. Children over 5 welcome. Garden. Car park.
Directions: From the airport, take the B4 south towards St Brelade's Bay, then the B6 (La Route de la Baie). Turn left into Rue de la Valeuse and the hotel is on the left. (Map 4, F7)

St Martin

Le Frère Restaurant

Rozel Hill, St Martin, Jersey JE3 6AN
Telephone: +44 (0)1534 861000
lefrere@jerseymail.co.uk
www.lefrerejersey.com

For years, Le Frère was known as a bistro but, following an extensive refurbishment, new owner Simon Dufty has created a casually elegant feel to his much more exciting restaurant. Le Frère's location in the north east of the island makes it the closest restaurant to France, and the menu, superbly executed by head chef Olivier Imbert, gives more than a nod to the noble cooking of that country. Under Imbert's deft hand, the amazing seafood and other local ingredients are used to great effect in the table d'hôte, lunch and carte menus. From the extensive carte, there are Jersey oysters, salmon and crab fishcakes with a chickpea dressing and pineapple salsa to start, followed by a middle course of, say, duo of artichoke soup, with mains of Jersey lobster on Jersey Royal mash, fillet of beef Wellington, or pavé of brill tutti verde served with a split pea and watercress jus. There is something for everyone, including a degustation menu and an excellent, exclusive selection of wines from around the world. From the restaurant, you can enjoy the most breathtaking views, and dining alfresco here is a joy. It is licensed for weddings and has three luxury self-contained suites.

Prices: Set lunch from £16.50. Set dinner from £23.50.
Restaurant main course from £15.50. Bar/snack main course from £7. House wine £12/50
Last orders: Food: lunch 14.00; dinner: 21.00 (Tuesday to Saturday).
Closed: Monday all day and Sunday night.
Food: Modern British.
Other points: No-smoking area. Garden. Children welcome. Car park. Licensed for civil weddings. Wheelchair access.
Directions: (Map 4, F7)

Sark

La Sablonnerie

Little Sark, Sark GY9 0SD
Telephone: +44 (0)1481 832061

As soon as you set foot on Sark, you enter a world of tranquillity and luxury. The fact that the island is car-free creates the peace and quiet, while La Sablonnerie ensures the ultimate get-away-from-it-all experience. A break here is magical from the start, as the hotel sends a horse-drawn barouche to collect you from the tiny harbour to take you to Little Sark at the southernmost tip. The 16th-century farmhouse and cottages that make up La Sablonnerie are delightful and set in extensive grounds. The buildings have been discreetly modernised for maximum comfort. Owned and run by the Perrée family since 1946, daughter Elizabeth is now at the helm. The heart of the hotel is the low-beamed bar with its granite walls and massive fireplace that has roaring fires in winter. All the traditional charm has been maintained in the public rooms and individually decorated bedrooms. This is a top place to dine, too, as its own farm supplies fresh fruit, vegetables, dairy produce and meat for the restaurant, while locally caught lobsters, scallops and oysters are a regular feature on the menu. Dinner begins with canapés in the bar, followed by roasted scallops with garlic butter, fillet of home-reared beef and crème brulée with exotic fruits and berries.

Rooms: 22, 12 ensuite. Rooms £30-£60 per person.
Prices: Set lunch £19.80 and dinner £20.80. House wine £7.50.
Last orders: Food: lunch 14.30; dinner 21.30.
Closed: Mid October-Easter.
Food: Modern French.
Other points: No-smoking area. Children welcome. Dogs welcome overnight. Garden.
Directions: Fly to Guernsey and take the boat to Sark. (Map 4, E6)

FOOD
PRODUCER'S

The recipes you cook are only as good as the ingredients you use, and we can help you source the best. Our directory of food producers and farm shops around the country brings you a market garden of fresh produce, the best local cheeses, meats and products. So, whether you want to pick your own fruits, buy a picnic hamper of goodies or garden plants, we have pinpointed the top suppliers.

Ely, Cambridgeshire

La Hogue Farm Shop and Delicatessen

La Hogue Farm, Chippenham, Ely,
Cambridgeshire CB7 5PZ
Tel: +44(0)1638 751128
info@lahogue.co.uk
www.lahogue.co.uk

Hours: Tuesday-Friday 10.00-19.00. Saturday 10.00-17.30.
Sunday 10.00-16.00. Closed Monday.
Other Points: Farm shop. Commercial kitchen. Car park.
Directions: From London/Cambridge take the A11 to Thetford and
Norwich. Take the first turning left to Chippenham. The
farm shop is 500 yards on the right.

Opened in 2002, La Hogue was named after a naval battle of the same name. This battle was fought off the shores of France and timbers from some of the ships were used to build the main farmhouse. You will find only the freshest East Anglian produce is stocked at Chris and Jo Reeks' family-owned farm shop and delicatessen. On offer are local fruits, vegetables, meats, game and venison from Suffolk estates, more than 60 types of cheese, Norfolk and continental hams, home-baked breads, antipasti, wines and ales. The farm's kitchen uses local ingredients in its tempting array of home-cooked dishes, which range from cakes to hearty frozen ready-meals.

Thurstaston, Cheshire

Church Farm Organics

Church Lane, Thurstaston, Wirral,
Cheshire CH61 0HW
Tel: +44(0)151 6487838
www.churchfarm.org.uk

Hours: Tuesday-Friday 10.00-17.00. Saturday 9.00-17.00. Sunday 11.00-17.00. Closed Monday.
Other Points: Coffee shop. Car park. Plants and shrubs for sale. Farm animals. Wheelchair access.
Directions: Exit 4/M53. Take the A540 Chester to Heswall road. Continue until you reach Thurstaston, then follow the brown signs to the farm.

It's set in a conservation area and has fabulous views of the River Dee, but the main reason to visit this family-run farm shop is that it stocks around 2,000 products. All the fruit and vegetables are organic and so too is the majority of the meats, cheese and grocery lines. You will find all the top brands here, from Belvoir cordials to The Village Bakery breads and Royal Warrant holder Richard Woodall's bacons, sausages and hams. The shop also sells fair trade products where possible, and runs an organic box scheme in the Wirral area. It also has a caravan and camping site.

Grasmere, Cumbria

Sarah Nelson's Original Celebrated Grasmere Gingerbread

The Gingerbread Shop, Church Cottage,
Grasmere, Cumbria LA22 9SW
Tel: +44(0)15394 35428
sarahnelson@grasmeregingerbread.co.uk
www.grasmeregingerbread.co.uk

Hours: Monday-Saturday 9.15-17.30. Sunday
12.30-17.30. (Shorter hours in Winter).
Other Points: Shop. Mail order.
Directions: From the south, take exit 36/M6,
then the A590 north, onto the A591, through
Windermere and Ambleside into Grasmere.

You can't visit Grasmere without visiting William Wordsworth's home Dove Cottage and the famous Grasmere Gingerbread Shop. Tucked away in the picturesque village, this tiny shop was built in 1630, originally as the village school. The gingerbread business has been in operation for 151 years, and has been in the same family for the last 80 years; the little girl pictured with her grandmother in the photo on the shop wall

is Joanne, who now runs the shop. Many have tried to copy the world-famous secret gingerbread recipe, but no one has ever come close to the intensely flavoured biscuit that comes traditionally wrapped in a classic blue-and-white pure parchment paper.

Kendal, Cumbria

Low Sizergh Barn

Low Sizergh Farm, Sizergh,
Kendal, Cumbria LA8 8AE
Tel: +44(0)15395 60426
apark@lowsizerghbarn.co.uk
www.lowsizerghbarn.co.uk

Hours: 9.00-17.30.
Other Points: Car park. Farm shop.
Farm trail. Craft gallery. Tearoom.
Directions: Situated on the A591,
three miles south of Kendal and
three miles from exit 36/M6. Follow
the A590 brown signs for Sizergh
Castle then Low Sizergh Barn.

Three floors of speciality foods, crafts
and gifts await you at this 17th-
century barn shop. It was awarded
UK Farm Retailer of the Year 2005
by FARMA (the Farmers' Retail &
Markets Association), and it's easy
to see why. Not only is it well-
appointed, with stylish interiors and
exposed brickwalls, but its shelves
are laden with speciality Cumbrian
foods. There are cheeses and ice cream
made from the farm's organic milk,
eggs and organic vegetables and fruits
from the fields and orchards. The tearoom uses the homegrown ingredients
to good effect in its breads, cakes and a selection of savoury dishes. To see
the cows being milked from the large viewing windows above, aim to arrive
around 3.45pm. Downstairs, in the craft shop, there are local ceramics,
paintings, baskets and rugs aplenty to buy. The two-mile farm trail for those
interested in organic farming is a must.

Penrith, Cumbria

The Old Smokehouse

Brougham Hall, Brougham,
Penrith, Cumbria CA10 2DE
Tel: +44(0)1768 867772
enqs@the-old-smokehouse.
co.uk

Hours: 10.00-16.00.
Other Points: Shop.
Directions: Brougham Hall is
signposted from the A6, one
mile south of Penrith.

If you thought smoked fish
began and finished with salmon,
get along to Richard Muirhead's
shop. Here you will find all
manner of fresh produce given
the smoked treatment, including
trout, meat, poulty, game,
venison, sausage and cheese.
The smokehouse is housed
within the walls of 14th-century
Brougham Hall. All the products
are carefully hand-smoked and
brined with their own recipes
of herbs and spices, and then
either cold-smoked or smoked-
roasted over oak. Fishermen
will be pleased to learn that the smokehouse will smoke your trout and salmon catch,
if it is already cleaned. Another quite different, but delicious, facet of this business is
its range of homemade gourmet chocolate truffles and coffee chocolates.

Penrith, Cumbria

The Watermill

Little Salkeld, Penrith,
Cumbria CA10 1NN
Tel: +44(0)1768 881523
organicflour@aol.com
www.organicmill.co.uk

Hours: 10.30-17.00.
Other Points: Mail order. Shop.
Directions: Six miles from exit 40/M6.
Take the A686 for five miles to
Langwathby. Turn left at the village
green. The mill is two miles on.

Ana and Nick Jones's shop majors
in the organic flours that are milled
at their restored watermill. The
wholesome range inclues wheatmeal,
wholewheat, barley flour, a special
blend, grain flour and a no-knead
variety. There is also Miller's Magic,
a blend of wheat and rye flours, made
using a traditional medieval recipe.
The flours are supplemented by a
host of other ingredients such as oats,
different styles of muesli, dried fruit,
nuts, seeds, pasta, herbs, spices, beans
and peas, chocolate, coffee, teas,
herbs, herb teas, spices and books.
You can buy these products online,
and book one of their numerous
cookery courses. Their Gallery shop
sells knits and crafts.

Cirencester, Gloucestershire

Chesterton Farm Shop

Chesterton Farm, Cirencester,
Gloucestershire GL7 6JP
Tel: +44(0)1285 653003
www.chestertonfarm.co.uk

Hours: 8.30-17.00. Saturday 8.00-16.00.
Closed Sunday.
Other Points: Farm shop. Rare-breed
butchers.
Directions: Situated on the southern
outskirts of Cirencester, off Chesterton
Lane. Follow the A433 out of Cirencester
in the direction of Tetbury. Chesterton
Lane is on the left between the last two
roundabouts.

This farm shop majors in traditional British and rare-breed meats and it is accredited by the Rare Breeds Survival Trust. It has a policy of only selling fully traceable meats. The butchers are happy to prepare meats and advise on recipes. Among its prime meat choices are Gloucester Old Spot pork, Tamworth pork, Dorset Down lamb, its famous dry-cured bacon and ribs of beef. Alongside the butchers is a well-stocked fruit and vegetable farm shop offering an excellent choice of locally grown fresh produce. It also sells delicious home-baked cakes, ice cream, free-range eggs, nibbles and olives. You can 'scoop' buy frozen fruits and vegetables.

...for topical features

Set in a traditional Cotswold threshing barn, Longborough Farm Shop, surrounded by its fields of fruits and vegetables and orchards, is a most pleasurable location to stock up on what's fresh and good in the region. You'll find a wide range of produce from its own farm and small local suppliers – most of the produce is sourced within a 30-mile radius. Throughout the summer, there are plentiful supplies of pick-your-own crops such as asparagus, strawberries, raspberries, red and blackcurrants, gooseberries, plums, greengages, apples, and pears. The shop is also a veritable feast of artisan English cheeses, local beef, pork, lamb and handmade sausages, fresh bread, deli items and gourmet ready meals.

Moreton-in-Marsh, Gloucestershire

Longborough Farm Shop

Longborough, Moreton-in-Marsh, Gloucestershire GL56 0QZ
Tel: +44(0)1451 830441
mail@longboroughfarmshop.com
www.longboroughfarmshop.com

Hours: January-Easter 10.00-17.00. Easter-Christmas 10.00-18.00. Closed Sunday.
Other Points: Farm shop. Car park. PYO.
Directions: Take the A424 out of Stow towards Broadway. The shop is three miles down on the left, past the Candicote turning.

Blackmoor, Hampshire

Blackmoor Farm Shop

Honey Lane, Blackmoor,
Hampshire GU33 6BS
Tel: +44(0)1420 473782

Hours: Monday-Saturday 9.00-17.00. Sunday 10.00-14.00.
Other Points: Farm Shop.
Directions: At the junction of the A3 and A3006 head towards Selbourne. Take the first right to Blackmoor and then a left. The farm shop is on the right.

Blackmoor Farm Shop is set in the heart of a family-owned estate and it is well stocked with local and British produce. In the farm's orchards, they grow old-fashioned and new varieties of English apples, pears and plums, all of which you can buy in the farm shop. In the summer, they also grow and sell strawberries. There is much more on offer than fruit though, as the shop sells fresh breads, homemade cakes, pies and savoury flans, which are

all cooked on the premises. In addition, they stock English cheeses, eggs, butter and other dairy produce, fresh vegetables, additive-free meat, jams and pickles, local honey, fudges and chocolates. There's also a tempting drinks line-up – a variety of ciders, local English wine and several choices of apple juice. You can sample many of its homebaked treats in the farm's coffee shop.

Ledbury, Herefordshire

Just Rachel Quality Desserts

The Old Dairy, Churches Farm,
Eggs Tump, Bromsberrow,
near Ledbury,
Gloucestershire HR8 1SA
Tel: +44(0)1531 650639
info@justrachel.com
www.justrachel.com

Hours: No direct sales. Check the website or call for a list of retail outlets.
Other Points: Mail order. Delivery service. Wholesaler.
Directions: Just off the A417, five mile south-east of Ledbury.

Rachel Hicks looked to cookery books by Mrs Beeton and Eliza Acton to find inspiration for her authenic, additive-free range of fabulous ice creams. Her ices and sorbets are popular in Herefordshire, and now, thanks to mail order, they can be enjoyed countrywide. The recipes are made using wholesome ingredients, local where possible. Some of the more unusual and enticing recipes include: butterscotch and orange liqueur; damson and sloe gin; gooseberry and elderflower; and plum, cinnamon and amaretto. Fans of unadulterated vanilla and chocolate won't be disappointed either. Indeed, all the sorbets and desserts come highly recommended. A different ice cream flavour is introduced every month, and there's one made especially for Cheltenham Race Week, held annually in March, that contains whisky, ginger and fresh orange juice.

Market Harborough, Leicestershire

Farndon Fields Farm Shop

Farndon Road, Market Harborough,
Leicestershire LE16 9NP
Telephone: +44(0)1858 464838
office@farndonfields.co.uk

Hours: Monday-Saturday 8.00-18.00. Sunday and
Bank Holidays 10.00-16.00. Closed Christmas
and New Year.
Other Points: Farm shop. Café. Butchery.
DIrections: J21/M1, Lutterworth. Take the A427
to Market Harborough. Turn right at the first
roundabout and right again at the next. The farm
is quarter of a mile on the right.

Originally selling potatoes and other vegetables, this centre long outgrew its farmhouse garage and is now housed in a large purpose-built shop. The range of produce has taken off too, and includes a wider choice of vegetables and a full selection of salads and fruits grown on the 250-acre site. These are supplemented by locally baked cakes and bread, meat, cheeses, jams, chutneys, honey, pickles, sauces and other deli products. The garden centre sells cut flowers plus plants, composts and pots.

Corbridge, Northumberland

Brocksbushes Fruit Farm

Brocksbushes Farm, Corbridge,
Northumberland NE43 7UB
Telephone: +44(0)1434 633100
acd@brocksbushes.co.uk
www.brocksbushes.co.uk

Hours: 9.30-18.00 in winter.
9.30-19.00 in summer.
Other Points: Farm shop. Parking.
Picnic area.
DIrections: 16 miles west of Newcastle
-upon-Tyne and five miles east of
Hexham, on the A69. The entrance is off
the Styford roundabout.

With Brocksbushes on your doorstep, all your dinner party dilemmas are solved. Its range of homemade foods, including savoury pies to decadent puddings, are irresistible and made to order. Farm fresh poultry and game in season is another draw, as are the fresh berry fruits. If you're not local, you can order one of its fabulous food hampers packed with goodies to be delivered by post. Alternatively, drop by to stock up on its grocery lines, fresh fruit and vegetables, much of it organic, and wines from around the world. This would also be the ideal place to fill your picnic basket, as there is a wonderful selection of cheese, smoked salmon and freshly baked breads and cakes. You can sample the farm's homemade specialities in its tearoom, which is also licenced.

From May to October, Millets Farm has more than 50 acres of crops exclusively for pick-your-own harvesting. A choice of around 30 different fruits and vegetables can be picked throughout the summer months, with many new varieties of certain crops extending the season. But if you'd rather someone else did the hard work, the extensive farm shop stocks the same produce. Alongside is a bakery selling breads and cakes made from locally grown and milled wheat, a delicatessen with a good cheese counter, a butchers selling locally reared meats and a wet fish shop. There's also a wine department. As well as two restaurants and the farm shop, there is a garden centre, children's zoo, trout lake and maze – more than than enough to make Millets a fun day out.

Abingdon, Oxfordshire

Millets Farm Centre

Kingston Road, Frilford, Abingdon,
Oxfordshire OX13 5PD
Telephone: +44(0)1865 391266
www.milletsfarmcentre.com

Hours: 9.00-17.00.
Other Points: Car park. Farm shop. Play
area. Children's farm. Restaurants.
Garden centre. Picnic area. PYO fruit
and vegetables available June-
September.
DIrections: Four miles west of
Abingdon on the A415 (follow
the brown signs).

Hailey, Oxfordshire

Shaken Oak Products

Shaken Oak Farm, Old North
Leigh Lane, Hailey, Witney,
Oxfordshire OX29 9UX
Tel: +44(0)1993 868043
shakenoak@lycos.co.uk
www.shakenoak.co.uk

Hours: Weekends and by appointment.
Other Points: Mail order. Farmers' market.
Delivery service.
Directions: From Witney take the B4022.
Before Hailey, turn right into Poffley End. Turn
right at the next crossroads (about one mile).
Take the left fork up the lane to the farm.

Mustard lovers should head for this farm on the edge of the Cotswolds. The owners started making mustard as a hobby for family and friends, but word soon spread and their mustard production has become a full-time business. What started in the farmhouse kitchen, then expanded into a purpose-built unit in an adjoining barn, is now set up in a dedicated Mustard House. Only the best ingredients are used in the range, which includes: original; mustard with garlic; honey mustard; mustard with herbs; Old Hooky beer mustard; Arthur's peppercorn mustard; and mustard with ginger. Each mustard comes with serving recommendations. In addition, a picanté south American-style sauce and a mustard and garlic dressing complete the offering. All the products are free from preservatives, colouring or artificial ingredients.

Market Drayton, Shropshire

Buttercross Farm Foods

Shiffords Grange Farm, Red Bull,
Market Drayton,
Shropshire TF9 2QS
Tel: +44(0)1630 656670
buttercross@farmersweekly.net
www.buttercross.com

Hours: 8.30-17.00.
Other Points: Farm shop. Mail order.
Suppliers to specialist retail outlets and
catering establishments.
Directions: Approximately one and a
half miles east of Market Drayton on
the A53.

Animal welfare has always been important to Buttercross Farm Foods, which specialises in fresh, free-range pork, dry-cured bacon, quality hams and gammons, speciality sausages and black pudding. All the produce is prepared on the farm from the specially selected outdoor-reared pigs, which are all RSPCA Freedom Food Accredited. The aim of owners Martyn and Helen Rowley is to 'revive the links between farmer and consumer for fresher, local food.' The new farm shop, which opened in summer 2005, offers a full range of local produce and a dedicated butchers offering, beef, lamb and poultry, as well as the pork.

Good old-fashioned bacon with real flavour can be hard to find at your local supermarket, but Maynards' dry-cured bacon will restore your faith in this key component of the great British breakfast. Its bacons and hams are cured to traditional methods and to recipes that date back to the 17th-century. The flavour of the British pork is enhanced by the curing process, which uses a mix of unrefined sugars and syrups imported from Mauritius, plus herbs and salts. You can buy sweet and medium flavour cures as well as several different cuts and flavours of hams. Also worth tasting are the superior sausages that come in Shropshire, Staffordshire and Cumberland varieties.

Shrewsbury, Shropshire

Maynards Farm Bacon

Hough Farm, Weston under
Redcastle, Shrewsbury,
Shropshire SY4 5LR
Tel: +44(0)1948 840252
sales@maynardsfarm.co.uk
www.maynardsfarm.co.uk

Hours: Monday-Saturday
9.00-18.00.
Other Points: Farm shop.
Mail order.
Directions: 10 miles north of
Shrewsbury on the A49.

Lichfield, Staffordshire

The Old Stables Farm Shop & Bakery

Packington Moor Farm, Packington,
Lichfield, Staffordshire WS14 9QB
Tel: +44(0)1543 481223
johnandrosemarybarnes@
  btopenworld.com
www.packingtonmoor-events.com

Hours: Tuesday-Friday 8.00-18.00. Saturday
8.00-17.30. Closed Sunday and Monday.
Other Points: Farmers' market. Farm shop.
Delivery service. Car park. Play area.
Picnic area.
Directions: Between the A51 and the A5,
near Whittington Army Barracks.

John and Rosemary Barnes's farm provides a rich harvest of pick-your-own fruits throughout the summer. Their fruity line-up includes blackcurrants, redcurrants, strawberries, raspberries and gooseberries. You can also buy these in the farm shop along with a winning selection of cheeses, cream, free-range eggs, meat and poultry, locally baked breads, cakes, pies, homemade ice creams and other grocery lines. Light refreshments are served, alfresco in good weather, and there's a large picnic area and playground as well as ample parking and a camping area.

Woodbridge, Suffolk

Tastebuds

The Street, Earl Soham,
Suffolk IP13 7RT
Tel: +44(0)1728 685557
tastebudssuffolk@yahoo.com
www.tastebudsfood.com

Hours: Monday-Friday 8.30-18.30.
Saturday 9.00-17.00. Closed Sunday.
Other Points: Shop. Mail order.
Farmers' market. Car park.
Directions: Situated on the A1120 on
the east Suffolk tourist route, halfway
between Yoxford and Stowmarket.

This delicatessen brings together many Suffolk and regional speciality foods that you won't find in the supermarket. Worth noting are the locally smoked fish and shellfish from Orford, seasonal organic fresh fruit and vegetables, a wide selection of British cheeses, homemade cakes, deli and takeaway party foods. You

can also order bespoke cakes. They are happy to make up weekend grocery packs or picnics, a handy service if you are self-catering. Also worth adding to your shopping list are the cask and bottle conditioned real ales from the nearby brewery. The deli is constantly on the look out for new and interesting products, so there's always something new to try. Sample its light lunches, cream teas and other refreshments in the attractive Coffee Yard.

Godalming, Surrey

Secretts

Hurst Farm, Chapel Lane, Milford,
Godalming, Surrey GU8 5HU
Telephone: +44(0)1483 520500
kathy@secretts.co.uk
www.secretts.co.uk

Hours: Farm shop, flower shop and garden centre;
Monday-Saturday 9.00-17.30. Farm shop; Sunday
11.00-17.00. Flower shop; Sunday 11.00-13.00.
Garden centre; Sunday 11.00-16.30.
Other Points: Farm shop. Flower shop and garden
centre. PYO. Ample parking. Play area. Picnic area.
Directions: Just off the A3, 40 minutes' drive
from London.

This farm shop is supplied with market garden produce by third-generation farmers. The shop stocks an extensive range of herbs, fruits, vegetables and salads produced outdoors and under glass on 150 acres of sandy loam. Home-grown tulips are available from January to April, and a pick your own fruit and vegetable section from June to September. Garden furniture, barbecues and other horticultural items can be bought at the garden centre, where there is also a self-service restaurant. And that's not all, next to the farm shop is Eliza's Tea Room, a recreation of a 1930s' tearoom, serving speciality teas and coffees, delicious sandwiches, light lunches and afternoon teas.

Hastings, East Sussex

Carr Taylor Wines Ltd

Wheel Lane, Westfield, Hastings,
East Sussex TN35 4SG
Tel: +44(0)1424 752501
sales@carr-taylor.co.uk
www.carr-taylor.com

Hours: 10.00-17.00. Closed 25 December-2 January.
Other Points: Vineyard. Shop. Mail order.
Tours available.
Directions: From the A21/A28 junction, just north of
Hastings, follow the A28 for two miles to Westfield.
Turn left by The Old Courthouse pub. The Vineyards
are three quarters of a mile on the left.

Turners Hill, West Sussex

Tulley's Farm Shop

Turners Hill Road, Turners Hill, near Crawley,
West Sussex RH10 4PD
Tel: +44(0)1342 718472
info@tulleysfarm.com
www.tulleysfarm.com

Hours: Shop 9.00-18.00 in summer, until 17.00 in winter.
Tearoom 10.00-17.00 in summer, until 16.50 in winter.
PYO June-October 9.00-18.00.
Other Points: Farm shop. PYO. Tearoom.
Directions: J10/M23 Take the A264 direct to East Grinstead.
At the B2928 head for Turners Hill. At the centre, take the
B2110 and then turn right at the church in the direction
for Worth. The PYO is on the right, the shop is on the left.

PYO soft fruits and vegetables are available at this well-stocked
farm shop in a converted dairy. It also sells a range of fresh and
local produce and gifts. A tearoom serves homemade foods.

In 2003, the National Farmers' Union
gave Turkey Talk a Farming Business
of the Year award for its cooked meat
products. Set in rural Warwickshire,
traditional turkey farming methods are
used to produce its premium products,
and the family business is now in its
third generation. The birds are reared
naturally and fed on natural corn-based
foods to produce quality products. The
range includes raw turkey products, such
as crowns and boneless turkey breast,
and many styles of cooked turkey: oak-
smoked turkey, honey and mustard turkey
breast and The Claverdon, a rolled turkey
breast using an age-old family recipe. At
Christmas, they sell a comprehensive
range, including hen turkeys and long-
legged Bronze hen turkeys.

Coventry, Warwickshire

Turkey Talk

Pheasant Oak Farm, Hob Lane,
Balsall Common, Coventry,
Warwickshire CV7 7GX
Tel: +44(0)1676 532681
esme@turkeytalk.co.uk
www.turkeytalk.co.uk

Hours: Monday-Friday 8.00-17.00.
Other Points: Delivery service.
Directions: Off the A452, near
Coventry.

Marlborough, Wiltshire

Everleigh Farm Shop

Old Rectory Farm, Everleigh,
Marlborough, Wiltshire SN8 3EY
Tel: +44(0)1264 850344
info@everleighfarmshop.co.uk
www.everleighfarmshop.co.uk

Hours: 8.00-16.00, until 17.00 on
Thursday and Friday.
Other Points: Mail order. Farm shop.
Delivery service. Car park.
Directions: Next to the church in
Everleigh, on the A342 Andover to
Devizes Road.

You will find an amazing selection of fully traceable meats and fresh farm produce all year round at this farm shop and butchers. Game turkeys, geese and duck are available in winter, then in late-summer and autumn there is oven-ready partridge, mallard, pheasants, rabbits, hares and venison. These are in addition to the other meats, poultry and homemade sausages, burgers and kebabs, which are ideal for parties and barbecues. Other foods include fruit and vegetables, smoked fish, bread and pastries, cheese, pâtés and wines from France. Christmas hampers packed in Somerset wicker baskets are another speciality. In the Nursery Garden, you will find pelargoniums and geraniums plus seasonal bedding plants for sale.

Warminster, Wiltshire

Boyton Farm

Boyton, Warminster,
Wiltshire BA12 0SS
Tel: +44(0)1985 850208
caroline@boytonfarm.co.uk
www.boytonfarm.co.uk

Hours: Wednesday-Friday 10.00-16.00. Saturday 10.00-13.00.
Other Points: Mail order. Farmers' market. Farm shop. Car park.
Directions: From the A36 (three miles east of Warminster), take the unclassified road south (half a mile) to Boyton.

You know exactly what you are getting at Boyton Farm, as all the meat sold is from animals born, reared and fed on the farm. Caroline and Thomas Wheatley-Hubbard sell succulent pork from their herd of traditional Tamworth pigs – the oldest in the country – as well as beef from their traditional Sussex/Hereford cattle and lamb from their Hampshire Down/Suffolk X sheep. Game is also available in season. The quality of the meat is due to the fact the animals are reared slowly on conservation land and fed on home-milled wheat and barley with GM-free soya and without growth promoters or antibiotics. The couple plan to move within the village, so that they can expand the butchery and meet the increased demand for cooked products.

Dumfries, Dumfries and Galloway

Loch Arthur Creamery

Camphill Village Trust, Beeswing,
Dumfries DB2 8JQ
Tel: +44(0)1387 760296
creamery@locharthur.org.uk
www.locharthur.org.uk

Hours: Monday-Friday 9.00-17.30. Saturday
10.00-15.00.
Other Points: Farm shop.
Directions: Take the A711 from Dumfries to
Dalbeattie. In Beeswing, turn left after the church.
The creamery is signposted.

RECIPES

Around the country, Les Routiers members are cooking up regional specialities every day of the week. We asked several to share their most popular and requested recipes to give you a taste of what's available in the regions. We have included starters, main courses, desserts and cakes so you can devise a complete menu or bake an indulgent afternoon tea. All our recipes have been adapted for the home cook by Les Routiers chefs and are easy to replicate at home.

Seared tuna with a tomato and red onion salad

This recipe for tuna from the **Mussel & Crab** restaurant in Tuxford makes an excellent supper dish, as it involves the minimum of cooking. It's also a good choice for a summer barbecue. Tuna has a meaty texture and is best eaten underdone.

Serves 4

Measure it
4 x 175-200g 6-7oz tuna steaks
1 tsp green pesto, to serve

For the marinade
½ tbsp crushed black pepper
1 tbsp chopped fresh parsley
juice of ½ lemon
4 tbsp olive oil, plus extra to serve

For the salad
4 ripe tomatoes
1 red onion
½ tbsp chopped fresh coriander
2 tbsp olive oil
1 tbsp balsamic vinegar
1 tsp chopped garlic
1 tsp sugar
salt and freshly ground black pepper

Make it

1 Mix the marinade ingredients together, and coat the tuna steaks all over with the mixture. Cover with foil and chill in the fridge for about an hour.

2 Prepare the salad: thinly slice the tomatoes and onion. In a mixing bowl add the rest of salad the ingredients, then mix with the tomato-and-onion mixture (can be made ahead and stored covered in the fridge).

3 Cook the tuna on a hot griddle for 1½-2 minutes on each side.

4 Arrange the salad in the middle of each of four plates, and place a tuna steak on top. Drizzle with some pesto mixed with olive oil.

Organic chicken breast in asparagus sauce

*The dish features on **Strattons**' menu when the local asparagus crop is in season; the Brecks area of Norfolk is one of the great asparagus-producing regions of the world, helped by light sandy soils and dry climate. **Castle Acre Organics** provides the kitchen with free-range chickens and eggs, and the wild mushrooms are gathered on the heathland and woodland in the hotel's grounds.*
Serves 6

Measure it
For the chicken

5 large spring green leaves
fungi or olive oil, for drizzling
6 organic skinless chicken breasts
6 rashers unsmoked Norfolk bacon
125g/4oz asparagus spears
2/3 shallots
25g/1oz butter
275ml/½ pint chicken stock
150ml/¼ pint Jersey cream
3 tbsp dry white wine
salt and freshly ground black pepper

For the stuffing

125g/4oz oyster mushrooms or
  chicken of the woods fungi
125g/4oz white onions
125g/4oz chicken livers
25g/1oz butter
2 tbsp chopped fresh young fleshy
  rosemary shoots

Make it

1 Make the stuffing: finely chop the oyster mushrooms or chicken of the woods fungi, onions and chicken livers and fry lightly in a pan with the butter and rosemary until soft but not brown. Season and leave to stand.

2 Cut the spring greens into thin strips and lay in a baking tray. Drizzle with olive oil and sprinkle with salt and pepper, and then crisp in a hot oven for 5 minutes. Set aside.

3 Create a pocket in the breast of each chicken with a knife, fill with the stuffing and close the pocket opening. Stretch each bacon rasher with the flat of a knife and wrap one rasher around each chicken fillet. Drizzle with a little fungi or olive oil and season. Brown under a hot grill for 10 minutes, turning and basting.

4 Slice the asparagus spears finely, setting the tips aside. Slice the shallots. Steam the asparagus tips for 3 minutes and set aside. Using a deep pan big enough to fit the chicken, melt the butter and gently fry the asparagus and shallots, taking care not to brown them, for 10 minutes.

5 Mix in the chicken stock, cream and wine. Add the chicken breasts and let them simmer for 15 minutes. Remove and set aside to rest.

6 Liquidise the rest of the creamy mixture and season to taste. Warm the sauce mixture through, adding the crisped greens and steamed asparagus tips and serve with the chicken.

Pillow of smoked salmon with herbed goat's cheese

This is a popular dish at **The White Horse**, Brancaster, Staithe, and was created by the head chef of its restaurant, Nicholas Parker. For the best flavour, he uses top-quality locally smoked salmon and a soft rindless goat's cheese made by **Mrs Temple** from nearby village Wighton.

Serves 4

Measure it

250g/8oz goat's cheese
100ml/3½fl oz double cream
chopped fresh dill
4 large slices of smoked salmon
1 bag of mixed salad leaves
olive oil mixed with a dash of
   fresh lemon juice
balsamic vinegar
4 sprigs of chervil, to garnish
salt and freshly ground black
   pepper

Make it

1 Break up the goat's cheese with a fork and mash in the cream slowly until you have a smooth paste. Mix in the chopped dill. Season with salt and pepper to taste.

2 Spoon the mixture equally into the middle of each salmon slice, then fold over the top and tuck the flaps underneath to form a pillow shape.

3 Place the salmon parcel, seam-side down, in the centre of each serving dish. Dress the salad leaves with a little lemon oil and arrange on top of parcel. Grind over some black pepper and drizzle with a little balsamic vinegar. Garnish with the chervil.

TYMSBORO
Made by Mary Holbrook in Tymsbury, near Bath.
£3·35

Apple and plum crumble

The fact that fruit crumble has appeared on almost every **Food For Thought** menu since 1974 testifies to the enduring popularity of this simple, but comforting, dessert, says the restaurant's Vanessa Garrett. Ring the changes to the recipe by using seasonal combinations of fruit, nuts and sweet spices, for example: pear and toasted hazelnut; rhubarb and ginger; apple and blackberry; apricot and almond; and sherried fig and apple, for example.

Serves 4

Measure it

450g/1lb Bramley apples, cored and cut into good bite-sized chunks

350g/12oz Victoria plums, stoned and cut into quarters

juice of 1 orange

½ tsp cinnamon

50g/2oz demerara sugar

For the topping

50g/2oz butter or sunflower margarine

50g/2oz demerara sugar, plus extra

50g/2oz medium rolled oats

50g/2oz large rolled oats

25g/1oz plain flour

25g/1oz ground almonds

3 tsp water, if a more textured, less crumbly topping is preferred, optional

Make it

1 Preheat the oven to 200°C (Gas mark 6). Wash and prepare the fruit. Place in a greased ovenproof dish with the orange juice, cinnamon and sugar. Cover with foil and bake for around 20 minutes, or until just soft.

2 Place all the topping ingredients (excluding the water) in a mixing bowl. Rub the fat into the oats as you would for pastry, until a good crumbly texture is achieved. (You can now add water to stiffen the mix if you wish.)

3 Layer on top of the fruit. A little more sugar may be sprinkled on top for the sweet-toothed, if desired. Bake for 20 minutes more until golden brown. Serve hot or cold with whipped cream, custard or Greek yogurt.

This recipe is from the New Food For Thought cookbook ISBN: 0-233-05071-X. You can buy a copy from Food For Thought, 31 Neal Street, WC2H 9PR, or from good book shops.

Cullen Skink

This stew is a meal in itself if you serve it with crusty bread, as Fran Sweeney does at her guesthouse, **Balkissock Lodge**. The dish gets its name from the village where it was created, Cullen, while skink is the Gaelic word for soup or broth.
Serves 4

Measure it

1 stick of celery
1 onion, chopped
50g/2oz butter
1 bay leaf
1.2 litres/2 pints milk
275ml/½ pint fish stock
150ml/¼ pint cream
700g/1½lb floury potatoes, peeled and diced
450g/1lb Finnan haddock, or natural smoked
  haddock fillets
chopped fresh parsley
salt and freshly ground black pepper

Make it

1 Sweat off the celery and onion in the butter until softened, then add the bay leaf, milk, fish stock and cream and bring to the boil.

2 Reduce to a simmer and add the potatoes and fish. Simmer until the fish is just cooked.

3 Remove the fish and place on a plate to cool, then flake it. Remove the bay leaf from the pan. Crush some of the potatoes against the side of the pan to thicken the soup.

4 Add the fish and parsley and season to taste. Serve with warm, crusty, wholegrain rolls and butter.

The Hive's Welshcakes

This recipe makes a big batch, as you will want to eat at least three each, says Sarah Holgate, who runs **Hive on the Quay**. She says they are best eaten while still warm, but definitely on the same day.
Makes 30

Measure it

165g/5½oz soft margarine
60g/2½oz butter
450g/1lb white self-raising flour, plus extra
175g/6oz currants
210g/7½oz granulated sugar
1 pinch of baking powder
1 pinch of salt
1 large egg, beaten
2 tbsp milk

Make it

1 In a mixing bowl, rub the margarine and butter into the flour. Add the currants, sugar, baking powder and salt, and work into a soft dough with the beaten egg and milk.

2 Turn onto a floured surface. Roll out to 5mm/¼ inch thick (no thinner or they become like biscuits). Cut with a 5cm/2inch round cutter.

3 Cook for 3-4 minutes on both sides on a lightly greased bakestone or heavy frying pan over a moderate heat.

Leek and Croglin cheese souffles

*These soufflés by **The Jumble Room**'s chef Andy Hill have a distinctive flavour as they are made using a local ewe's cheese, but you can use a flavoursome goat's cheese instead. They can be made in advance and reheated as twice-baked soufflés. After cooking, cool the soufflés and turn out of the ramekins (use a small knife to go around the edge of the dish to loosen). They will keep well in the fridge for up to the three days. Reheat the soufflés in a white-wine cream sauce (having arranged them in a buttered ovenproof dish) in a medium oven for 10-12 minutes, until hot.*

Serves 4-6

Measure it
For the soufflés

250ml/9fl oz full-fat milk
sprig of fresh thyme
pinch of freshly grated nutmeg
1 medium leek, finely diced and washed
olive oil
75g/3oz butter
50g/2oz flour
4 eggs, separated
150g/5oz goat's cheese or Croglin ewe's
   cheese, grated
squeeze of fresh lemon juice

To serve

handful of wild rocket, washed
couple of bunches of baby beetroots,
   washed, cooked, peeled and sliced
vinaigrette
fresh chervil, basil or chives, chopped

Make it

1 Preheat the oven to 180°C (Gas mark 4). Bring the milk to the boil with the thyme and grated nutmeg. Remove from the heat and leave to infuse.

2 Meanwhile, cook the leek in a little olive oil until soft and translucent. Add 50g/2oz of the butter to the pan with the leeks and, then stir in the flour to make a smooth roux. Gradually strain the infused milk onto the roux, stirring all the time, until the sauce thickens. Stir in the egg yolks and grated cheese. Check for seasoning and leave to cool for a few minutes.

3 In the meantime, whisk the egg whites with the lemon juice until they just start to peak. Using a large metal spoon, fold gently into the cheese-leek mixture. Divide between four to six buttered ramekins and transfer to a bain-marie, or sit the ramekins in a roasting tin and fill with water to come halfway up the sides of the dishes. Cook in the preheated oven for approximately 15-18 minutes. Once ready, the soufflés will be fluffy, golden and not too firm in the centre. While they're cooking, prepare a simple salad.

4 Toss together the rocket and beetroot with a drizzle of vinaigrette and fresh herbs. Divide between four to six plates, leaving a space for each soufflé ramekin.

Roast lamb with honeyed-parsnip purée

This dish, served at **Riverdale Hall Hotel** is very popular, simple to make and tastes wholesome and rich. Most of the restaurant's ingredients are produced locally. The butcher knows the farmers who supply its beef and lamb, and the vegetable supplier grows a great deal of the fresh produce he sells himself.

Serves 6

Measure it

6 lamb chump steaks

new potatoes roasted in
  garlic and rosemary,
  to serve

For the parsnip purée

12 parsnips (more if very
  small)

55ml/2fl oz olive oil

55ml/2fl oz clear honey

salt and freshly ground black
  pepper

For the red-wine sauce

570ml/1 pint red wine

570ml/1 pint water

1 lamb stock cube (beef will
  do if lamb is hard to find)

2 tbsp redcurrant jelly

Make it

1 Preheat the oven to 170°C (Gas mark 3). First make the parsnip purée. Peel and chop the parsnips, then rub with the olive oil, honey and salt and pepper. Tip into a roasting tin and roast for 50 minutes (40 minutes covered with foil, 10 minutes without). If still not soft, cook for an extra 10 minutes. Put into a food processor and purée. Set aside.

2 Meanwhile prepare the meat. Score the fat on top and seal the steaks on both sides in a dry, hot frying pan. Transfer to the oven in a dish, cover with foil and bake for 25 minutes. The steaks should still be pink in the middle. Allow them to rest for 10 minutes.

3 Make the sauce: put all the sauce ingredients in a pan and bring to the boil. Boil rapidly for 5 minutes, then simmer until reduced by half and the sauce starts to thicken.

4 Divide the parsnip purée between six plates, carve each steak into slices and place on top, then trickle the sauce round. Serve with small new potatoes roasted in garlic and rosemary.

Sticky toffee pudding

Dorothy Stubley serves this delicious and popular pudding at **Hazelmere Café** *in Grange over Sands. She says the quantities for the sauce serve four generously, so any leftover can be stored in the fridge and gently reheated to serve over ice cream or other desserts. It is especially good with anything containing apples or pears.*

Serves 4

Measure it

140ml/scant ¼ pint of water
95g/3½oz stoned and chopped dates
25g/1oz butter
95g/3½oz soft dark brown sugar
95g/3½oz self-raising flour
1 large free-range egg
¼ tsp vanilla essence

For the sauce

225g/8oz soft dark brown sugar
110g/4oz unsalted butter
275ml/½ pint double cream
¼ tsp vanilla essence

Make it

1 Preheat the oven to 180°C (Gas mark 4). In a pan, bring the water, dates and butter to the boil and then leave to cool.

2 Mix the sugar and flour together in a mixing bowl, then add the egg and vanilla essence and finally the cold date mixture. Mix together thoroughly. Pour into a 20x13cm/ 8x5inch ovenproof container and bake for 30-40 minutes until risen and firm.

3 Meanwhile, make the sauce. Bring all the sauce ingredients except the vanilla essence to the boil in a pan. Once boiling point has been reached, reduce the heat and simmer gently for 5 minutes. Remove from the heat and add the vanilla essence. Pour over the baked pudding or serve separately in a jug.

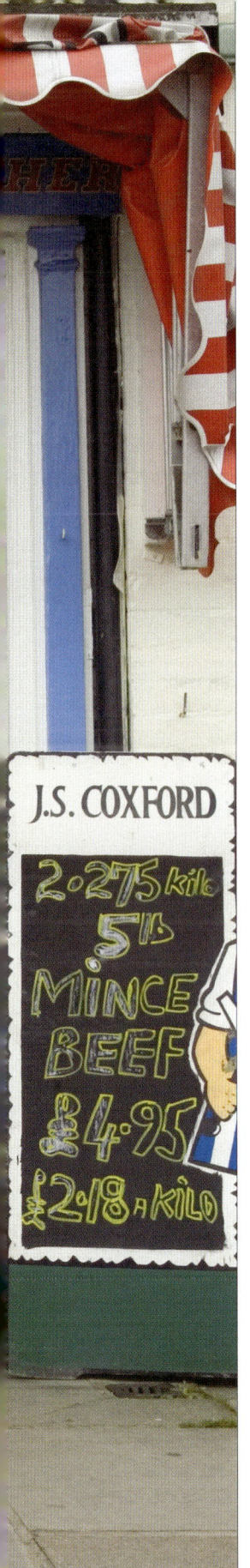

Shortcrust steak, kidney and mushroom pie

*This recipe by chef Mark Armes is a firm favourite on **The Wig and Pen** menu.*

Serves 6

Measure it

For the pastry
625g/1lb 6oz plain flour
365g/13oz margarine or butter
pinch of salt
2 eggs, beaten
cold water

For the filling
2 tbsp vegetable oil
1kg/2lb 4oz diced stewing steak
250g/9oz diced ox kidneys
2 litres/3½ pints beef stock
200g/7oz plain flour
pinch of chopped fresh oregano
pinch of chopped fresh basil
275ml/½ pint of rich, dark ale
250g/9oz quartered mushrooms
1 egg, beaten
salt and freshly ground black pepper

Make it

1 Heat the oil for the filling in a pan, then add the steak and kidneys. Stir with a wooden spoon, allowing the meat to brown and the juices to ooze from the beef. Continue cooking until all the juices have reduced, then cover with the stock, reduce the heat and simmer for an hour.

2 Meanwhile, prepare the pastry. In a large bowl or food processor, add the flour, margarine and salt and blend to a fine sandy texture. Add the eggs and water and form into a firm, but not over dry pastry. On a floured surface, roll out half the pastry to around 3mm thick and line a lightly oiled 25.5cm/10 inch round pie dish.

3 After an hour of simmering the meat, check if it is tender. If tender, drain, saving any remaining stock. Add the flour and stir into the beef. Return to a low heat, stirring continually for 5 minutes to cook the flour.

4 Add the chopped herbs, ale and enough stock to cover the meat. Add the mushrooms, season to taste and simmer on a low heat for 15-20 minutes longer.

5 Preheat the oven to 180°C (Gas mark 4). Transfer the prepared filling to the pastry-lined dish, and moisten the pastry edge with cold water. Roll out the other half of the pastry and lay across the top of the pie. Press down gently to seal the pastry, crimp the join and trim off any excess pastry from the outside of the dish.

6 Brush the top with beaten egg, make four incisions to allow steam to escape and bake for 50 minutes to an hour until the pastry is cooked and the top is golden brown.

Marion's Devon scones

Guests arriving at **Tor Cottage**, a small country house which was Les Routiers National Winner of Bed & Breakfast of the Year 2005, are often welcomed with a real Devonshire cream tea, compliments of the house. They are made by Marion, its housekeeper, and guests have described her scones as 'heavenly.' She cooks them in Tor Cottage's Aga, but they taste just as good from a conventional oven.
Makes 12

Measure it

250g/9oz self-raising flour
½ tsp baking powder
pinch of salt
2oz/50g butter
2oz/50g caster sugar
150ml/¼ pint milk, plus extra

Make it

1 Preheat the oven to 230°C (Gas mark 8). Sieve the flour into a large mixing bowl and add the baking powder and a pinch of salt.

2 Lightly rub in the butter until the mix resembles fine breadcrumbs. Mix in the sugar.

3 Add the milk and stir to a soft spongy dough, taking care not to make the dough too wet and sticky.

4 On a floured surface roll out the dough to 2cm/¾inch thick and cut out scone shapes with a ring cutter.

5 Place on a greased baking tray and brush the tops of the scones with a little milk. Bake for around 10 minutes, until risen and golden brown. Serve with Devonshire clotted cream and strawberry conserve.

Bread-and-butter pudding

This traditional British classic is a perennial favourite on **Monsieur's** takeaway menu, created by proprietors Guy and Anita Jenkinson. This pudding used to be a way of using up stale bread, combining it with milk and eggs, but using fresh bread gives a much spongier texture.
Serves 4-6

Measure it

5 whole eggs
1.5 litres/2½ pints full-cream milk
3 tbsp sugar
1 tbsp cornflour
9 slices of buttered white bread, crusts removed and each slice cut into four triangles
2 heaped tbsp sultanas
freshly ground nutmeg

Make it

1 Preheat the oven to 180°C (Gas mark 4). Whisk the eggs thoroughly, then add the milk, sugar and cornflour and whisk again until well blended.

2 Place 12 triangles of buttered bread, slightly overlapping, evenly over the base of a shallow 1.75-litre/3-pint ovenproof dish. Scatter one tablespoon of sultanas over these slices.

3 Repeat this layer once more and then finish with a final layer of bread and butter, but no sultanas this time.

4 Briefly whisk the eggs, milk, sugar and cornflour mix again to make sure it is well blended, pour over the bread and sultanas and finish with an even scattering of ground nutmeg. Bake for approximately 30 minutes at the top of the oven, and then move down to the middle shelf for another 30 minutes, or until set and golden. Serve hot with fresh cream or vanilla ice cream.

JUST OFF THE MOTORWAY

Les Routiers establishments just a short detour off the motorway.

Just off the Motorway

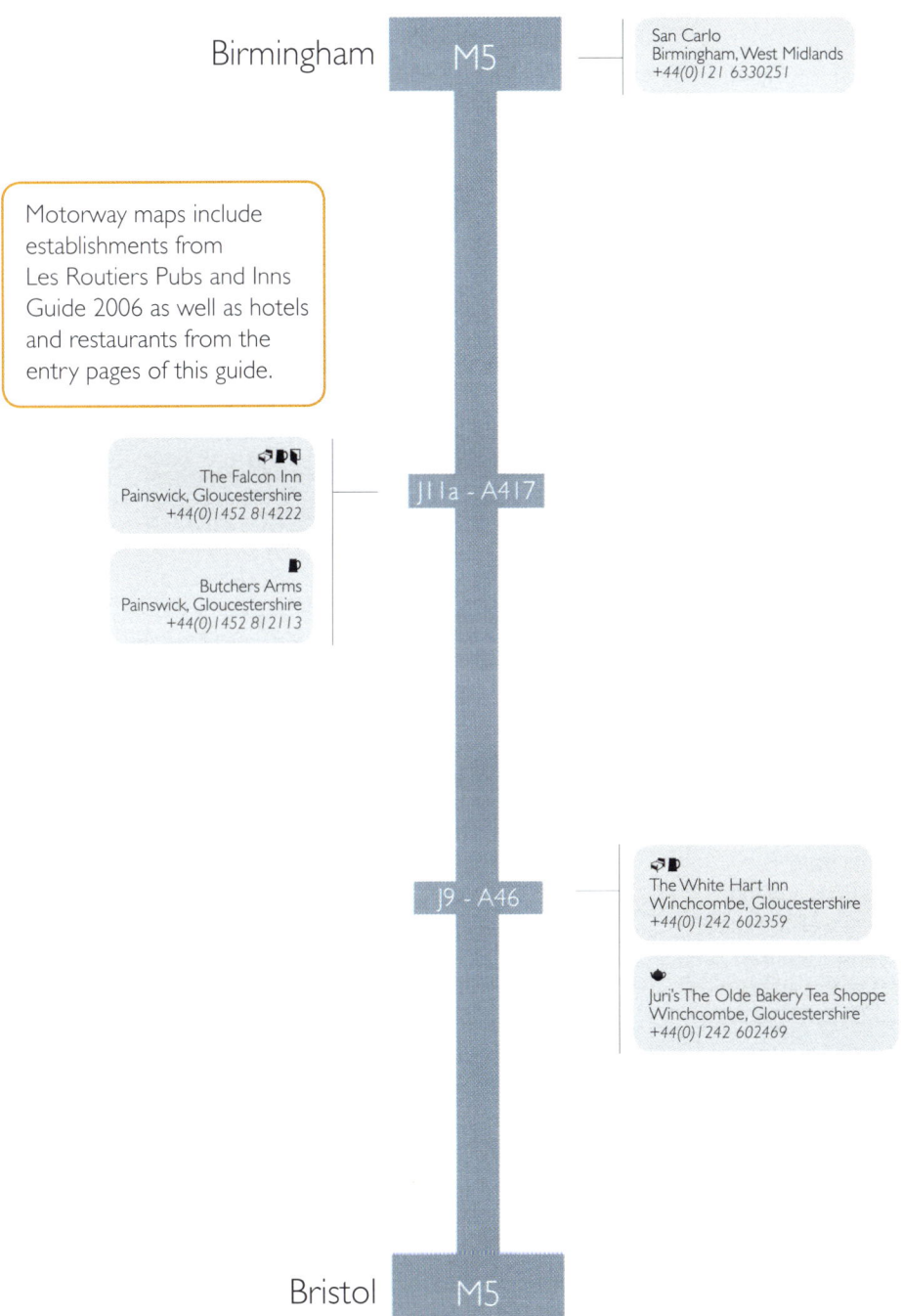

Birmingham **M5**

San Carlo
Birmingham, West Midlands
+44(0)121 6330251

Motorway maps include
establishments from
Les Routiers Pubs and Inns
Guide 2006 as well as hotels
and restaurants from the
entry pages of this guide.

The Falcon Inn
Painswick, Gloucestershire
+44(0)1452 814222

J11a - A417

Butchers Arms
Painswick, Gloucestershire
+44(0)1452 812113

J9 - A46

The White Hart Inn
Winchcombe, Gloucestershire
+44(0)1242 602359

Juri's The Olde Bakery Tea Shoppe
Winchcombe, Gloucestershire
+44(0)1242 602469

Bristol **M5**

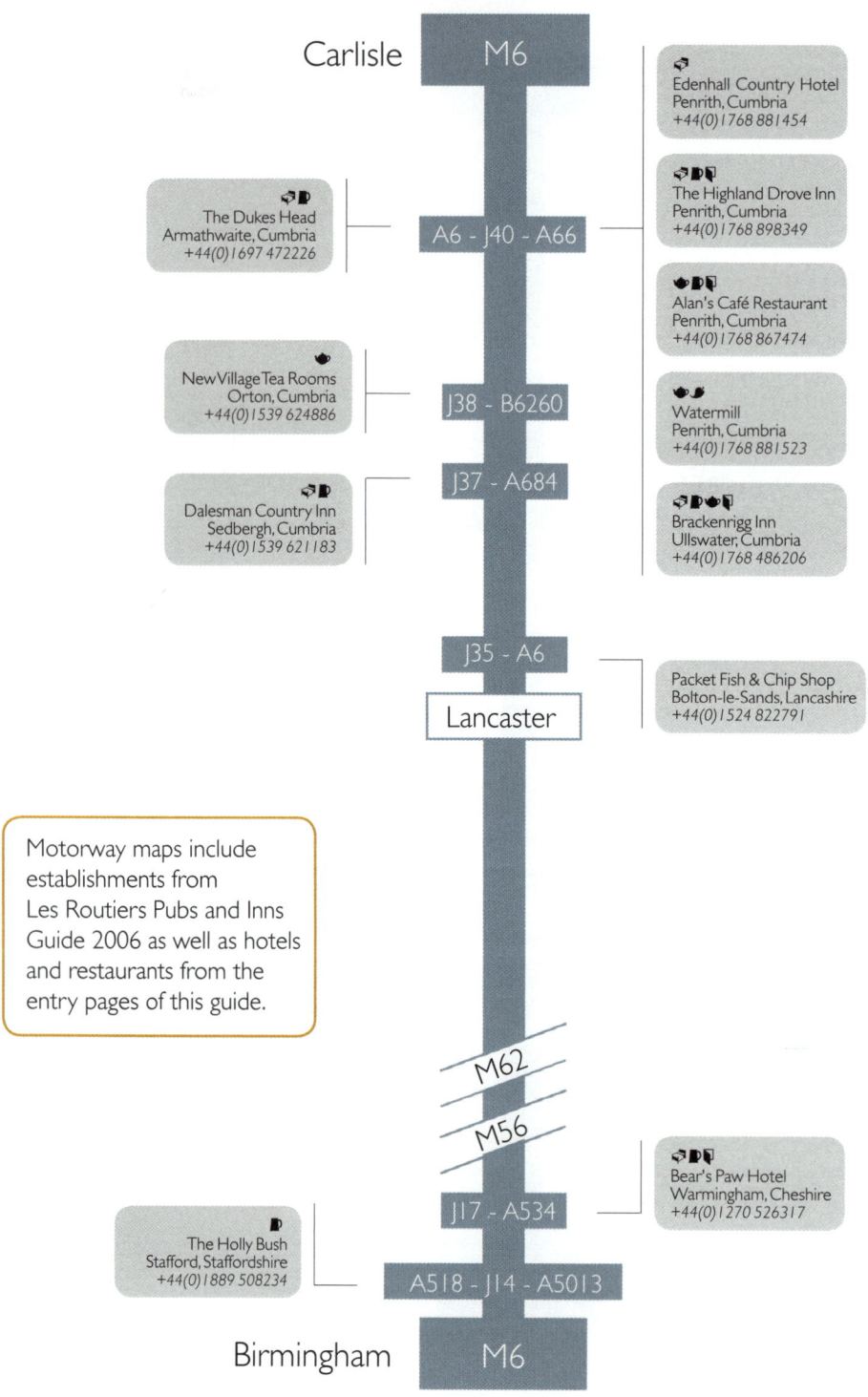

Carlisle

M6

Edenhall Country Hotel
Penrith, Cumbria
+44(0)1768 881454

The Dukes Head
Armathwaite, Cumbria
+44(0)1697 472226

A6 - J40 - A66

The Highland Drove Inn
Penrith, Cumbria
+44(0)1768 898349

Alan's Café Restaurant
Penrith, Cumbria
+44(0)1768 867474

New Village Tea Rooms
Orton, Cumbria
+44(0)1539 624886

J38 - B6260

Watermill
Penrith, Cumbria
+44(0)1768 881523

Dalesman Country Inn
Sedbergh, Cumbria
+44(0)1539 621183

J37 - A684

Brackenrigg Inn
Ullswater, Cumbria
+44(0)1768 486206

J35 - A6

Lancaster

Packet Fish & Chip Shop
Bolton-le-Sands, Lancashire
+44(0)1524 822791

Motorway maps include
establishments from
Les Routiers Pubs and Inns
Guide 2006 as well as hotels
and restaurants from the
entry pages of this guide.

M62

M56

Bear's Paw Hotel
Warmingham, Cheshire
+44(0)1270 526317

The Holly Bush
Stafford, Staffordshire
+44(0)1889 508234

J17 - A534

A518 - J14 - A5013

Birmingham

M6

Darlington to Edinburgh on the A68

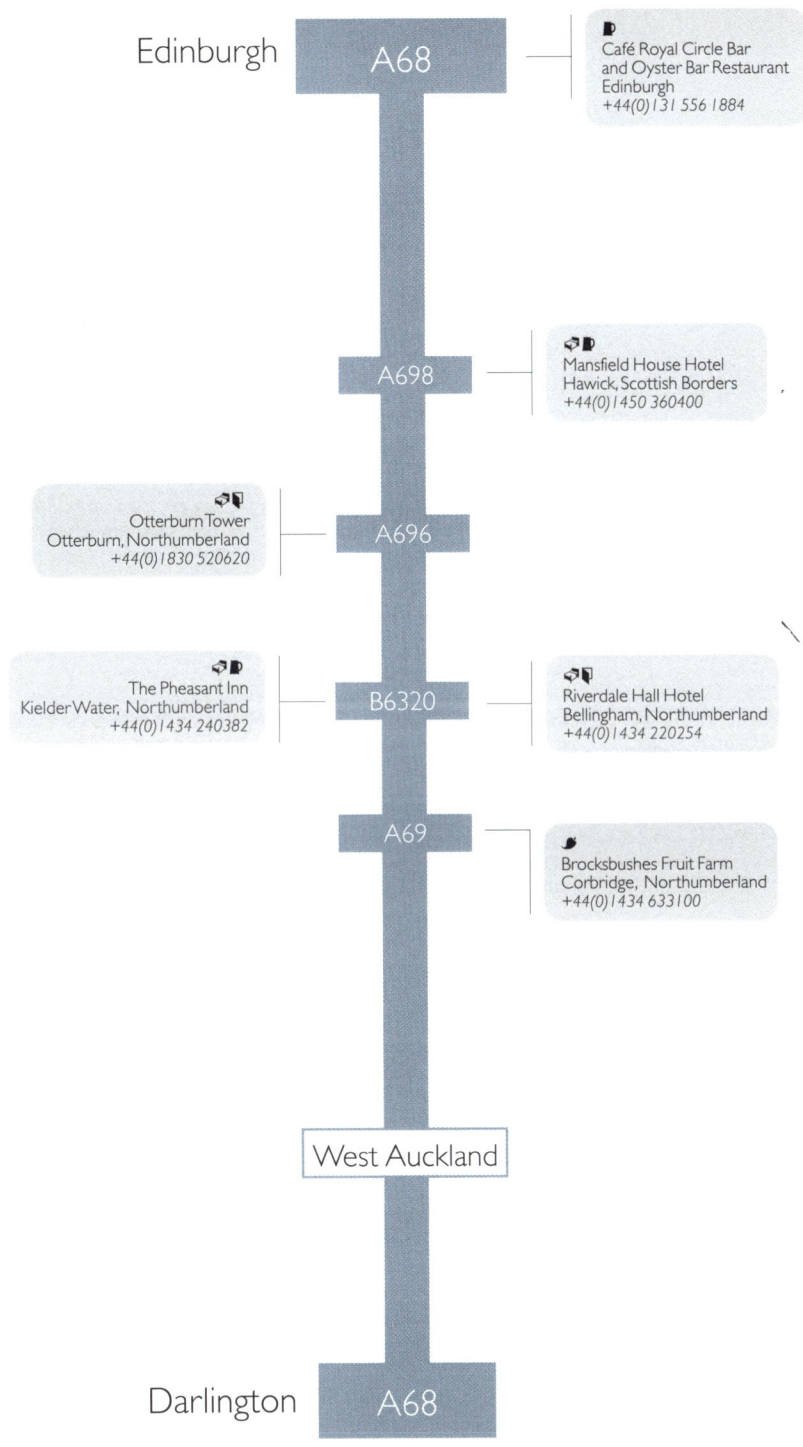

Edinburgh

A68

Café Royal Circle Bar
and Oyster Bar Restaurant
Edinburgh
+44(0)131 556 1884

A698

Mansfield House Hotel
Hawick, Scottish Borders
+44(0)1450 360400

Otterburn Tower
Otterburn, Northumberland
+44(0)1830 520620

A696

The Pheasant Inn
Kielder Water, Northumberland
+44(0)1434 240382

B6320

Riverdale Hall Hotel
Bellingham, Northumberland
+44(0)1434 220254

A69

Brocksbushes Fruit Farm
Corbridge, Northumberland
+44(0)1434 633100

West Auckland

Darlington

A68

...for special offers

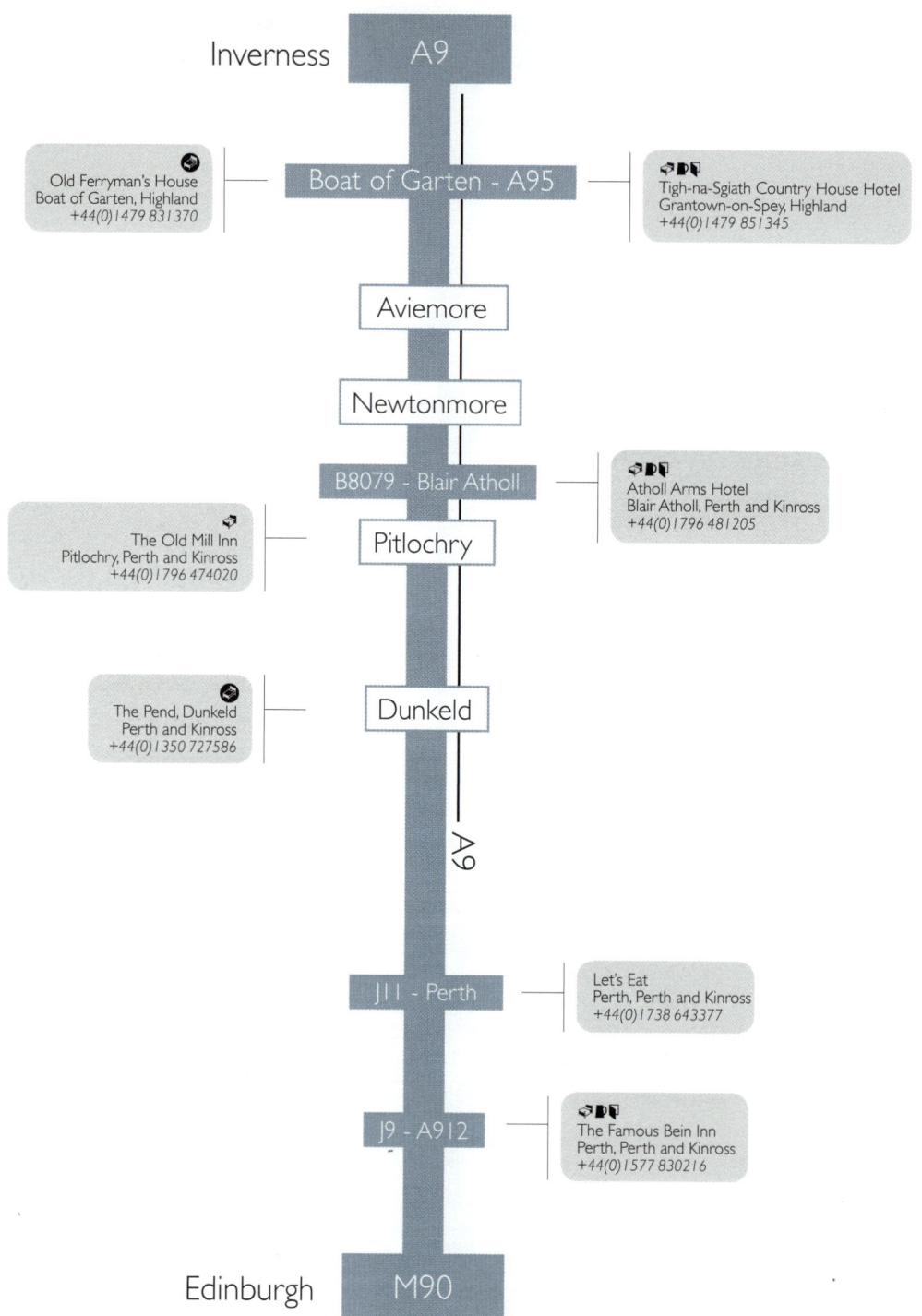

Inverness — A9

Old Ferryman's House
Boat of Garten, Highland
+44(0)1479 831370

Boat of Garten - A95

Tigh-na-Sgiath Country House Hotel
Grantown-on-Spey, Highland
+44(0)1479 851345

Aviemore

Newtonmore

B8079 - Blair Atholl

Atholl Arms Hotel
Blair Atholl, Perth and Kinross
+44(0)1796 481205

The Old Mill Inn
Pitlochry, Perth and Kinross
+44(0)1796 474020

Pitlochry

The Pend, Dunkeld
Perth and Kinross
+44(0)1350 727586

Dunkeld

A9

J11 - Perth

Let's Eat
Perth, Perth and Kinross
+44(0)1738 643377

J9 - A912

The Famous Bein Inn
Perth, Perth and Kinross
+44(0)1577 830216

Edinburgh — M90

Leicester to Norwich on the A47

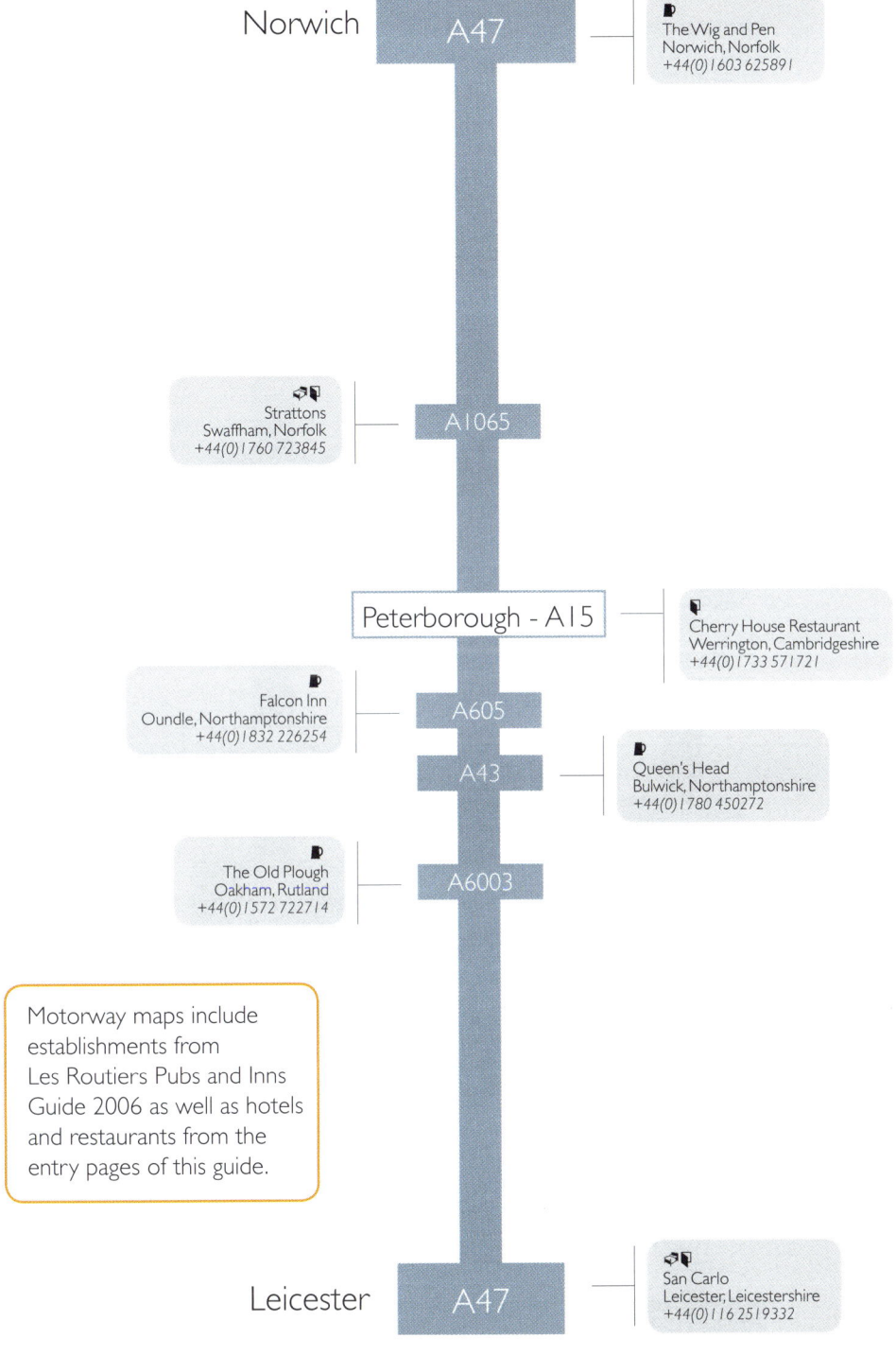

Norwich

A47

The Wig and Pen
Norwich, Norfolk
+44(0)1603 625891

Strattons
Swaffham, Norfolk
+44(0)1760 723845

A1065

Peterborough - A15

Cherry House Restaurant
Werrington, Cambridgeshire
+44(0)1733 571721

Falcon Inn
Oundle, Northamptonshire
+44(0)1832 226254

A605

A43

Queen's Head
Bulwick, Northamptonshire
+44(0)1780 450272

The Old Plough
Oakham, Rutland
+44(0)1572 722714

A6003

Motorway maps include
establishments from
Les Routiers Pubs and Inns
Guide 2006 as well as hotels
and restaurants from the
entry pages of this guide.

Leicester

A47

San Carlo
Leicester, Leicestershire
+44(0)116 2519332

...for the latest news

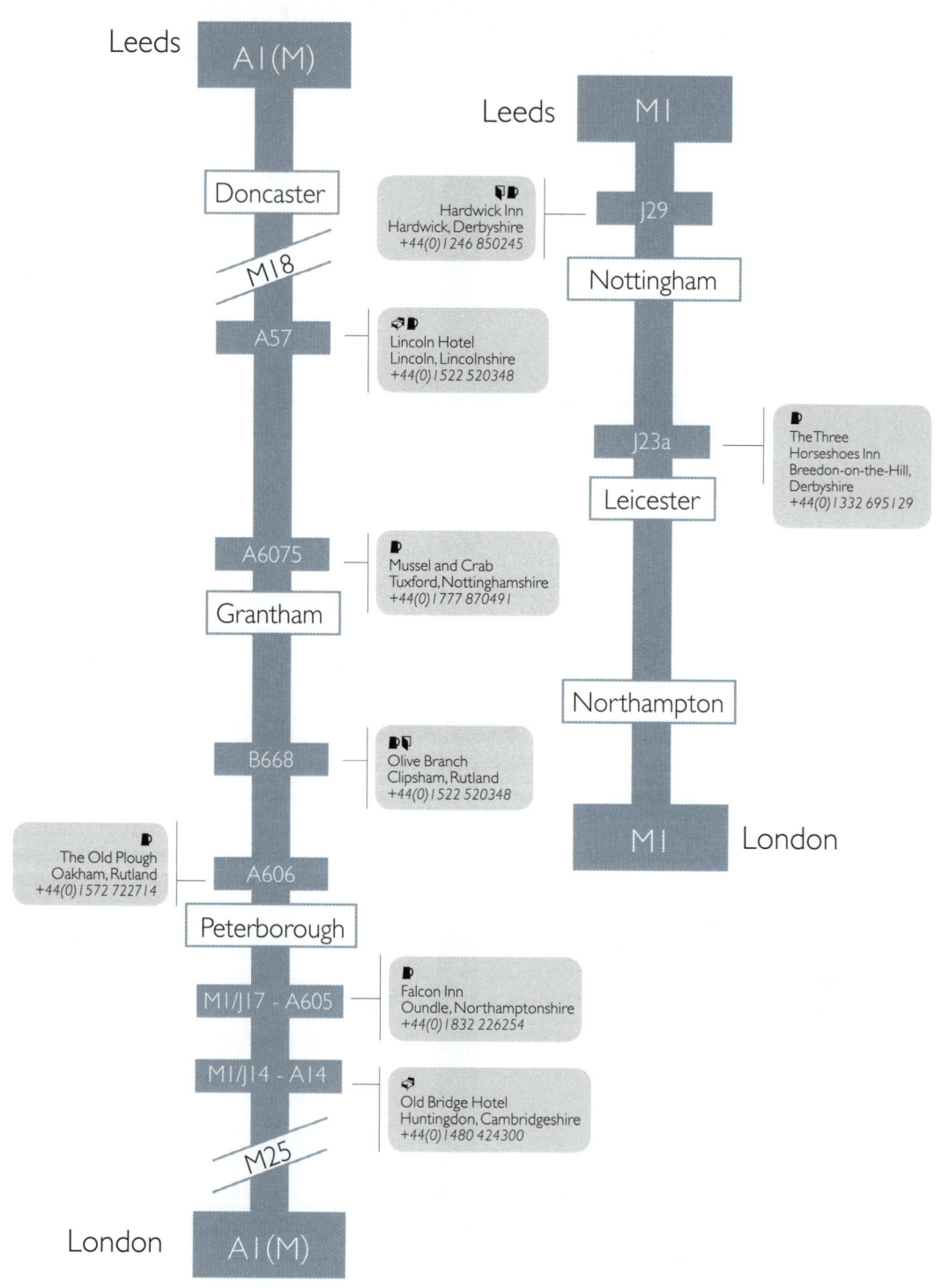

Leeds — A1(M)

Leeds — M1

Doncaster

Hardwick Inn
Hardwick, Derbyshire
+44(0)1246 850245

J29

Nottingham

M18

A57

Lincoln Hotel
Lincoln, Lincolnshire
+44(0)1522 520348

J23a

The Three
Horseshoes Inn
Breedon-on-the-Hill,
Derbyshire
+44(0)1332 695129

Leicester

A6075

Mussel and Crab
Tuxford, Nottinghamshire
+44(0)1777 870491

Grantham

Northampton

B668

Olive Branch
Clipsham, Rutland
+44(0)1522 520348

The Old Plough
Oakham, Rutland
+44(0)1572 722714

A606

M1 — London

Peterborough

M1/J17 - A605

Falcon Inn
Oundle, Northamptonshire
+44(0)1832 226254

M1/J14 - A14

Old Bridge Hotel
Huntingdon, Cambridgeshire
+44(0)1480 424300

M25

London — A1(M)

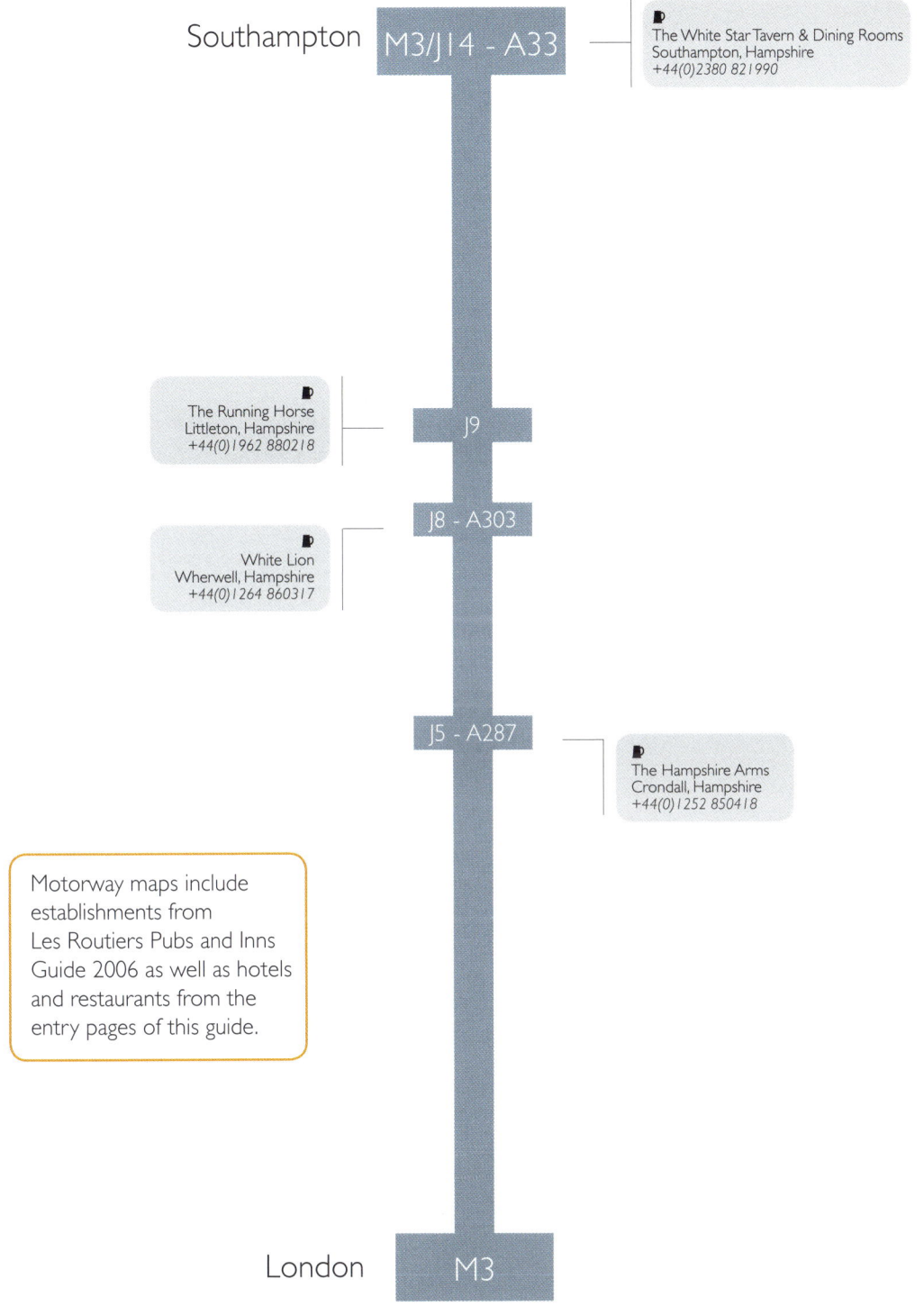

Southampton — M3/J14 - A33

The White Star Tavern & Dining Rooms
Southampton, Hampshire
+44(0)2380 821990

The Running Horse
Littleton, Hampshire
+44(0)1962 880218

J9

J8 - A303

White Lion
Wherwell, Hampshire
+44(0)1264 860317

J5 - A287

The Hampshire Arms
Crondall, Hampshire
+44(0)1252 850418

Motorway maps include
establishments from
Les Routiers Pubs and Inns
Guide 2006 as well as hotels
and restaurants from the
entry pages of this guide.

London — M3

...for topical features

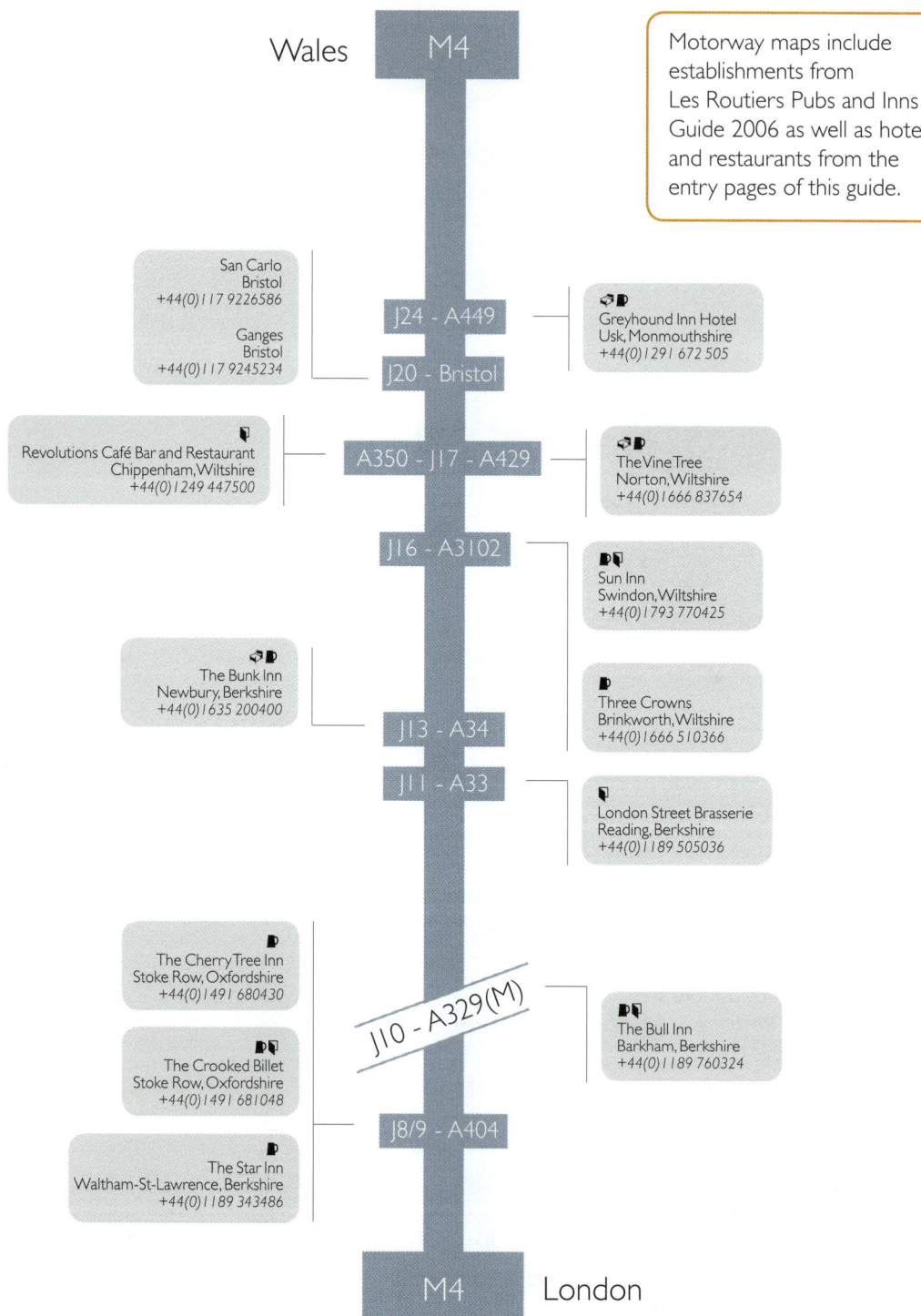

Motorway maps include establishments from Les Routiers Pubs and Inns Guide 2006 as well as hotels and restaurants from the entry pages of this guide.

Wales — M4

San Carlo
Bristol
+44(0)117 9226586

Ganges
Bristol
+44(0)117 9245234

J24 - A449

J20 - Bristol

Greyhound Inn Hotel
Usk, Monmouthshire
+44(0)1291 672 505

Revolutions Café Bar and Restaurant
Chippenham, Wiltshire
+44(0)1249 447500

A350 - J17 - A429

The Vine Tree
Norton, Wiltshire
+44(0)1666 837654

J16 - A3102

Sun Inn
Swindon, Wiltshire
+44(0)1793 770425

The Bunk Inn
Newbury, Berkshire
+44(0)1635 200400

Three Crowns
Brinkworth, Wiltshire
+44(0)1666 510366

J13 - A34

J11 - A33

London Street Brasserie
Reading, Berkshire
+44(0)1189 505036

The Cherry Tree Inn
Stoke Row, Oxfordshire
+44(0)1491 680430

J10 - A329(M)

The Bull Inn
Barkham, Berkshire
+44(0)1189 760324

The Crooked Billet
Stoke Row, Oxfordshire
+44(0)1491 681048

J8/9 - A404

The Star Inn
Waltham-St-Lawrence, Berkshire
+44(0)1189 343486

M4 — London

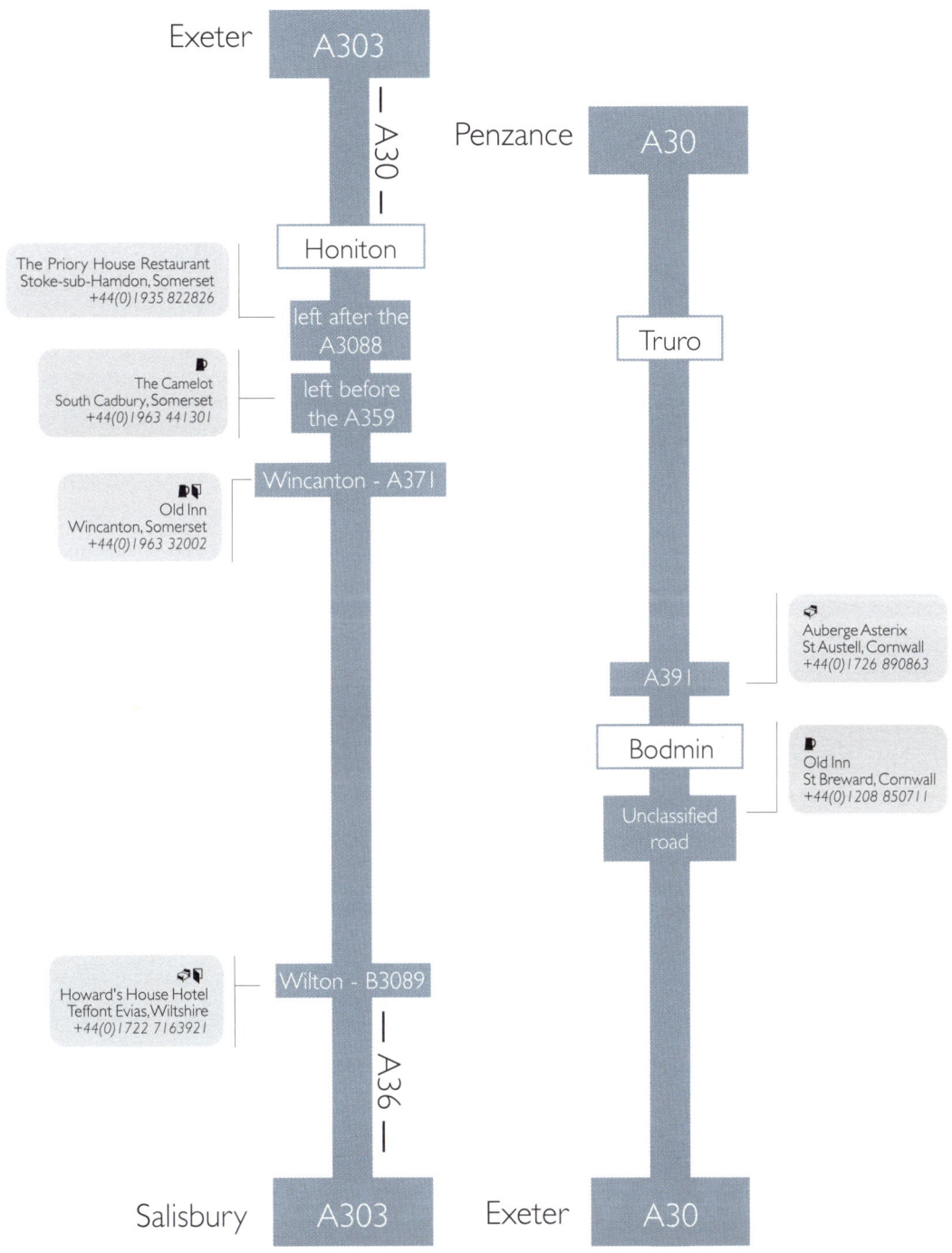

Exeter — A303 — A30

Penzance — A30

Honiton

The Priory House Restaurant
Stoke-sub-Hamdon, Somerset
+44(0)1935 822826

left after the A3088

Truro

The Camelot
South Cadbury, Somerset
+44(0)1963 441301

left before the A359

Wincanton - A371

Old Inn
Wincanton, Somerset
+44(0)1963 32002

Auberge Asterix
St Austell, Cornwall
+44(0)1726 890863

A391

Bodmin

Old Inn
St Breward, Cornwall
+44(0)1208 850711

Unclassified road

Howard's House Hotel
Teffont Evias, Wiltshire
+44(0)1722 7163921

Wilton - B3089

— A36 —

Salisbury — A303

Exeter — A30

WANTED

FOR COOKS WHO CAN STAND THE HEAT
(AND LOVE THE KITCHEN)

For the best route to a great meal simply visit

www.TABASCO.com

MAPS

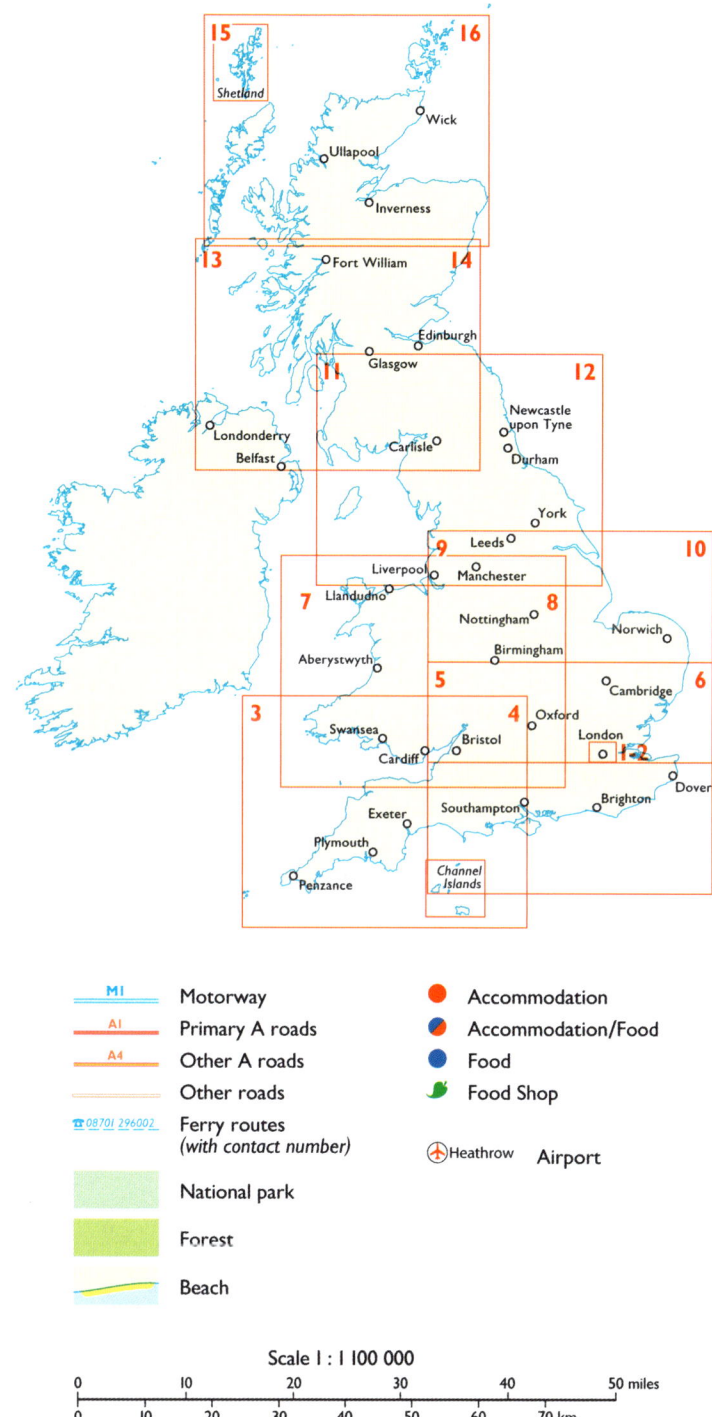

M1 Motorway	● Accommodation
A1 Primary A roads	◑ Accommodation/Food
A4 Other A roads	● Food
Other roads	🌿 Food Shop
☎ 08701 296002 Ferry routes (with contact number)	✈ Heathrow **Airport**
National park	
Forest	
Beach	

Scale 1 : 1 100 000

0	10	20	30	40	50 miles

0	10	20	30	40	50	60	70 km

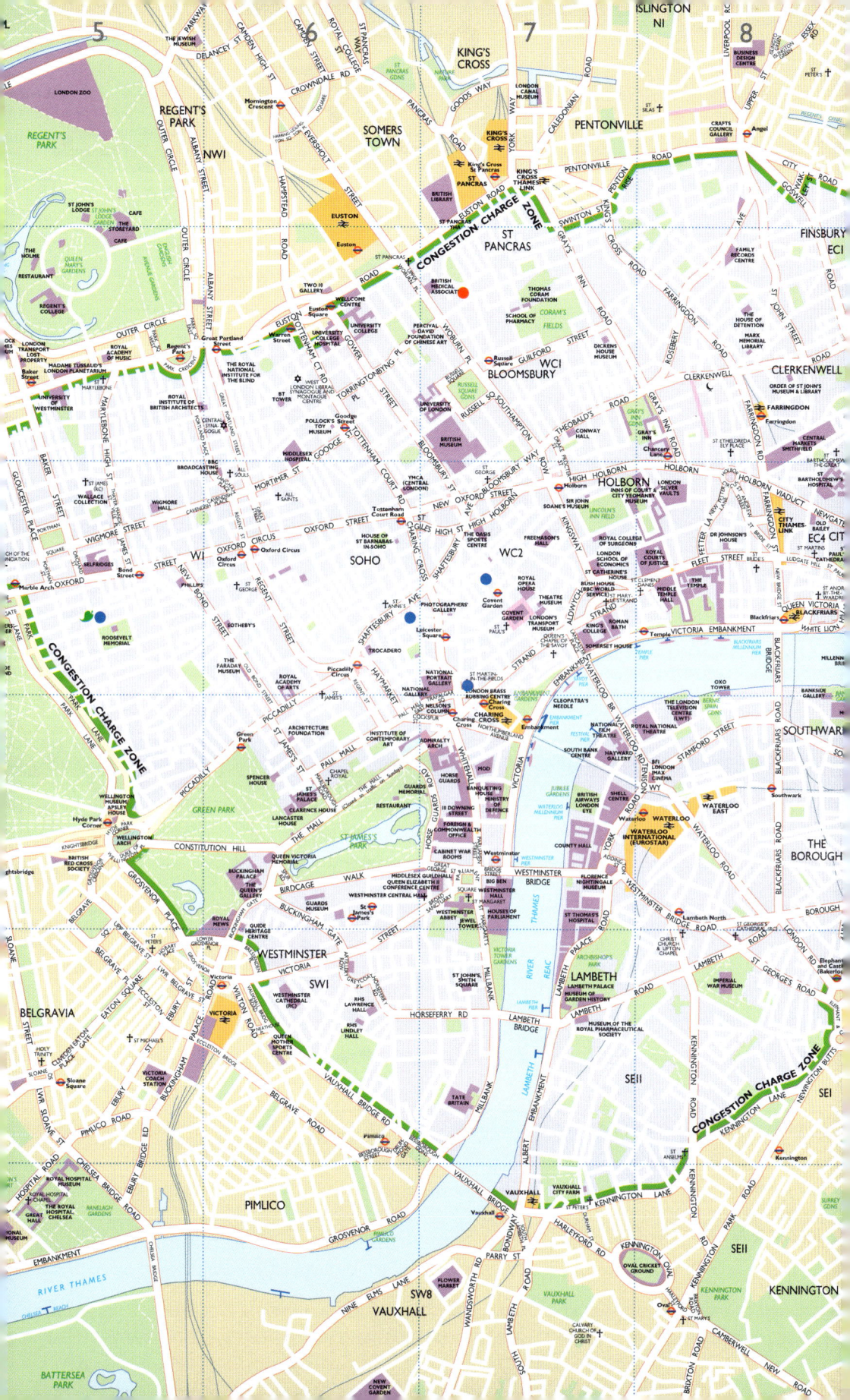

Whitehall Keighley Leeds/Bradford Tadcaster Weighton Beverley

Clitheroe WEST YORKSHIRE 12 Leeds Selby Howden NORTH

Burnley Bradford Sherburn in Elmet Goole Barton-upon-Humber

Preston Blackburn Sowerby Bridge Halifax Dewsbury Wakefield Castleford Pontefract Scunthorpe LINCOLNSHIRE

Leyland Ramsbottom Rochdale Huddersfield Slaithwaite Shelley Barnsley Doncaster

Ormskirk Bolton Oldham SOUTH YORKSHIRE Rotherham Bawtry

Wigan Manchester Glossop Sheffield Worksop Gainsborough

St Helens Stockport Marple Howden Reservoir Retford Lincoln

Liverpool Warrington Knutsford Prestbury Ladybower Reservoir Chesterfield Sherwood Forest Tuxford Thorpe on the Hill

Birkenhead Liverpool John Lennon Macclesfield Buxton Peak Hardwick Mansfield

Ellesmere Port Northwich CHESHIRE Eaton Bakewell Matlock Ollerton Newark-on-Trent

Chester Tarporley Congleton District DERBYSHIRE NOTTINGHAMSHIRE

Tattenhall Warmingham Leek Ashbourne Nottingham Grantham

Wrexham Crewe Nantwich Stoke-on-Trent Derby A52

Whitchurch Red Bull Uttoxeter East Midlands Loughborough Nether Broughton

Wem Market Drayton Salt Burton upon Trent Ashby-de-la-Zouch Melton Mowbray

Oswestry Stafford Rugeley Packington LEICESTERSHIRE RUTLAND Rutland Water Oakham A606

Shrewsbury Telford Lichfield Brownhills Tamworth Leicester Uppingham Corby Fotheringhay

Albrighton Walsall Sutton Coldfield Nuneaton M69 Kettering

7 Wolverhampton WEST MIDLANDS Heathton Dudley Birmingham Market Harborough

Bridgnorth Birmingham Coventry Rugby NORTHAMPTONSHIRE Wellingborough

SHROPSHIRE Kidderminster Knowle Balsall Common Kenilworth Northampton

Ludlow Bewdley Bromsgrove Royal Leamington Spa Daventry Newport Pagnell

Brimfield Tenbury Wells Redditch Droitwich Warwick Towcester Milton Keynes

Kington Leominster Worcester WARWICKSHIRE Brackley Leighton Buzzard Dunstable

Weobley WORCESTERSHIRE Stratford-upon-Avon Banbury Buckingham Bicester BUCKINGHAMSHIRE Waddesdon Mentmore

HEREFORDSHIRE Malvern Pershore Evesham Shipston on Stour Chipping Norton Aylesbury Ivinghoe

Hereford Chipping Campden Broadway Moreton-in-Marsh Flaunden

Ledbury Bromsberrow Tewkesbury Stow-on-the-Wold Chalfont St Giles Beaconsfield

Walterstone Hoarwithy Newent Winchcombe Hailey Witney Oxford Henley-on-Thames Marlow

Skenfrith Ross-on-Wye Cheltenham Burford Goring Maidenhead

Crickhowell Rockfield Monmouth Gloucester Painswick Northleach OXFORDSHIRE Abingdon Windsor Slough

Raglan Clearwell Forest of Dean GLOUCESTERSHIRE Cirencester Fairford Frilford Didcot Bracknell

Usk Llantrisant Frampton Mansell Ewen Faringdon Wantage Reading Wokingham

Cwmbran Chepstow Tetbury Thames Swindon Thatcham Newbury

Newport Chipping Sodbury Malmesbury M4 Hungerford

Portishead Clevedon Bristol Chippenham 5 Marlborough Melksham

Cosworth District Peak Chiltern Hills Cotswold Hills

15

1

2

3

4

INSET
not at same scale

Herma Ness
Haroldswick
Unst
Belmont
Gutcher
Fetlar

SHETLAND
North Roe
Yell
Ulsta

Shetland Islands

Esha Ness
Hillswick
Mossbank
Lunna Ness

Papa Stour
Whalsay

Sandness
Walls

Mainland
Scalloway
Lerwick
Bressay

Foula

☎ 01234 572665
to Torshavn (Faroe Islands)
to Seyðisfjörður (Iceland)

☎ 01234 572613
to Bergen

to Hanstholm

Sumburgh Head
Sumburgh
to Aberdeen

Cape Wrath

Durness

A838

Butt of Lewis
Port of Ness

Borve

A857

Barvas

Tolsta Head

A858

Scourie

A838

Outer Hebrides

Gallan Head
Callanish
Stornoway

A837

Isle of Lewis

Loch Trealabhal

Rubha Coigeach
Loch Assynt
Lochinver
Inchnadamph

Loch Sionascaig

Loch Langabhat

Elphin

A835

Kebock Head

The Minch

☎ 01475 650100

Loch Lurgainn

Loch Lurgainn

A837

Càilleach Head

WESTERN ISLES
Tarbert
(NA H-EILEANAN AN IAR)

Manish

Laide

A835

Ullapool

A832

Leverburgh

Little Minch

North Uist

Rudha Hunish

Gairloch

Fionn Loch

Loch Maree

Loch Fannich

☎ 01475 650100

Lochmaddy

☎ 01475 650100

Uig

A855

Kinlochewe

A832

A837

Loch Luichart

Achnasheen

Balivanich

Benbecula

A850

Shieldaig

A890

A896

HIGHLAND

Loch Monar

Portree

Raasay

Strathcarron

Farrar

A835

Sconser

Stromeferry

Cannich

Loch Mullardoch

A890

Skye

Scalpay

Kyle of Lochalsh

A87

Affric

Loch Affric

South Uist

Rudha Hunish

A863

A863

A87

Loch Cluanie

A87

Lochboisdale

☎ 01475 650100

Sleat

Glenmoriston

Loch Loyne

Fort Augustus

Eriskay

Canna

13

Armadale

A851

Loch Quoich

A865

A887

A87

Barra

Kinloch

Mallaig

Loch Garry

A888

Castlebay

Rum

A-Z by establishment name

A-Z by listing town

Quick-reference guide

Alfresco eating

Fish & Seafood

Best views

Waterside locations

Game

Private dining facilities

Afternoon tea

Breakfast or brunch

Budget food

To the Editor, Les Routiers Guide 2007
Report Form

☐ From my personal experience the following establishment should be a member of Les Routiers.

☐ From my personal experience the following establishment should not be a member of Les Routiers.

PLEASE PRINT IN BLOCK CAPITALS

Establishment ....

Address ....

....

....

I had ☐ lunch ☐ dinner ☐ stayed there on (date) ....

Details ....

....

....

....

....

....

....

....

....

....

Reports received up to the end of **May 2006** will be used in the research of the **2007** edition.

☐ I am not connected in any way with management or proprietors.

Name ....

Address ....

....

....

As a result of your sending Les Routiers this report form, we may send you information on Les Routiers in the future.
If you would prefer not to receive such information, please tick this box ☐

To send your report...
Fax: Complete this form and fax it to 020 7370 4528
Post: Complete this form and mail it to
The Editor, FREEPOST, Les Routiers, 190 Earl's Court Road, London, SW5 9QG
Email: info@routiers.co.uk

To the Editor, Les Routiers Guide 2007
Report Form

☐ From my personal experience the following establishment should be a member of Les Routiers.

☐ From my personal experience the following establishment should not be a member of Les Routiers.

PLEASE PRINT IN BLOCK CAPITALS

Establishment ....

Address ....

....

....

I had ☐ lunch ☐ dinner ☐ stayed there on (date) ....

Details ....

....

....

....

....

....

....

....

....

....

....

Reports received up to the end of May 2006 will be used in the research of the 2007 edition.

☐ I am not connected in any way with management or proprietors.

Name ....

Address ....

....

....

As a result of your sending Les Routiers this report form, we may send you information on Les Routiers in the future.
If you would prefer not to receive such information, please tick this box ☐

To send your report...
Fax: Complete this form and fax it to 020 7370 4528
Post: Complete this form and mail it to
The Editor, FREEPOST, Les Routiers, 190 Earl's Court Road, London, SW5 9QG
Email: info@routiers.co.uk

To the Editor, Les Routiers Guide 2007
Report Form

☐ From my personal experience the following establishment should be a member of Les Routiers.

☐ From my personal experience the following establishment should not be a member of Les Routiers.

PLEASE PRINT IN BLOCK CAPITALS

Establishment ....

Address ....

....

....

I had ☐ lunch ☐ dinner ☐ stayed there on (date) ....

Details ....

....

....

....

....

....

....

....

....

....

....

Reports received up to the end of May 2006 will be used in the research of the 2007 edition.

☐ I am not connected in any way with management or proprietors.

Name ....

Address ....

....

....

As a result of your sending Les Routiers this report form, we may send you information on Les Routiers in the future.
If you would prefer not to receive such information, please tick this box ☐

To send your report...
Fax: Complete this form and fax it to 020 7370 4528
Post: Complete this form and mail it to
The Editor, FREEPOST, Les Routiers, 190 Earl's Court Road, London, SW5 9QG
Email: info@routiers.co.uk

To the Editor, Les Routiers Guide 2007
Report Form

☐ From my personal experience the following establishment should be a member of Les Routiers.

☐ From my personal experience the following establishment should not be a member of Les Routiers.

PLEASE PRINT IN BLOCK CAPITALS

Establishment ....

Address ....

....

....

I had ☐ lunch ☐ dinner ☐ stayed there on (date) ....

Details ....

....

....

....

....

....

....

....

....

Reports received up to the end of May 2006 will be used in the research of the 2007 edition.

☐ I am not connected in any way with management or proprietors.

Name ....

Address ....

....

....

As a result of your sending Les Routiers this report form, we may send you information on Les Routiers in the future.
If you would prefer not to receive such information, please tick this box ☐

To send your report...
Fax: Complete this form and fax it to 020 7370 4528
Post: Complete this form and mail it to
The Editor, FREEPOST, Les Routiers, 190 Earl's Court Road, London, SW5 9QG
Email: info@routiers.co.uk